TSUBASA

25

CLAMP

TRANSLATED AND ADAPTED BY
William Flanagan

LETTERED BY
Dana Hayward

DEL
REY

BALLANTINE BOOKS • NEW YORK

Tsubasa, volume 25 is a work of fiction. Names, characters, places, and incidents are the products of the author's imagination or are used fictitiously. Any resemblance to actual events, locales, or persons, living or dead, is entirely coincidental.

A Del Rey Manga/Kodansha Trade Paperback Original

Published in the United States by Del Rey, an imprint of The Random House Publishing Group, a division of Random House, Inc., New York.

Publication rights arranged through Kodansha Ltd.

First published in Japan in 2008 by Kodansha Ltd., Tokyo

ISBN 978-0-345-51716-6

Printed in the United States of America

www.delreymanga.com

9 8 7 6 5 4 3 2 1

Translator/Adapter—William Flanagan
Lettering—Dana Hayward

Contents

Tsubasa crosses over with *xxxHOLiC*. Although it isn't necessary to read *xxxHOLiC* to understand the events in *Tsubasa*, you'll get to see the same events from different perspectives if you read both series!

Honorifics Explained

Throughout the Del Rey Manga books, you will find Japanese honorifics left intact in the translations. For those not familiar with how the Japanese use honorifics and, more important, how they differ from American honorifics, we present this brief overview.

Politeness has always been a critical facet of Japanese culture. Ever since the feudal era, when Japan was a highly stratified society, use of honorifics—which can be defined as polite speech that indicates relationship or status—has played an essential role in the Japanese language. When you address someone in Japanese, an honorific usually takes the form of a suffix attached to one's name (example: "Asuna-san"), is used as a title at the end of one's name, or appears in place of the name itself (example: "Negi-sensei," or simply "Sensei!").

Honorifics can be expressions of respect or endearment. In the context of manga and anime, honorifics give insight into the nature of the relationship between characters. Many English translations leave out these important honorifics and therefore distort the feel of the original Japanese. Because Japanese honorifics contain nuances that English honorifics lack, it is our policy at Del Rey not to translate them. Here, instead, is a guide to some of the honorifics you may encounter in Del Rey Manga.

-san: This is the most common honorific and is equivalent to Mr., Miss, Ms., or Mrs. It is the all-purpose honorific and can be used in any situation where politeness is required.

-sama: This is one level higher than "-san" and is used to confer great respect.

-dono: This comes from the word "tono," which means "lord." It is an even higher level than "-sama" and confers utmost respect.

-kun: This suffix is used at the end of boys' names to express familiarity or endearment. It is also sometimes used by men among friends, or when addressing someone younger or of a lower station

-chan: This is used to express endearment, mostly toward girls. It is also used for little boys, pets, and even among lovers. It gives a sense of childish cuteness.

Bozu: This is an informal way to refer to a boy, similar to the English terms "kid" and "squirt."

Sempai/Senpai: This title suggests that the addressee is one's senior in a group or organization. It is most often used in a school setting, where underclassmen refer to their upperclassmen as "sempai." It can also be used in the workplace, such as when a newer employee addresses an employee who has seniority in the company.

Kohai: This is the opposite of "sempai" and is used toward underclassmen in school or newcomers in the workplace. It connotes that the addressee is of a lower station.

Sensei: Literally meaning "one who has come before," this title is used for teachers, doctors, or masters of any profession or art.

-[blank]: This is usually forgotten in these lists, but it is perhaps the most significant difference between Japanese and English. The lack of honorific means that the speaker has permission to address the person in a very intimate way. Usually, only family, spouses, or very close friends have this kind of permission. Known as *yobisute*, it can be gratifying when someone who has earned the intimacy starts to call one by one's name without an honorific. But when that intimacy hasn't been earned, it can be very insulting.

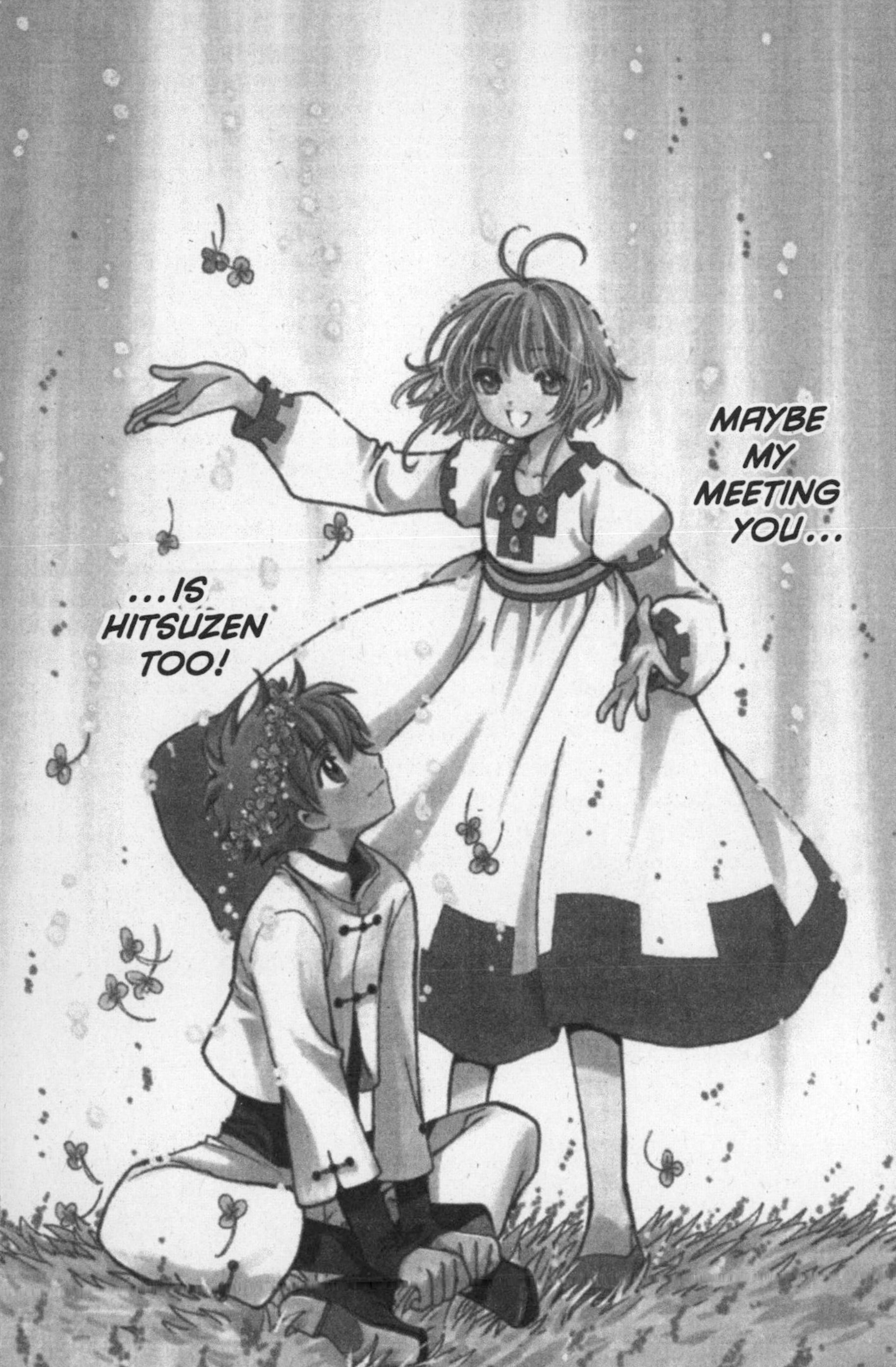
MAYBE MY MEETING YOU...
...IS HITSUZEN TOO!

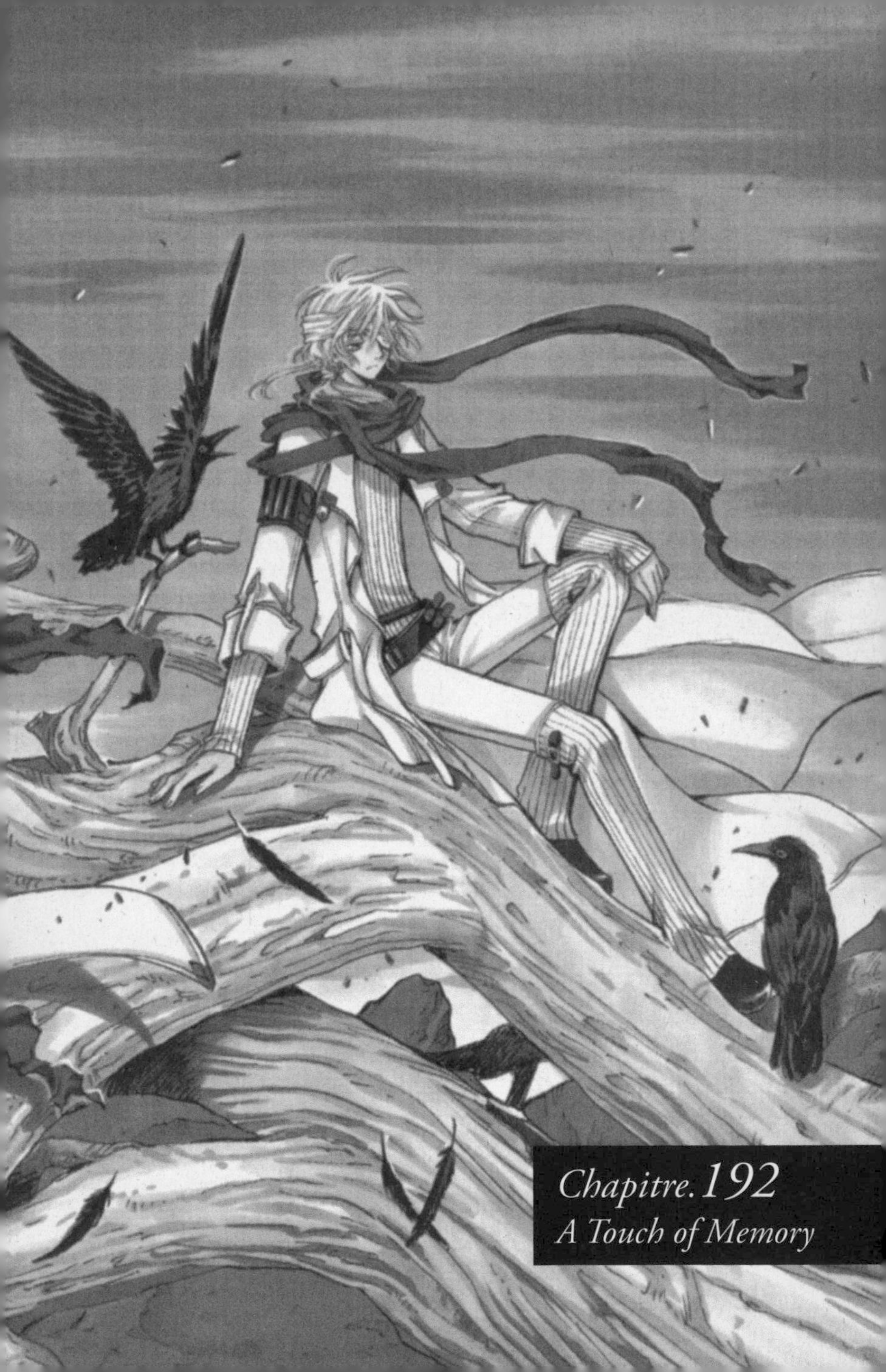
Chapitre. 192
A Touch of Memory

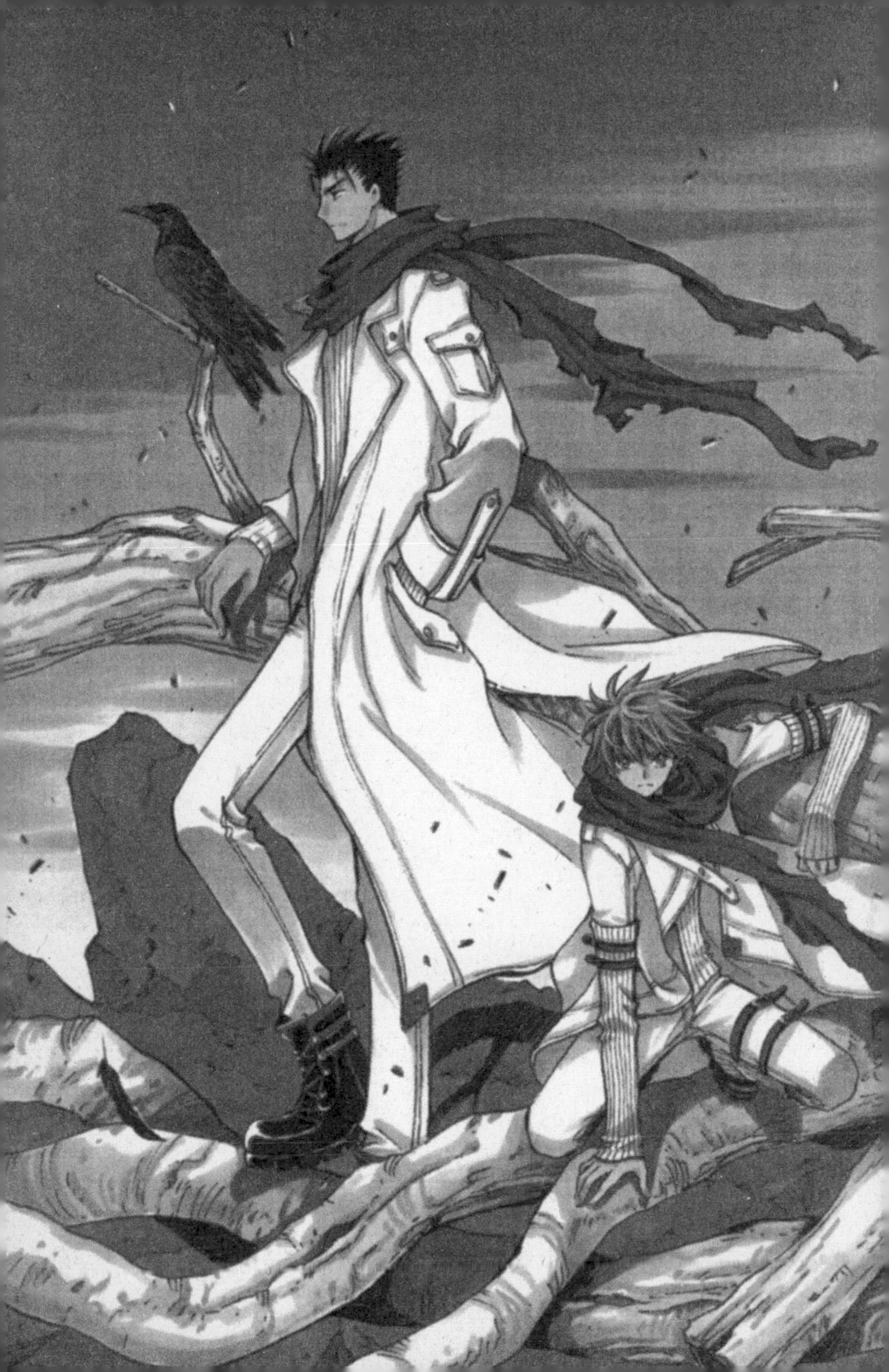

ツバサ

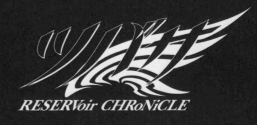

RESERVoir CHRoNiCLE

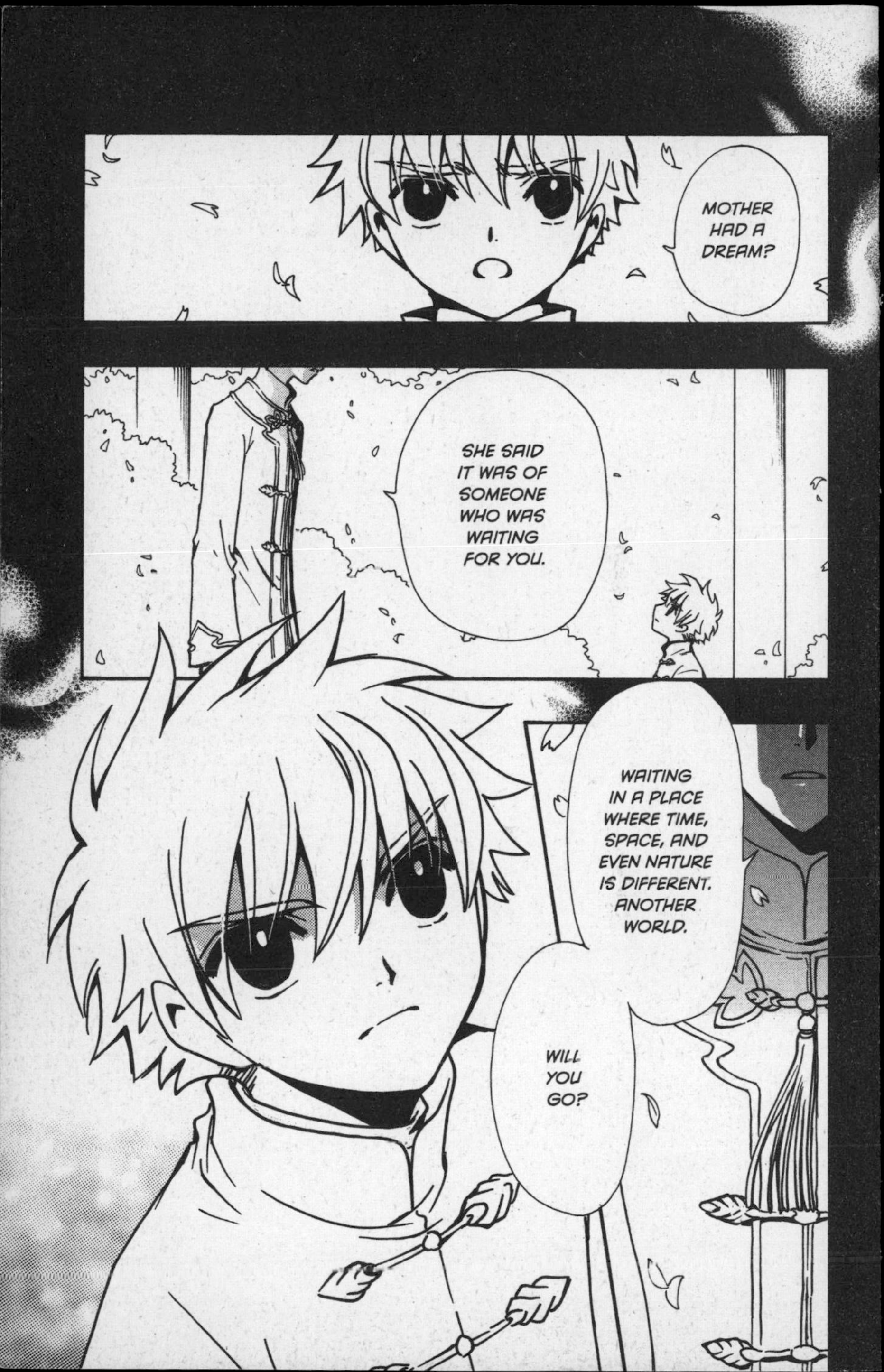
MOTHER HAD A DREAM?
SHE SAID IT WAS OF SOMEONE WHO WAS WAITING FOR YOU.
WAITING IN A PLACE WHERE TIME, SPACE, AND EVEN NATURE IS DIFFERENT. ANOTHER WORLD.
WILL YOU GO?

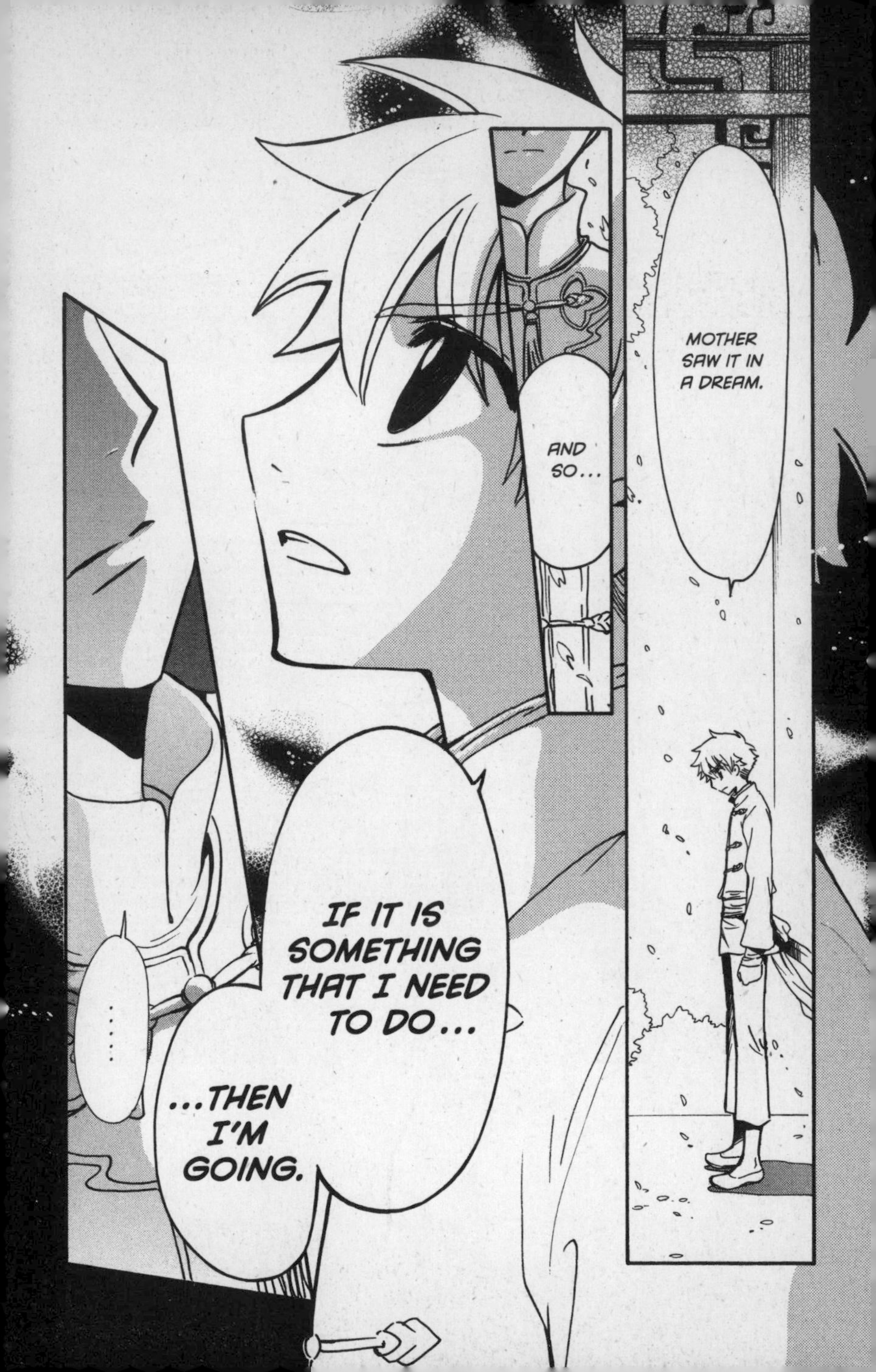
MOTHER SAW IT IN A DREAM.
AND SO...
IF IT IS SOMETHING THAT I NEED TO DO...
...THEN I'M GOING.
......

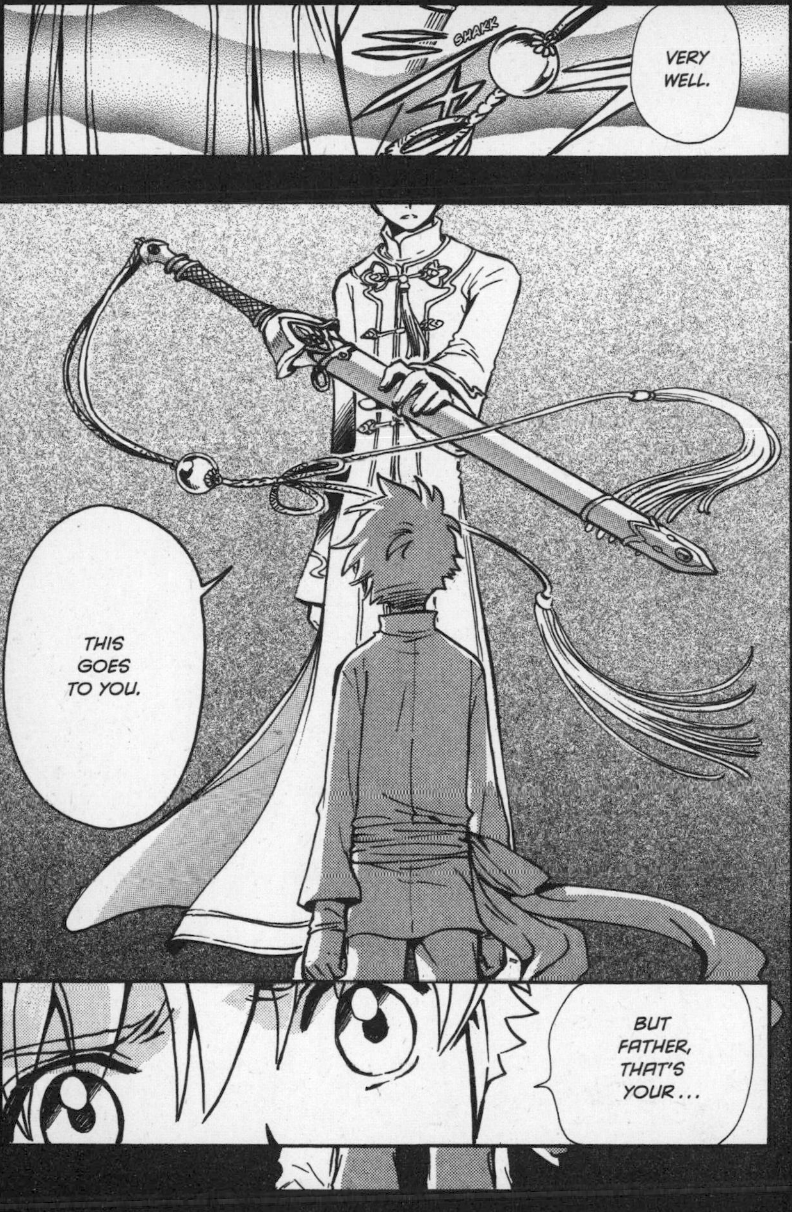
VERY WELL.
SHAKK
THIS GOES TO YOU.
BUT FATHER, THAT'S YOUR...

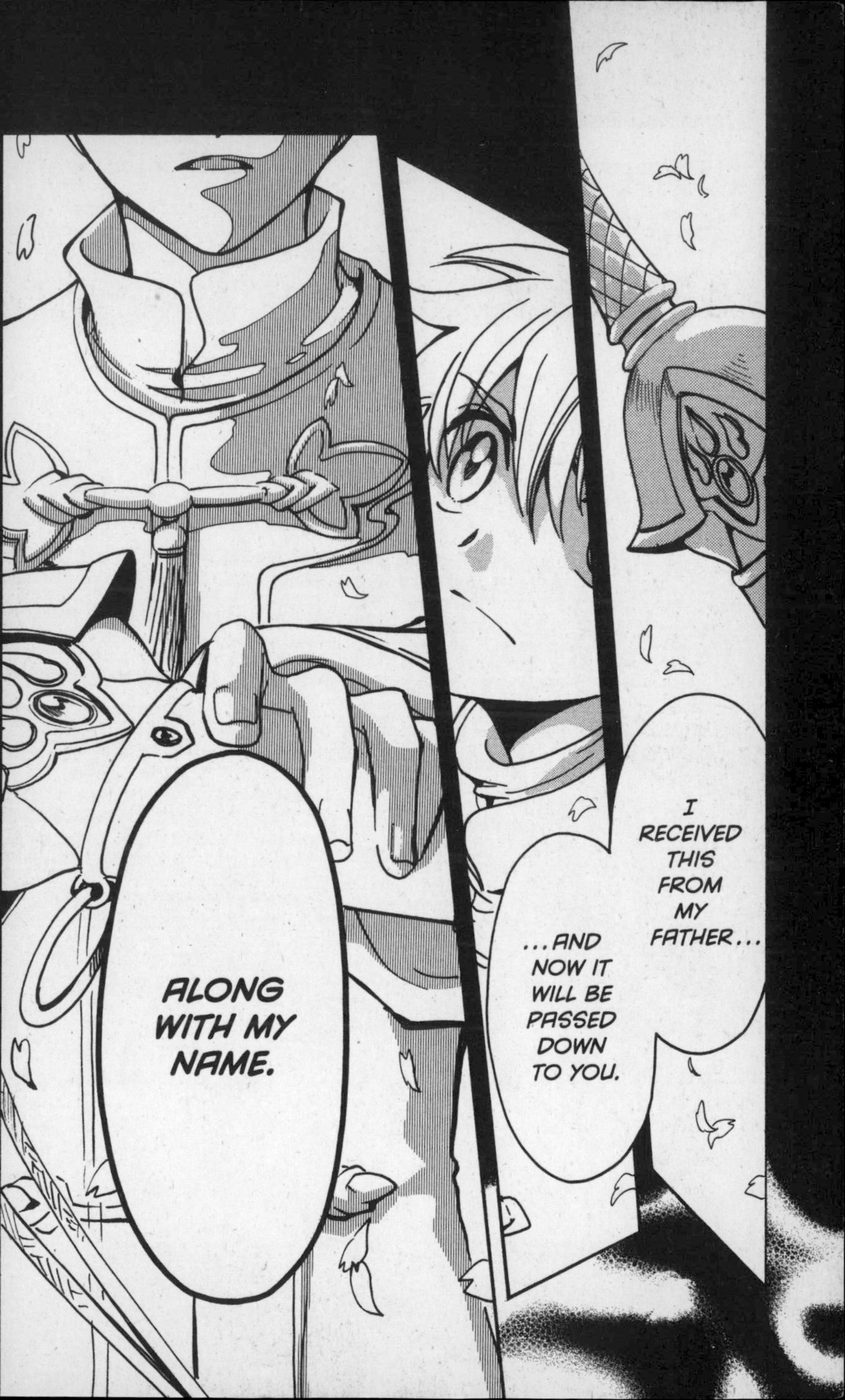
I RECEIVED THIS FROM MY FATHER...
...AND NOW IT WILL BE PASSED DOWN TO YOU.
ALONG WITH MY NAME.

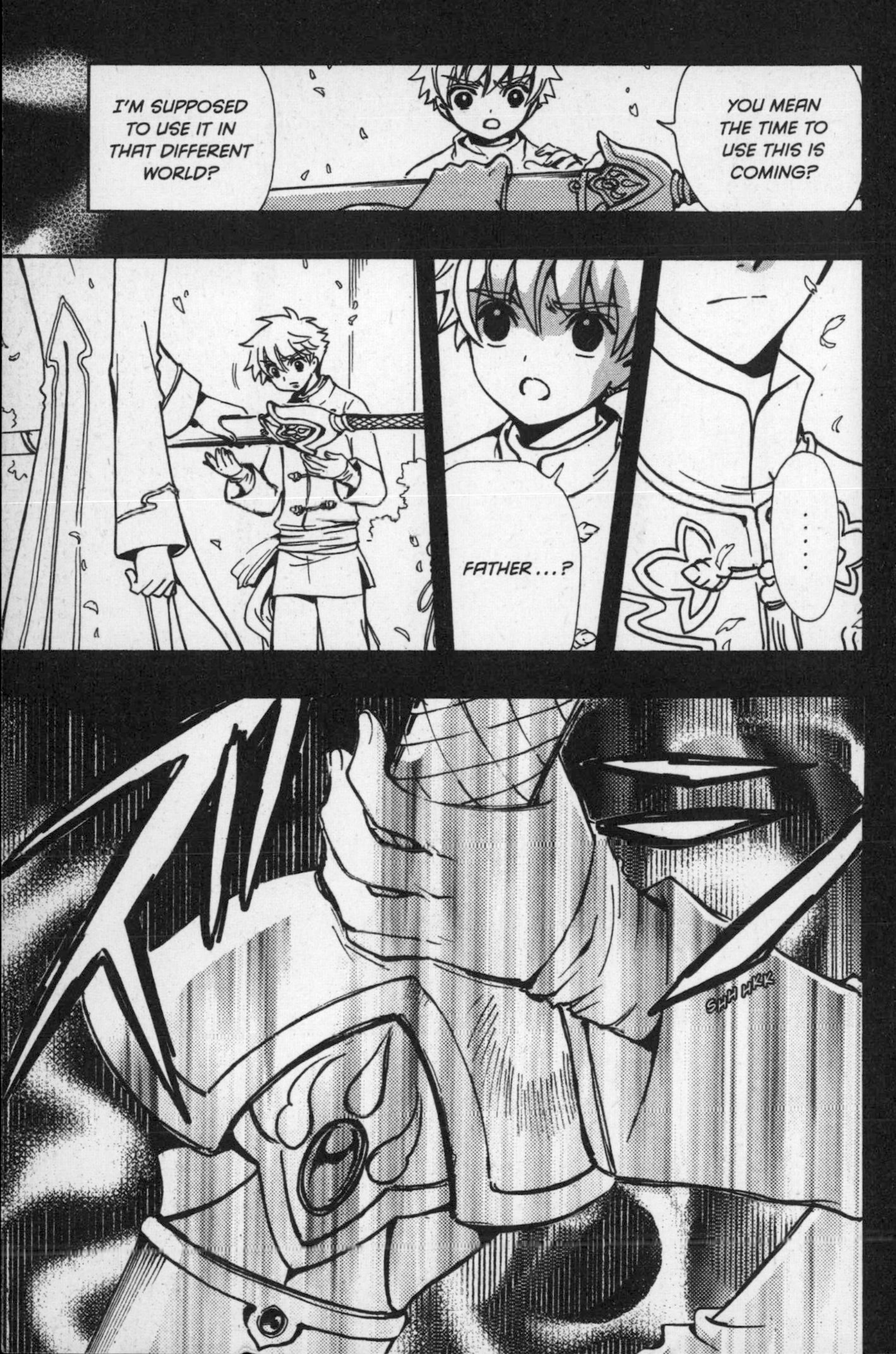
YOU MEAN THE TIME TO USE THIS IS COMING?
I'M SUPPOSED TO USE IT IN THAT DIFFERENT WORLD?
......
FATHER...?
SHH HKK

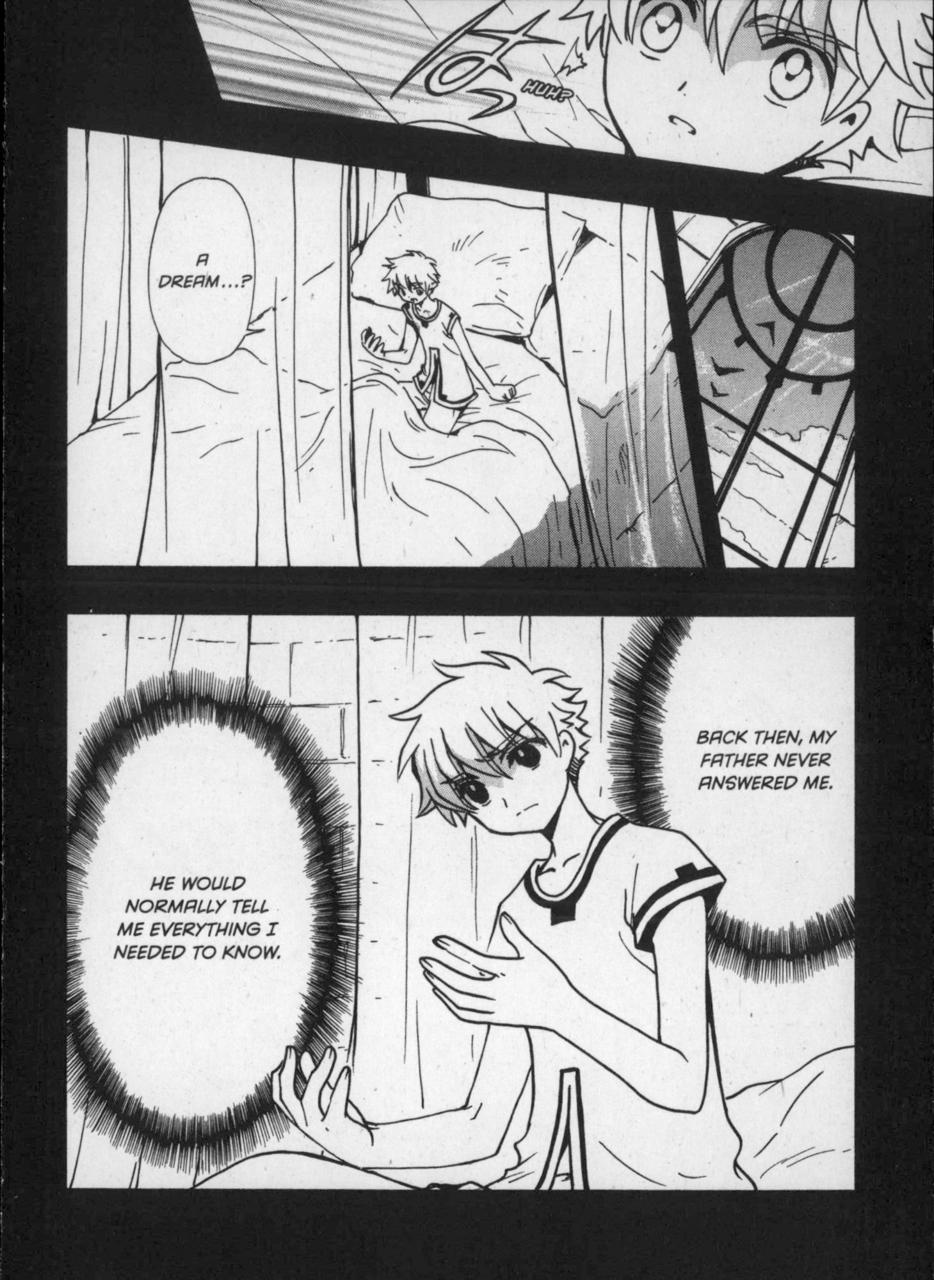
HUH?
A DREAM...?
BACK THEN, MY FATHER NEVER ANSWERED ME.
HE WOULD NORMALLY TELL ME EVERYTHING I NEEDED TO KNOW.

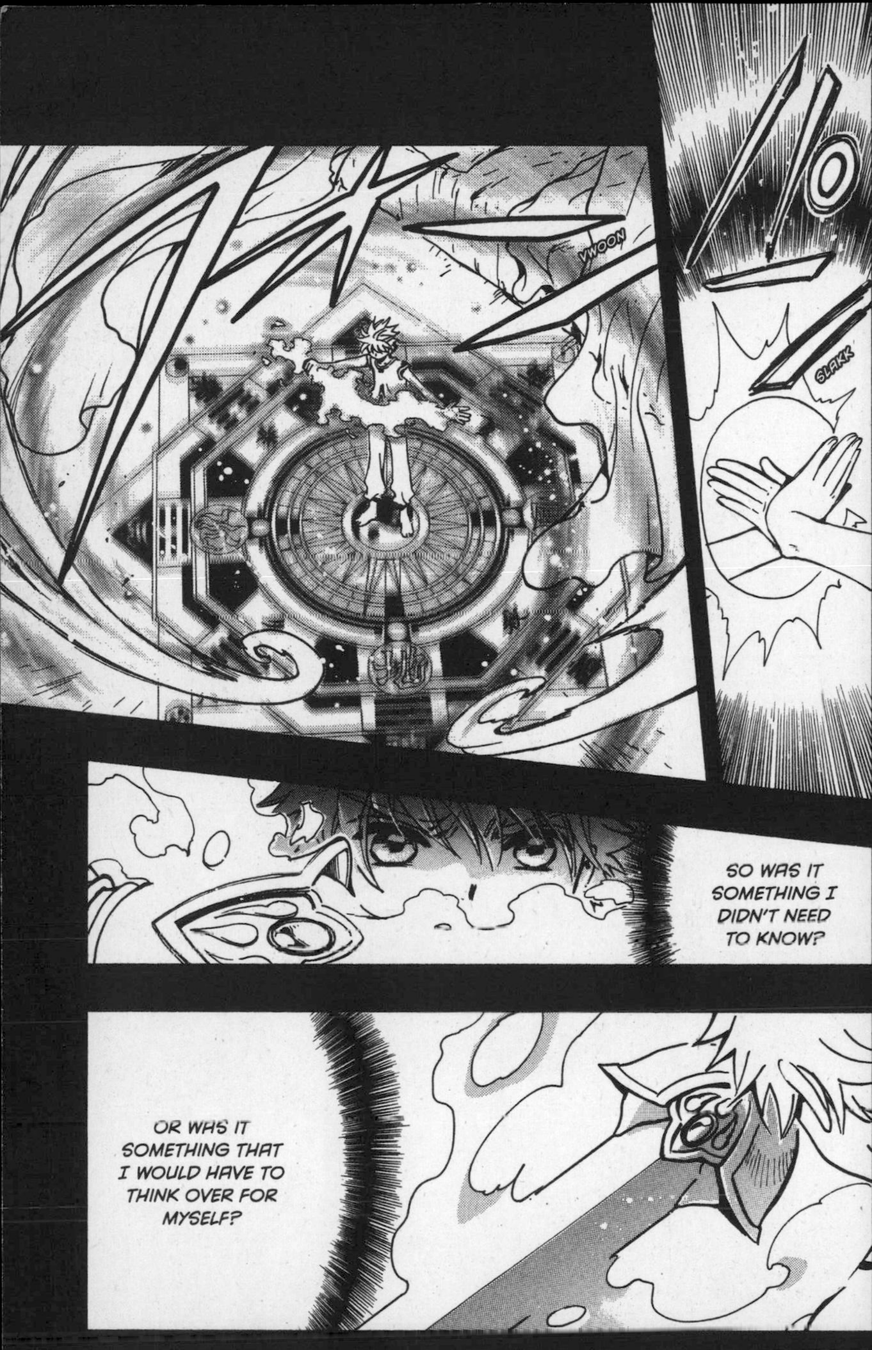
SLAKK
VWOON
SO WAS IT SOMETHING I DIDN'T NEED TO KNOW?
OR WAS IT SOMETHING THAT I WOULD HAVE TO THINK OVER FOR MYSELF?

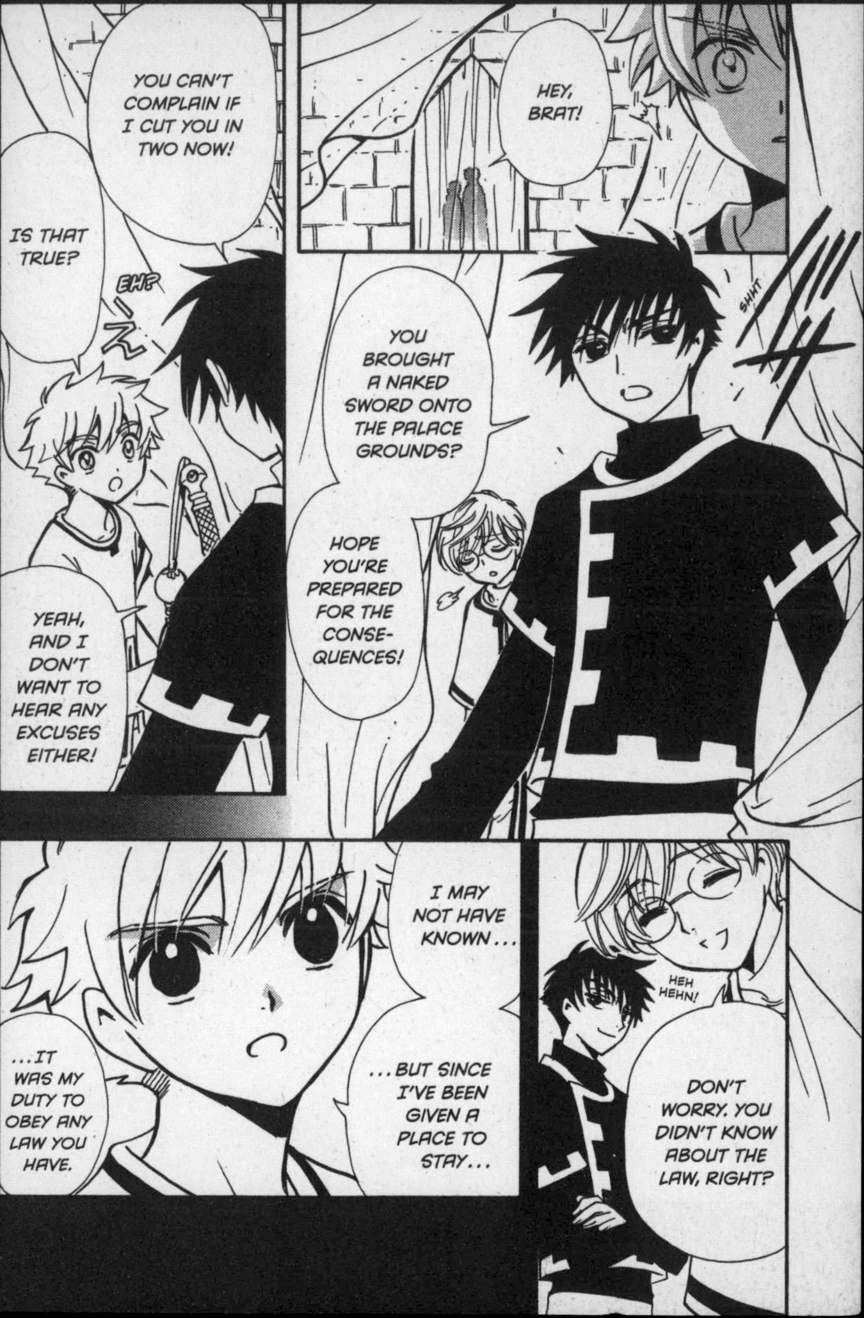
HEY, BRAT!
SHHT
YOU BROUGHT A NAKED SWORD ONTO THE PALACE GROUNDS?
HOPE YOU'RE PREPARED FOR THE CONSE- QUENCES!
YOU CAN'T COMPLAIN IF I CUT YOU IN TWO NOW!
IS THAT TRUE?
EH?
YEAH, AND I DON'T WANT TO HEAR ANY EXCUSES EITHER!
HEH HEHN!
DON'T WORRY. YOU DIDN'T KNOW ABOUT THE LAW, RIGHT?
I MAY NOT HAVE KNOWN...
...BUT SINCE I'VE BEEN GIVEN A PLACE TO STAY...
...IT WAS MY DUTY TO OBEY ANY LAW YOU HAVE.

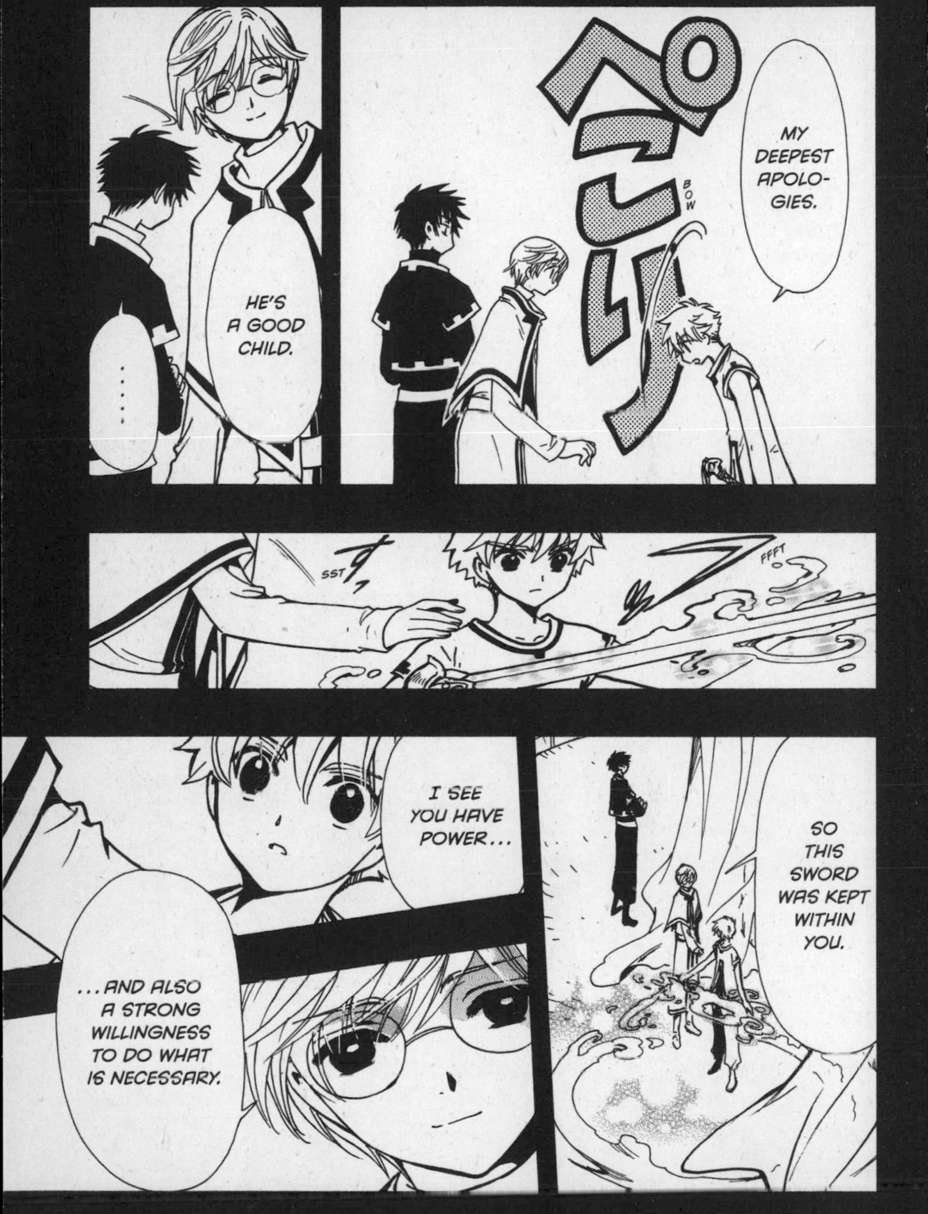
ぺこり
BOW
MY DEEPEST APOLOGIES.
HE'S A GOOD CHILD.
......
FFFT
SST
SO THIS SWORD WAS KEPT WITHIN YOU.
I SEE YOU HAVE POWER...
...AND ALSO A STRONG WILLINGNESS TO DO WHAT IS NECESSARY.

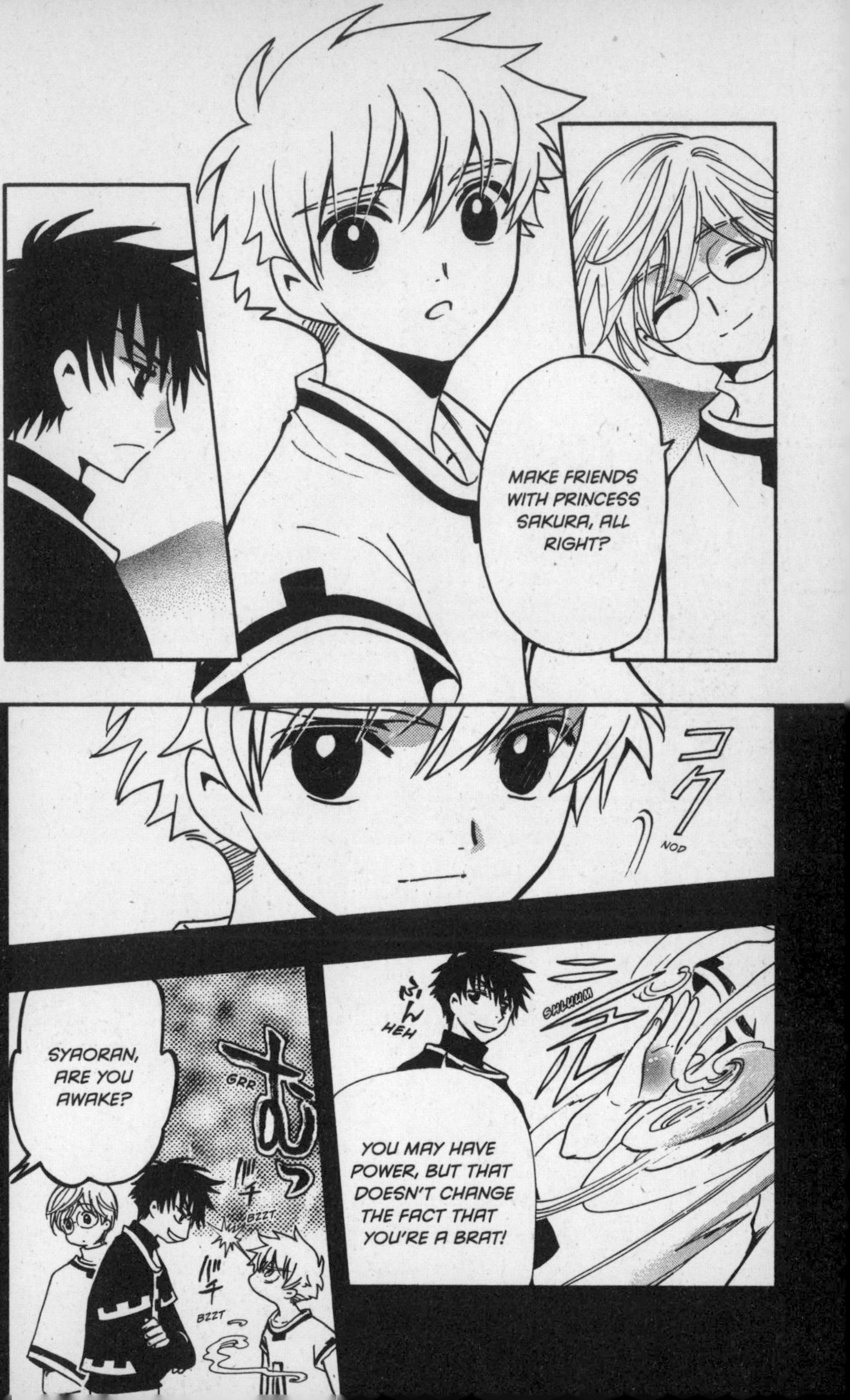
MAKE FRIENDS WITH PRINCESS SAKURA, ALL RIGHT?
コク
NOD
ぷん
HEH
SHLUUM
YOU MAY HAVE POWER, BUT THAT DOESN'T CHANGE THE FACT THAT YOU'RE A BRAT!
むっ
GRR
バチ
BZZT
バチ
BZZT
SYAORAN, ARE YOU AWAKE?

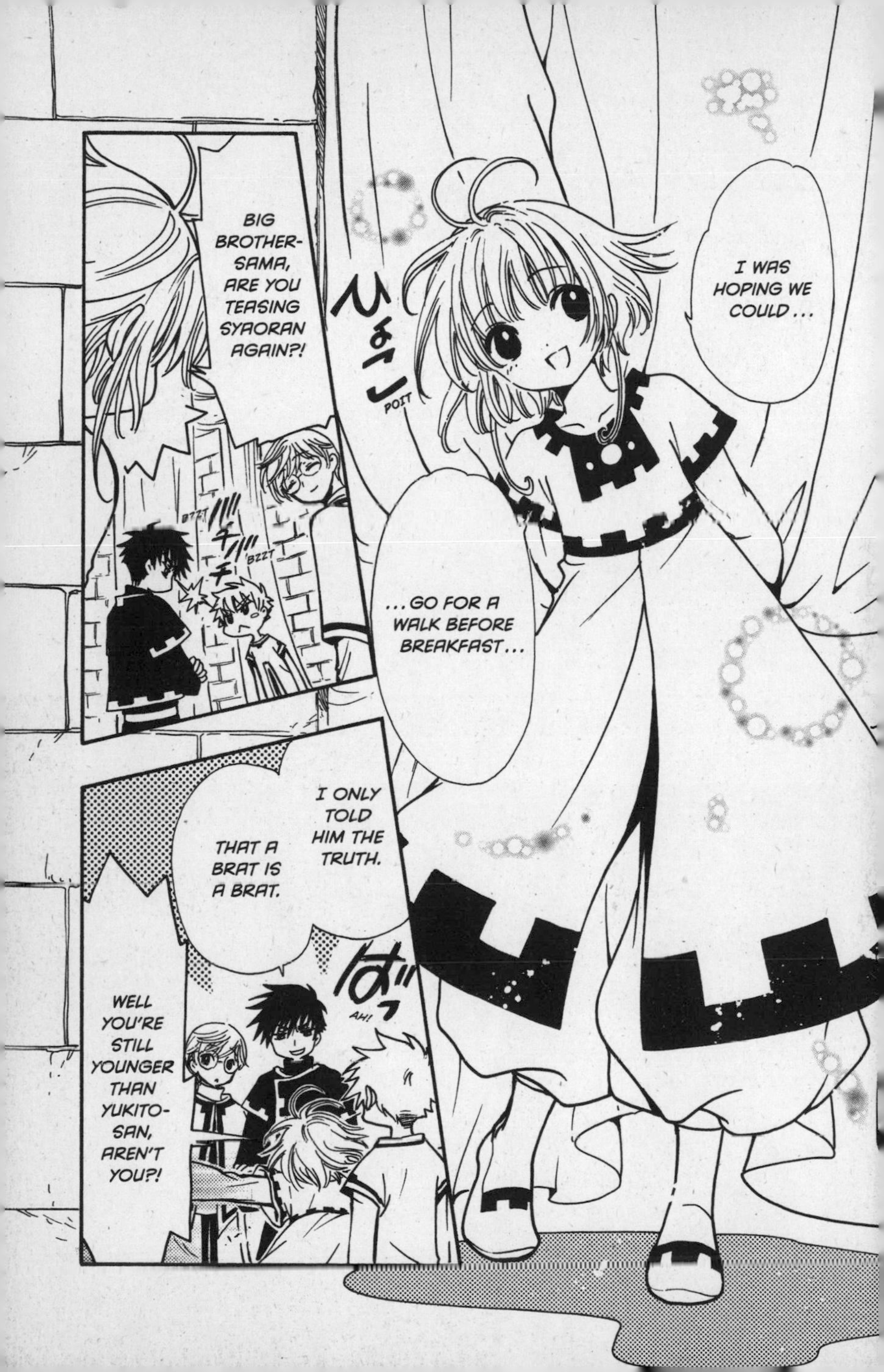
I WAS HOPING WE COULD...
ひょこ
POIT
...GO FOR A WALK BEFORE BREAKFAST...
BIG BROTHER-SAMA, ARE YOU TEASING SYAORAN AGAIN?!
BZZT
BZZT
I ONLY TOLD HIM THE TRUTH.
THAT A BRAT IS A BRAT.
はっ
AH!
WELL YOU'RE STILL YOUNGER THAN YUKITO-SAN, AREN'T YOU?!

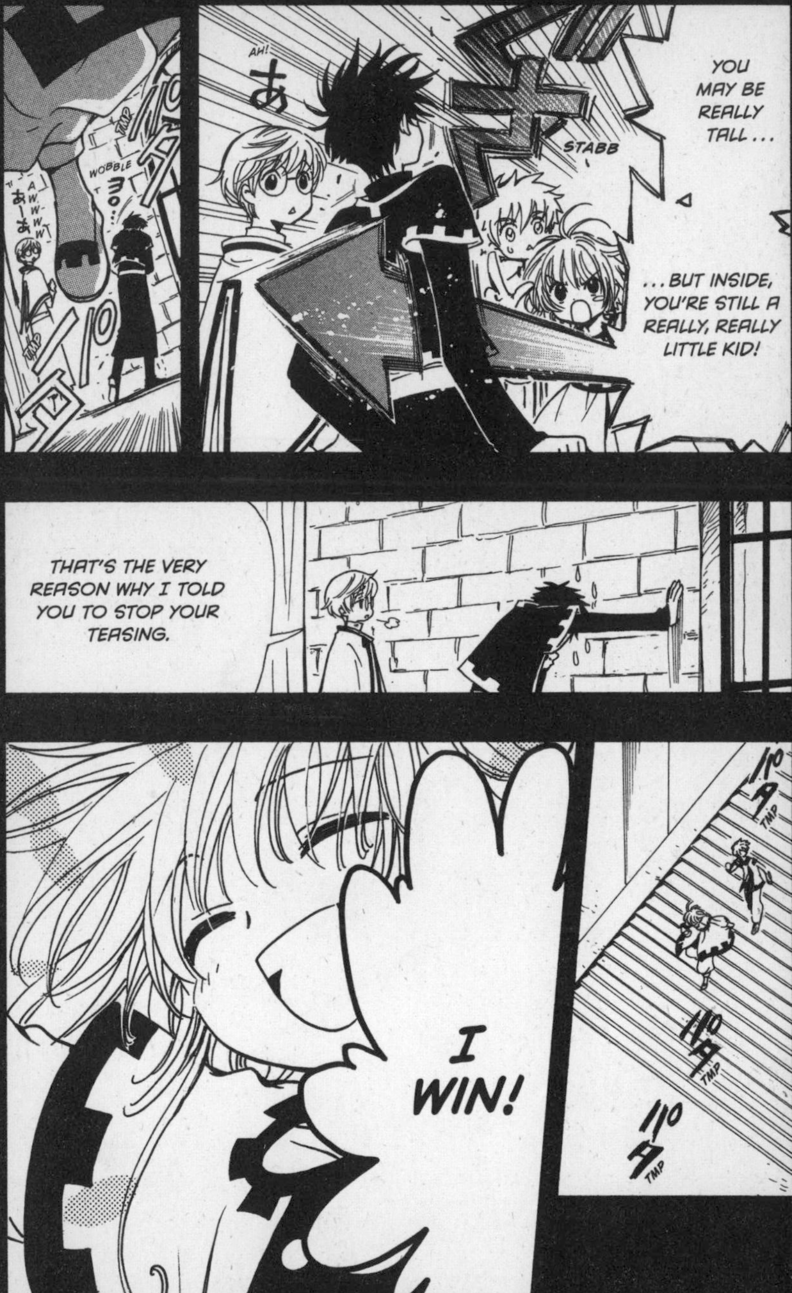
AH!
あ
STABB
YOU MAY BE REALLY TALL ...
... BUT INSIDE, YOU'RE STILL A REALLY, REALLY LITTLE KID!
TMP
WOBBLE
AWWWW
TMP
THAT'S THE VERY REASON WHY I TOLD YOU TO STOP YOUR TEASING.
TMP
TMP
TMP
I WIN!

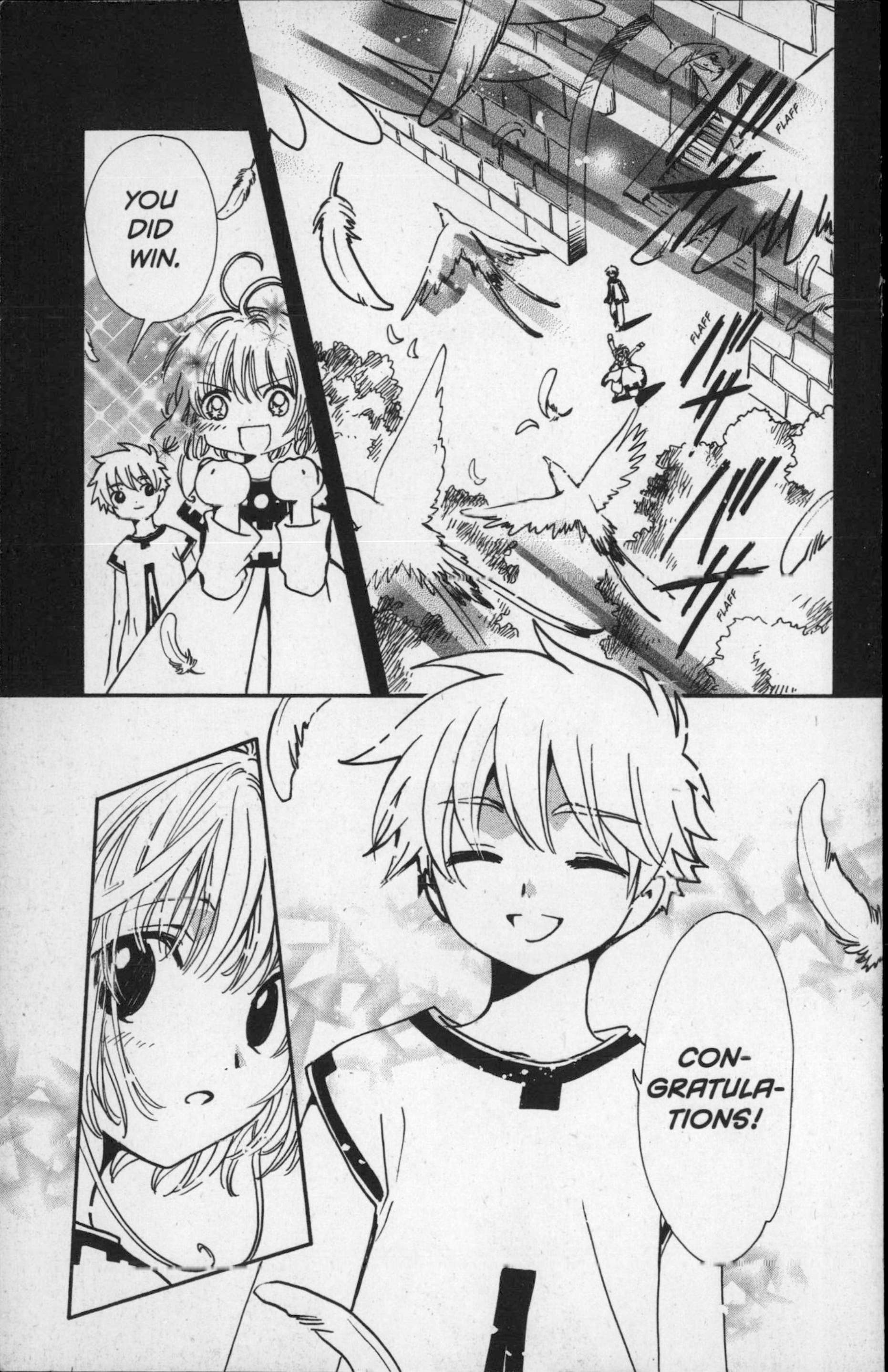
FLAFF
FLAFF
FLAFF
YOU DID WIN.
CON-GRATULA-TIONS!

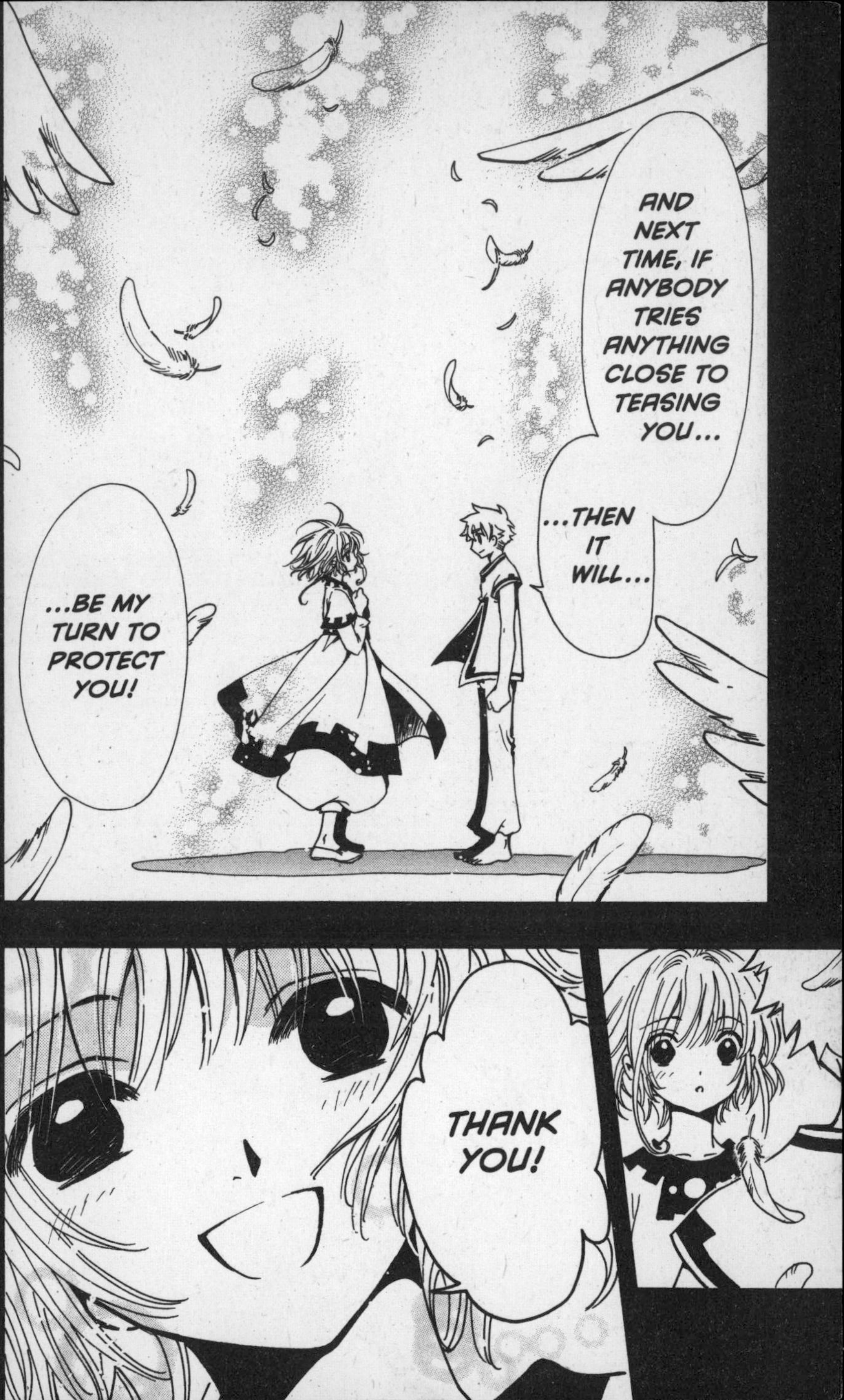
AND NEXT TIME, IF ANYBODY TRIES ANYTHING CLOSE TO TEASING YOU...
...THEN IT WILL...
...BE MY TURN TO PROTECT YOU!
THANK YOU!

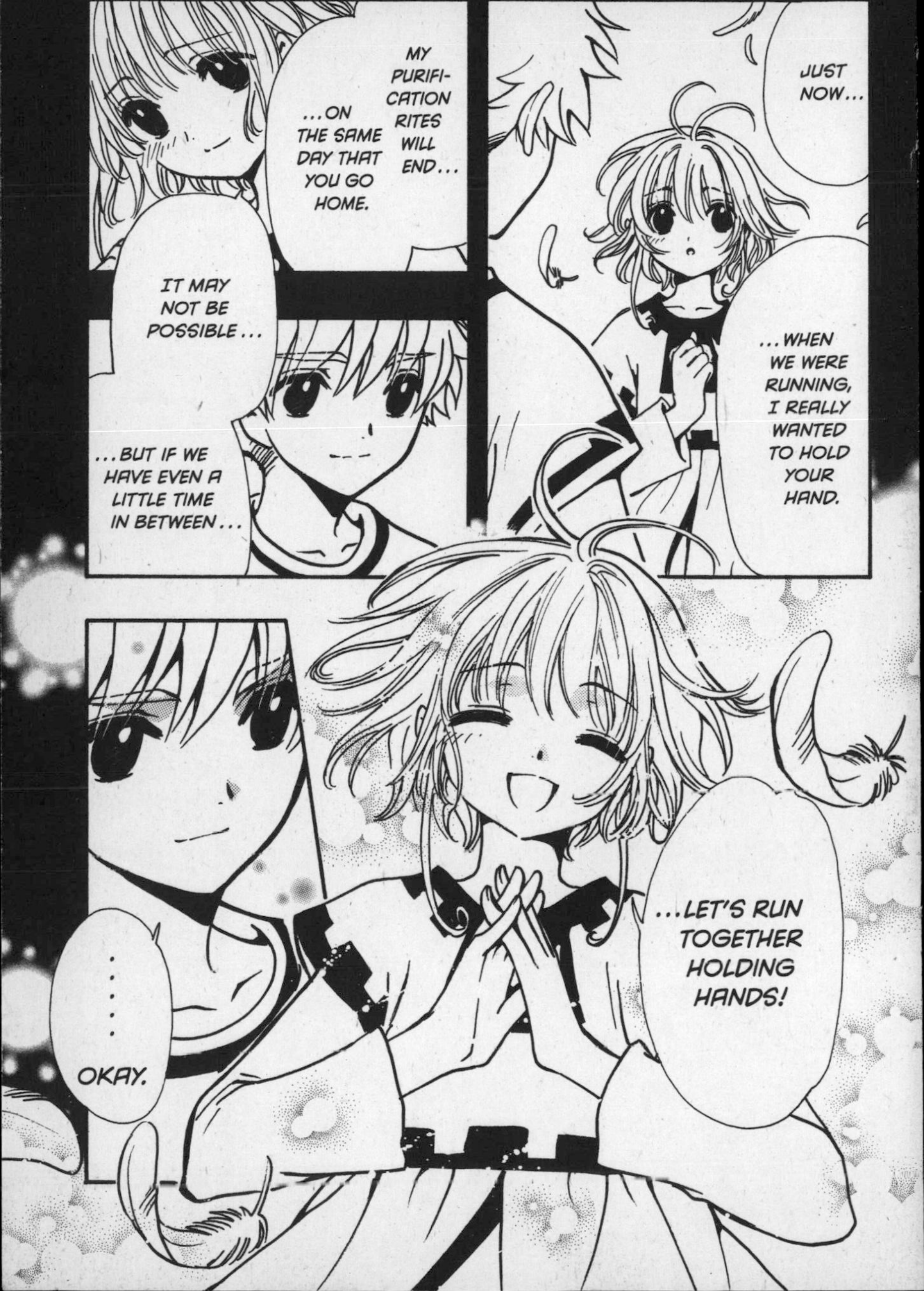
JUST NOW...
...WHEN WE WERE RUNNING, I REALLY WANTED TO HOLD YOUR HAND.
MY PURIFICATION RITES WILL END...
...ON THE SAME DAY THAT YOU GO HOME.
IT MAY NOT BE POSSIBLE...
...BUT IF WE HAVE EVEN A LITTLE TIME IN BETWEEN...
...LET'S RUN TOGETHER HOLDING HANDS!
......
OKAY.

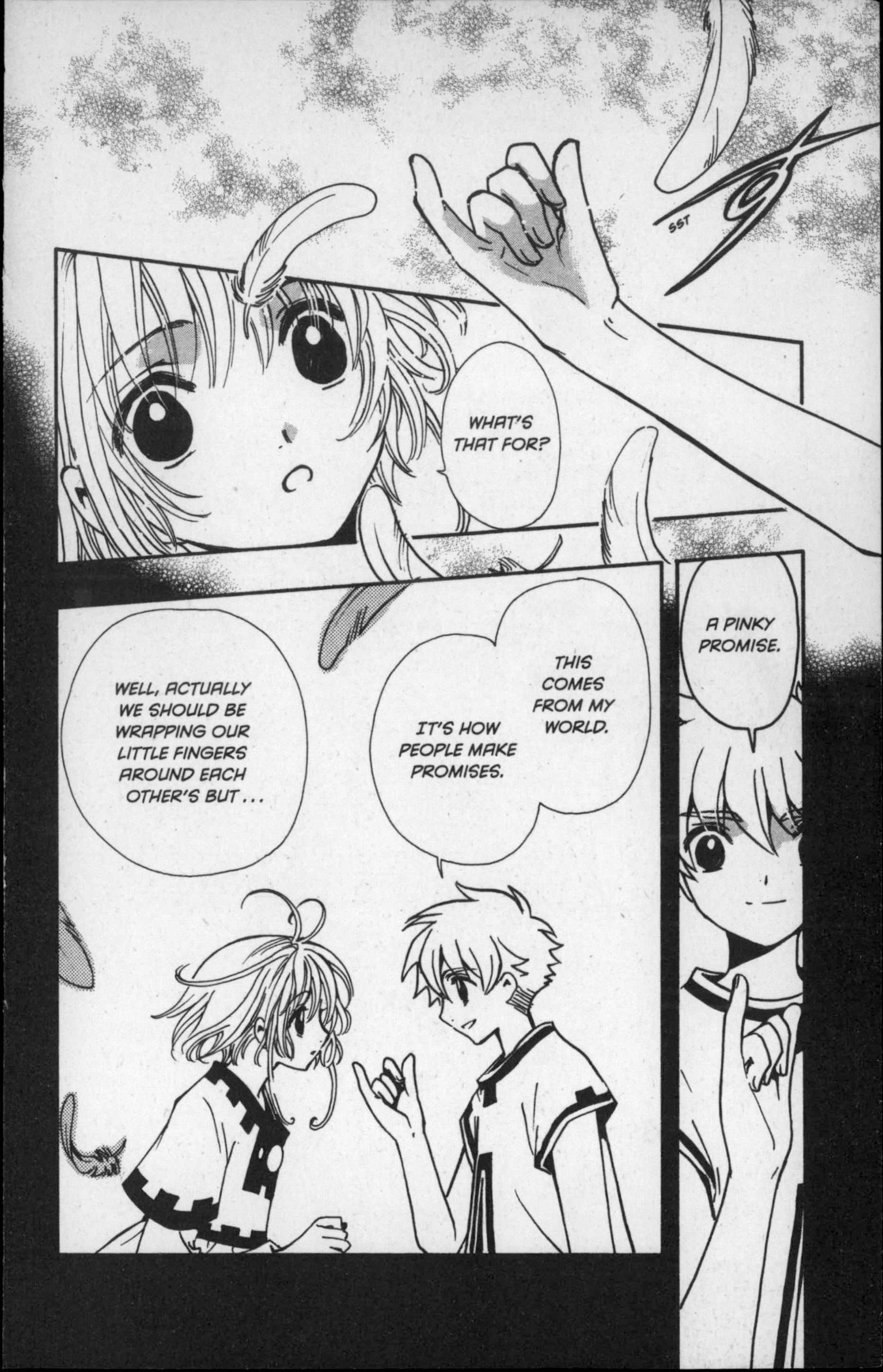
SST
WHAT'S THAT FOR?
A PINKY PROMISE.
THIS COMES FROM MY WORLD.
IT'S HOW PEOPLE MAKE PROMISES.
WELL, ACTUALLY WE SHOULD BE WRAPPING OUR LITTLE FINGERS AROUND EACH OTHER'S BUT . . .

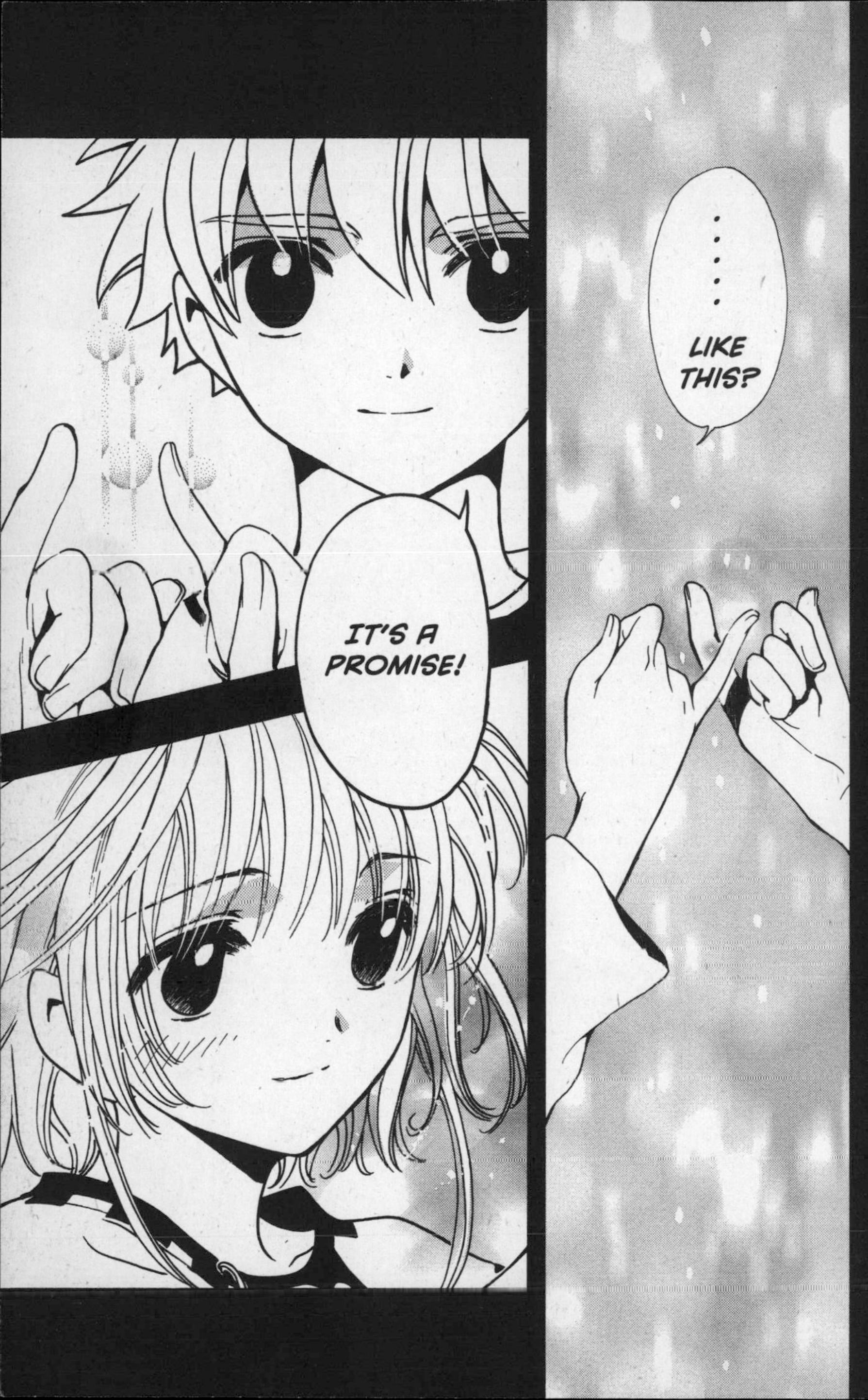
.....
LIKE THIS?
IT'S A PROMISE!

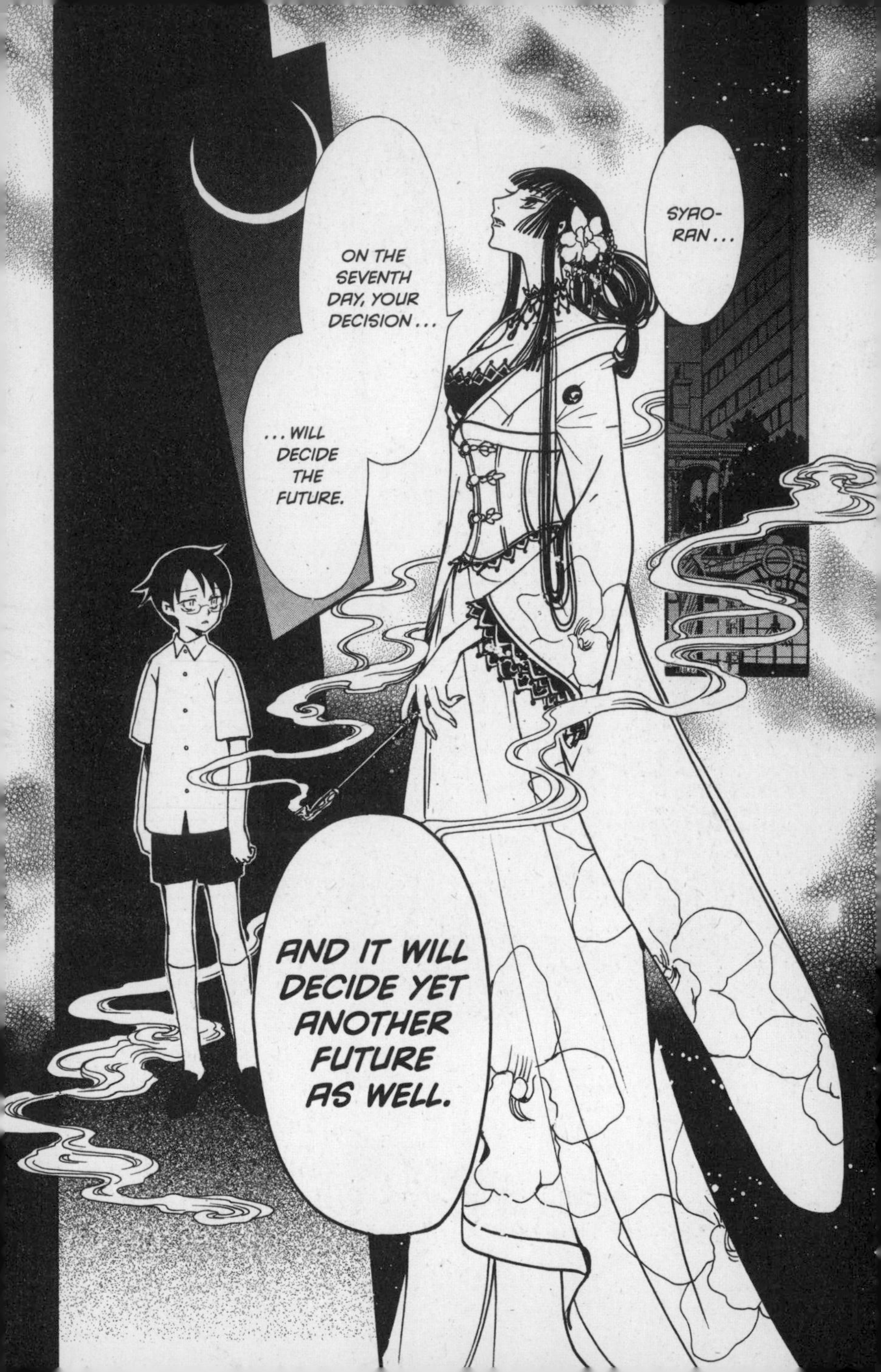
SYAO-RAN...
ON THE SEVENTH DAY, YOUR DECISION...
...WILL DECIDE THE FUTURE.
AND IT WILL DECIDE YET ANOTHER FUTURE AS WELL.

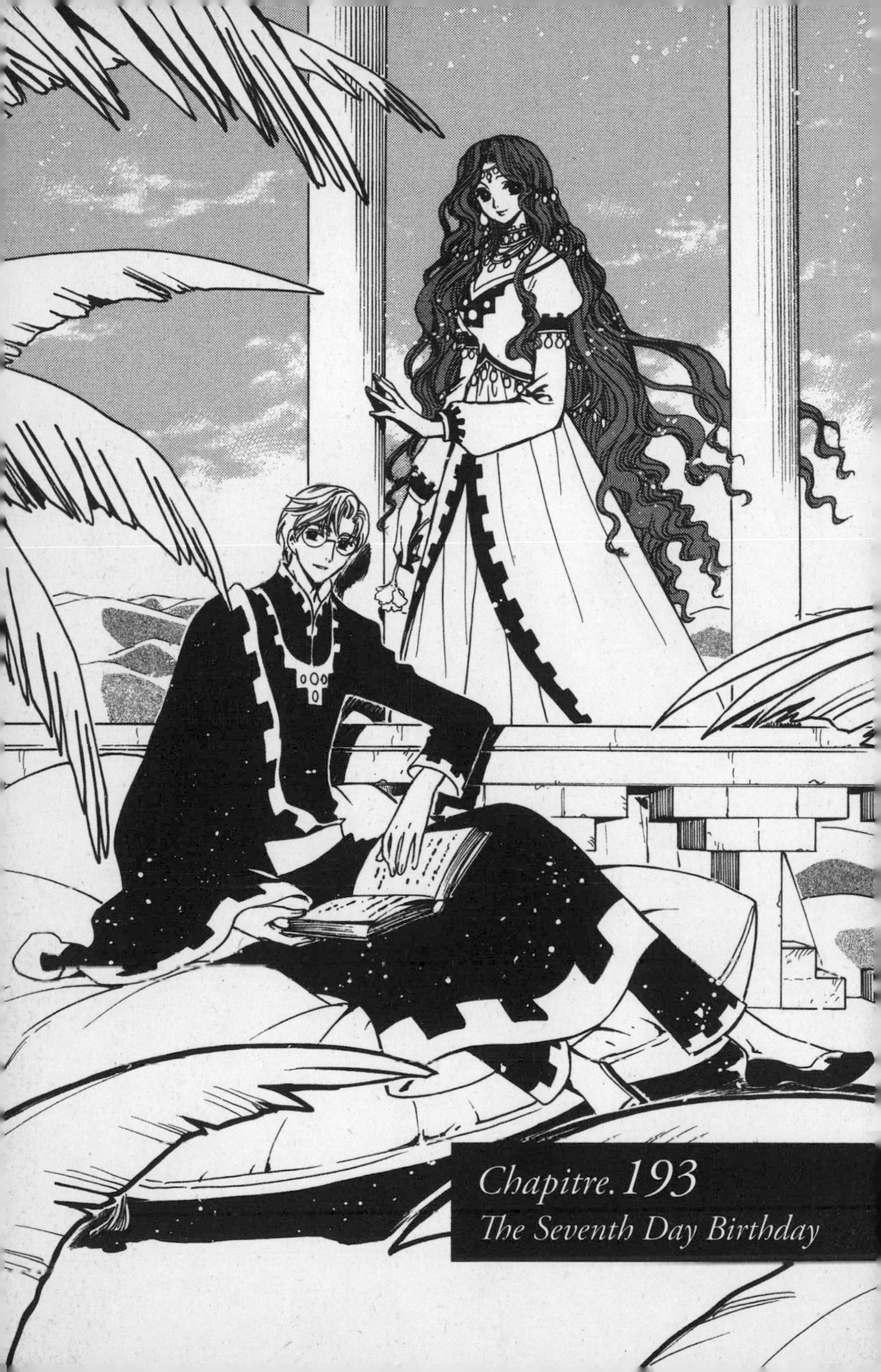
Chapitre. 193
The Seventh Day Birthday

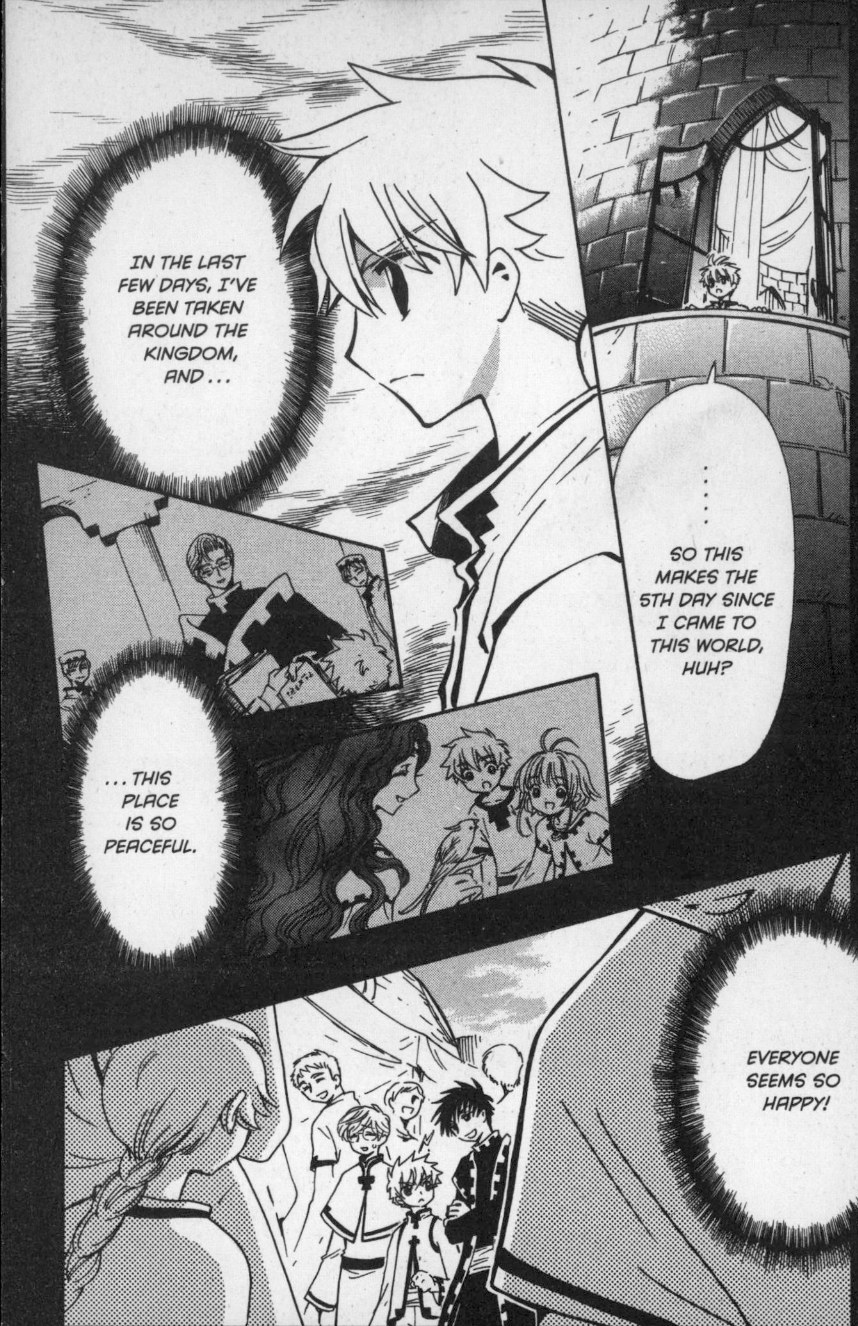
.....
SO THIS MAKES THE 5TH DAY SINCE I CAME TO THIS WORLD, HUH?
IN THE LAST FEW DAYS, I'VE BEEN TAKEN AROUND THE KINGDOM, AND . . .
. . . THIS PLACE IS SO PEACEFUL.
EVERYONE SEEMS SO HAPPY!

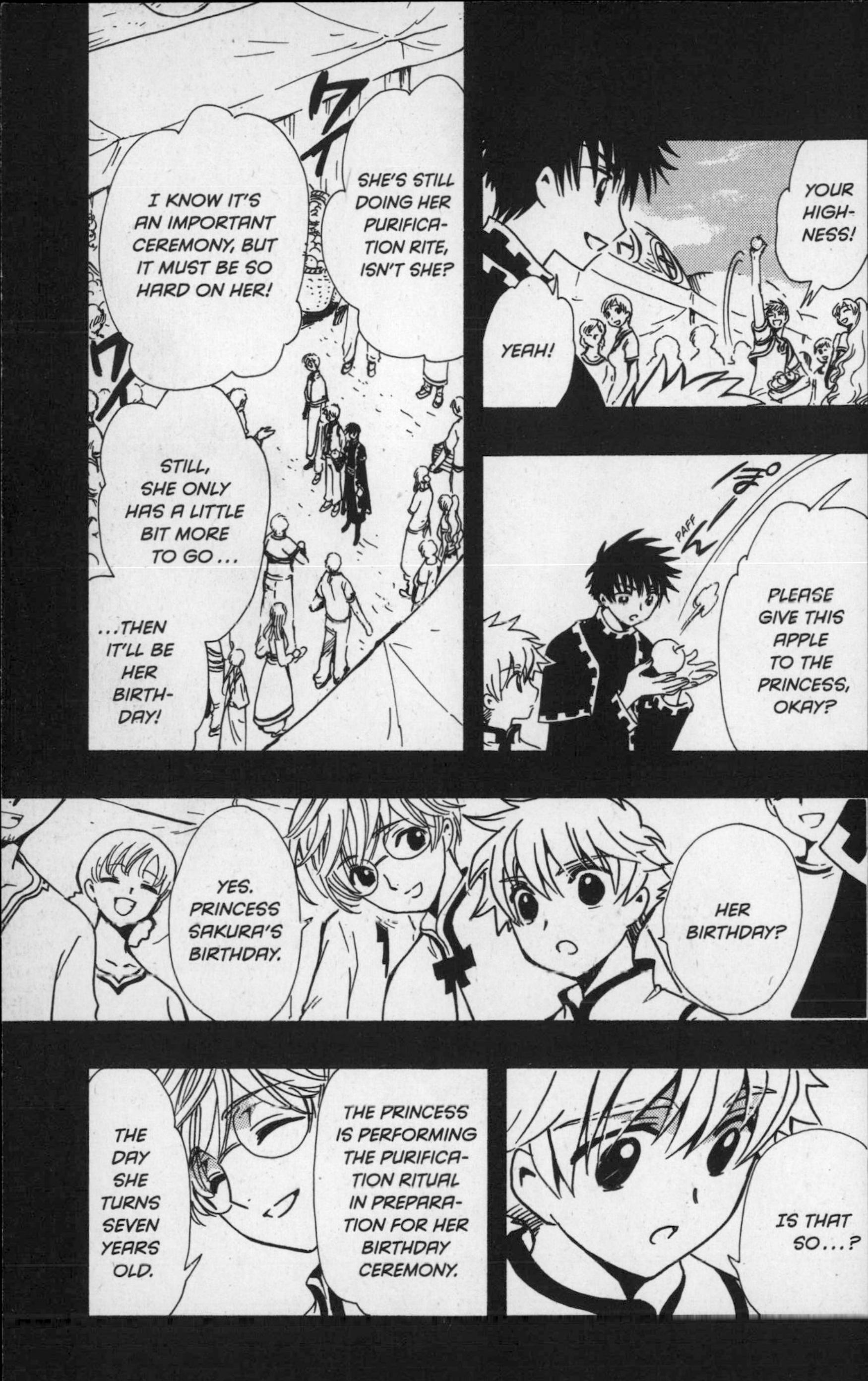
YOUR HIGHNESS!
YEAH!
PAFF
PLEASE GIVE THIS APPLE TO THE PRINCESS, OKAY?
SHE'S STILL DOING HER PURIFICATION RITE, ISN'T SHE?
I KNOW IT'S AN IMPORTANT CEREMONY, BUT IT MUST BE SO HARD ON HER!
STILL, SHE ONLY HAS A LITTLE BIT MORE TO GO...
...THEN IT'LL BE HER BIRTHDAY!
HER BIRTHDAY?
YES. PRINCESS SAKURA'S BIRTHDAY.
IS THAT SO...?
THE PRINCESS IS PERFORMING THE PURIFICATION RITUAL IN PREPARATION FOR HER BIRTHDAY CEREMONY.
THE DAY SHE TURNS SEVEN YEARS OLD.

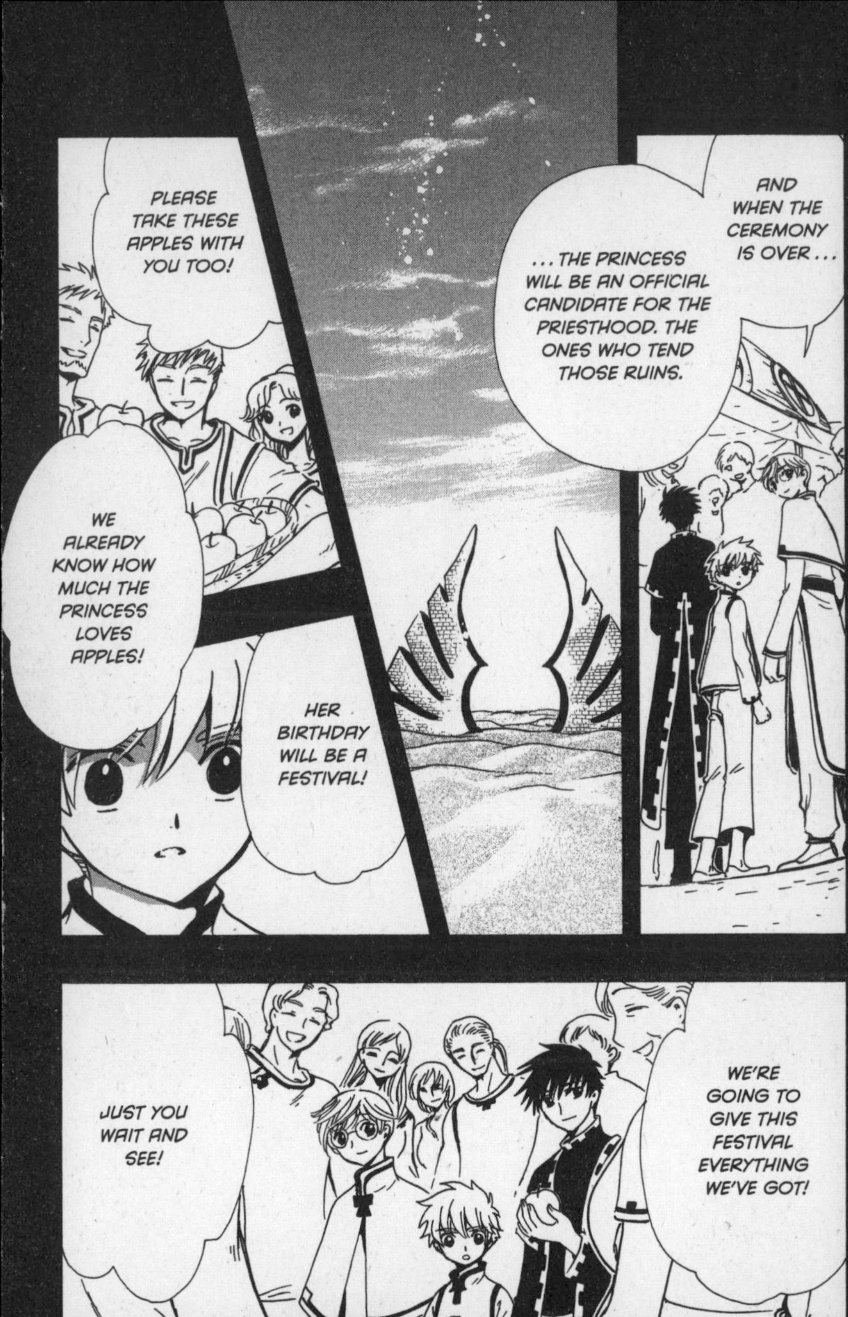
AND WHEN THE CEREMONY IS OVER...
...THE PRINCESS WILL BE AN OFFICIAL CANDIDATE FOR THE PRIESTHOOD. THE ONES WHO TEND THOSE RUINS.
PLEASE TAKE THESE APPLES WITH YOU TOO!
WE ALREADY KNOW HOW MUCH THE PRINCESS LOVES APPLES!
HER BIRTHDAY WILL BE A FESTIVAL!
WE'RE GOING TO GIVE THIS FESTIVAL EVERYTHING WE'VE GOT!
JUST YOU WAIT AND SEE!

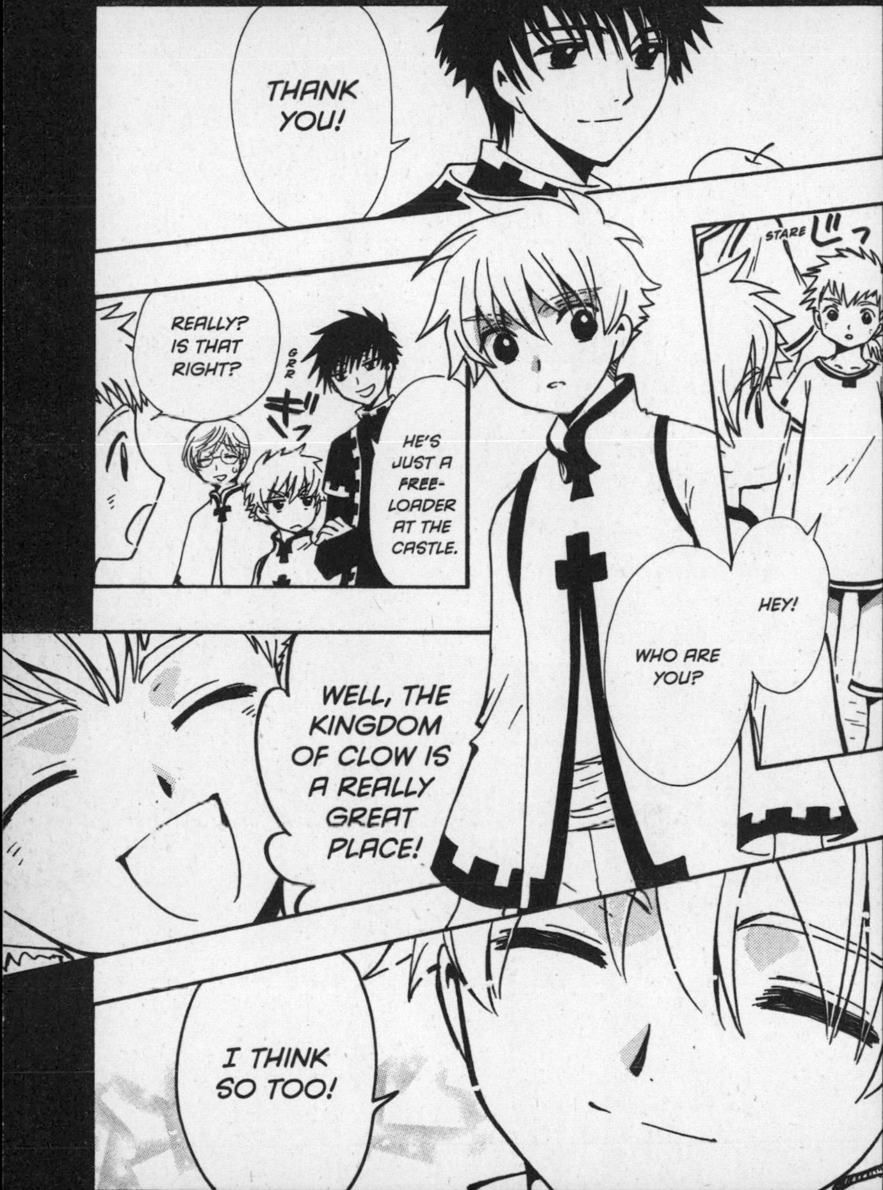
THANK YOU!
STARE
HEY!
WHO ARE YOU?
HE'S JUST A FREE-LOADER AT THE CASTLE.
GRR
REALLY? IS THAT RIGHT?
WELL, THE KINGDOM OF CLOW IS A REALLY GREAT PLACE!
I THINK SO TOO!

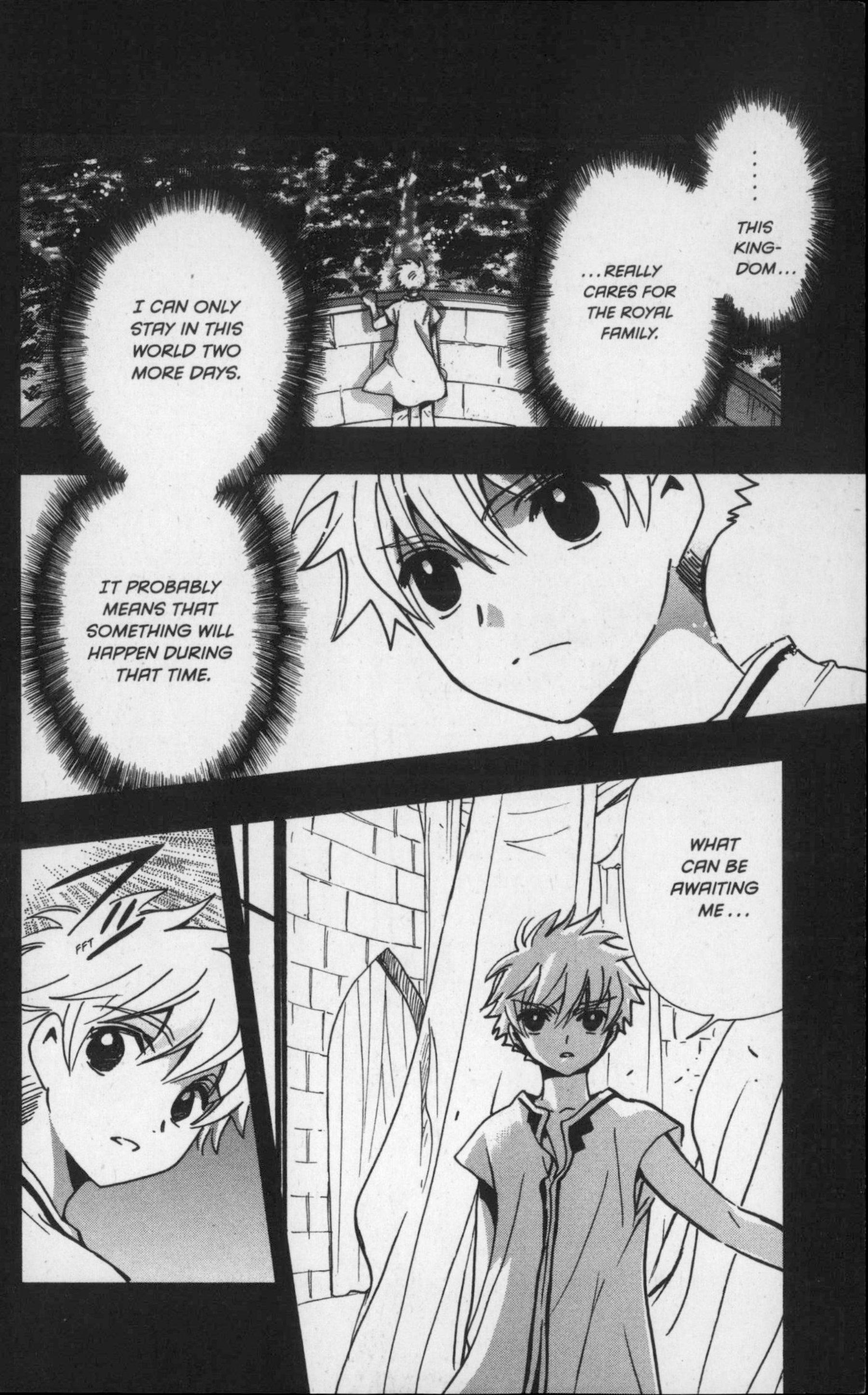

. . .
THIS KING-DOM...
...REALLY CARES FOR THE ROYAL FAMILY.
I CAN ONLY STAY IN THIS WORLD TWO MORE DAYS.
IT PROBABLY MEANS THAT SOMETHING WILL HAPPEN DURING THAT TIME.
WHAT CAN BE AWAITING ME...
FFT

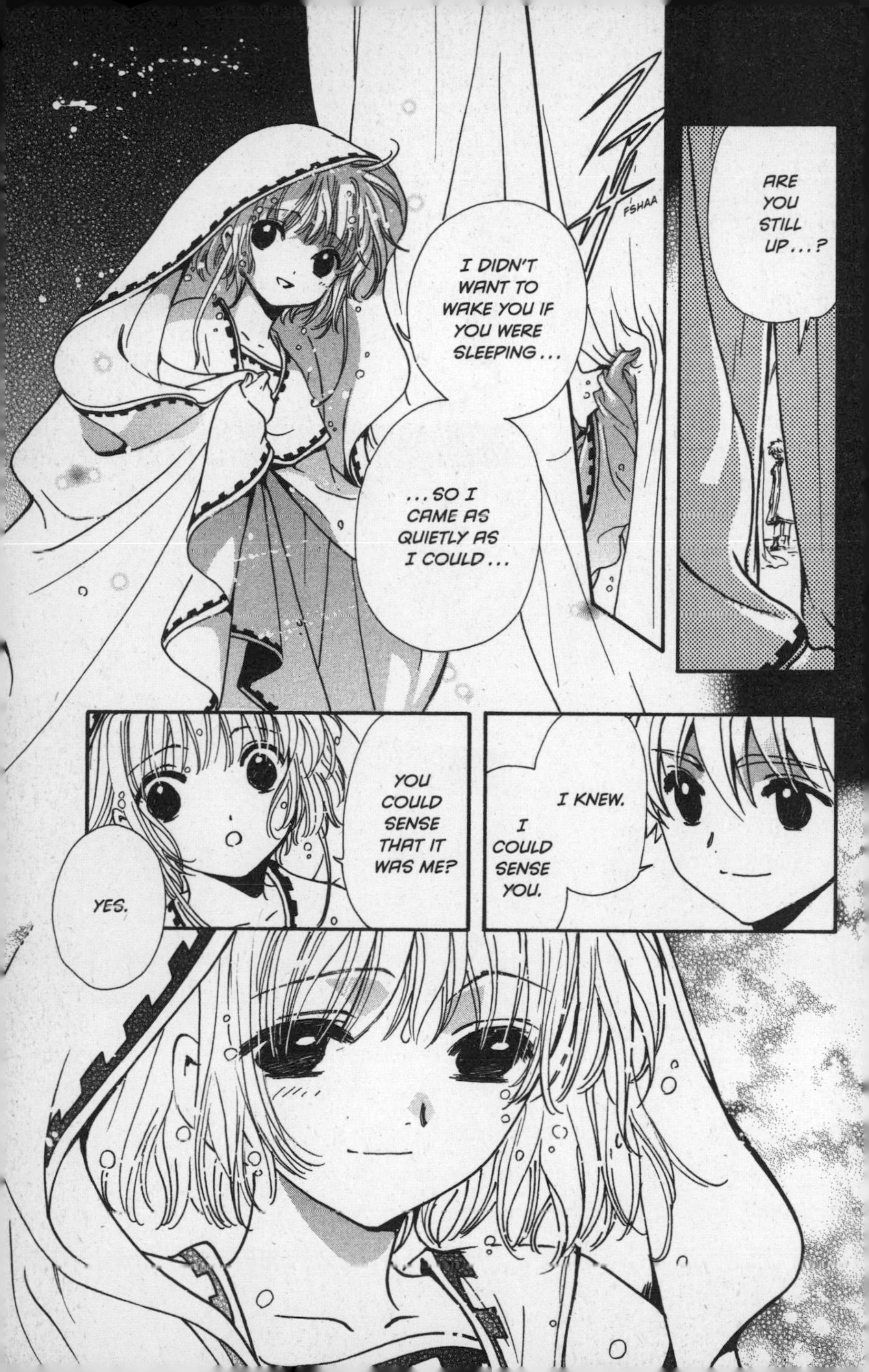
ARE YOU STILL UP...?
FSHAA
I DIDN'T WANT TO WAKE YOU IF YOU WERE SLEEPING...
...SO I CAME AS QUIETLY AS I COULD...
I KNEW.
I COULD SENSE YOU.
YOU COULD SENSE THAT IT WAS ME?
YES.

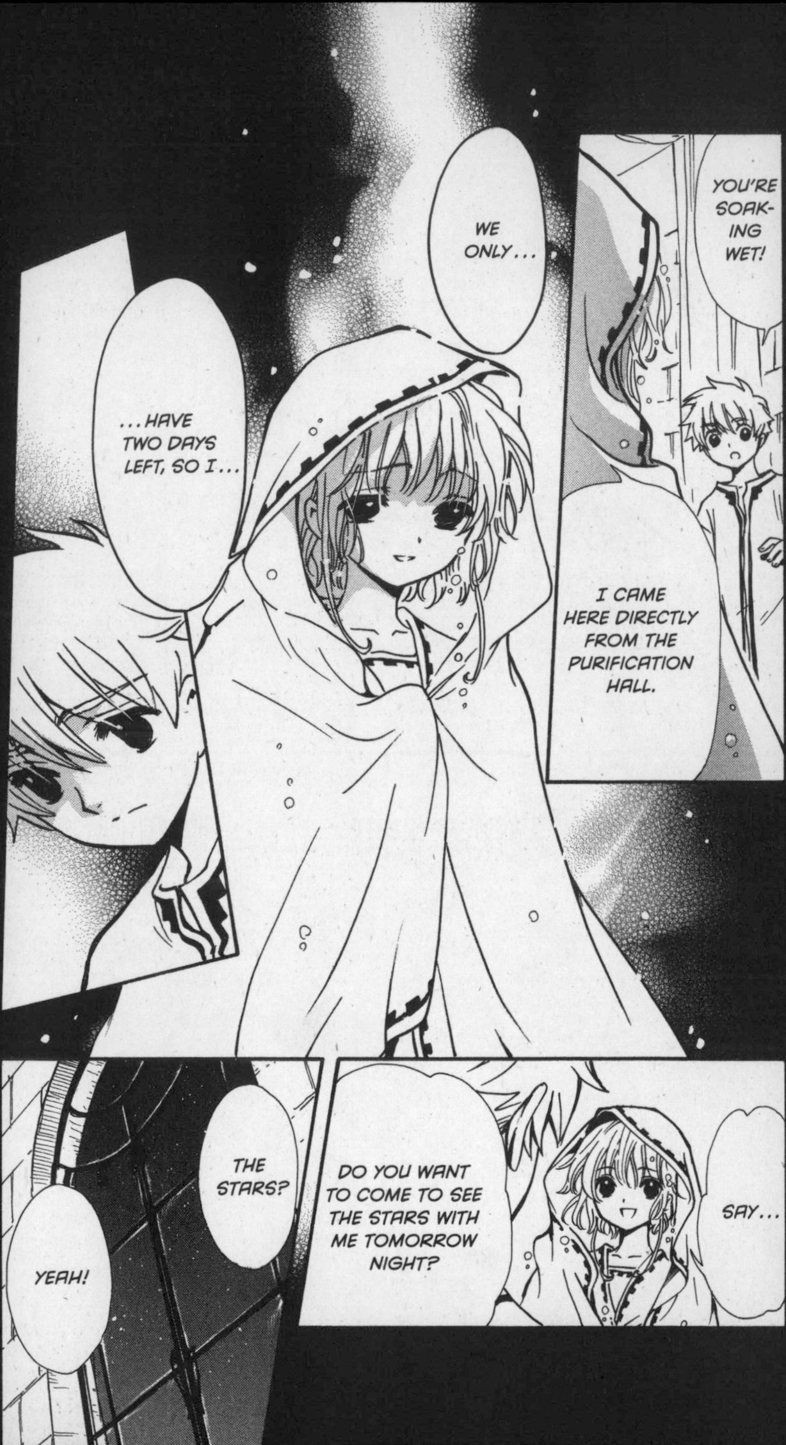
YOU'RE SOAK-ING WET!
I CAME HERE DIRECTLY FROM THE PURIFICATION HALL.
WE ONLY...
...HAVE TWO DAYS LEFT, SO I...
SAY...
DO YOU WANT TO COME TO SEE THE STARS WITH ME TOMORROW NIGHT?
THE STARS?
YEAH!

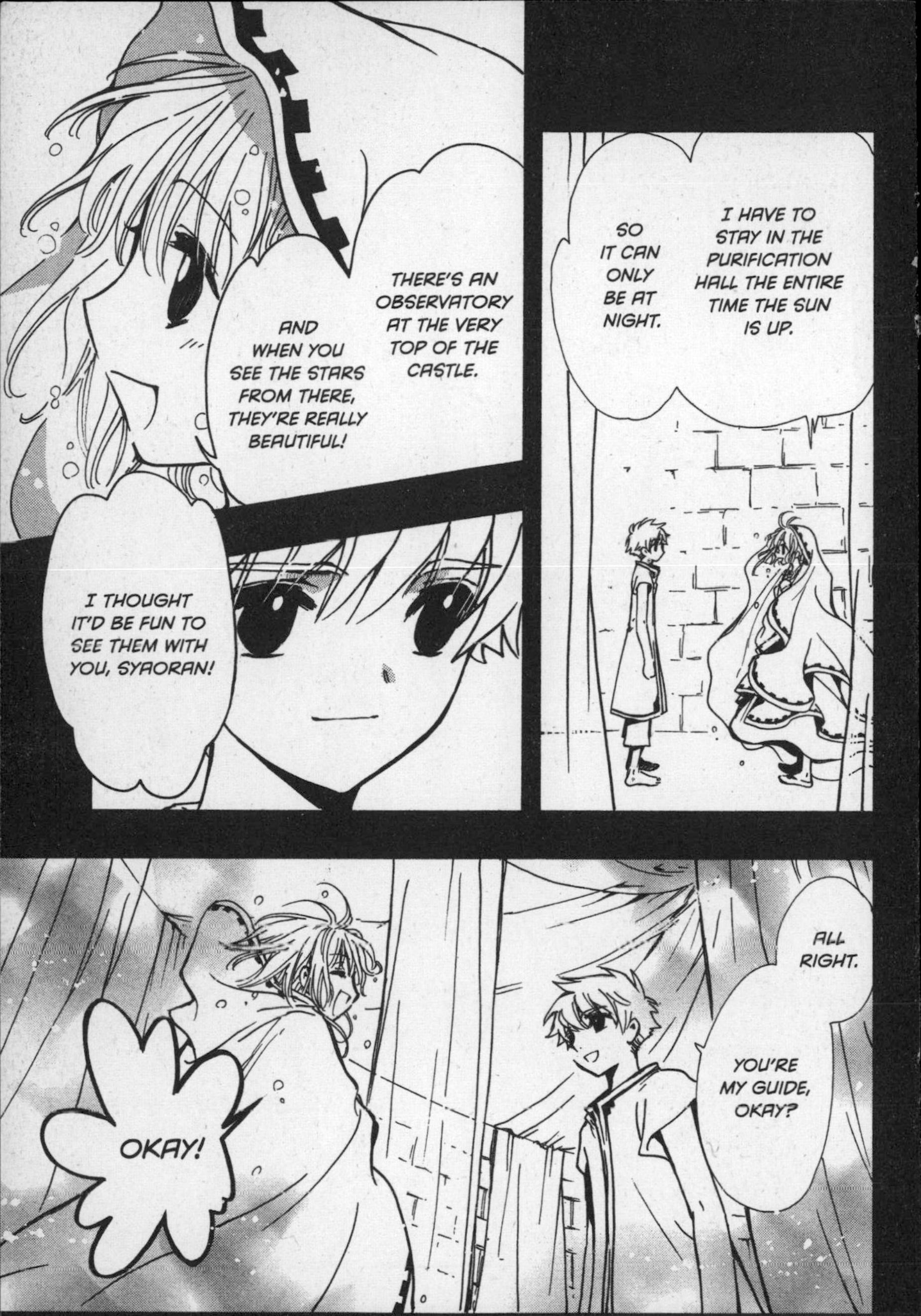
I HAVE TO STAY IN THE PURIFICATION HALL THE ENTIRE TIME THE SUN IS UP.
SO IT CAN ONLY BE AT NIGHT.
THERE'S AN OBSERVATORY AT THE VERY TOP OF THE CASTLE.
AND WHEN YOU SEE THE STARS FROM THERE, THEY'RE REALLY BEAUTIFUL!
I THOUGHT IT'D BE FUN TO SEE THEM WITH YOU, SYAORAN!
ALL RIGHT.
YOU'RE MY GUIDE, OKAY?
OKAY!

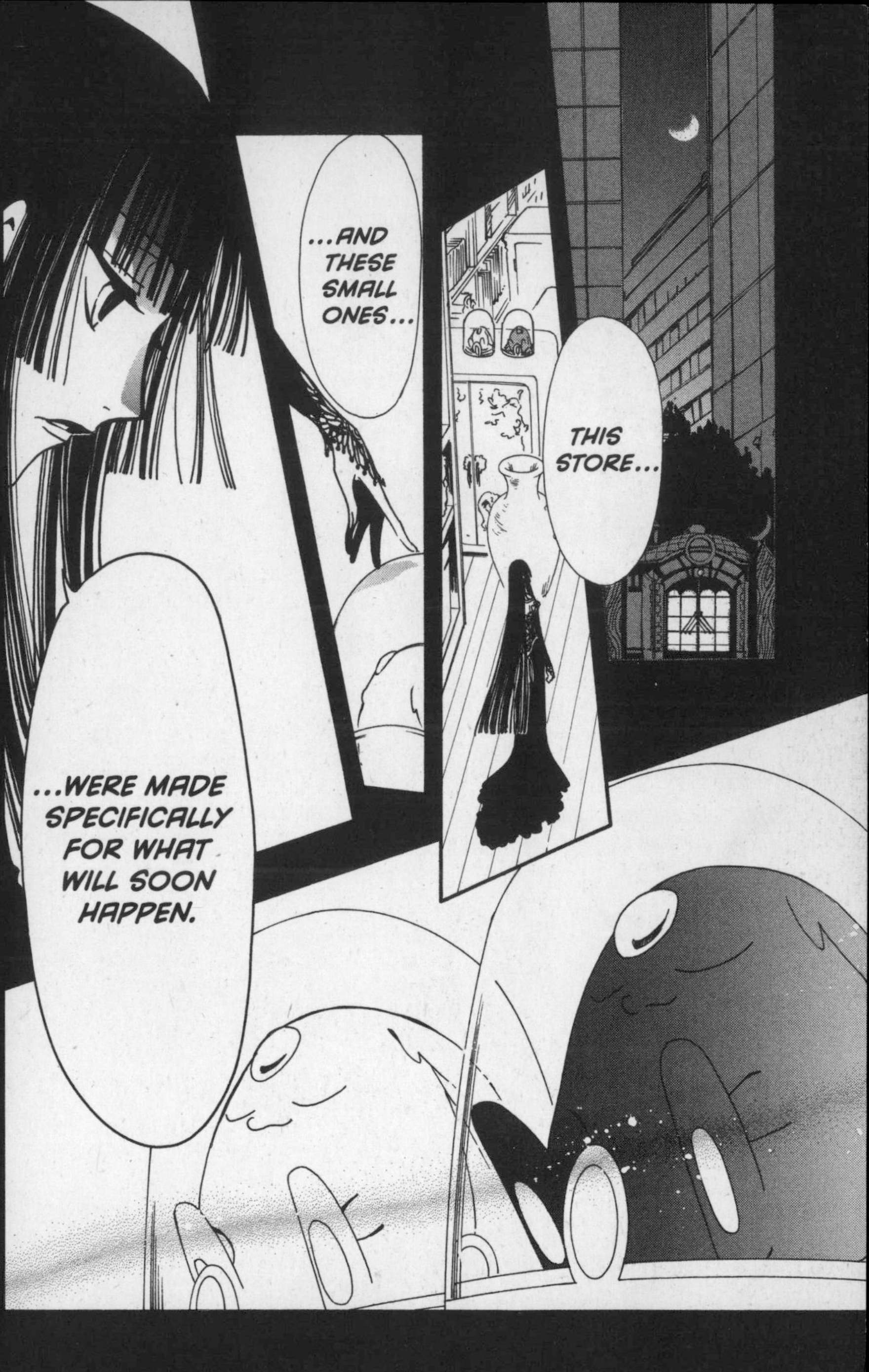
THIS STORE...
...AND THESE SMALL ONES...
...WERE MADE SPECIFICALLY FOR WHAT WILL SOON HAPPEN.

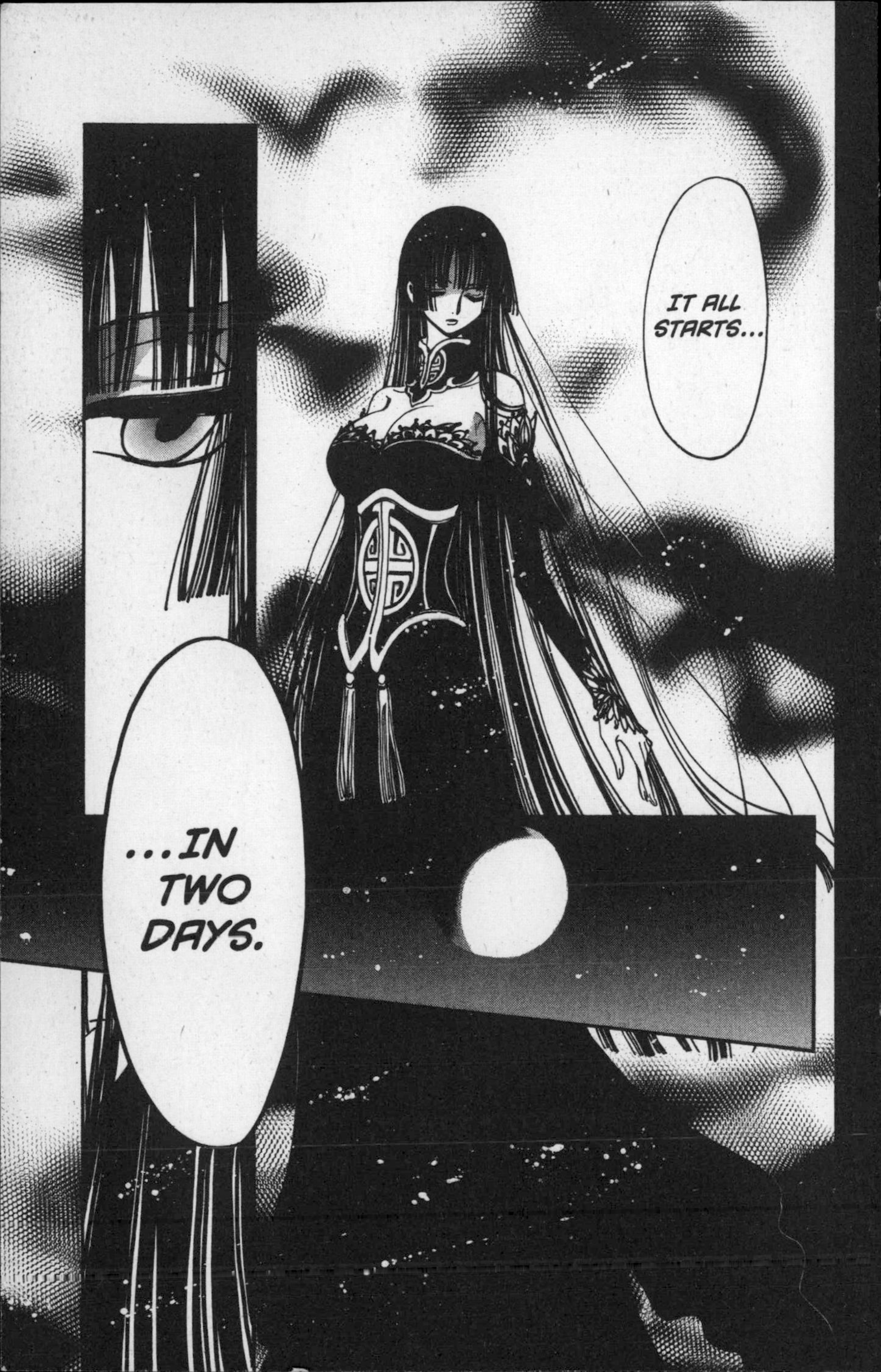
IT ALL STARTS...
...IN TWO DAYS.

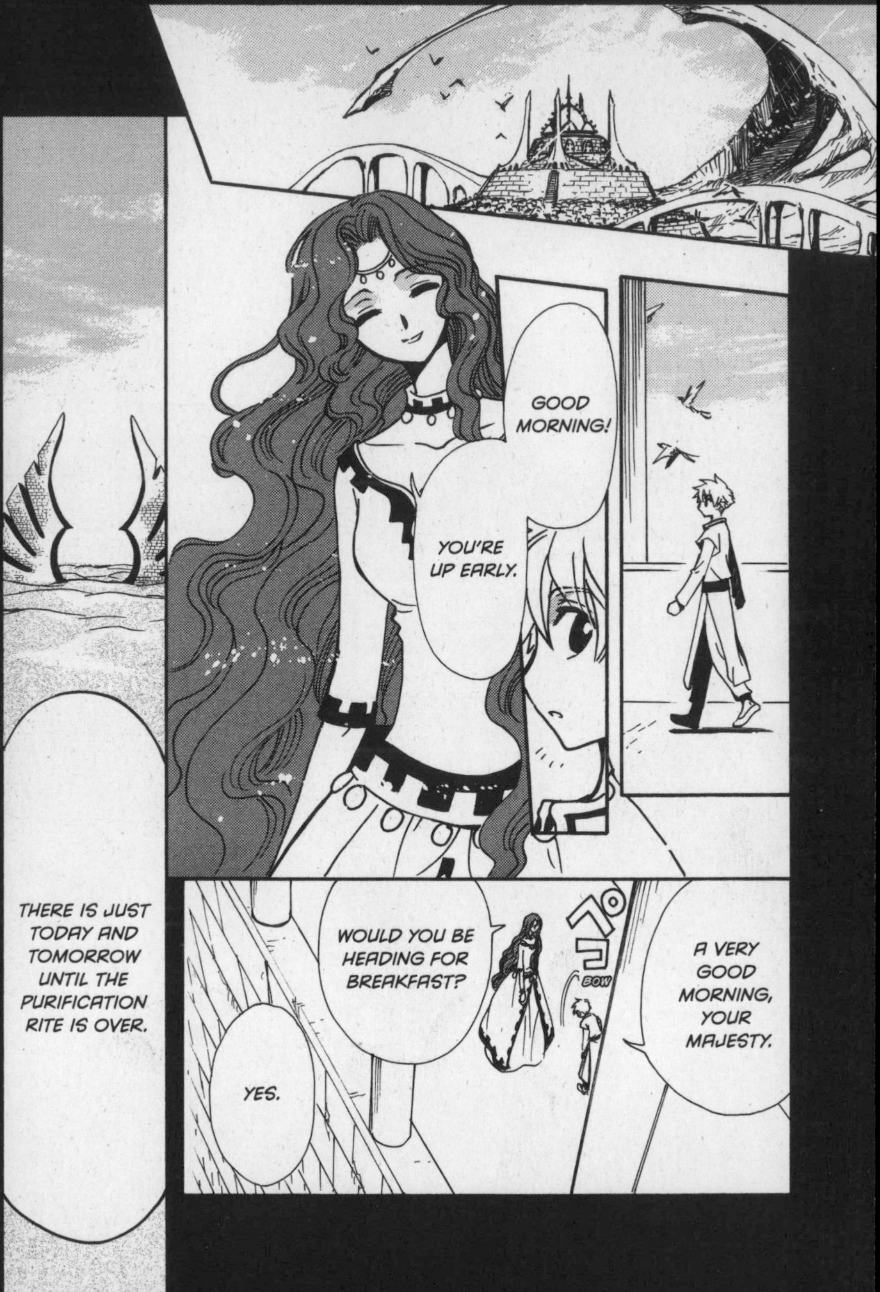
GOOD MORNING!
YOU'RE UP EARLY.
A VERY GOOD MORNING, YOUR MAJESTY.
ペコ
BOW
WOULD YOU BE HEADING FOR BREAKFAST?
YES.
THERE IS JUST TODAY AND TOMORROW UNTIL THE PURIFICATION RITE IS OVER.

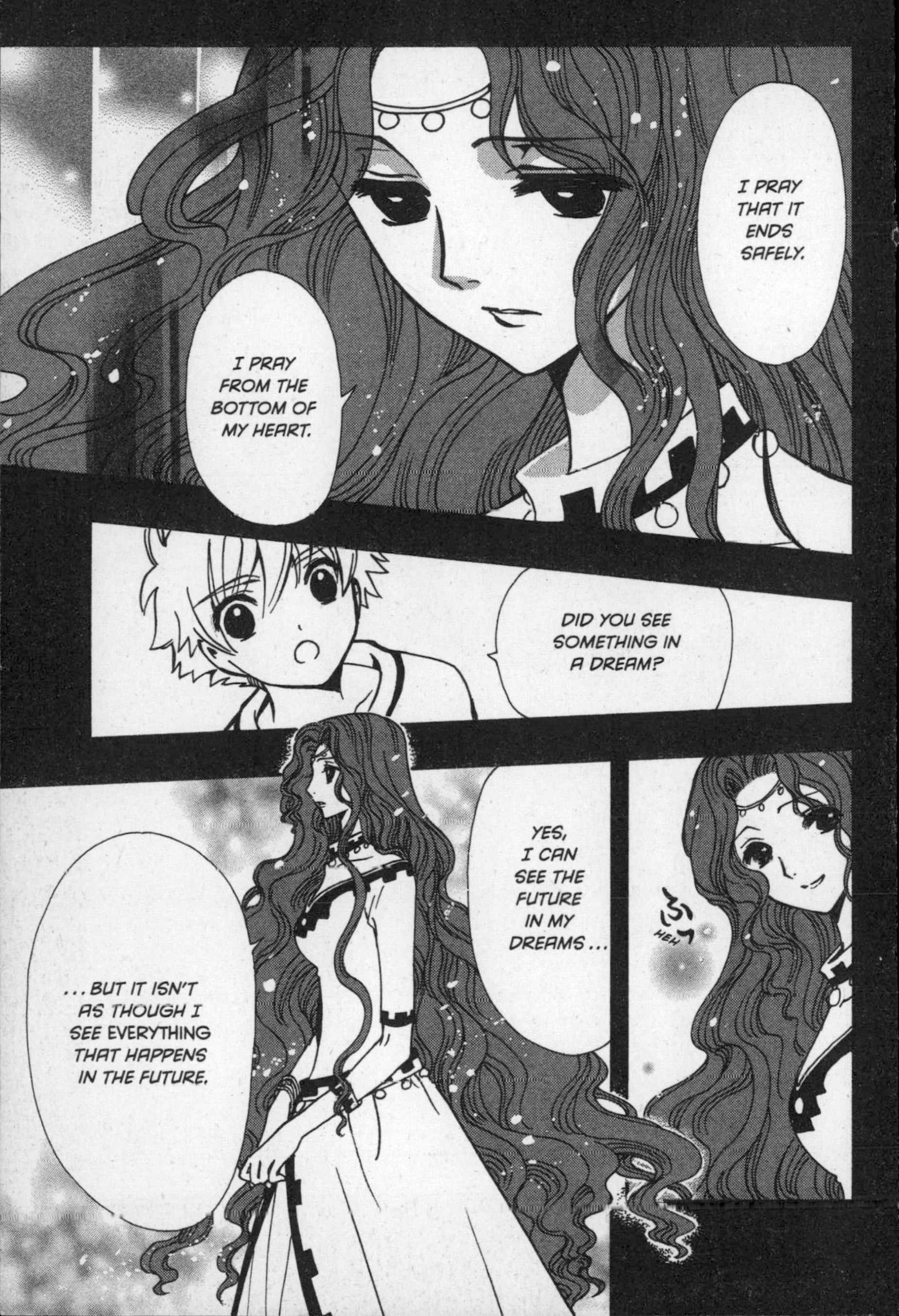
I PRAY THAT IT ENDS SAFELY.
I PRAY FROM THE BOTTOM OF MY HEART.
DID YOU SEE SOMETHING IN A DREAM?
ふっ HEH
YES, I CAN SEE THE FUTURE IN MY DREAMS...
...BUT IT ISN'T AS THOUGH I SEE EVERYTHING THAT HAPPENS IN THE FUTURE.

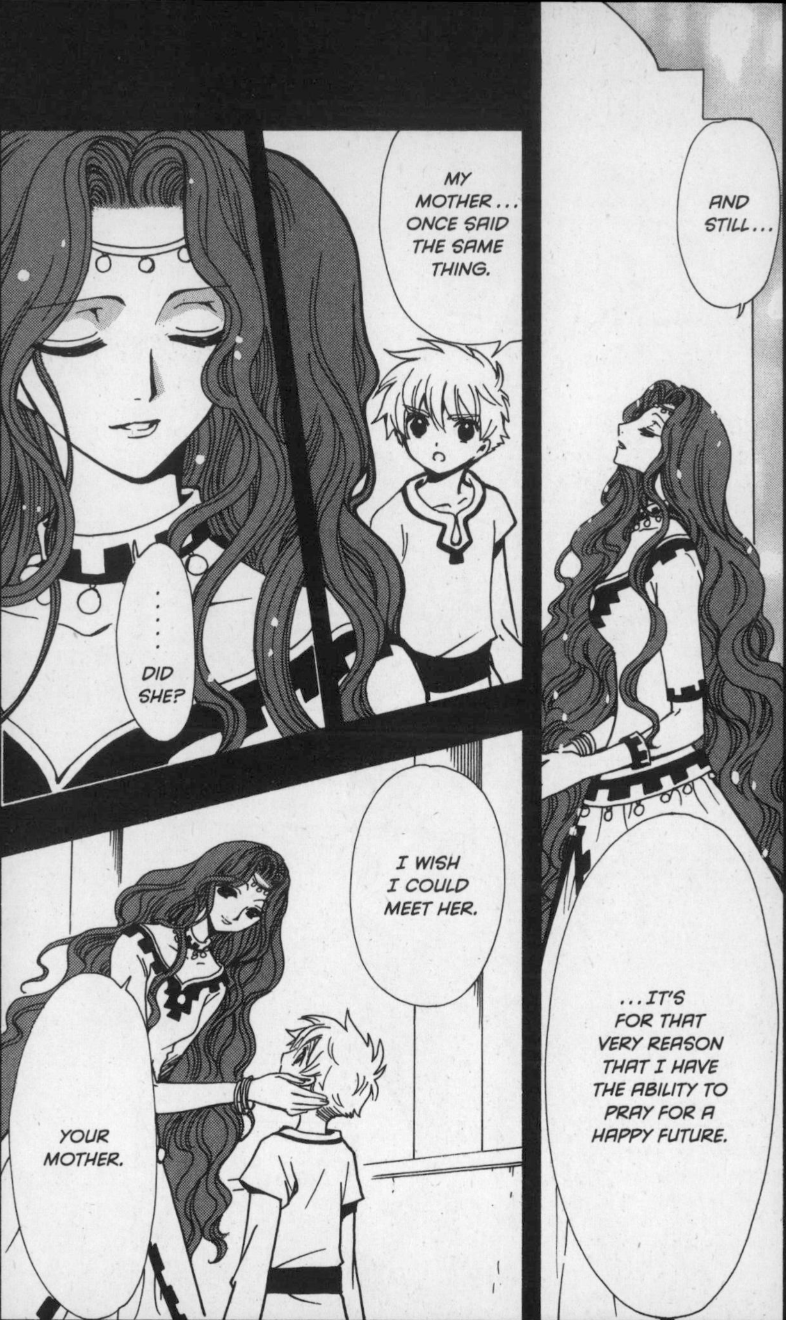
AND STILL...
...IT'S FOR THAT VERY REASON THAT I HAVE THE ABILITY TO PRAY FOR A HAPPY FUTURE.
MY MOTHER... ONCE SAID THE SAME THING.
......DID SHE?
I WISH I COULD MEET HER.
YOUR MOTHER.

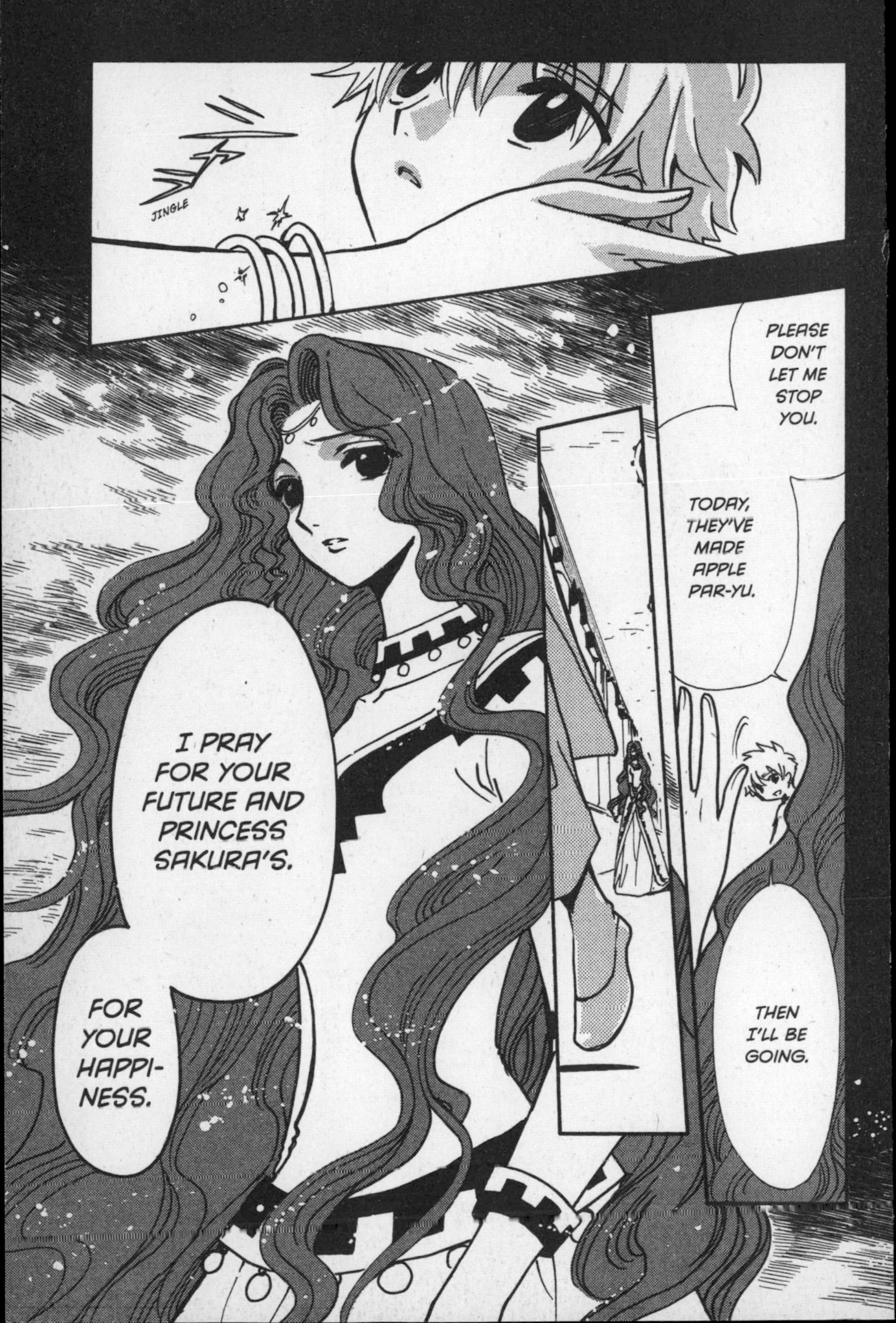
JINGLE
PLEASE DON'T LET ME STOP YOU.
TODAY, THEY'VE MADE APPLE PAR-YU.
THEN I'LL BE GOING.
I PRAY FOR YOUR FUTURE AND PRINCESS SAKURA'S.
FOR YOUR HAPPI-NESS.

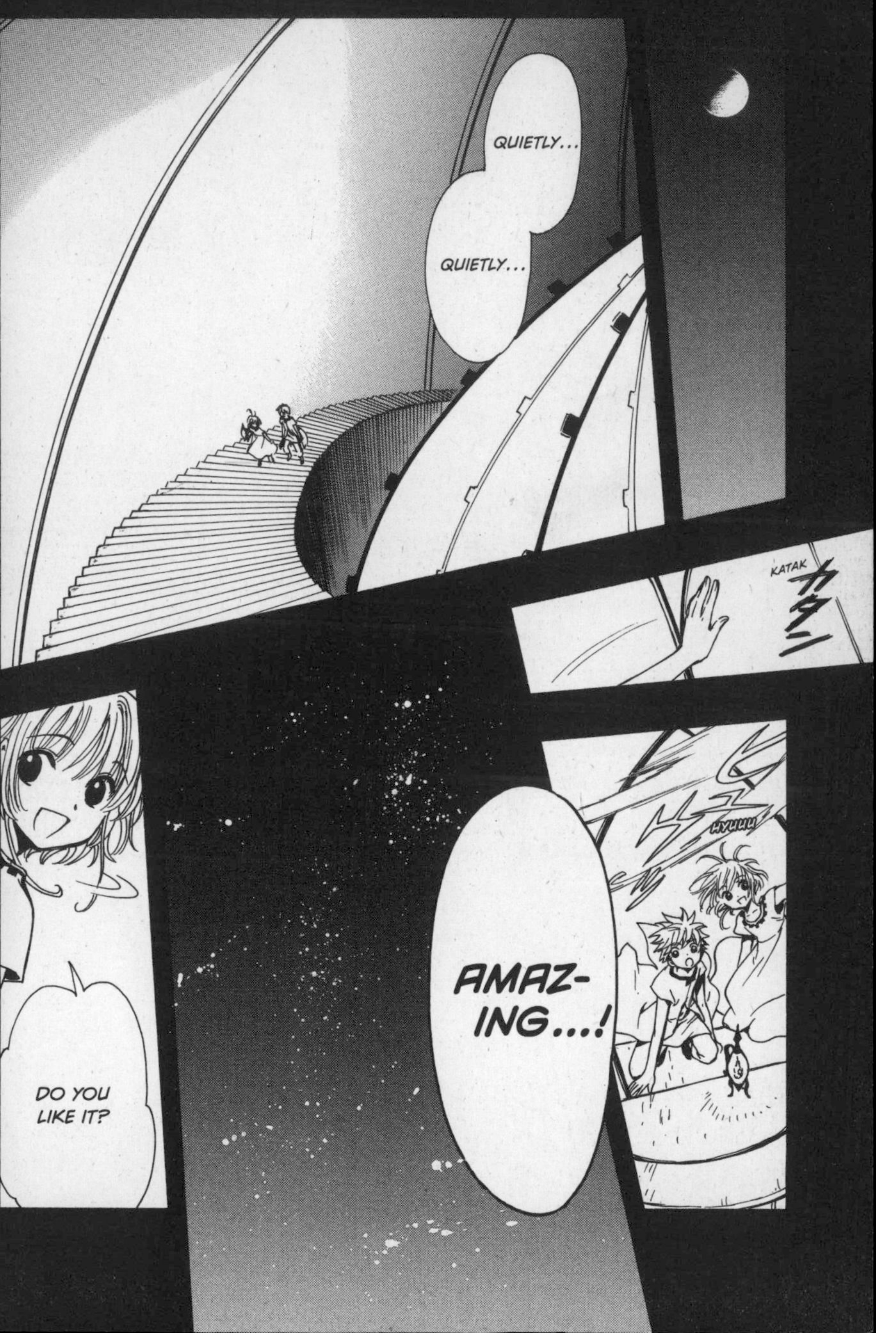
QUIETLY...
QUIETLY...
KATAK
HYUUU
AMAZ-ING...!
DO YOU LIKE IT?

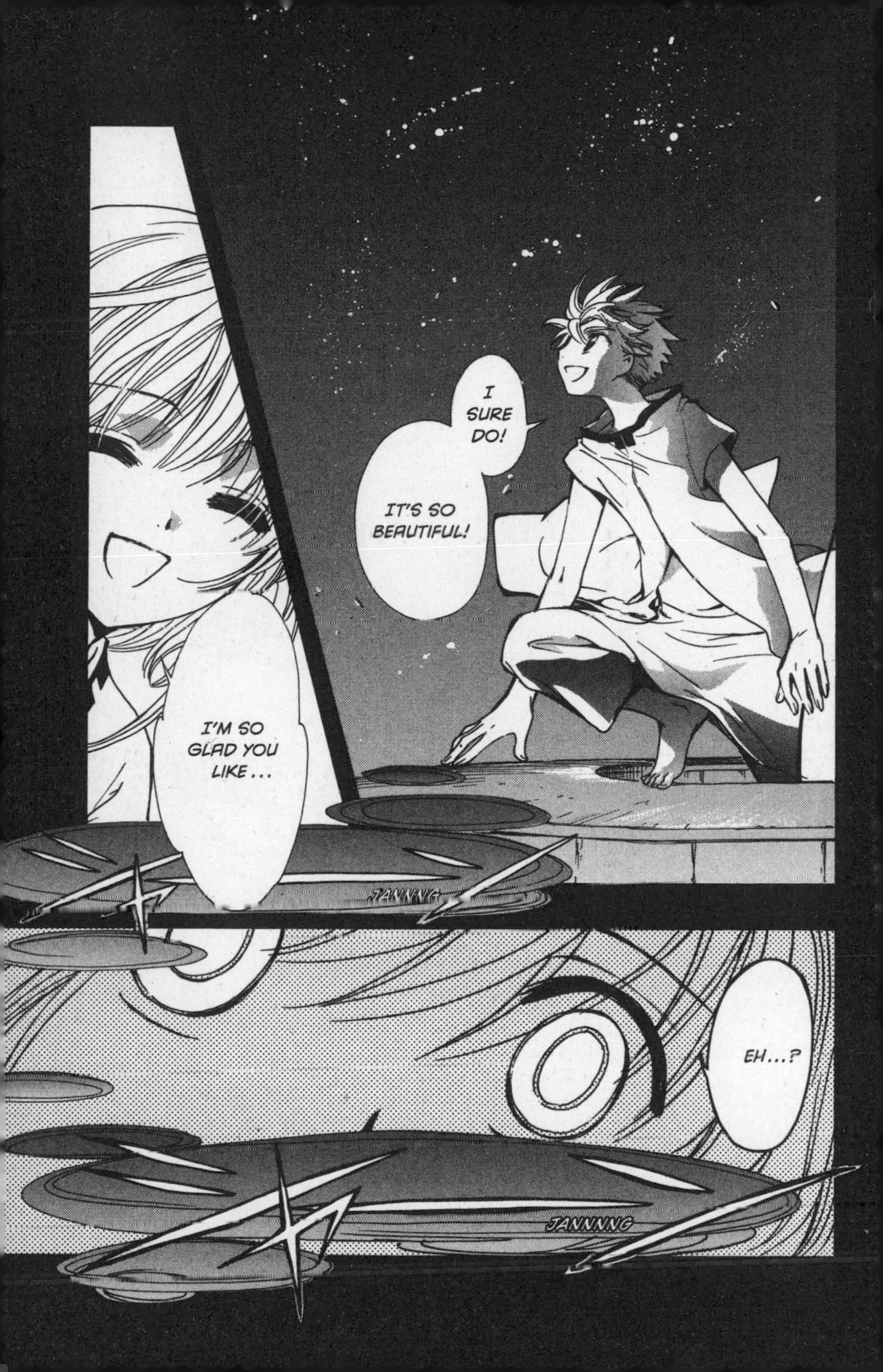
I SURE DO!
IT'S SO BEAUTIFUL!
I'M SO GLAD YOU LIKE...
JANNNG
EH...?
JANNNNG

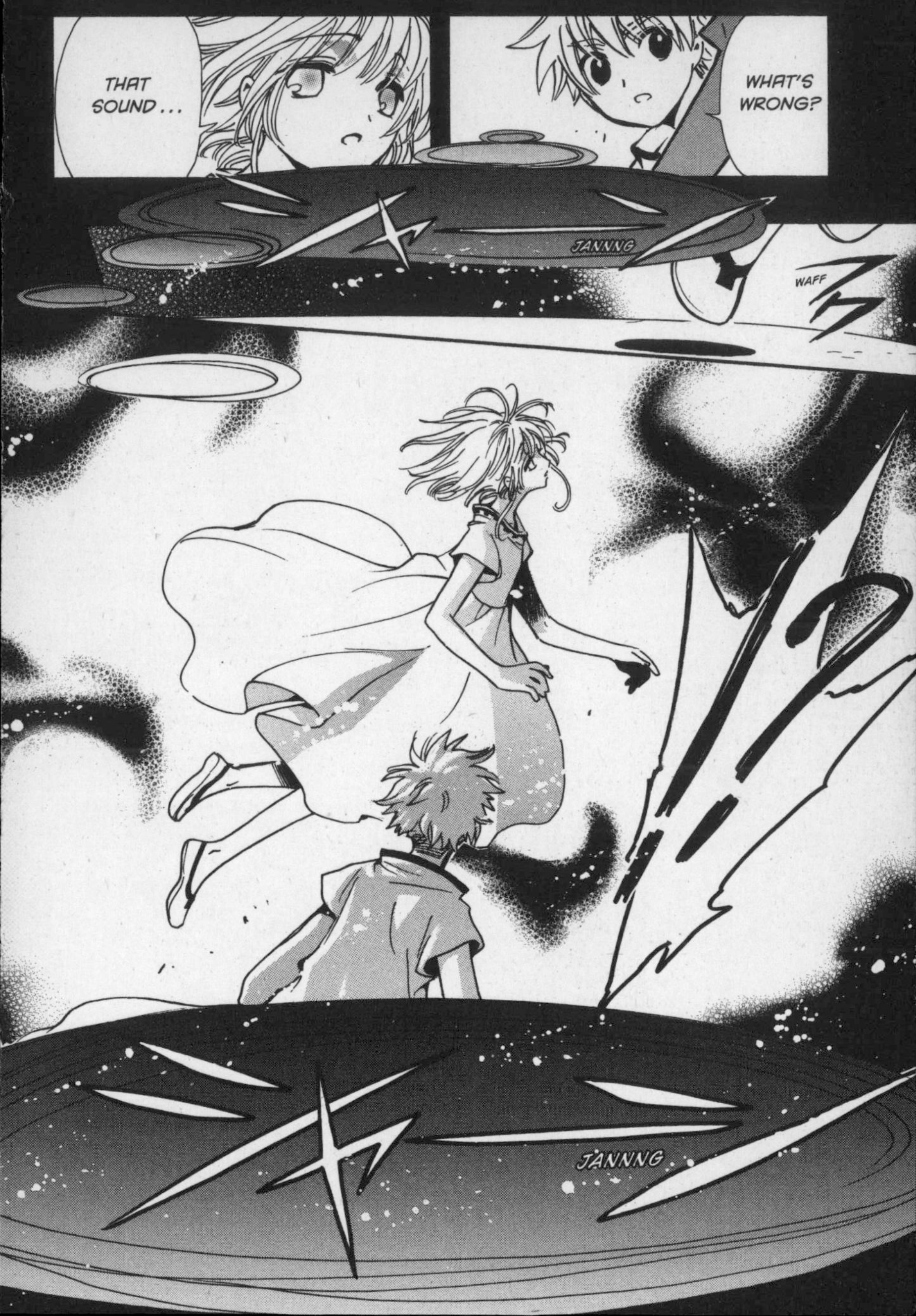
WHAT'S WRONG?
THAT SOUND...
WAFF
JANNNG
JANNNG

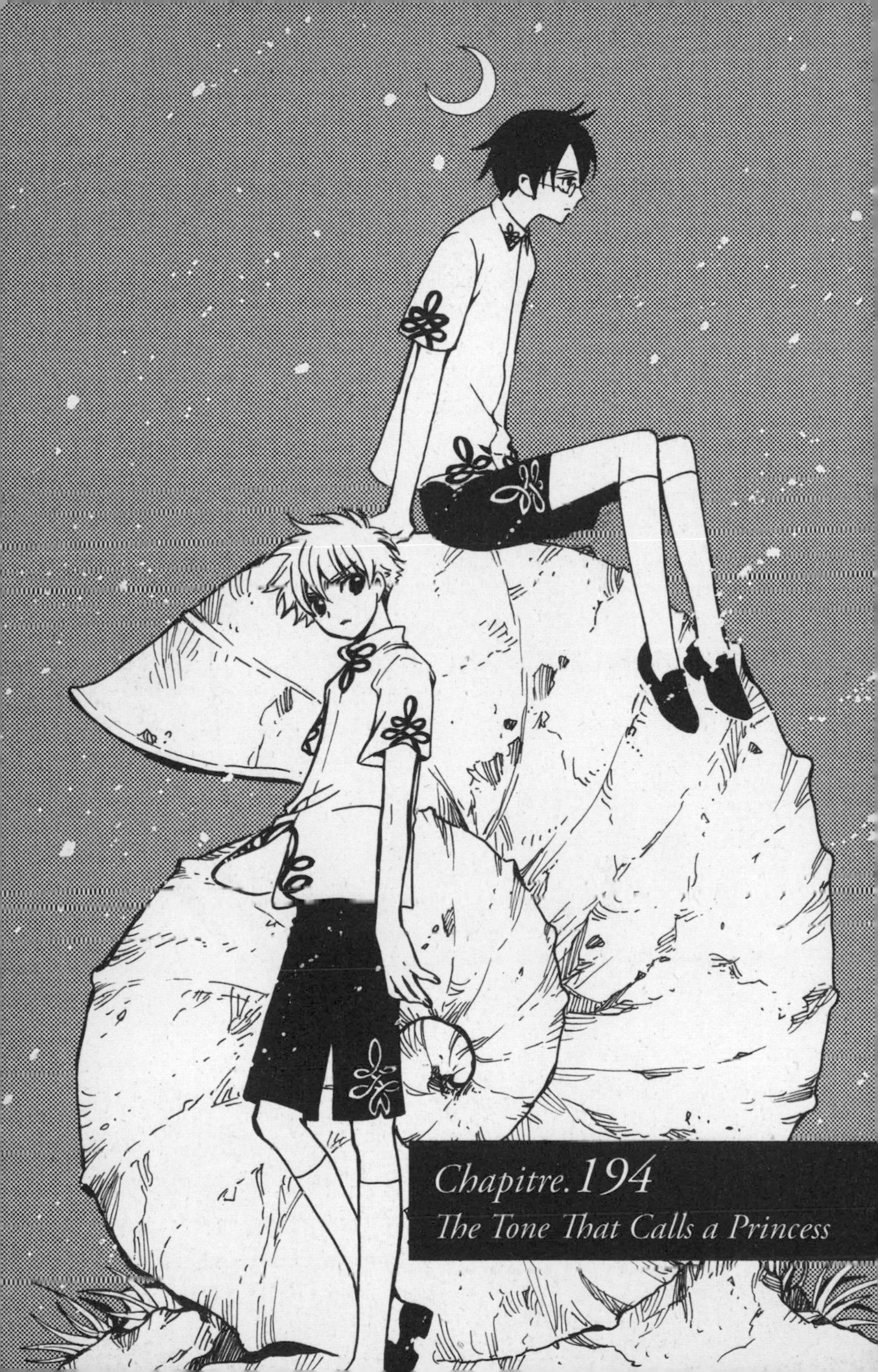

Chapitre. 194
The Tone That Calls a Princess

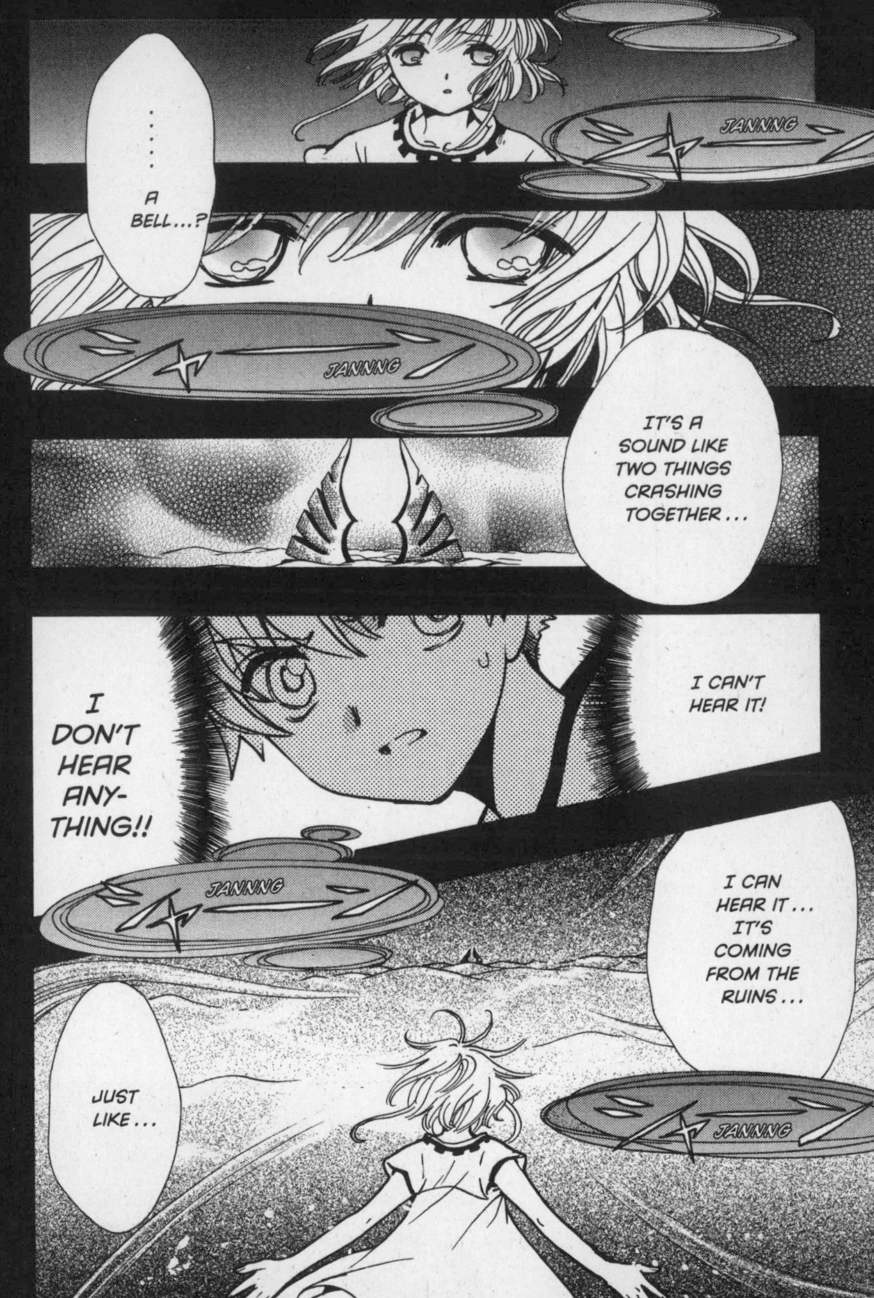
JANNNG
..... A BELL...?
JANNNG
IT'S A SOUND LIKE TWO THINGS CRASHING TOGETHER...
I CAN'T HEAR IT!
I DON'T HEAR ANYTHING!!
I CAN HEAR IT... IT'S COMING FROM THE RUINS...
JANNNG
JANNNG
JUST LIKE...

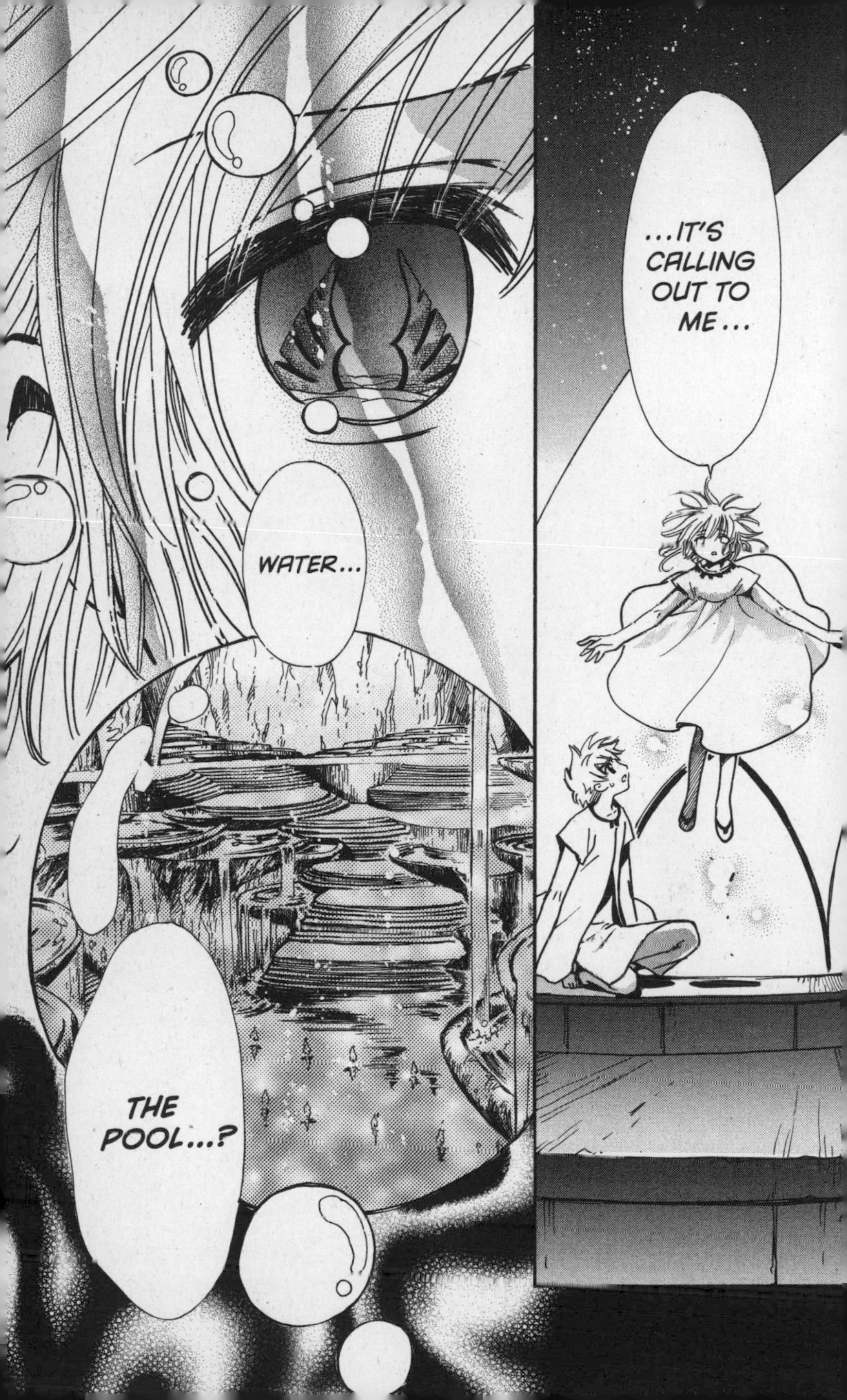
...IT'S CALLING OUT TO ME...
WATER...
THE POOL...?

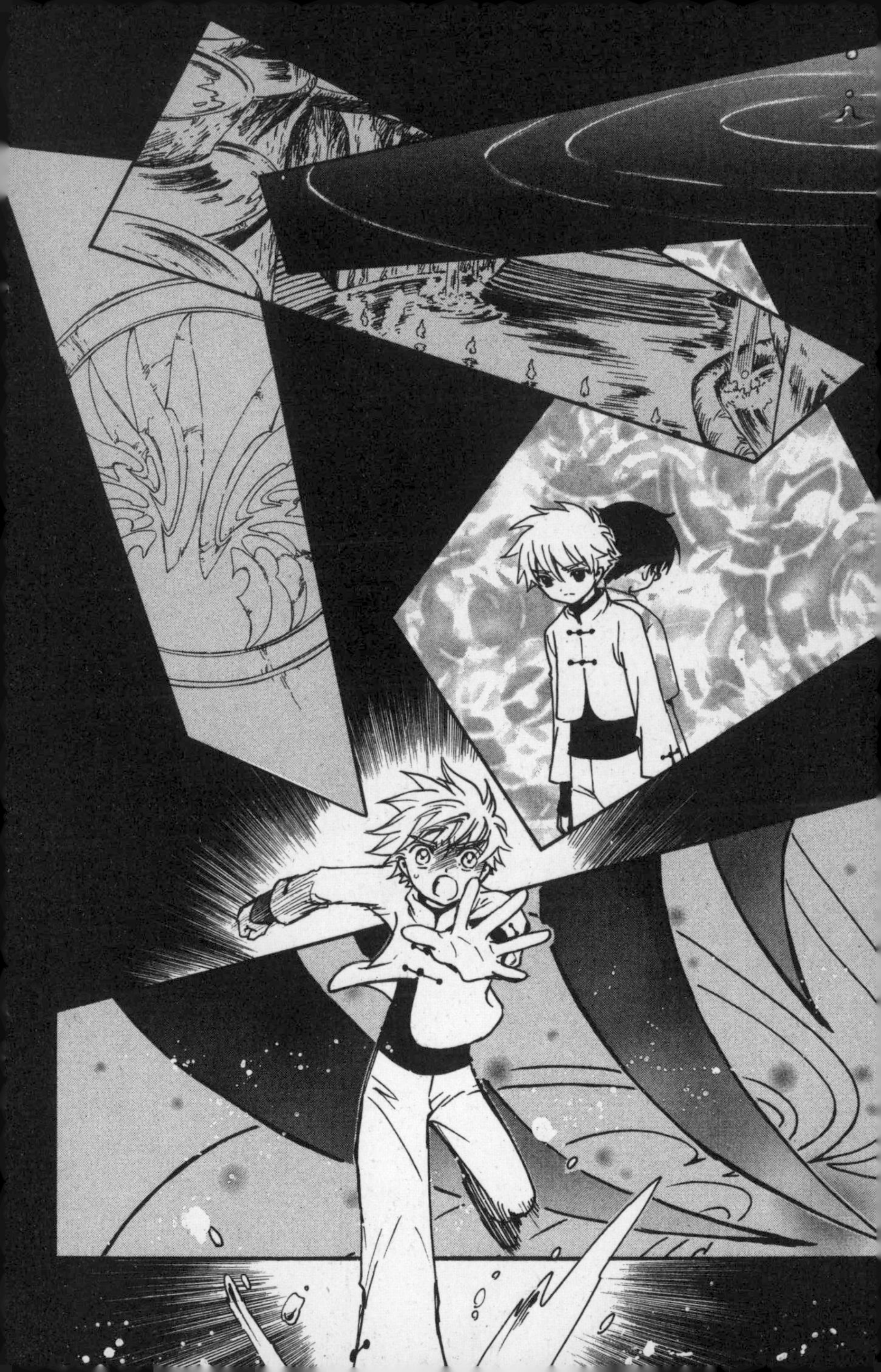

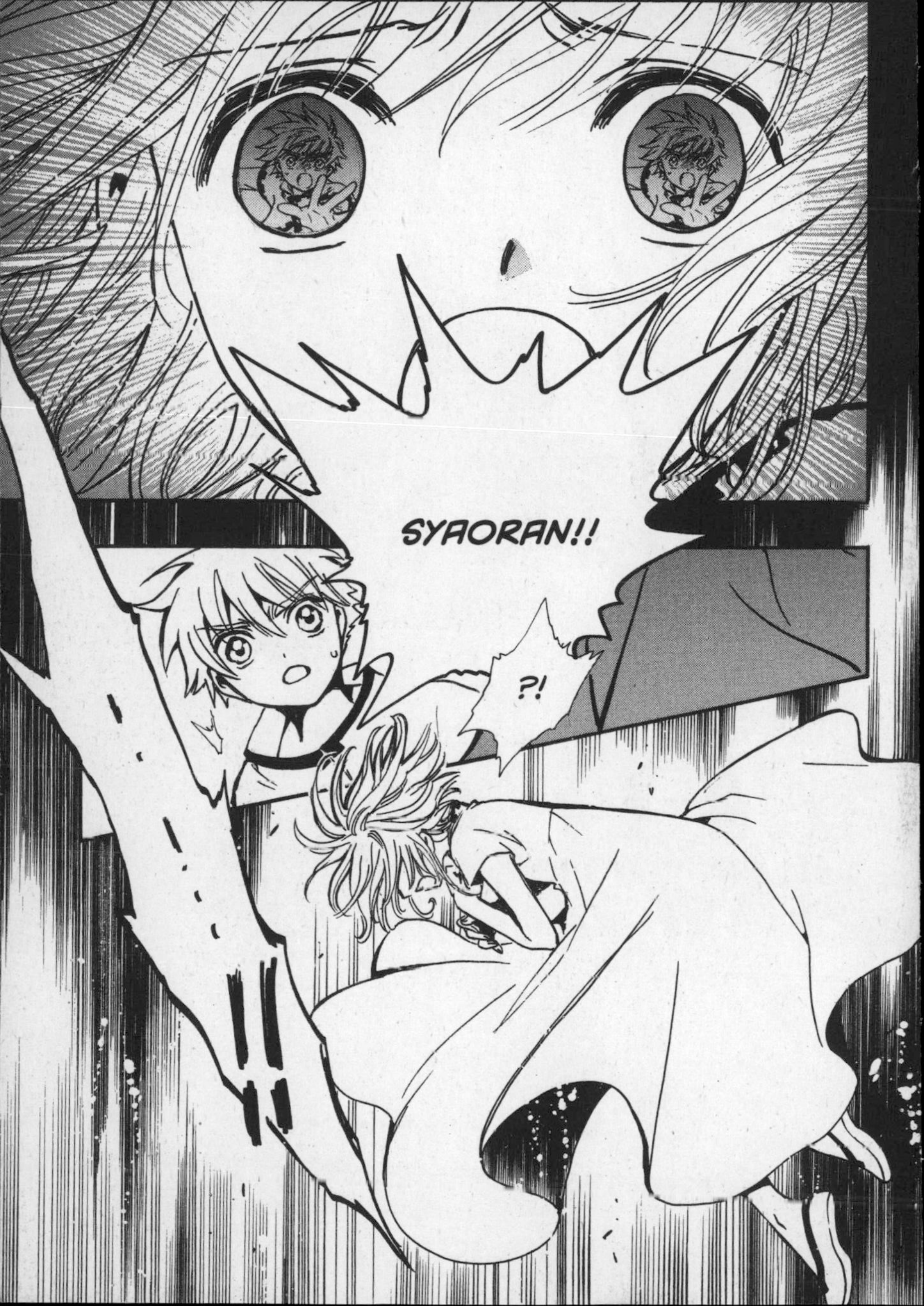
SYAORAN!!
?!

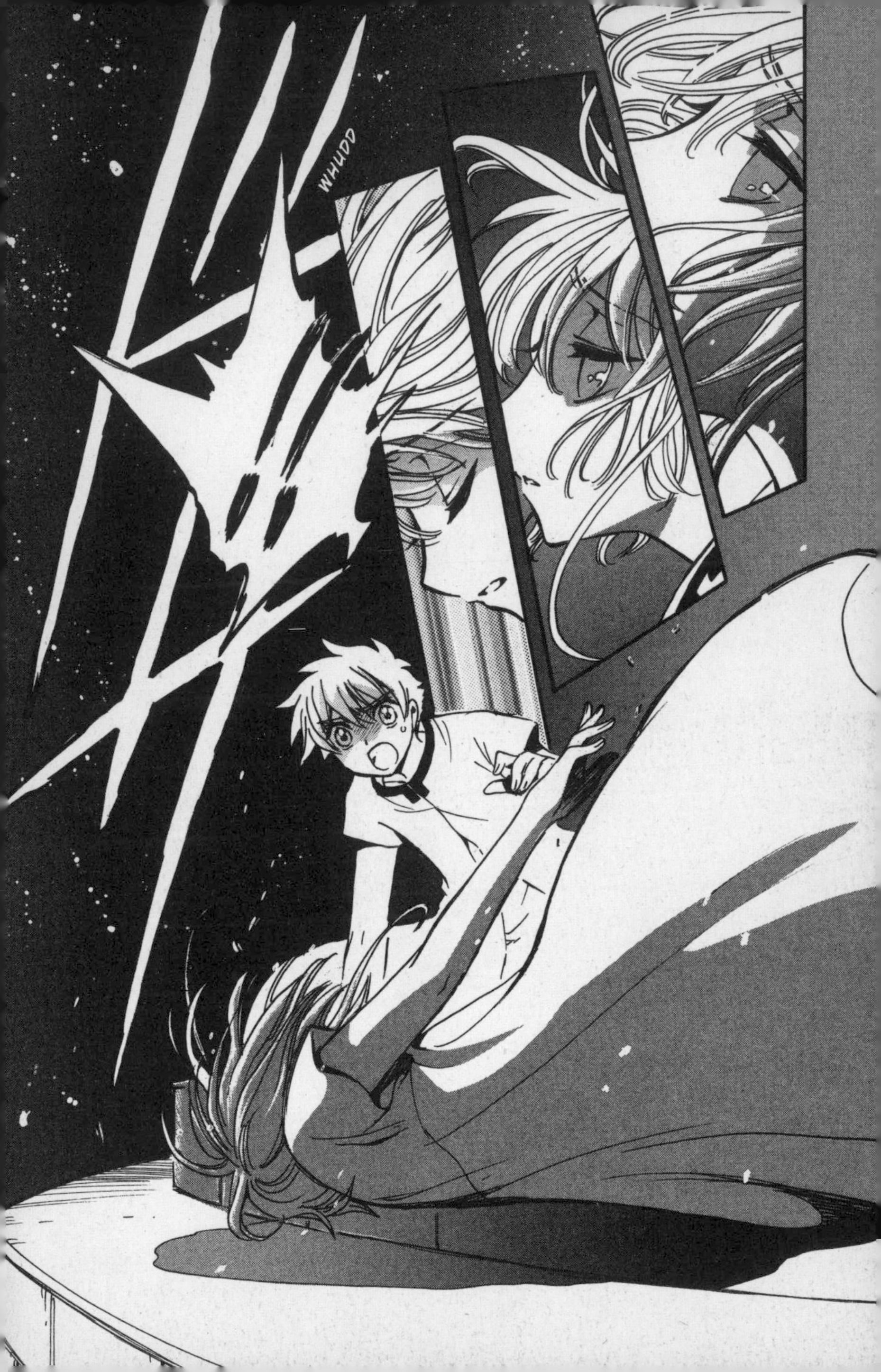
WHUDD

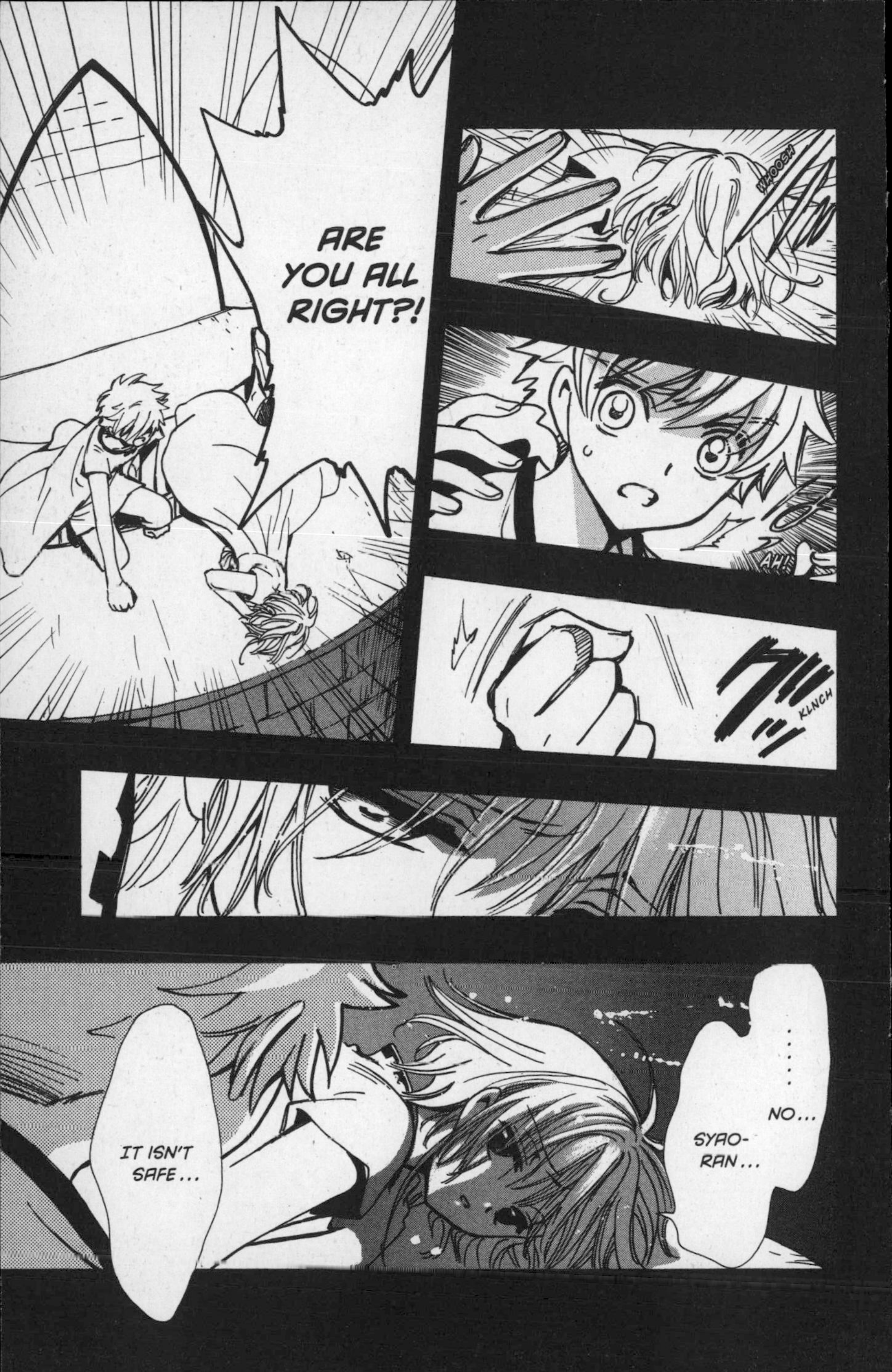
WHOOSH
AH!
KLNCH
ARE YOU ALL RIGHT?!
......
NO... SYAO-RAN...
IT ISN'T SAFE...

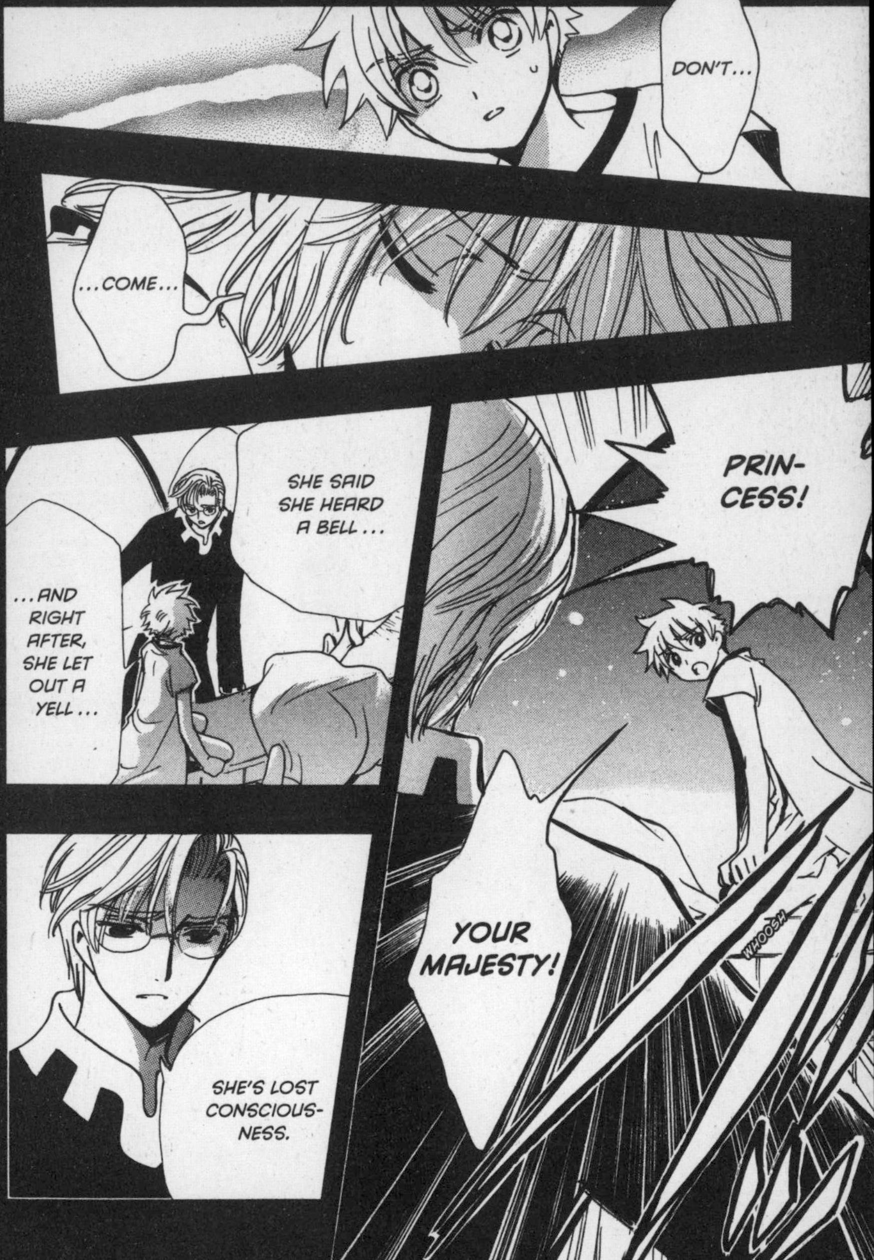
DON'T...
...COME...
PRIN-CESS!
YOUR MAJESTY!
WHOOSH
SHE SAID SHE HEARD A BELL...
...AND RIGHT AFTER, SHE LET OUT A YELL...
SHE'S LOST CONSCIOUS-NESS.

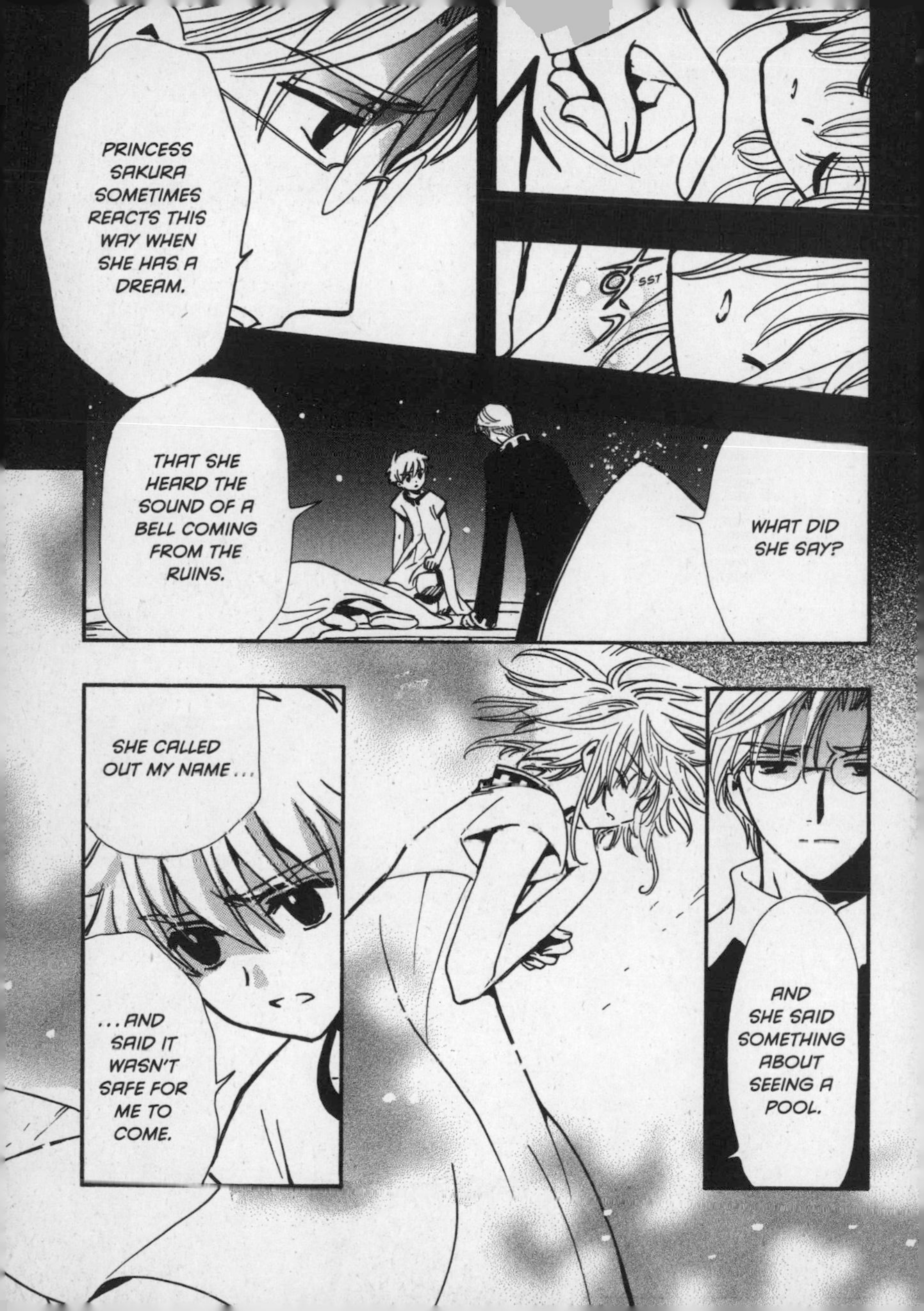
SST
PRINCESS SAKURA SOMETIMES REACTS THIS WAY WHEN SHE HAS A DREAM.
WHAT DID SHE SAY?
THAT SHE HEARD THE SOUND OF A BELL COMING FROM THE RUINS.
AND SHE SAID SOMETHING ABOUT SEEING A POOL.
SHE CALLED OUT MY NAME...
...AND SAID IT WASN'T SAFE FOR ME TO COME.

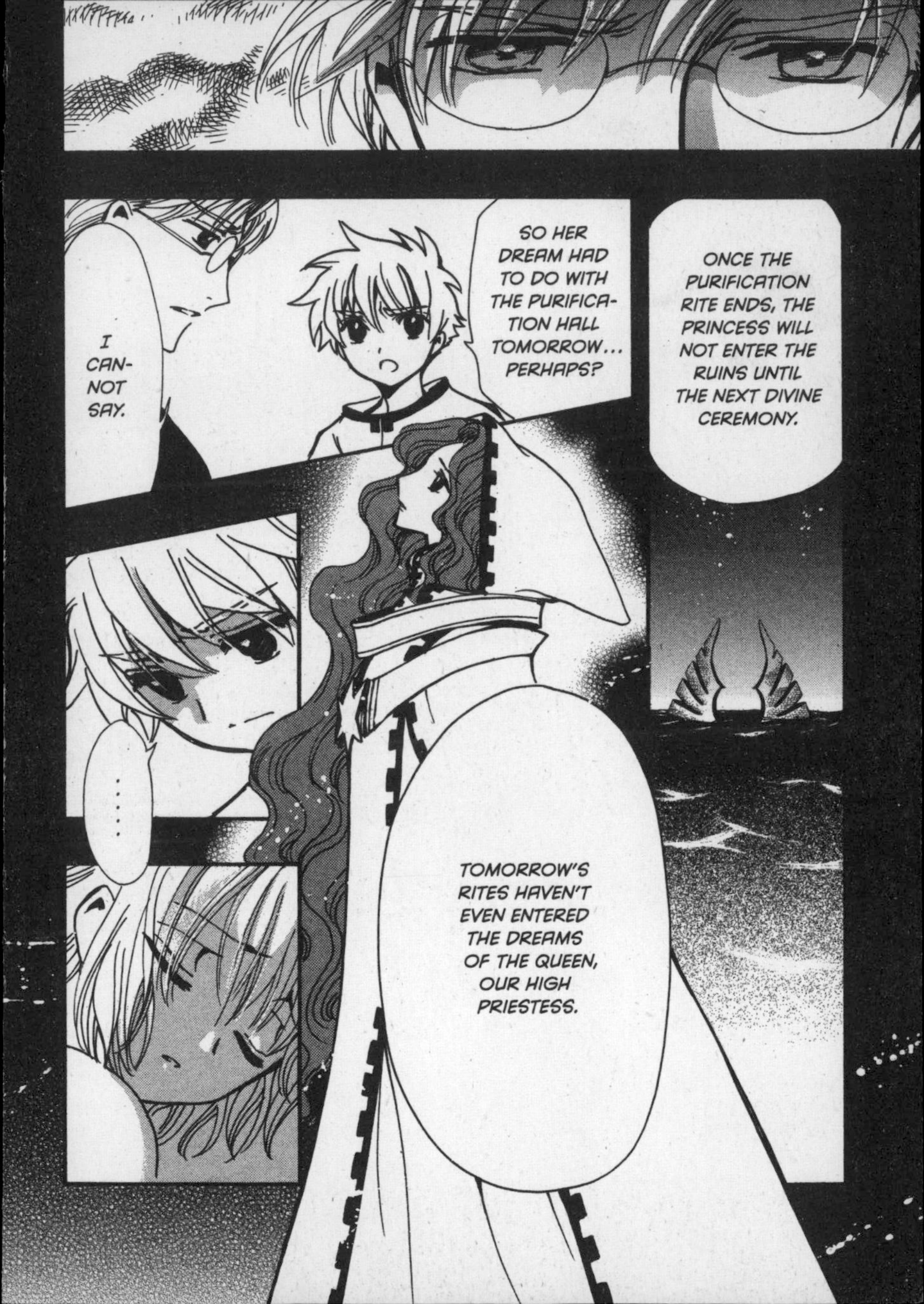
ONCE THE PURIFICATION RITE ENDS, THE PRINCESS WILL NOT ENTER THE RUINS UNTIL THE NEXT DIVINE CEREMONY.
SO HER DREAM HAD TO DO WITH THE PURIFICATION HALL TOMORROW... PERHAPS?
I CANNOT SAY.
TOMORROW'S RITES HAVEN'T EVEN ENTERED THE DREAMS OF THE QUEEN, OUR HIGH PRIESTESS.
......

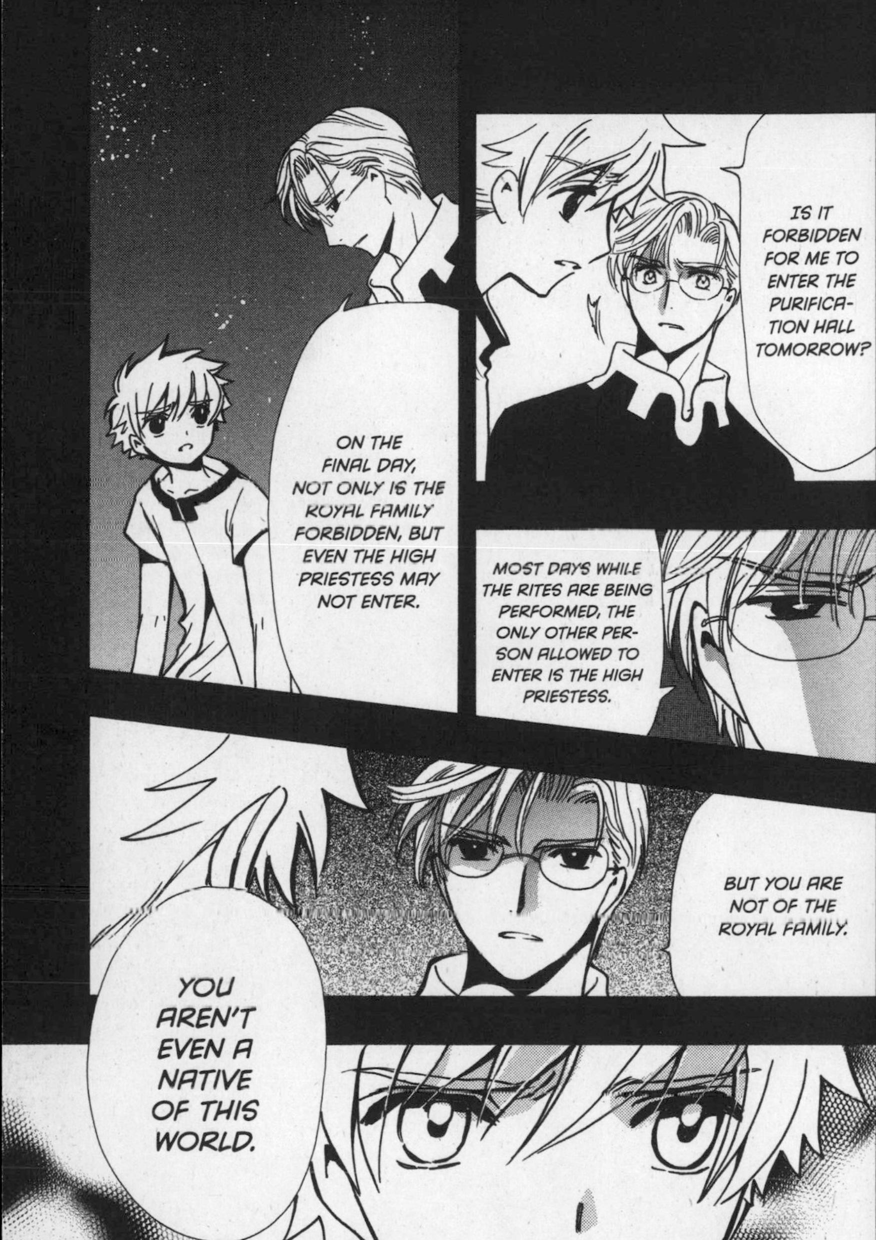
IS IT FORBIDDEN FOR ME TO ENTER THE PURIFICA- TION HALL TOMORROW?
MOST DAYS WHILE THE RITES ARE BEING PERFORMED, THE ONLY OTHER PER- SON ALLOWED TO ENTER IS THE HIGH PRIESTESS.
ON THE FINAL DAY, NOT ONLY IS THE ROYAL FAMILY FORBIDDEN, BUT EVEN THE HIGH PRIESTESS MAY NOT ENTER.
BUT YOU ARE NOT OF THE ROYAL FAMILY.
YOU AREN'T EVEN A NATIVE OF THIS WORLD.

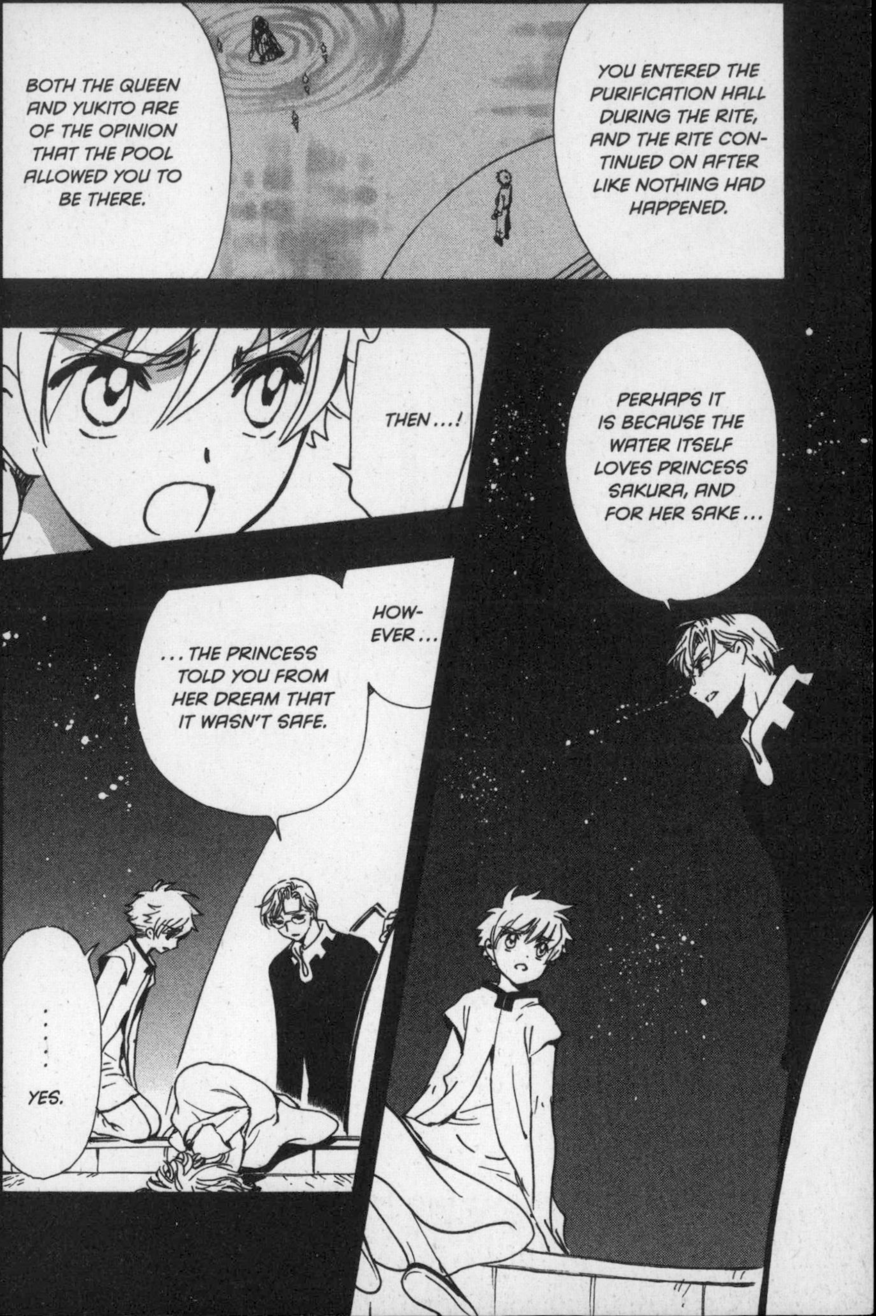
YOU ENTERED THE PURIFICATION HALL DURING THE RITE, AND THE RITE CONTINUED ON AFTER LIKE NOTHING HAD HAPPENED.
BOTH THE QUEEN AND YUKITO ARE OF THE OPINION THAT THE POOL ALLOWED YOU TO BE THERE.
PERHAPS IT IS BECAUSE THE WATER ITSELF LOVES PRINCESS SAKURA, AND FOR HER SAKE...
THEN...!
HOW-EVER...
...THE PRINCESS TOLD YOU FROM HER DREAM THAT IT WASN'T SAFE.
.....
YES.

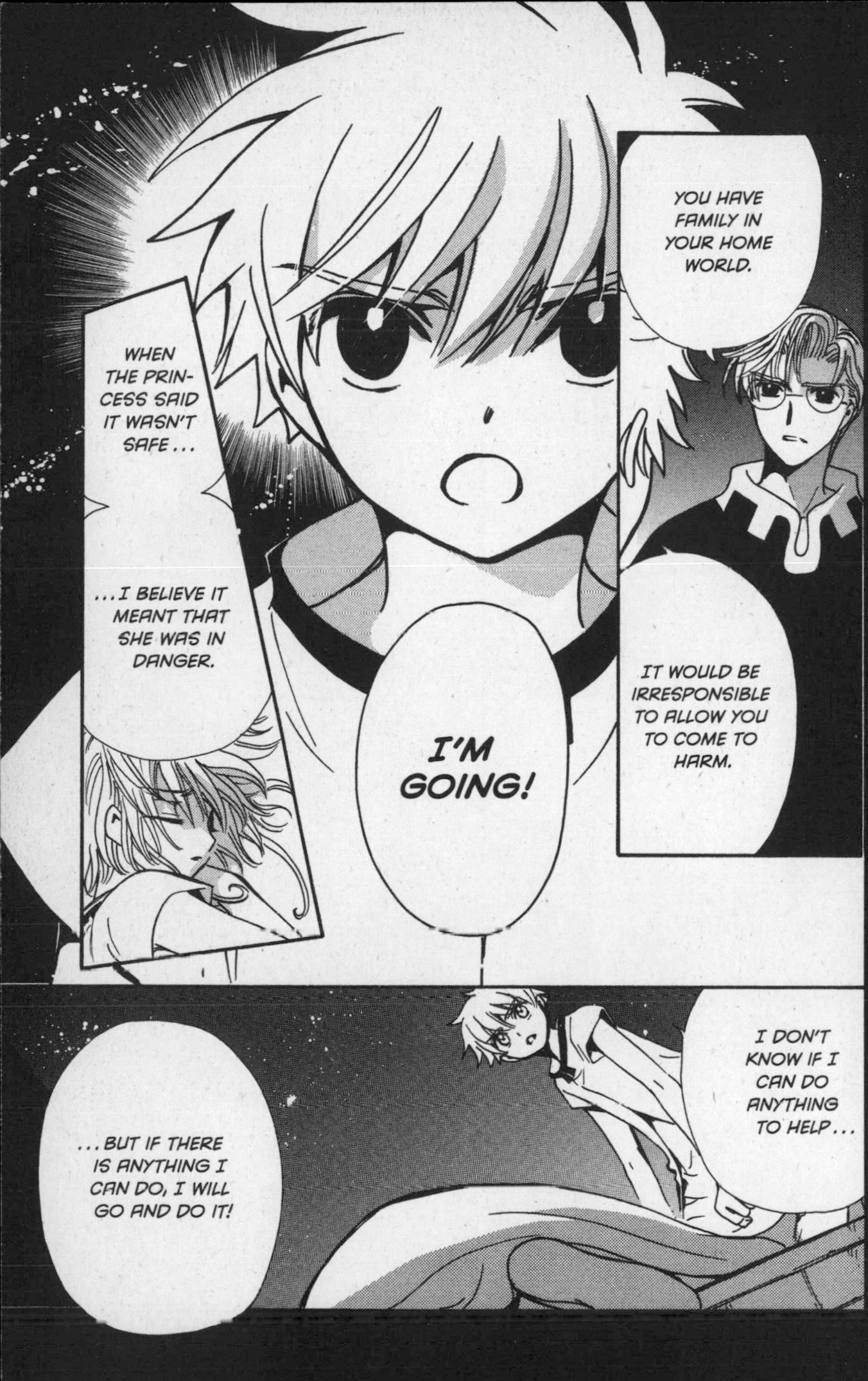
YOU HAVE FAMILY IN YOUR HOME WORLD.
IT WOULD BE IRRESPONSIBLE TO ALLOW YOU TO COME TO HARM.
WHEN THE PRIN-CESS SAID IT WASN'T SAFE...
...I BELIEVE IT MEANT THAT SHE WAS IN DANGER.
I'M GOING!
I DON'T KNOW IF I CAN DO ANYTHING TO HELP...
...BUT IF THERE IS ANYTHING I CAN DO, I WILL GO AND DO IT!

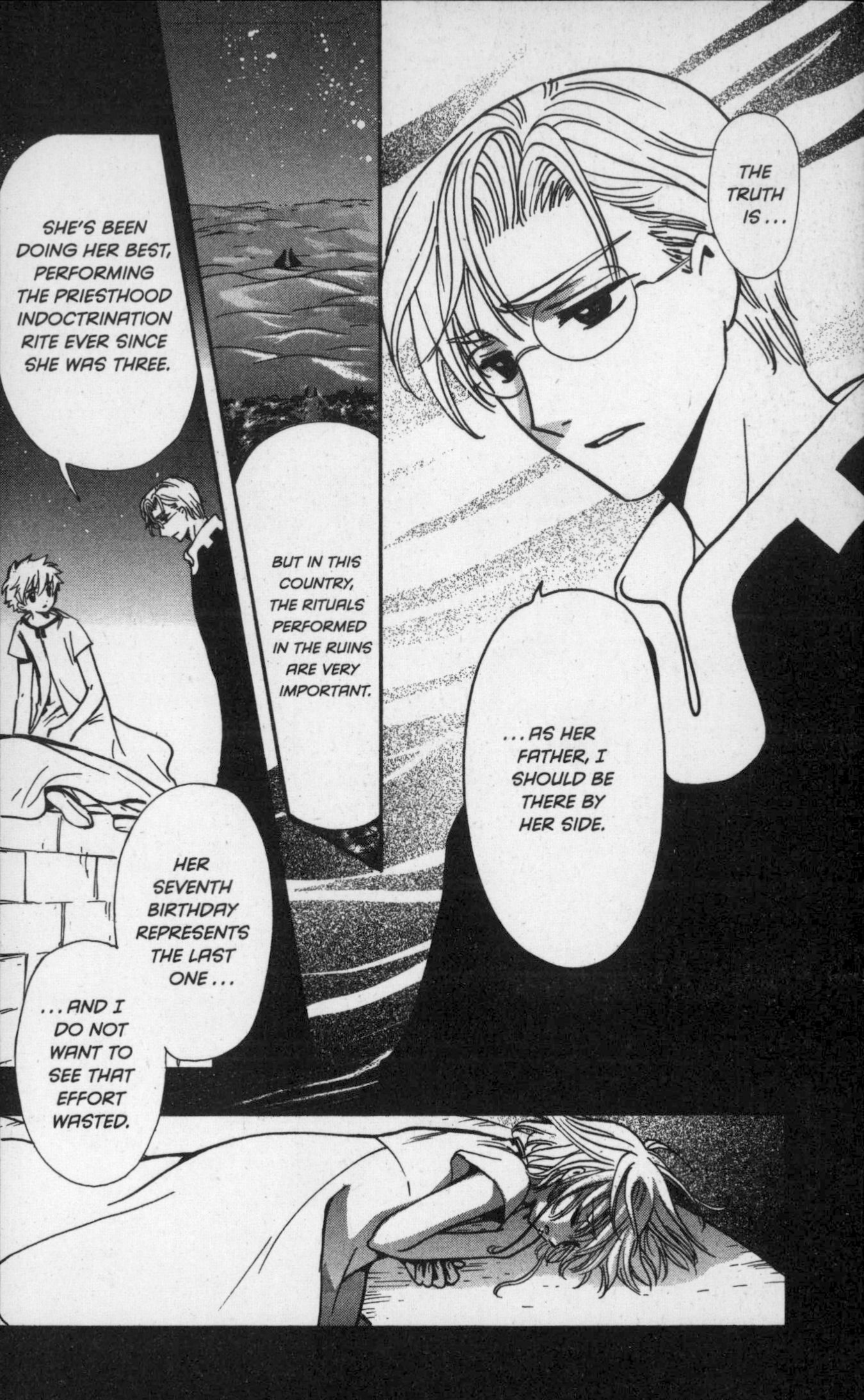
THE TRUTH IS...
...AS HER FATHER, I SHOULD BE THERE BY HER SIDE.
BUT IN THIS COUNTRY, THE RITUALS PERFORMED IN THE RUINS ARE VERY IMPORTANT.
SHE'S BEEN DOING HER BEST, PERFORMING THE PRIESTHOOD INDOCTRINATION RITE EVER SINCE SHE WAS THREE.
HER SEVENTH BIRTHDAY REPRESENTS THE LAST ONE...
...AND I DO NOT WANT TO SEE THAT EFFORT WASTED.

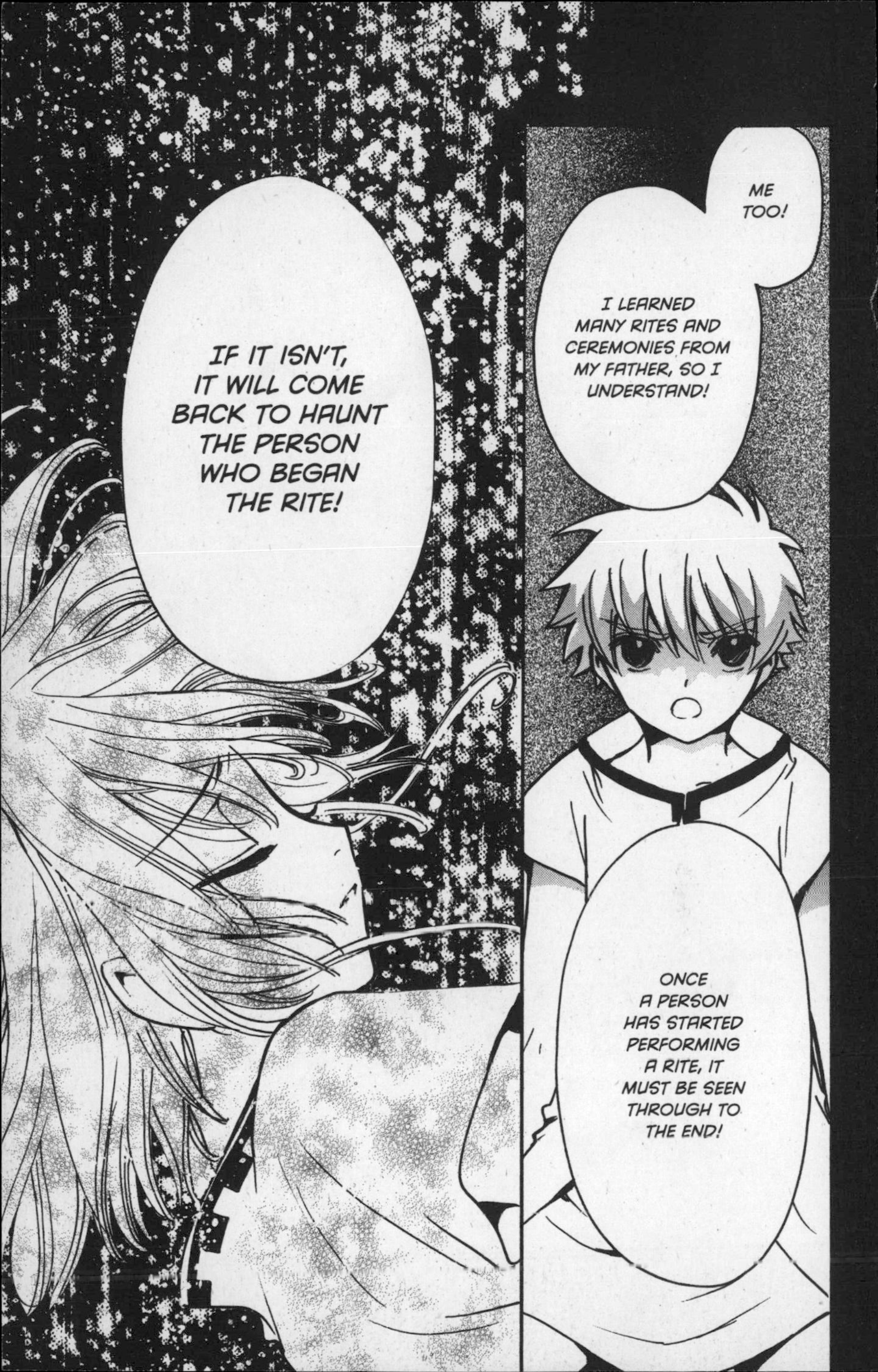
ME TOO!
I LEARNED MANY RITES AND CEREMONIES FROM MY FATHER, SO I UNDERSTAND!
ONCE A PERSON HAS STARTED PERFORMING A RITE, IT MUST BE SEEN THROUGH TO THE END!
IF IT ISN'T, IT WILL COME BACK TO HAUNT THE PERSON WHO BEGAN THE RITE!

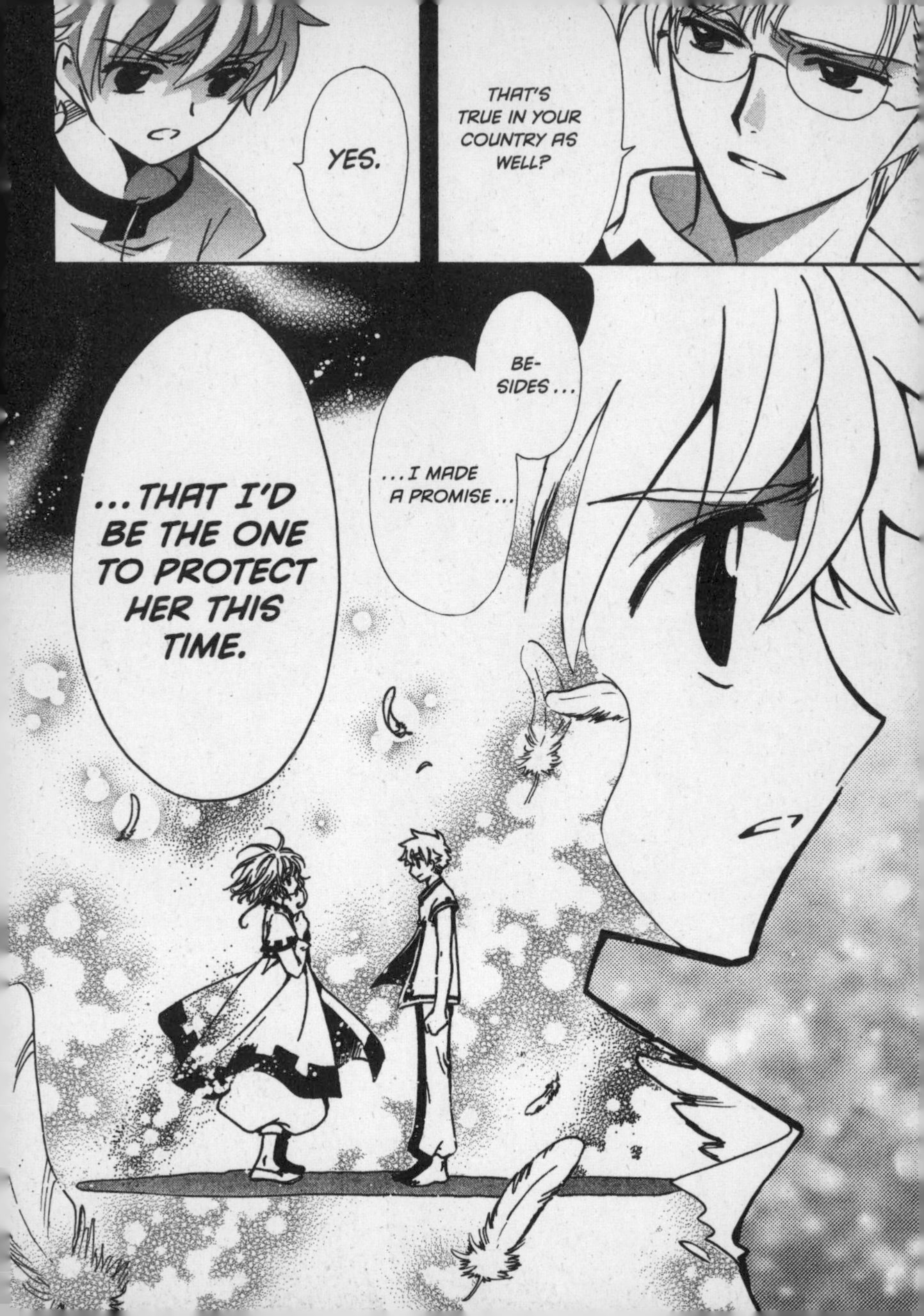
THAT'S TRUE IN YOUR COUNTRY AS WELL?
YES.
BE-SIDES...
...I MADE A PROMISE...
...THAT I'D BE THE ONE TO PROTECT HER THIS TIME.

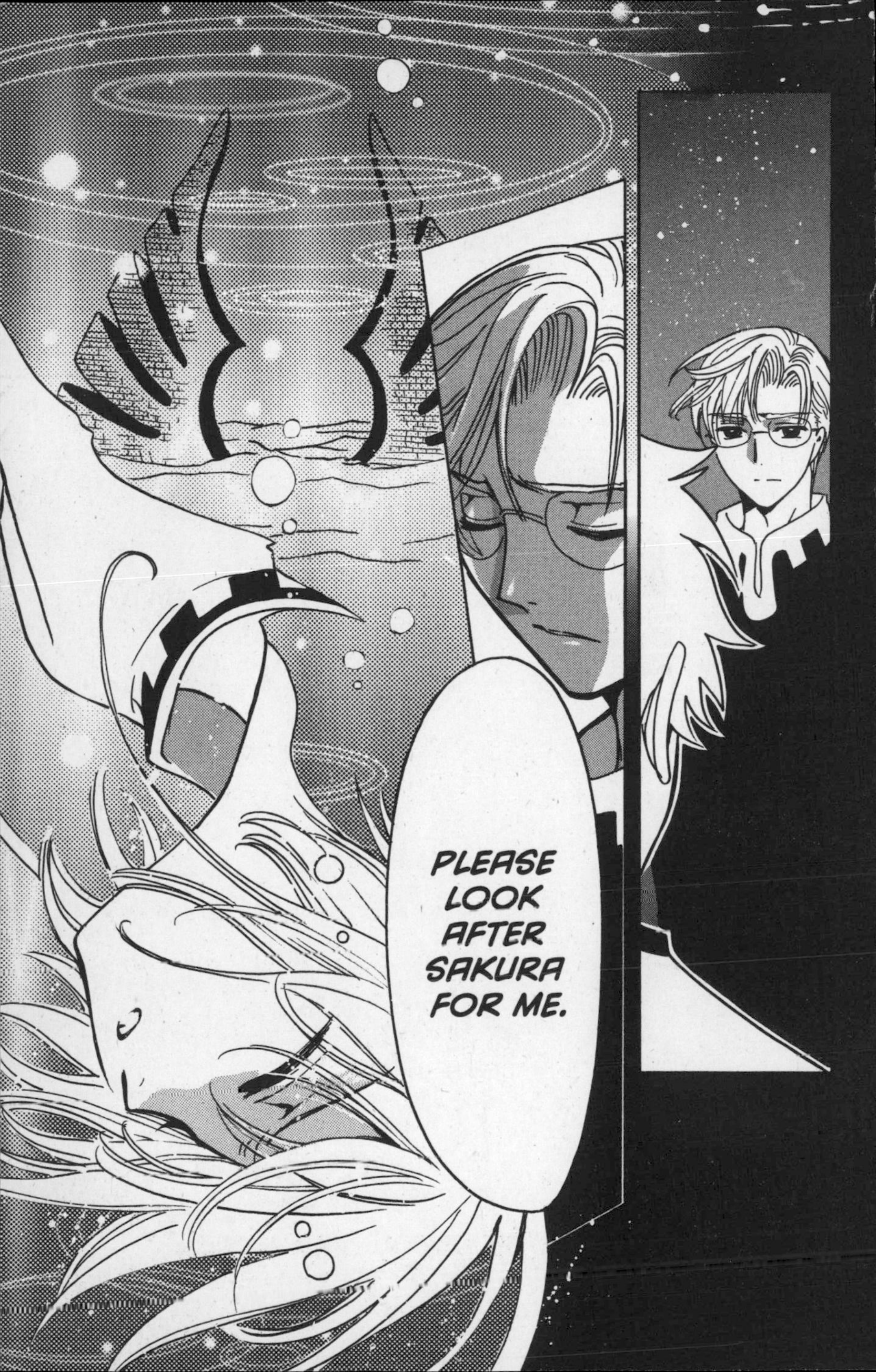
PLEASE LOOK AFTER SAKURA FOR ME.

ツバサ

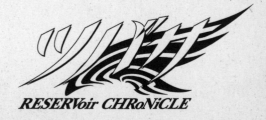

RESERVoir CHRoNiCLE

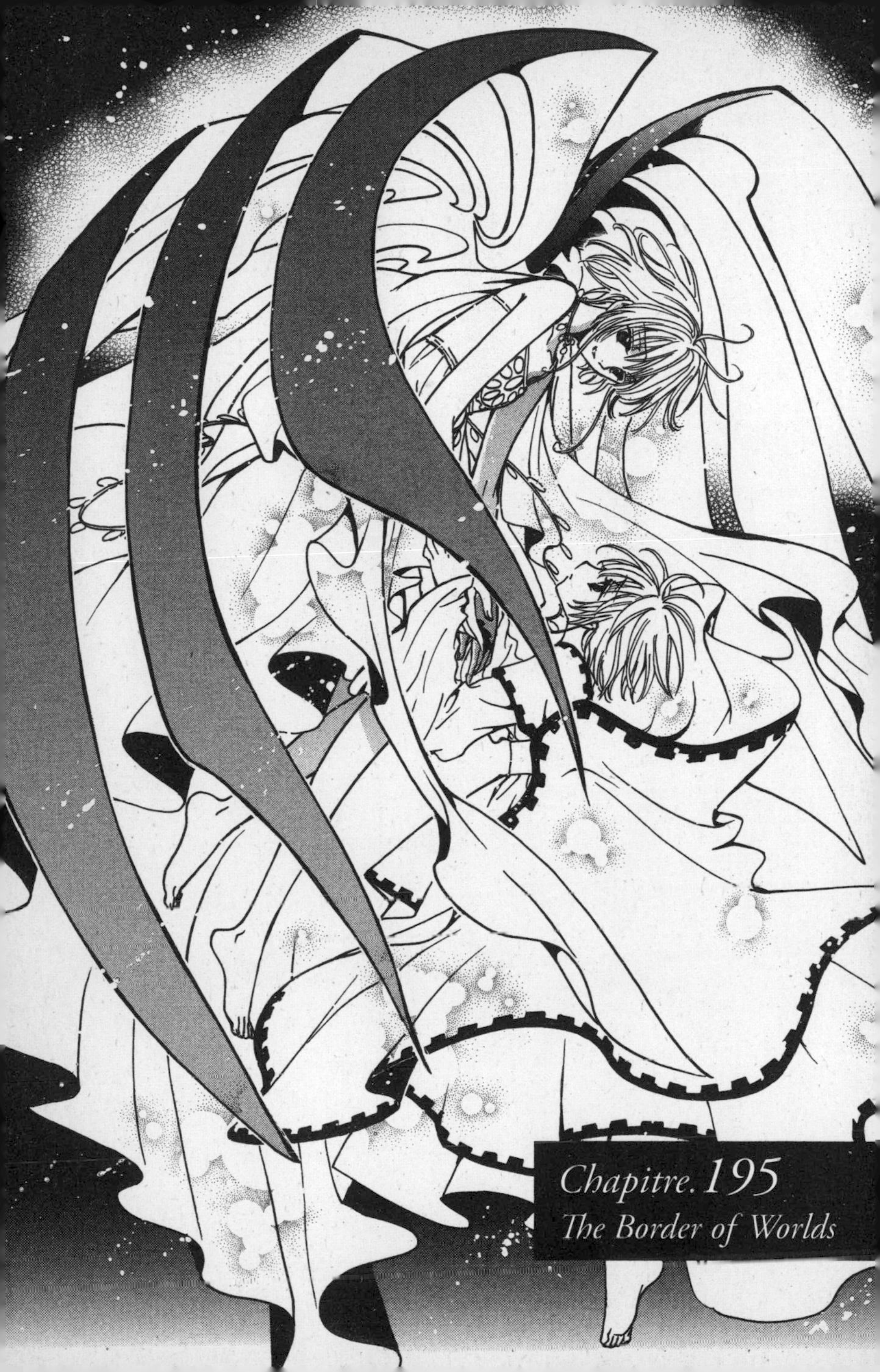
Chapitre. 195
The Border of Worlds

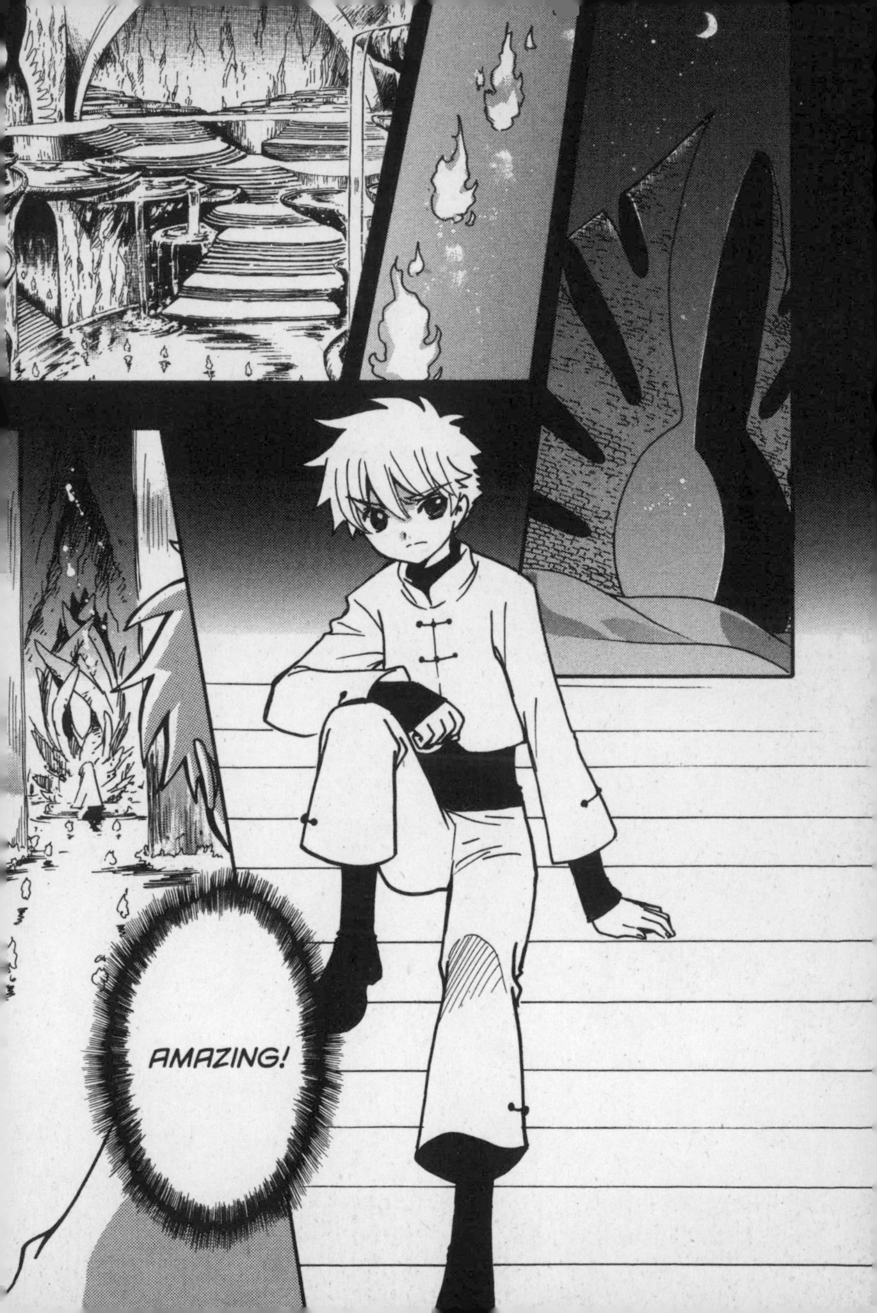
AMAZING!

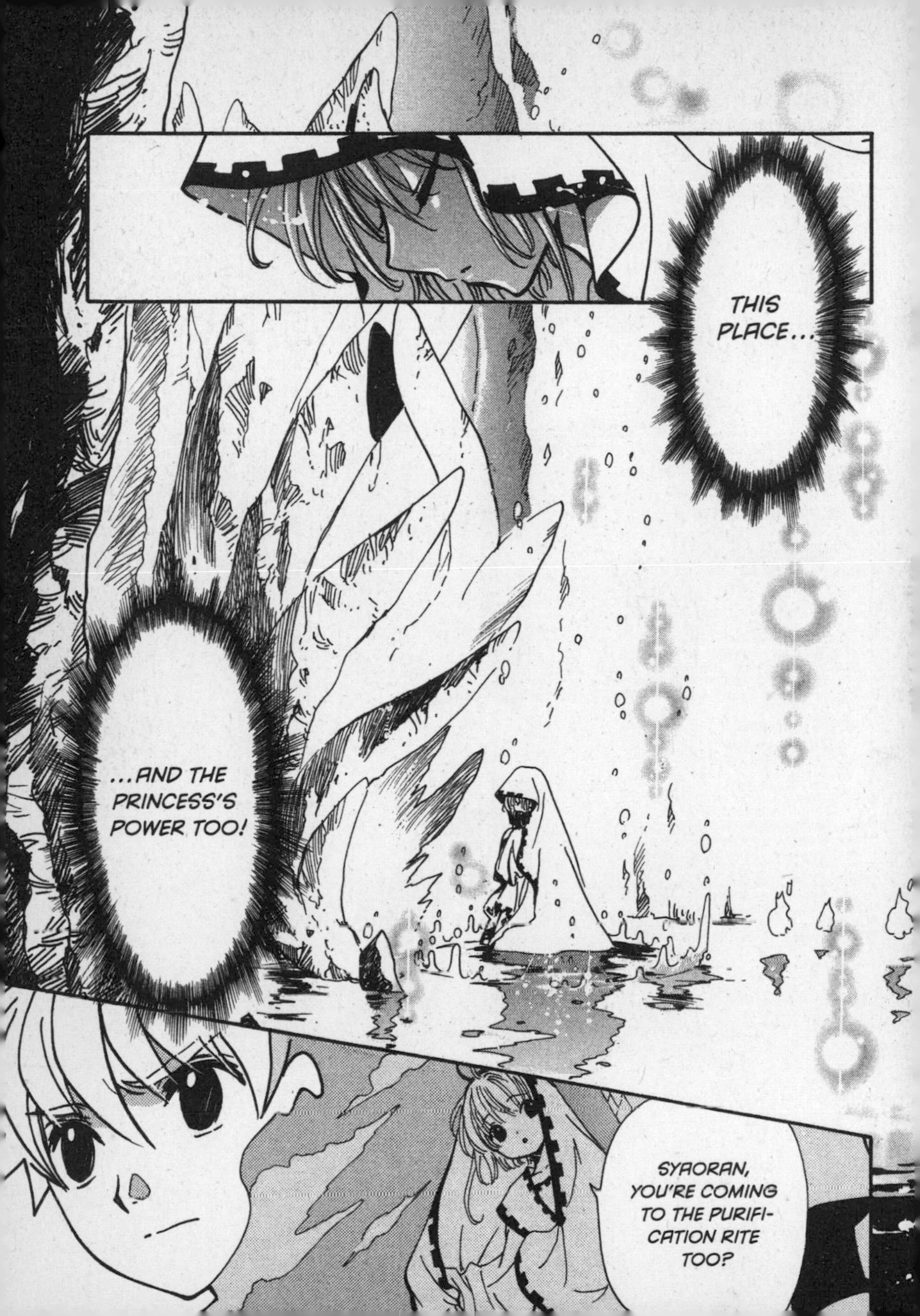
THIS PLACE...
...AND THE PRINCESS'S POWER TOO!
SYAORAN, YOU'RE COMING TO THE PURIFI-CATION RITE TOO?

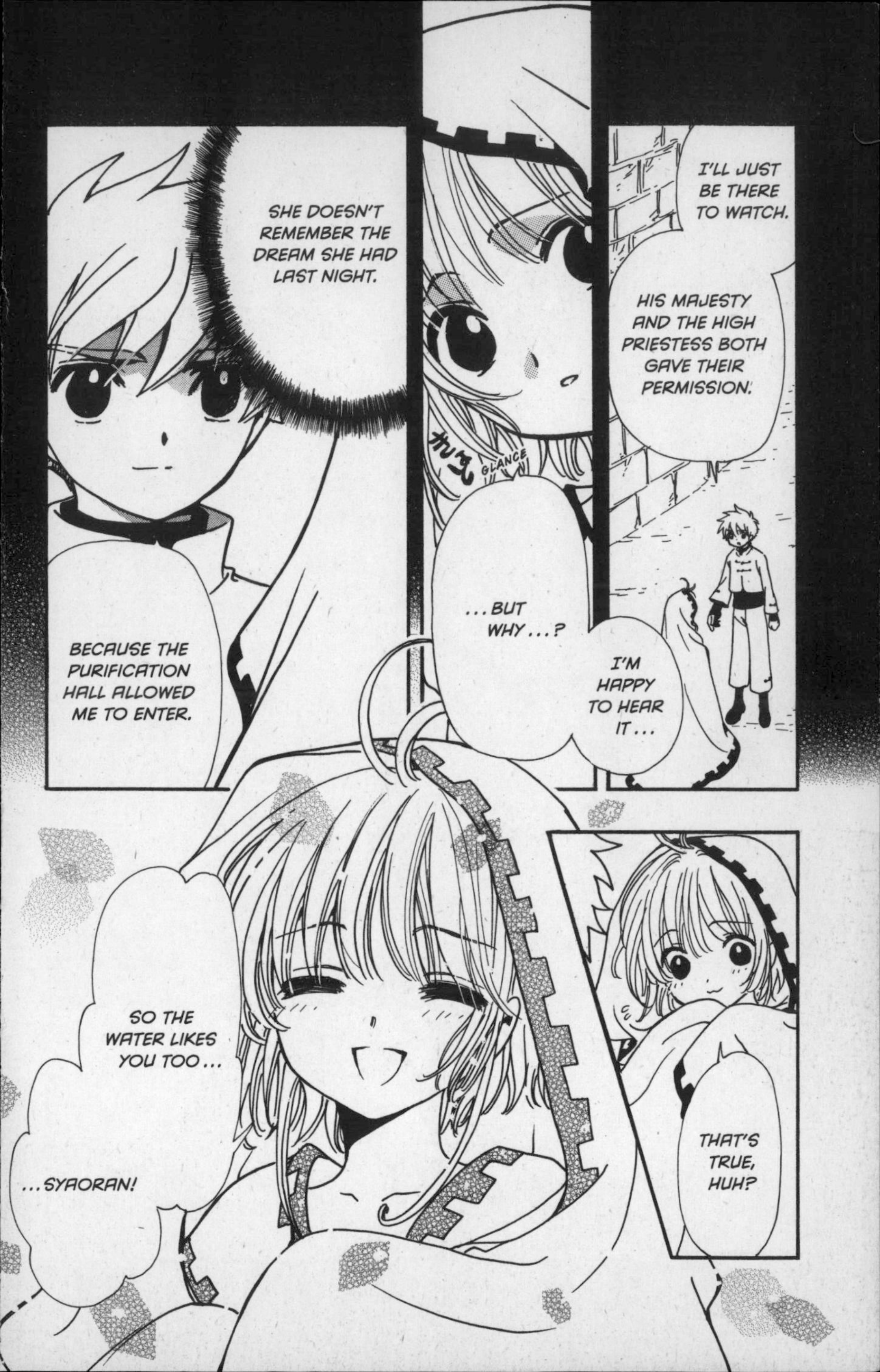
I'LL JUST BE THERE TO WATCH.
HIS MAJESTY AND THE HIGH PRIESTESS BOTH GAVE THEIR PERMISSION.
I'M HAPPY TO HEAR IT...
GLANCE
...BUT WHY...?
SHE DOESN'T REMEMBER THE DREAM SHE HAD LAST NIGHT.
BECAUSE THE PURIFICATION HALL ALLOWED ME TO ENTER.
THAT'S TRUE, HUH?
SO THE WATER LIKES YOU TOO...
...SYAORAN!

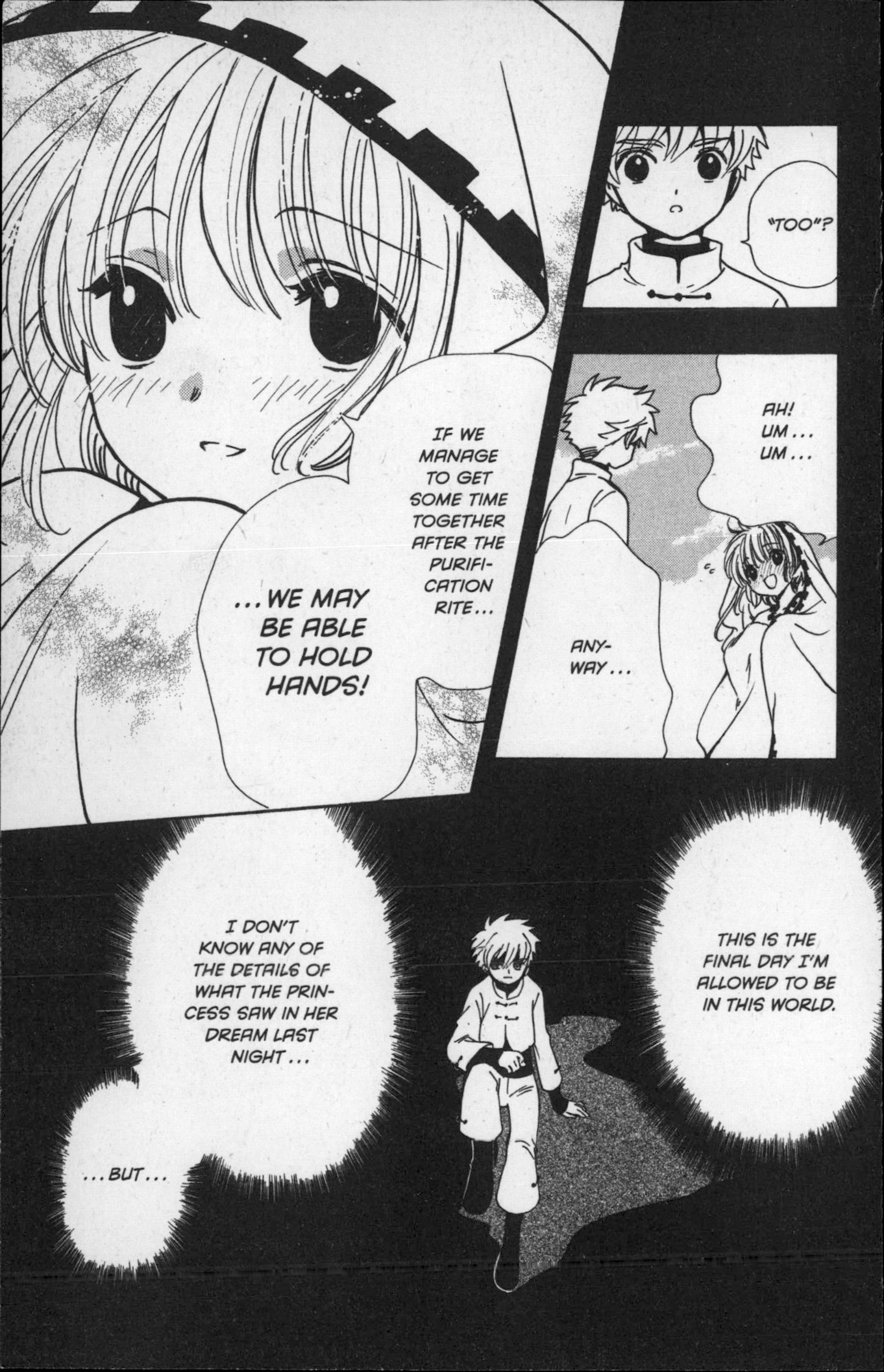
"TOO"?
AH! UM ... UM ...
ANY-WAY ...
IF WE MANAGE TO GET SOME TIME TOGETHER AFTER THE PURIFI-CATION RITE ...
... WE MAY BE ABLE TO HOLD HANDS!
THIS IS THE FINAL DAY I'M ALLOWED TO BE IN THIS WORLD.
I DON'T KNOW ANY OF THE DETAILS OF WHAT THE PRIN-CESS SAW IN HER DREAM LAST NIGHT ...
... BUT ...

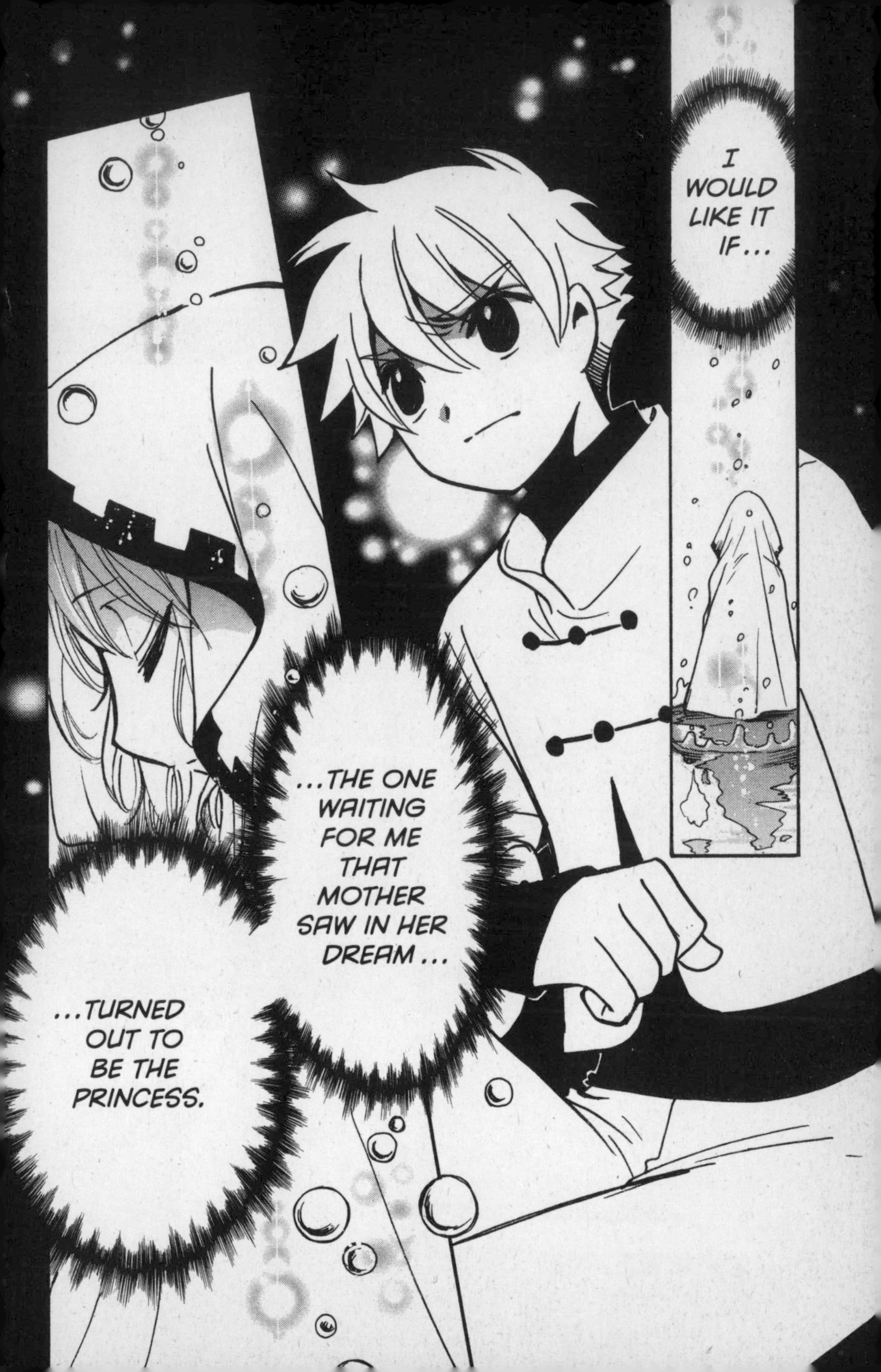
I WOULD LIKE IT IF...
...THE ONE WAITING FOR ME THAT MOTHER SAW IN HER DREAM...
...TURNED OUT TO BE THE PRINCESS.

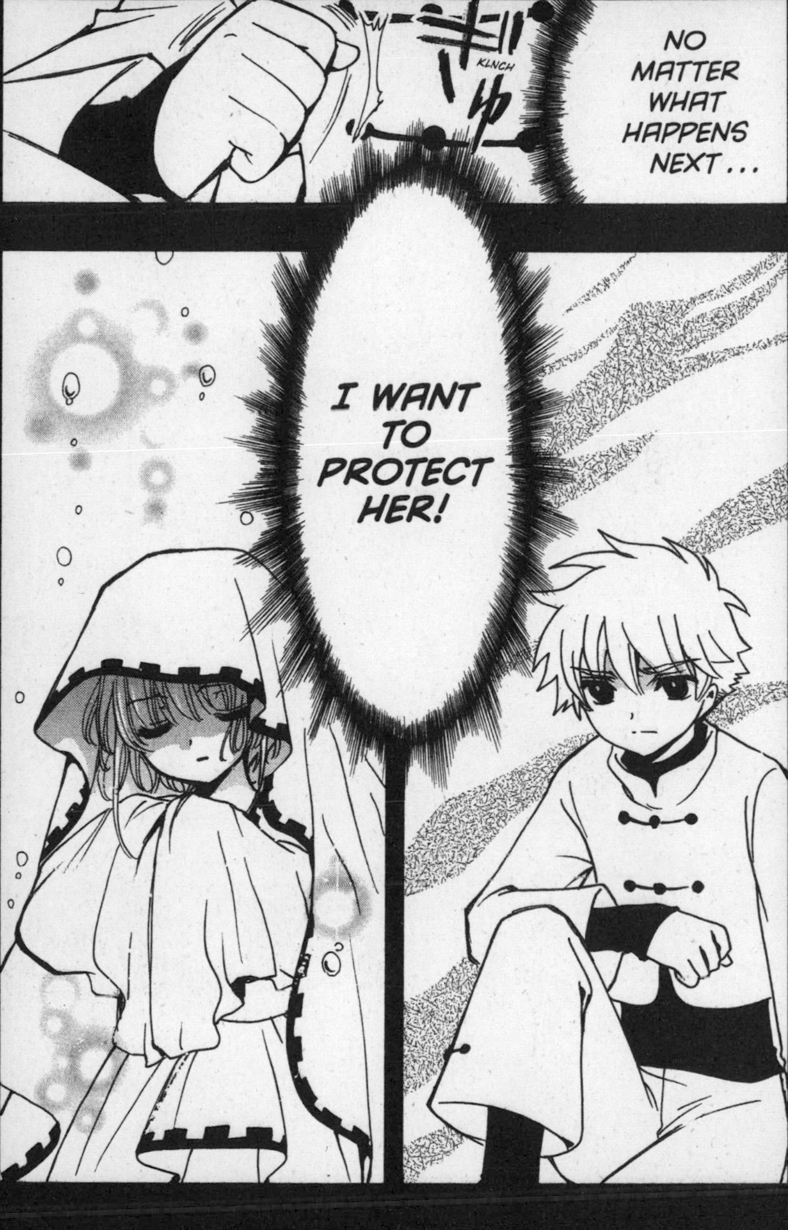
NO MATTER WHAT HAPPENS NEXT...
KLNCH
I WANT TO PROTECT HER!

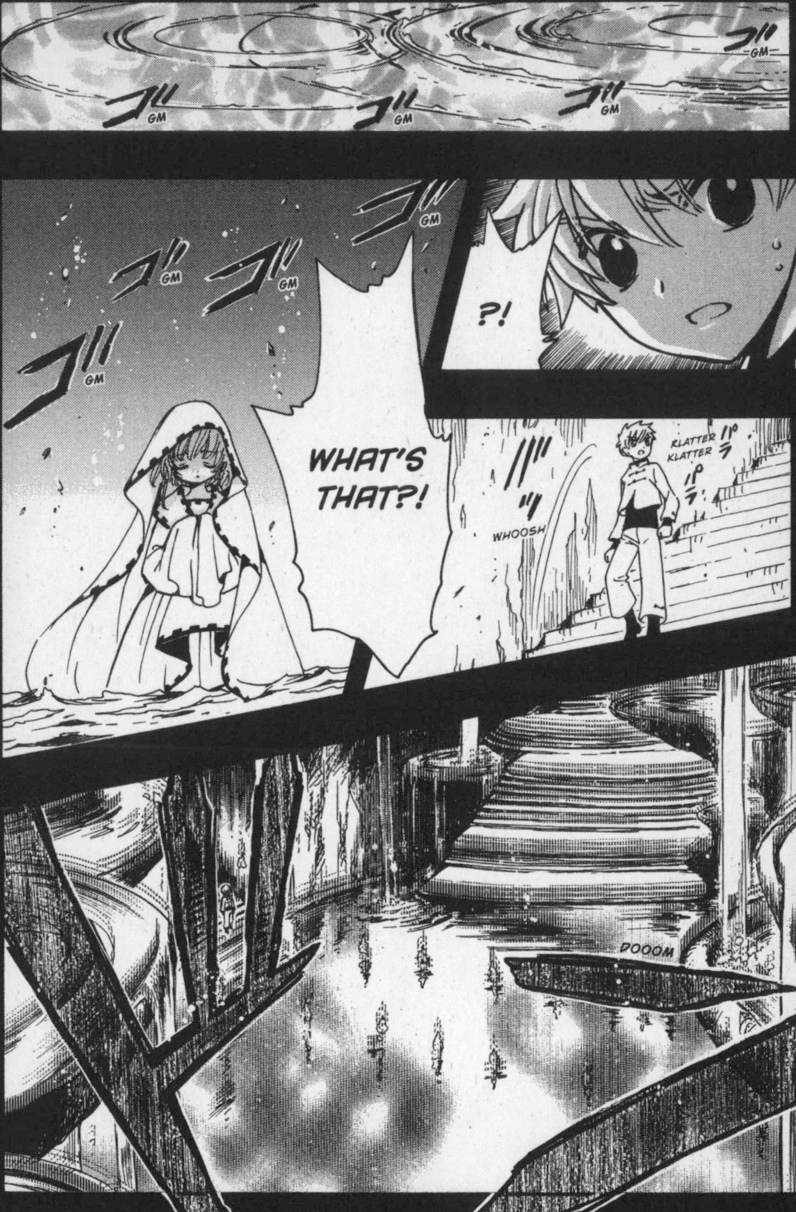
GM
GM
GM
GM
?!
GM
GM
GM
GM
KLATTER KLATTER
WHOOSH
WHAT'S THAT?!
DOOOM

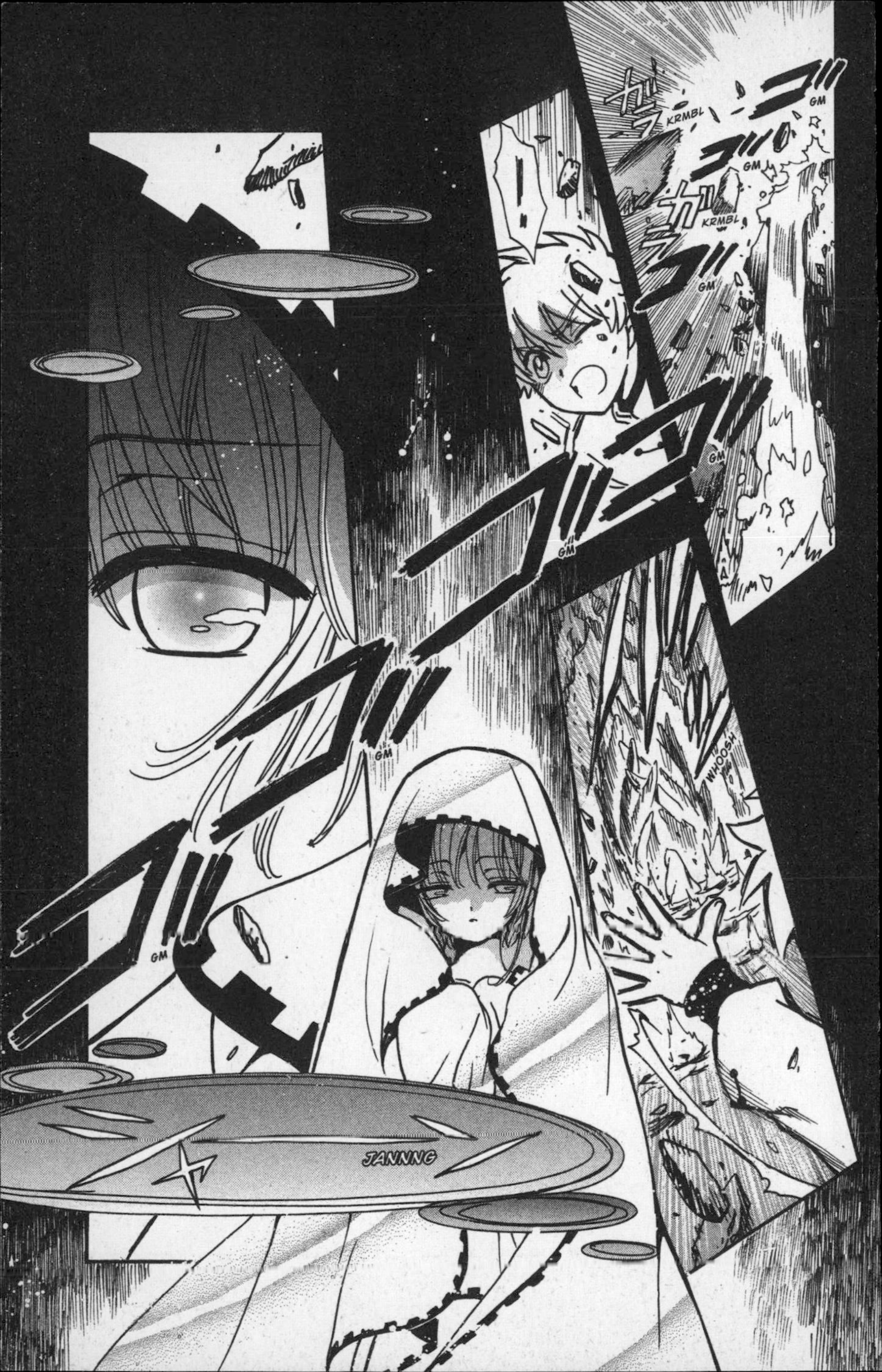
KRMBL
GM
GM
KRMBL
GM
GM
GM
GM
GM
WHOOSH
JANNNG

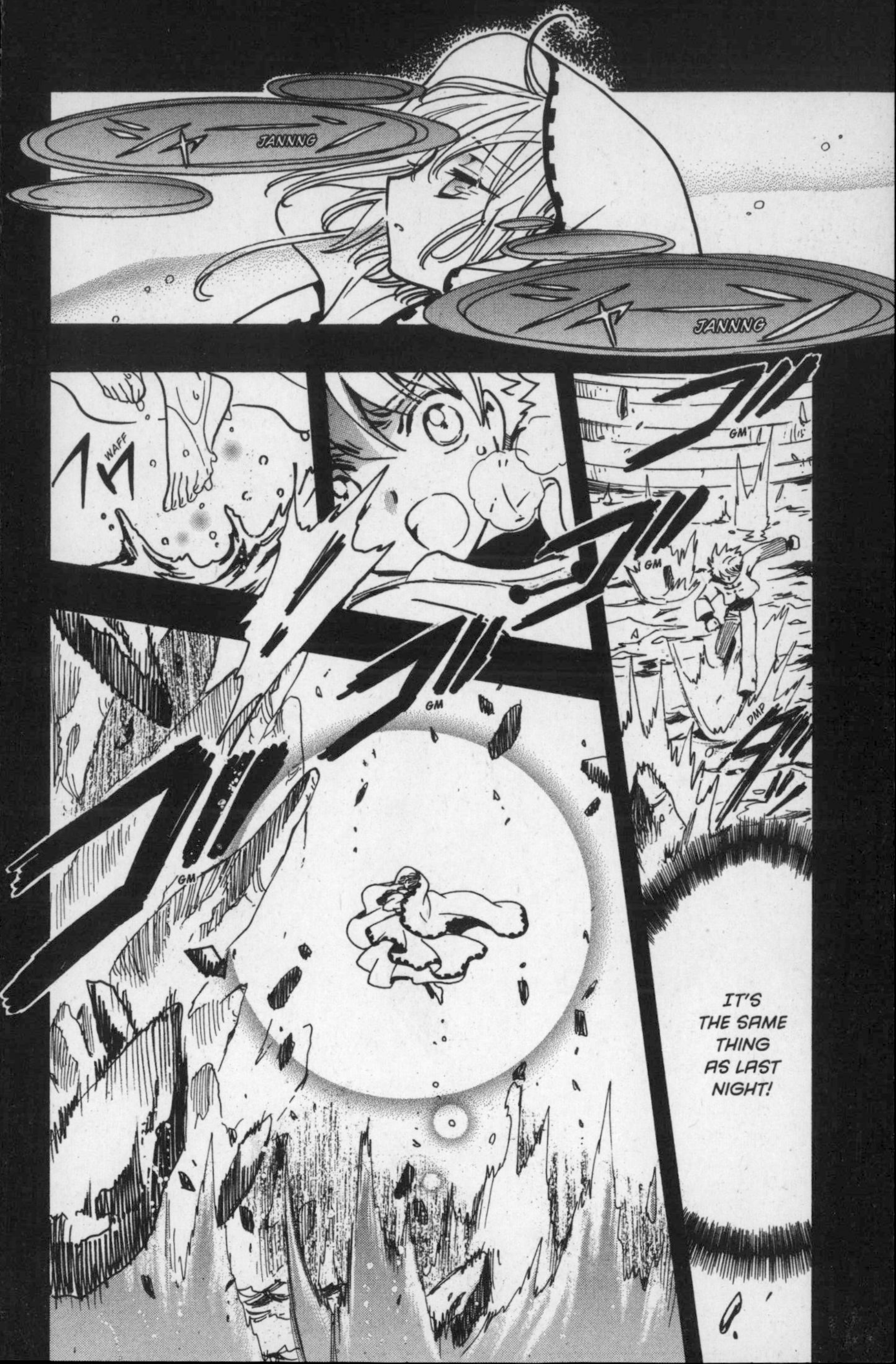
JANNNG
JANNNG
GM
GM
DMP
WAFF
GM
GM
IT'S THE SAME THING AS LAST NIGHT!

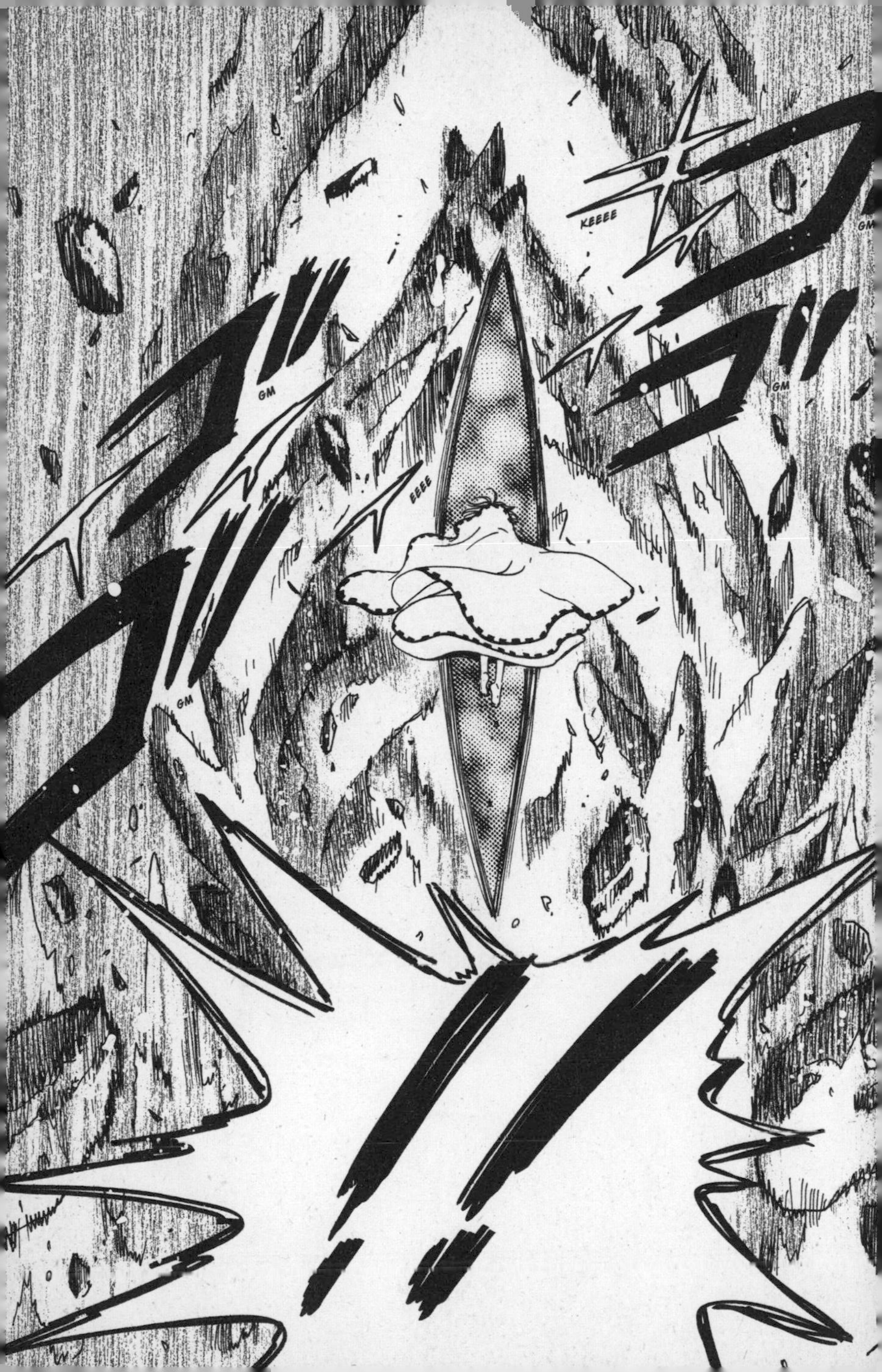
KEEEE
GM
GM
GM
EEEE
GM

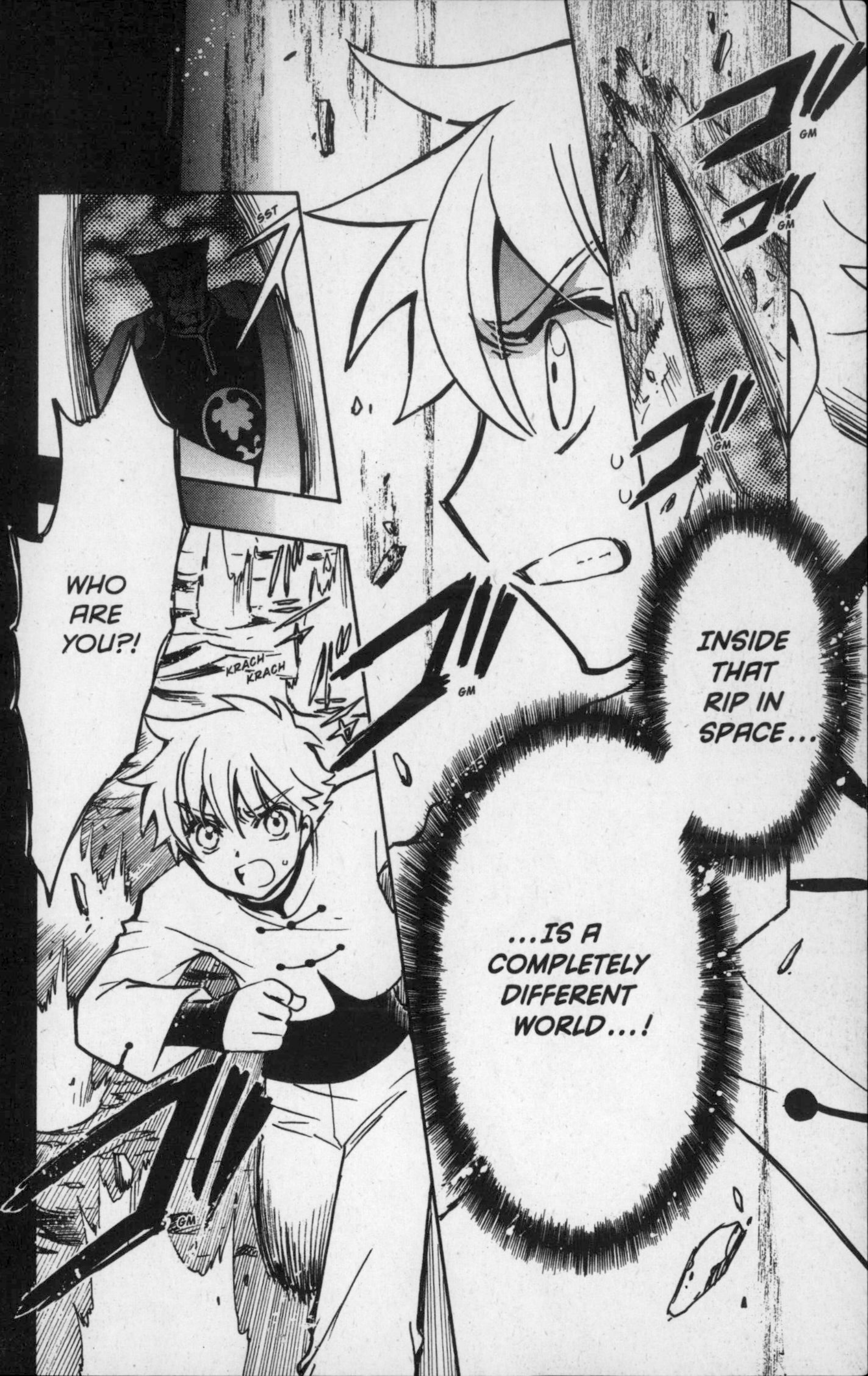
GM
GM
GM
SST
INSIDE THAT RIP IN SPACE...
...IS A COMPLETELY DIFFERENT WORLD...!
WHO ARE YOU?!
KRACH KRACH
GM
GM

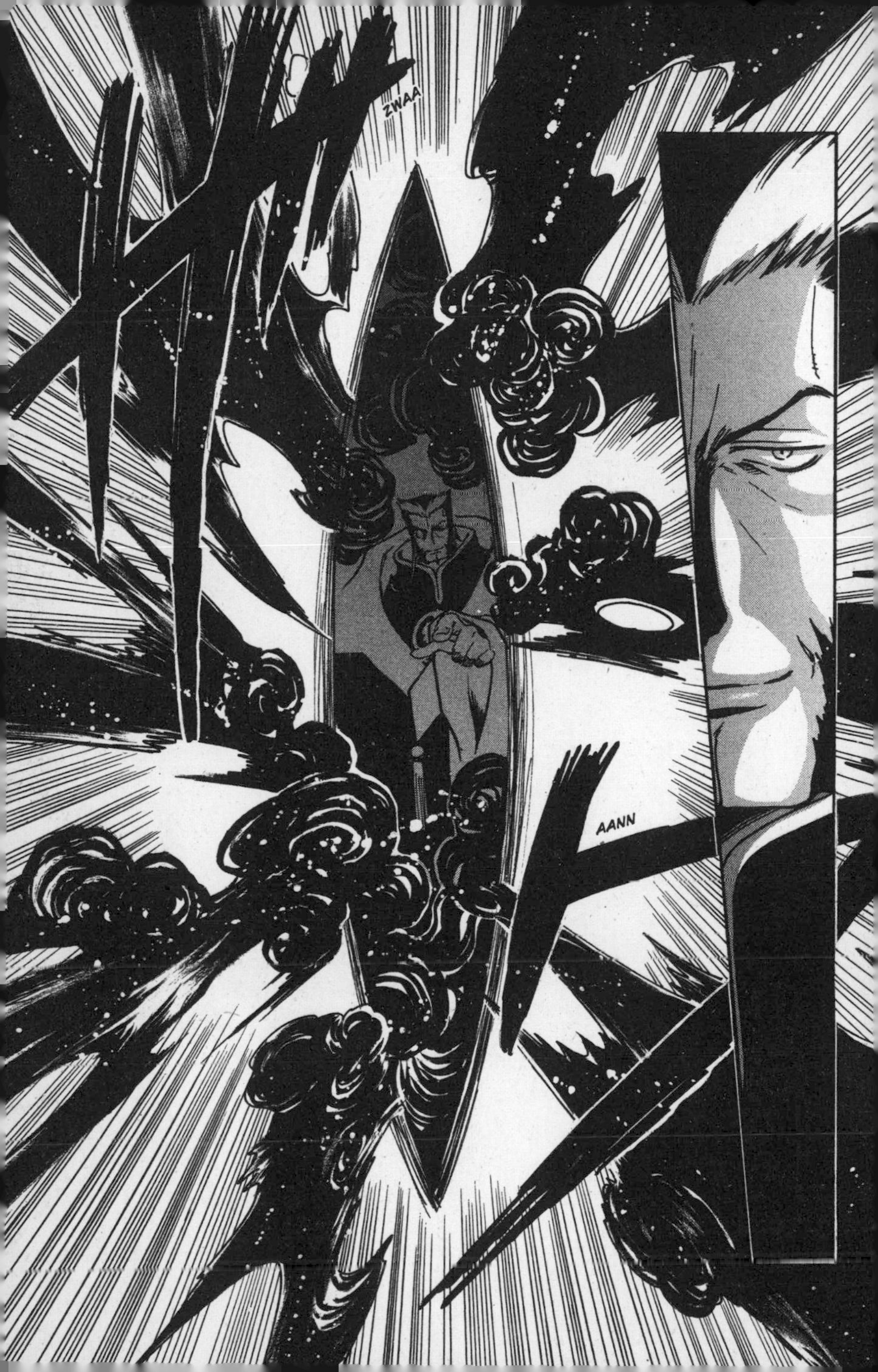
ZWAA
AANN

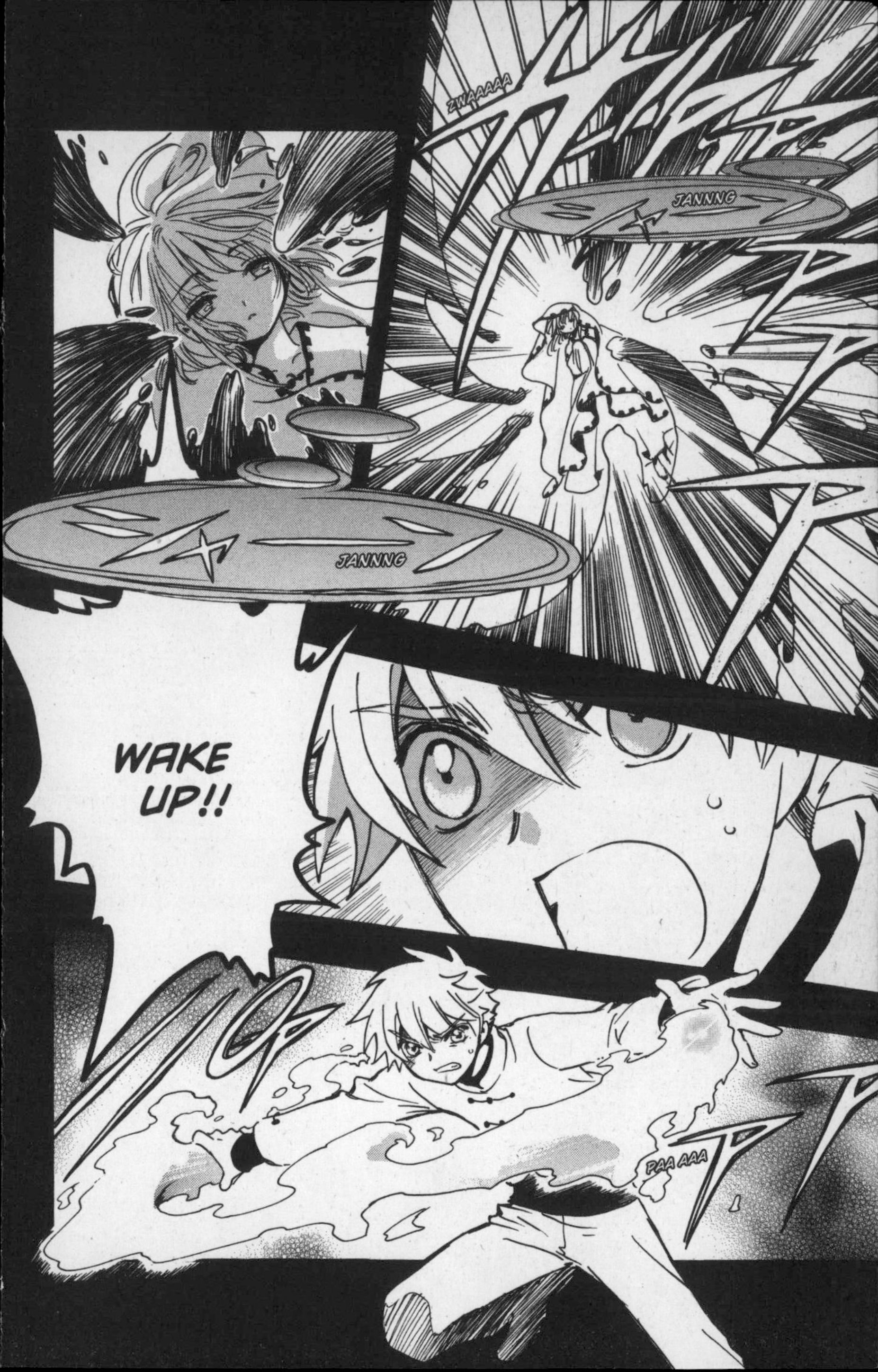
ZWAAAAA
JANNNG
JANNNG
WAKE UP!!
PAA AAA

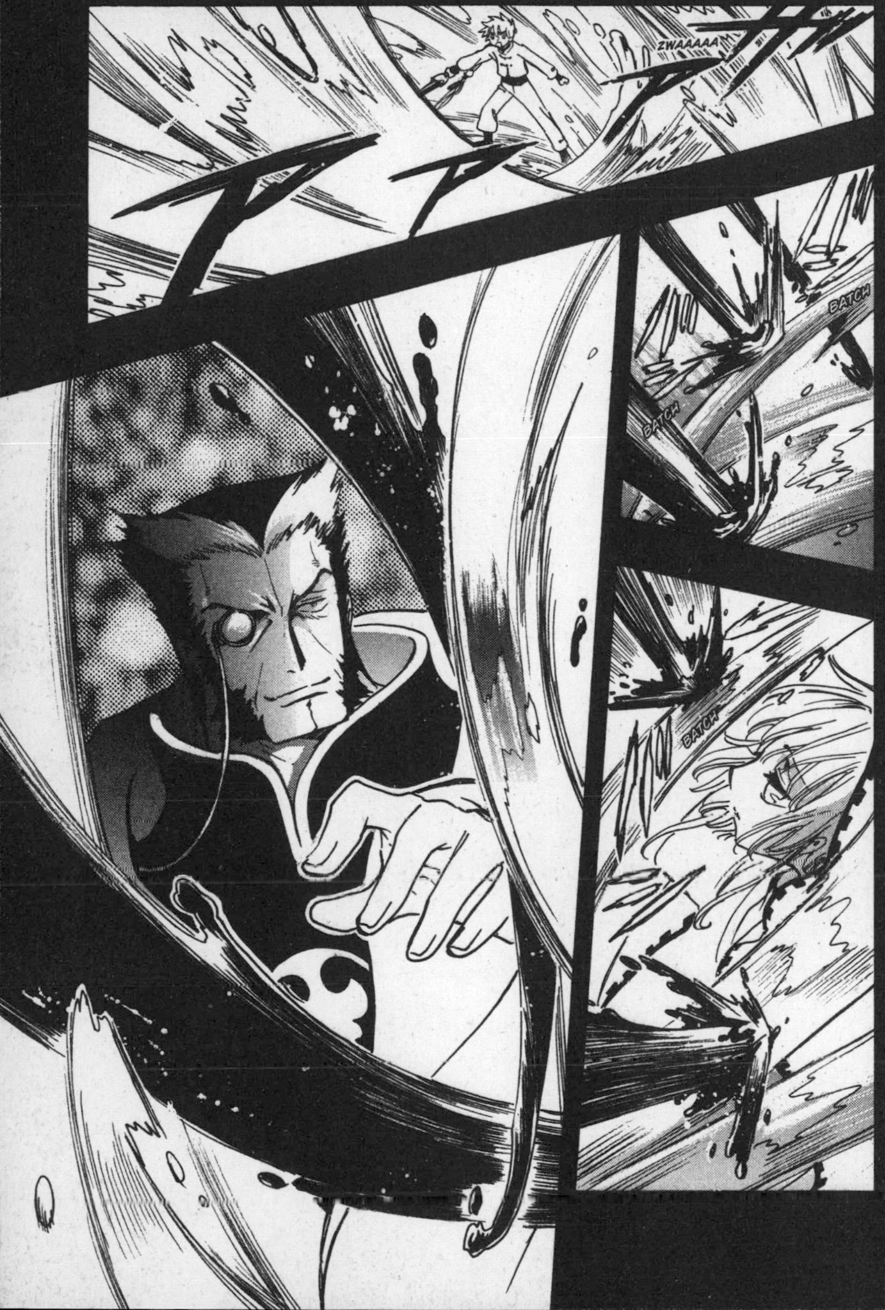
ZWAAAAAA
BATCH
BATCH
BATCH

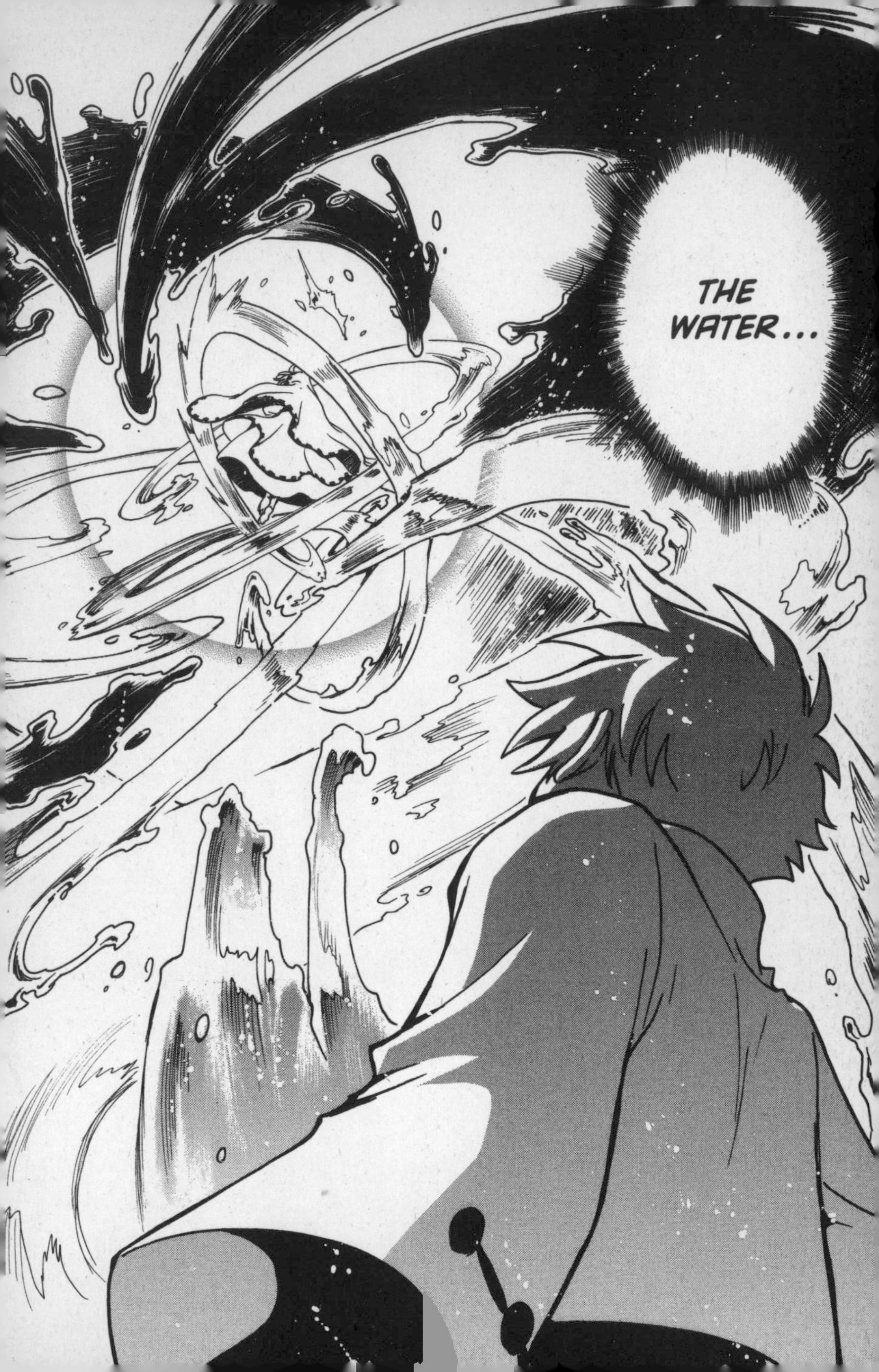
THE WATER...

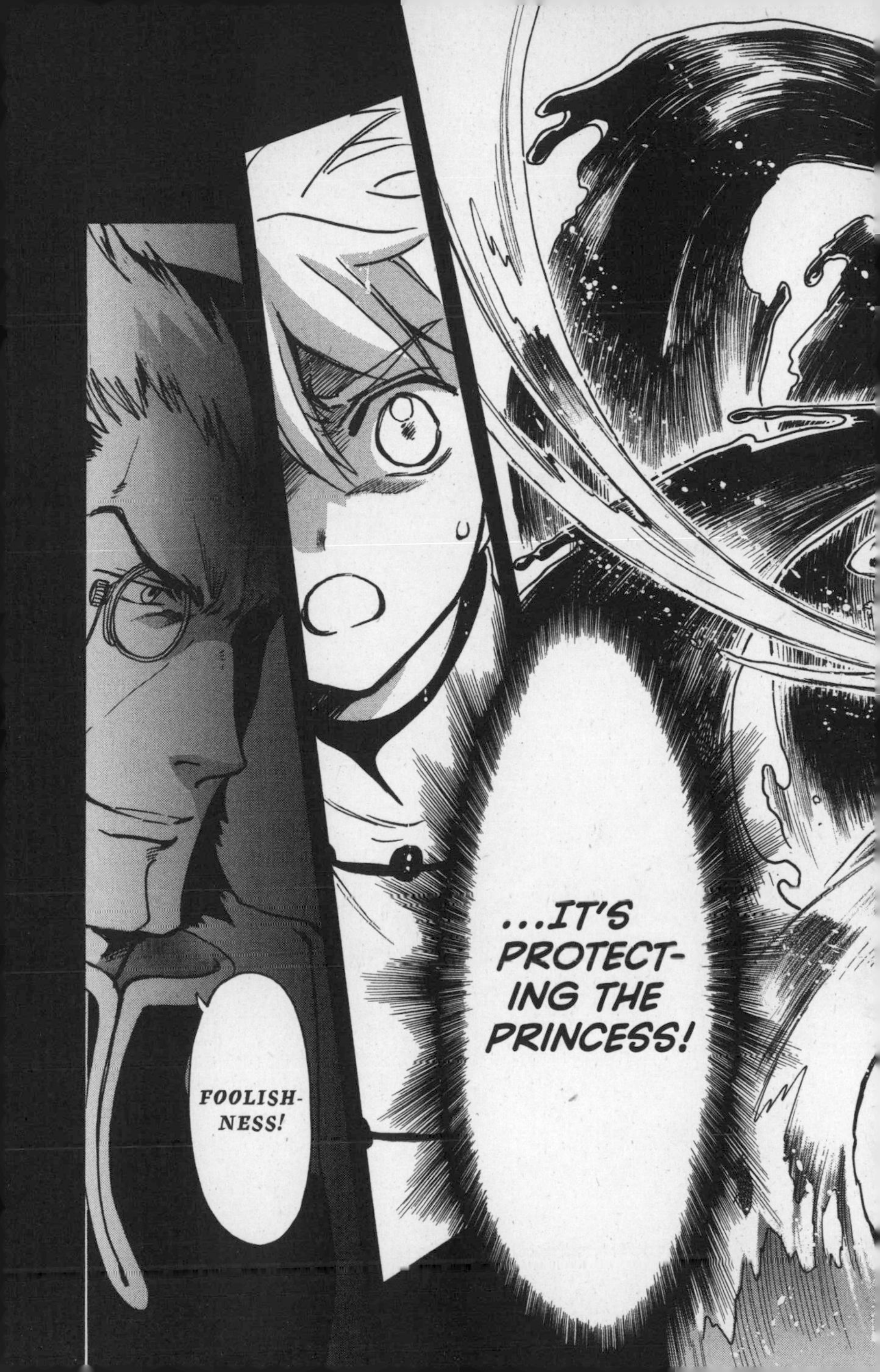
...IT'S PROTECT-ING THE PRINCESS!
FOOLISH-NESS!

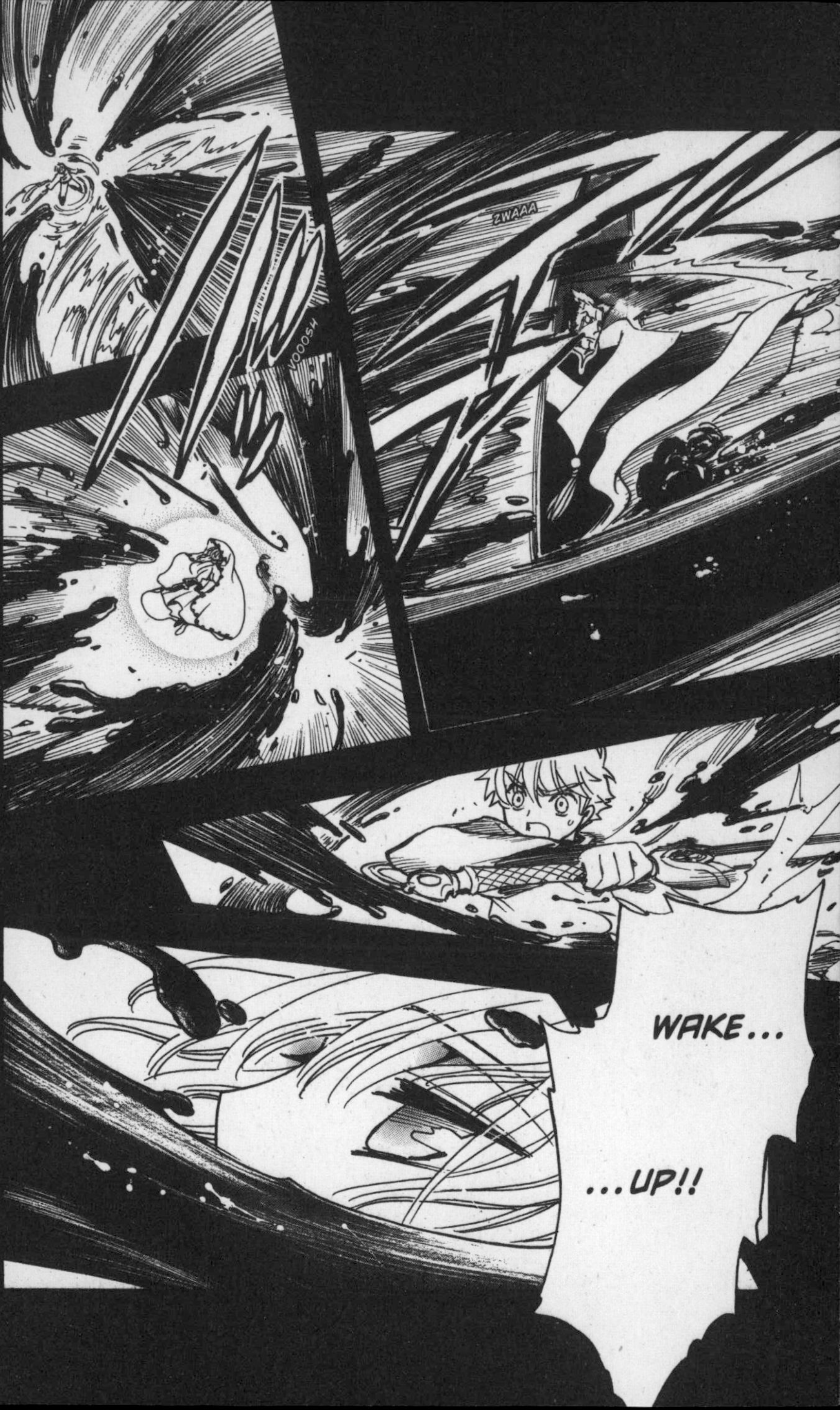
ZWAAA
VOOOSH
WAKE...
...UP!!

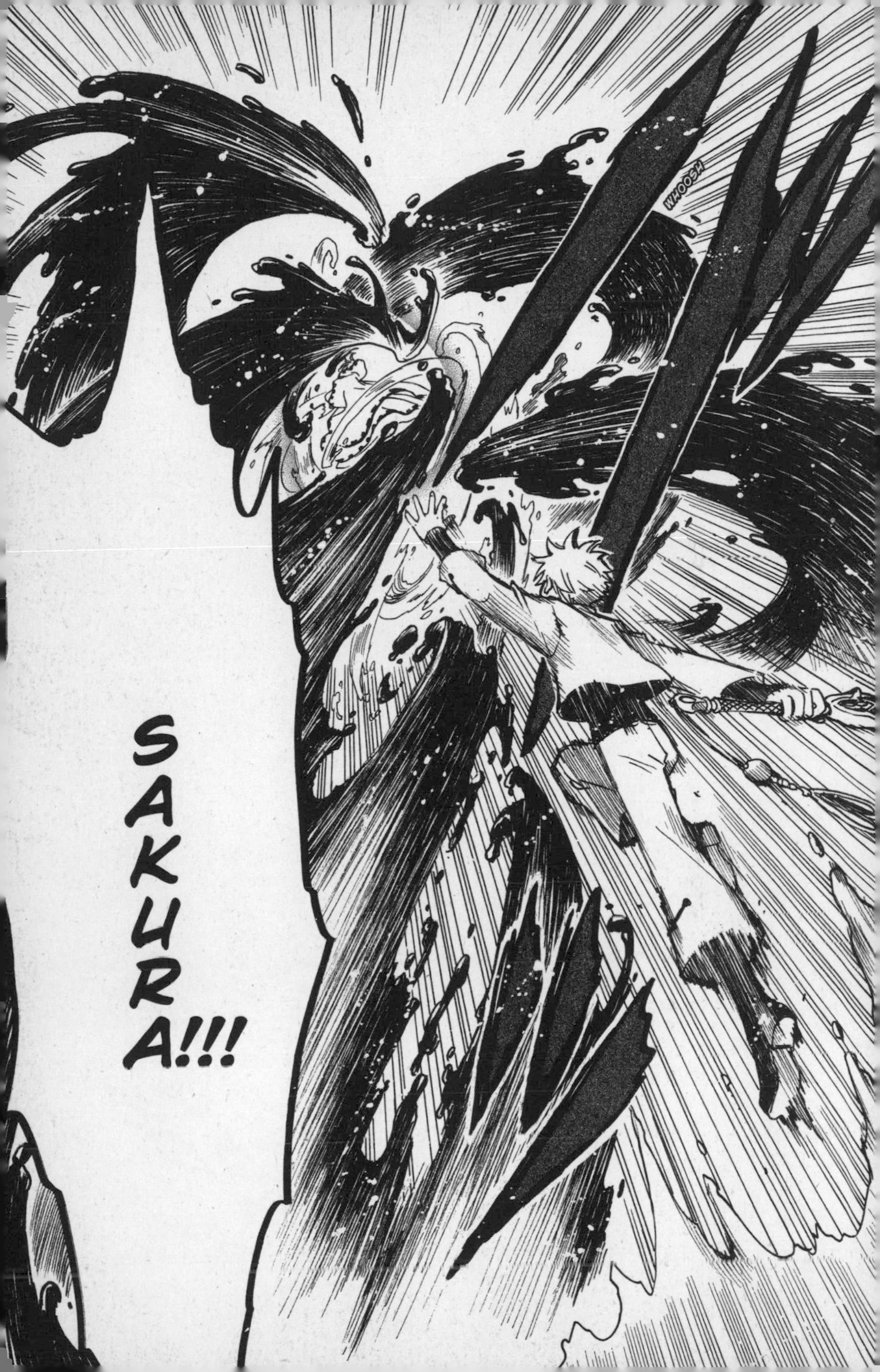
WHOOSH
SAKURA!!!

ツバサ
RESERVoir CHRoNiCLE

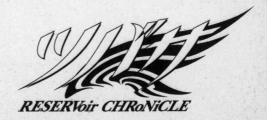

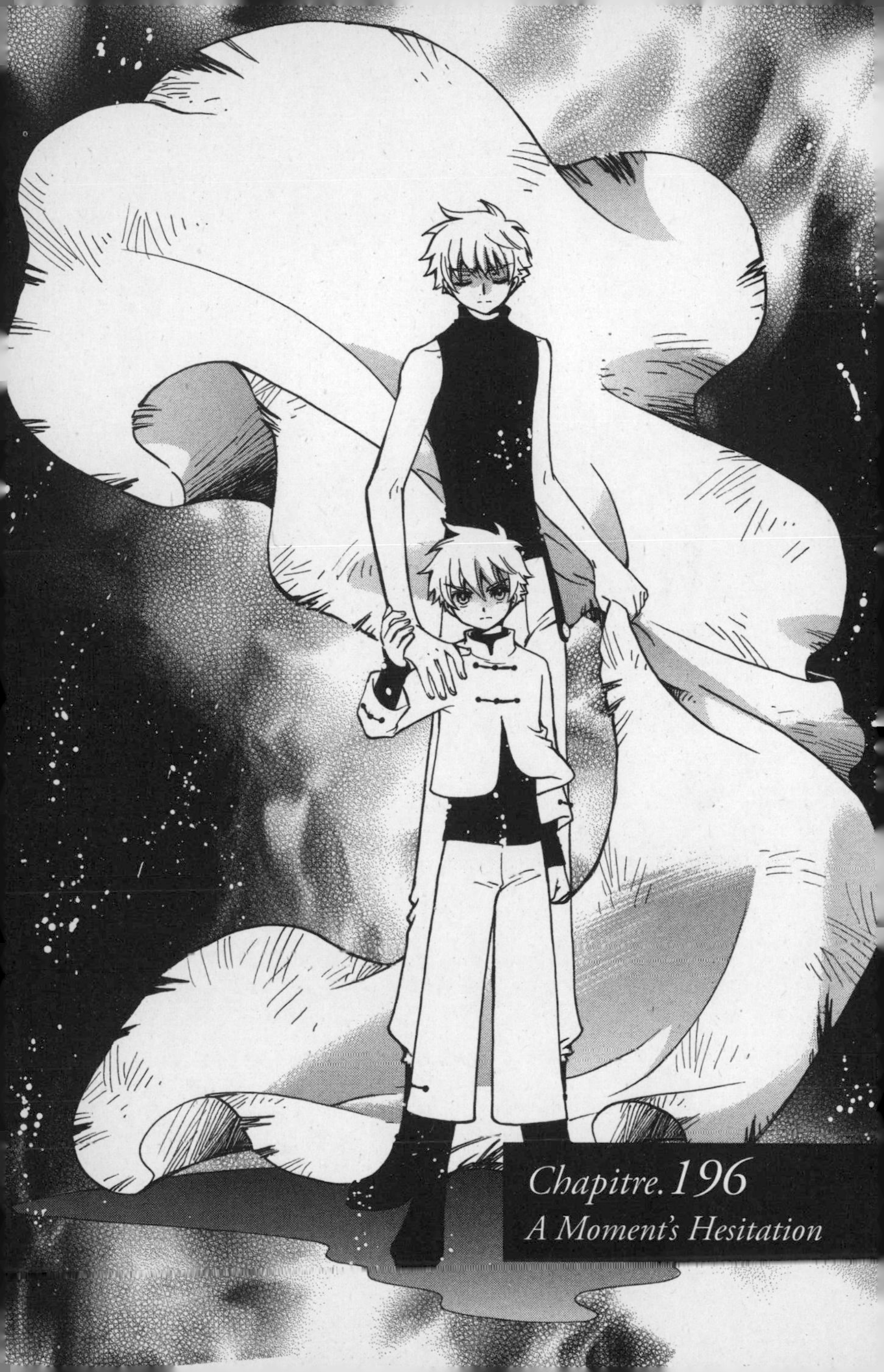
Chapitre. 196
A Moment's Hesitation

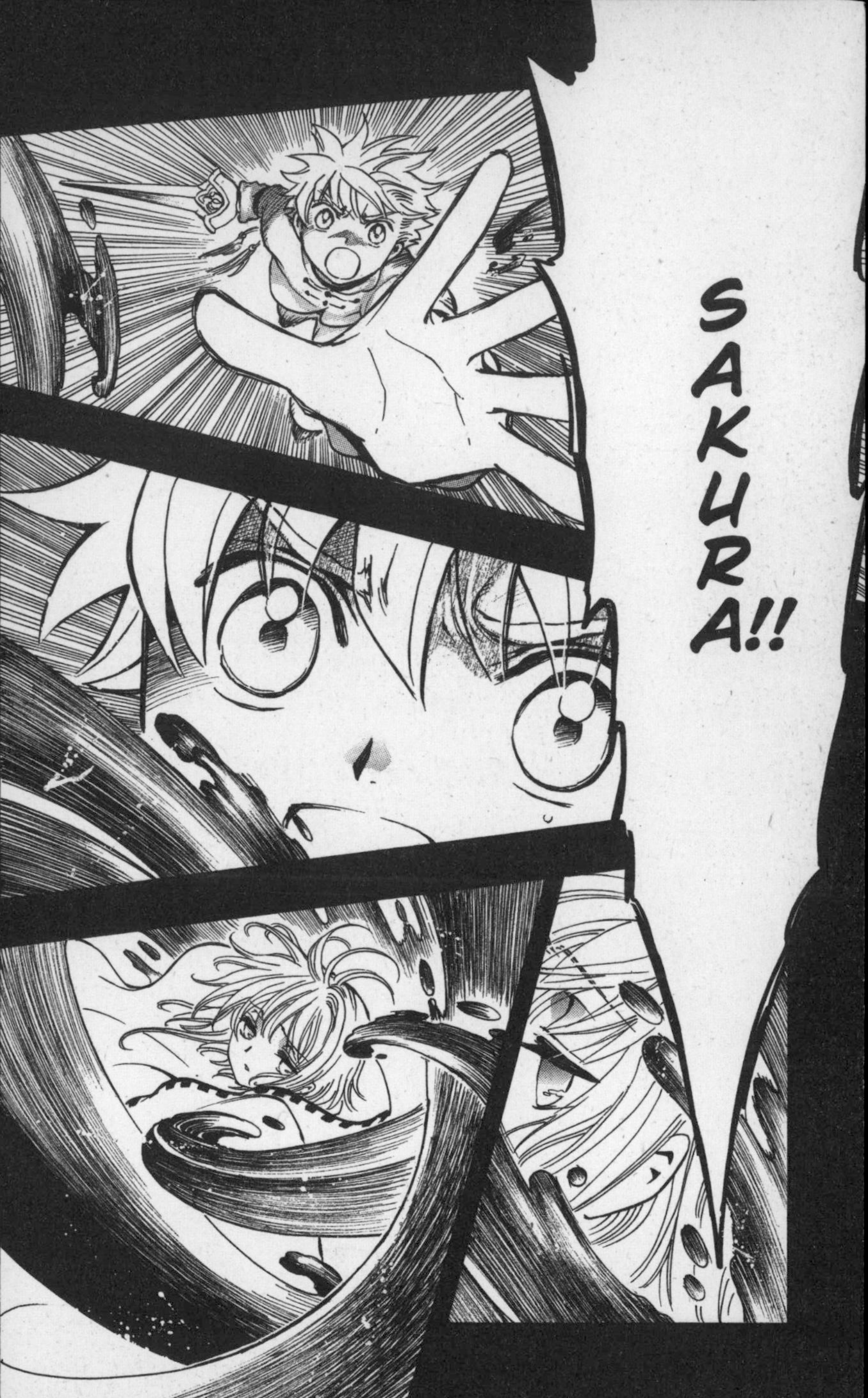
SAKURA!!

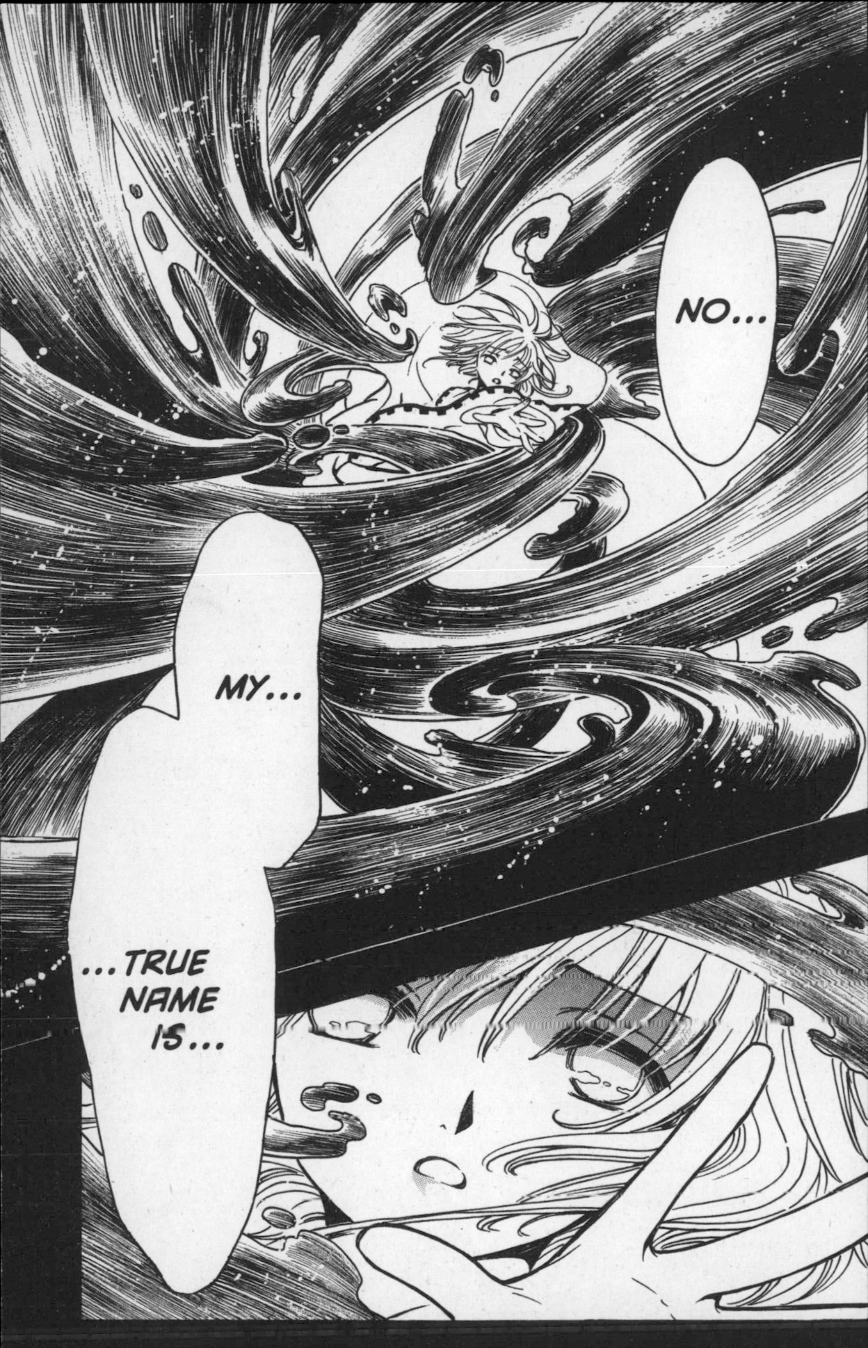
NO...
MY...
...TRUE NAME IS...

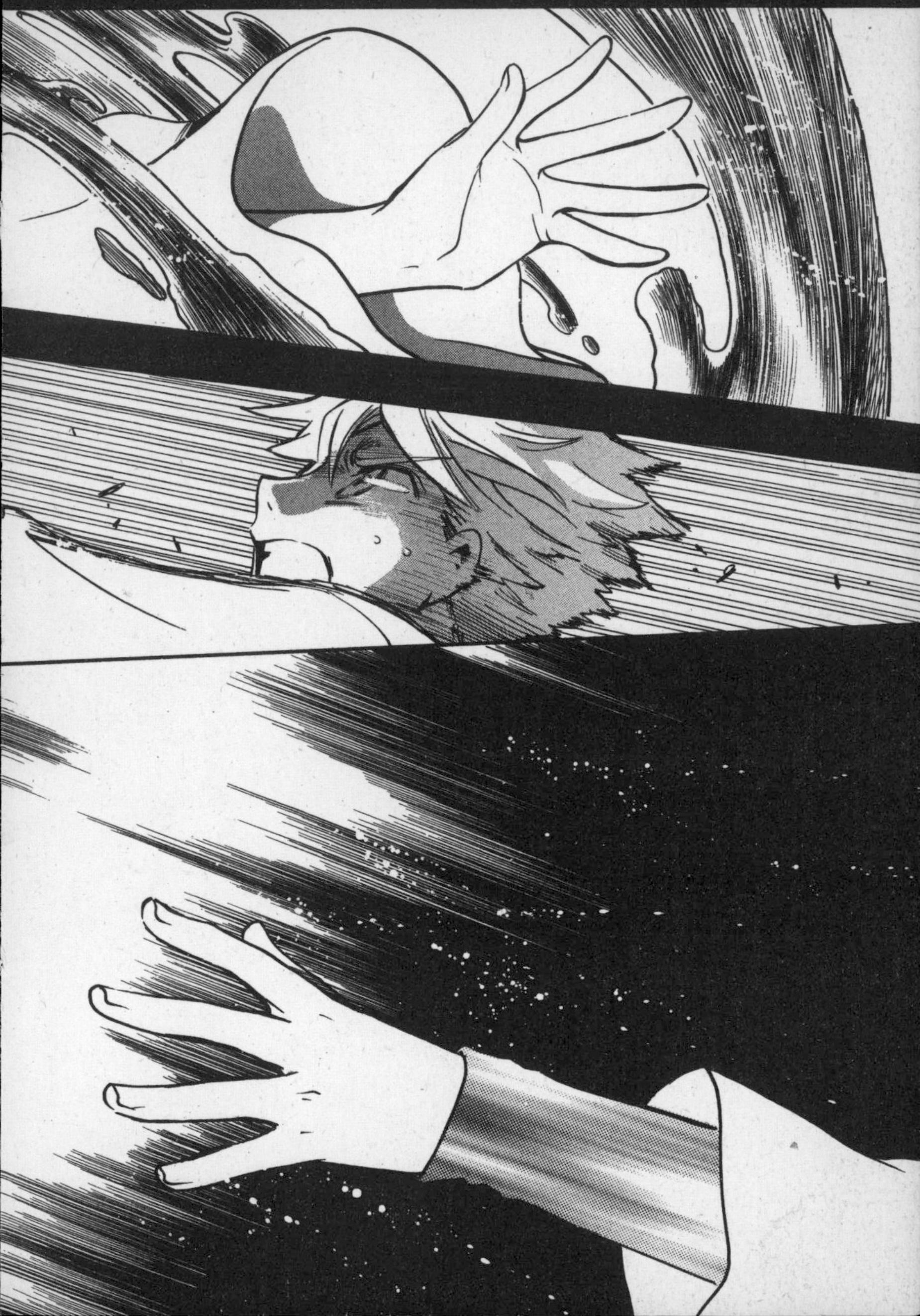

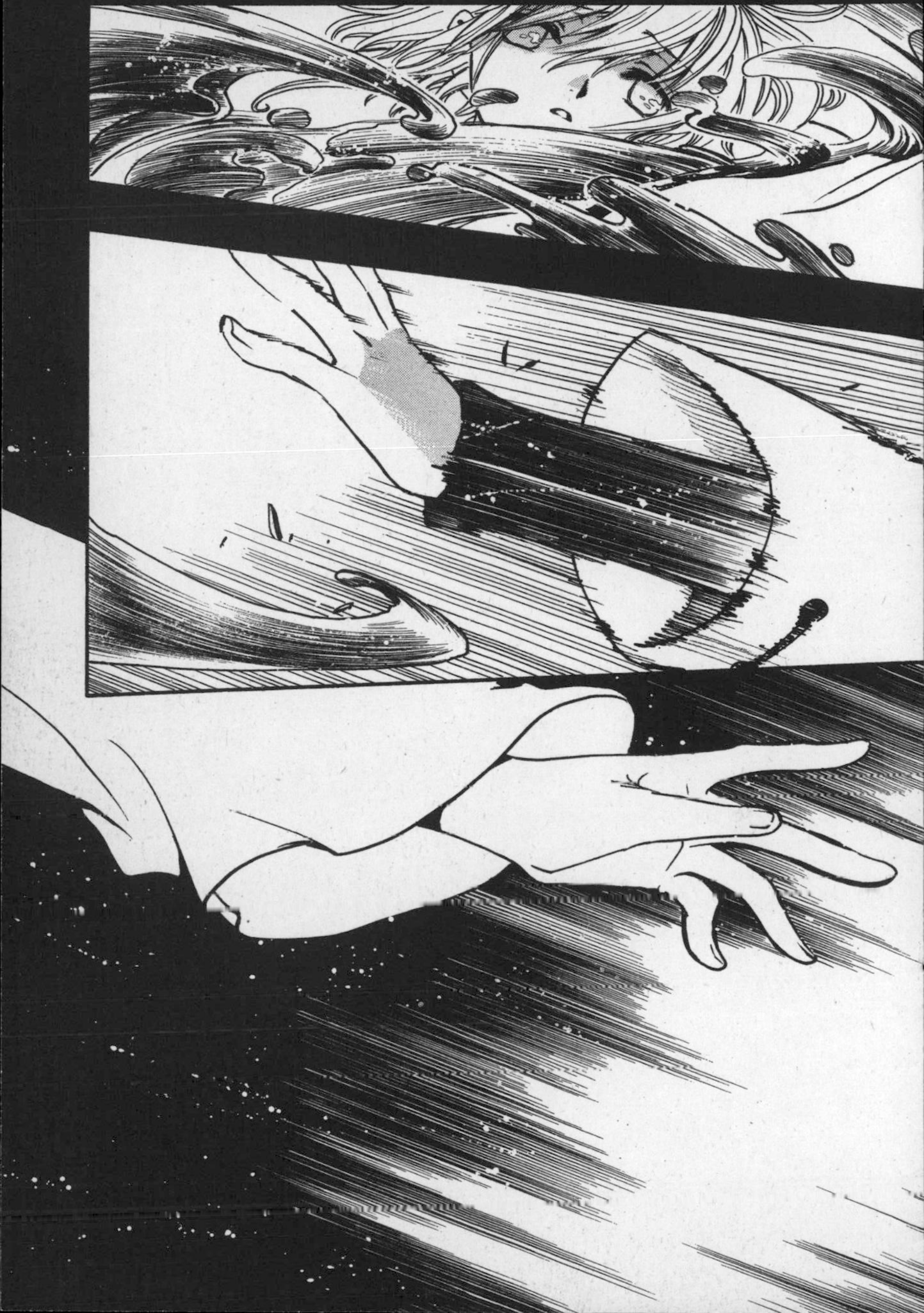

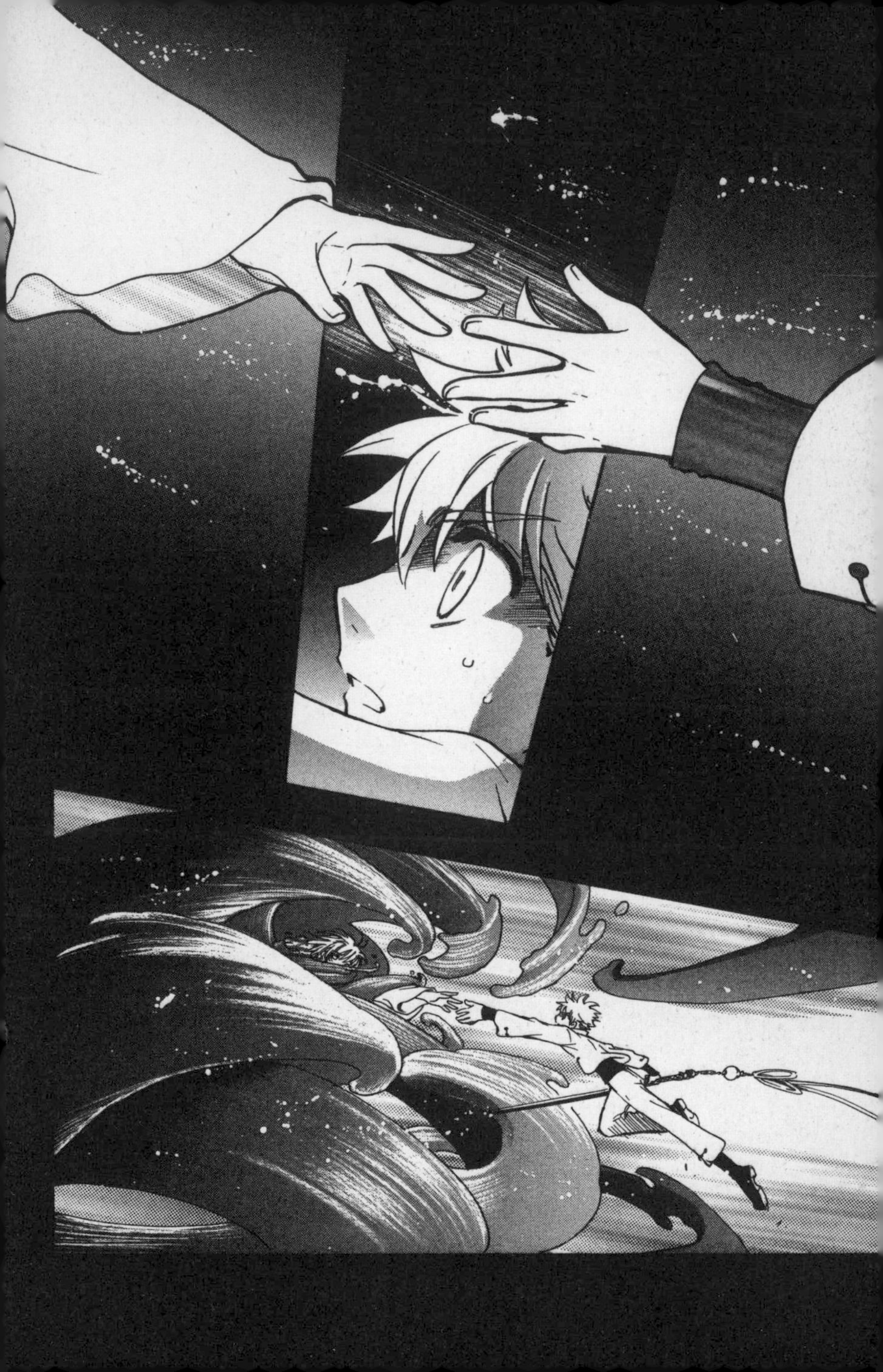

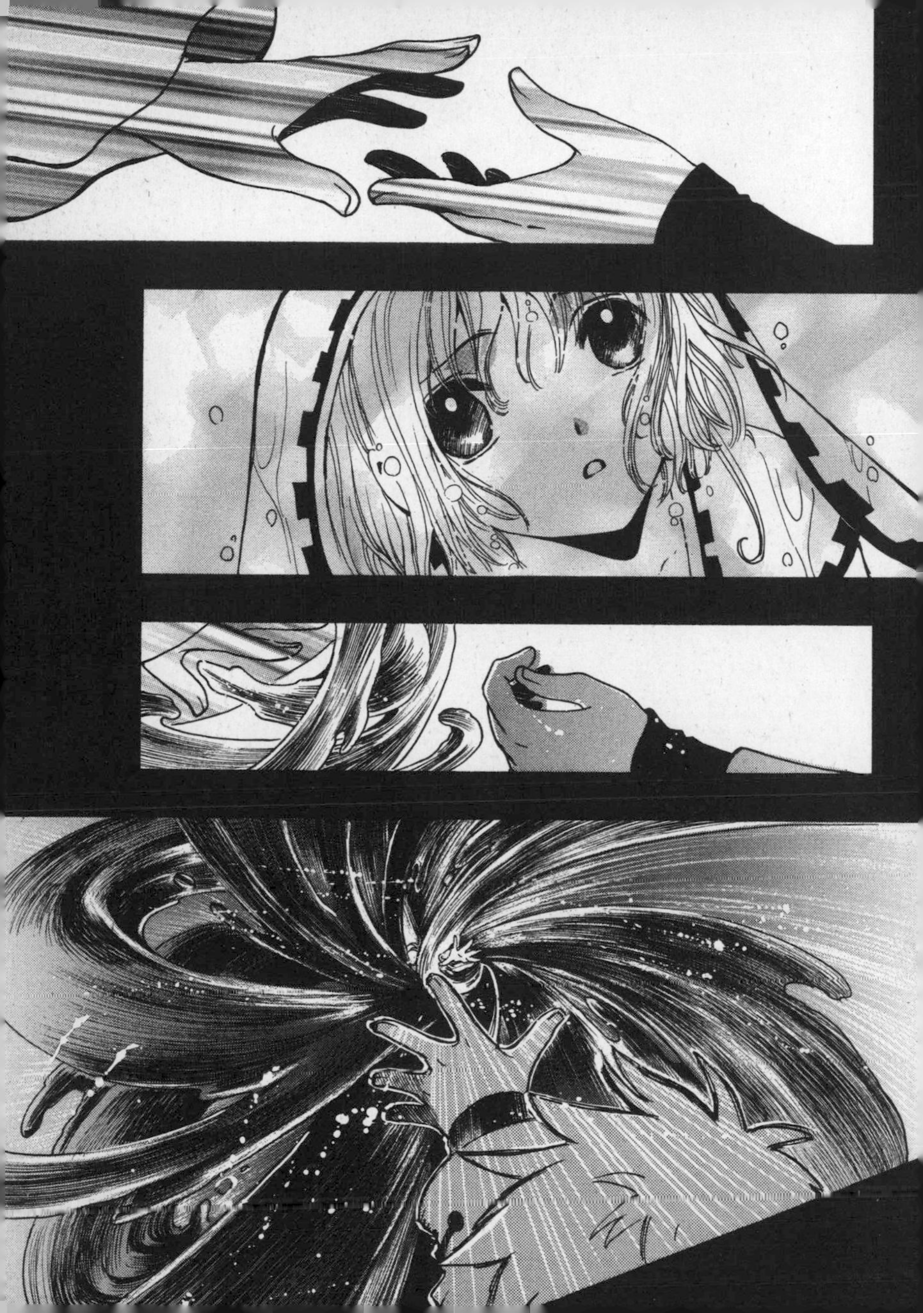

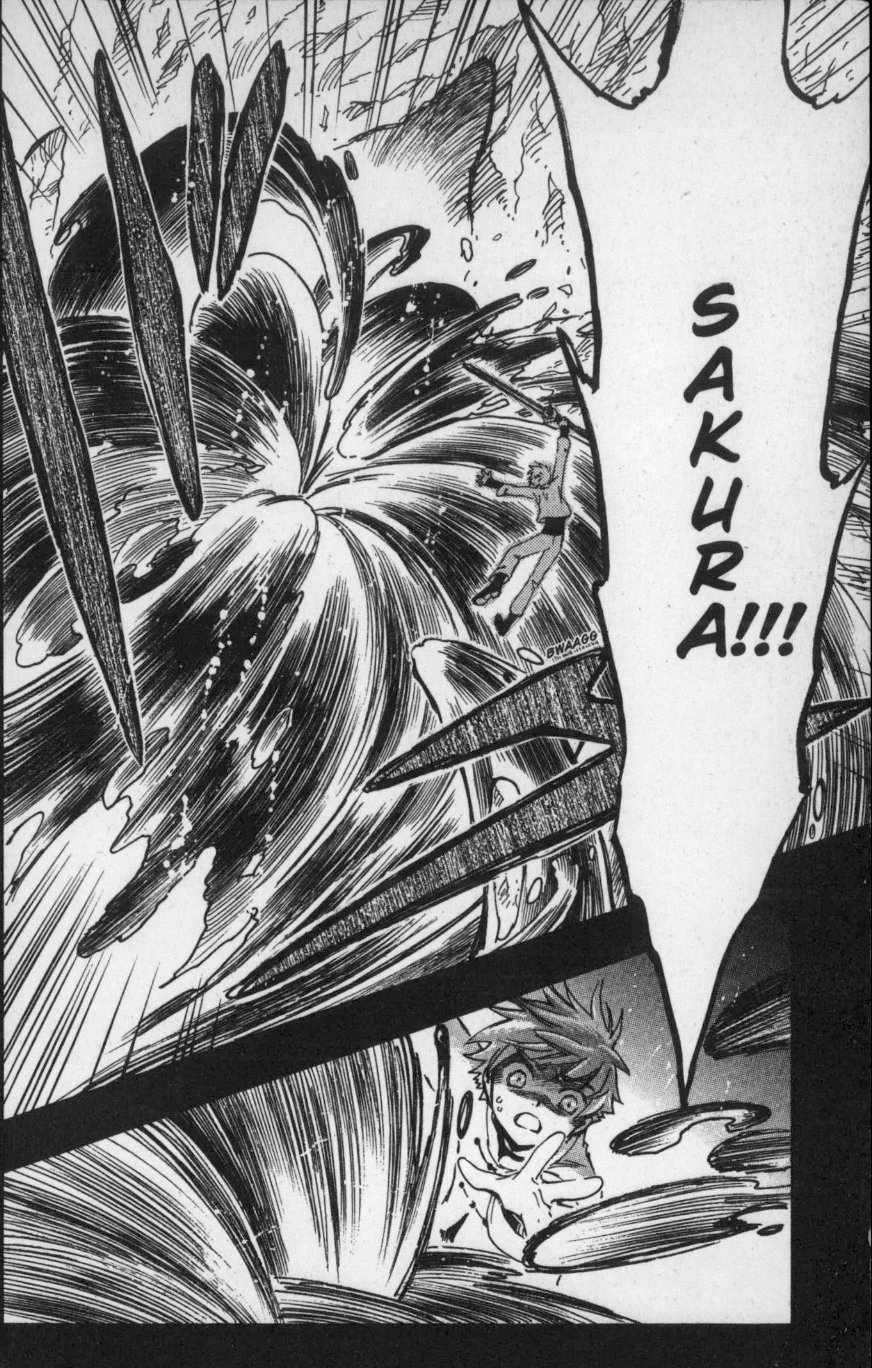
SAKURA!!!
BWAAGG

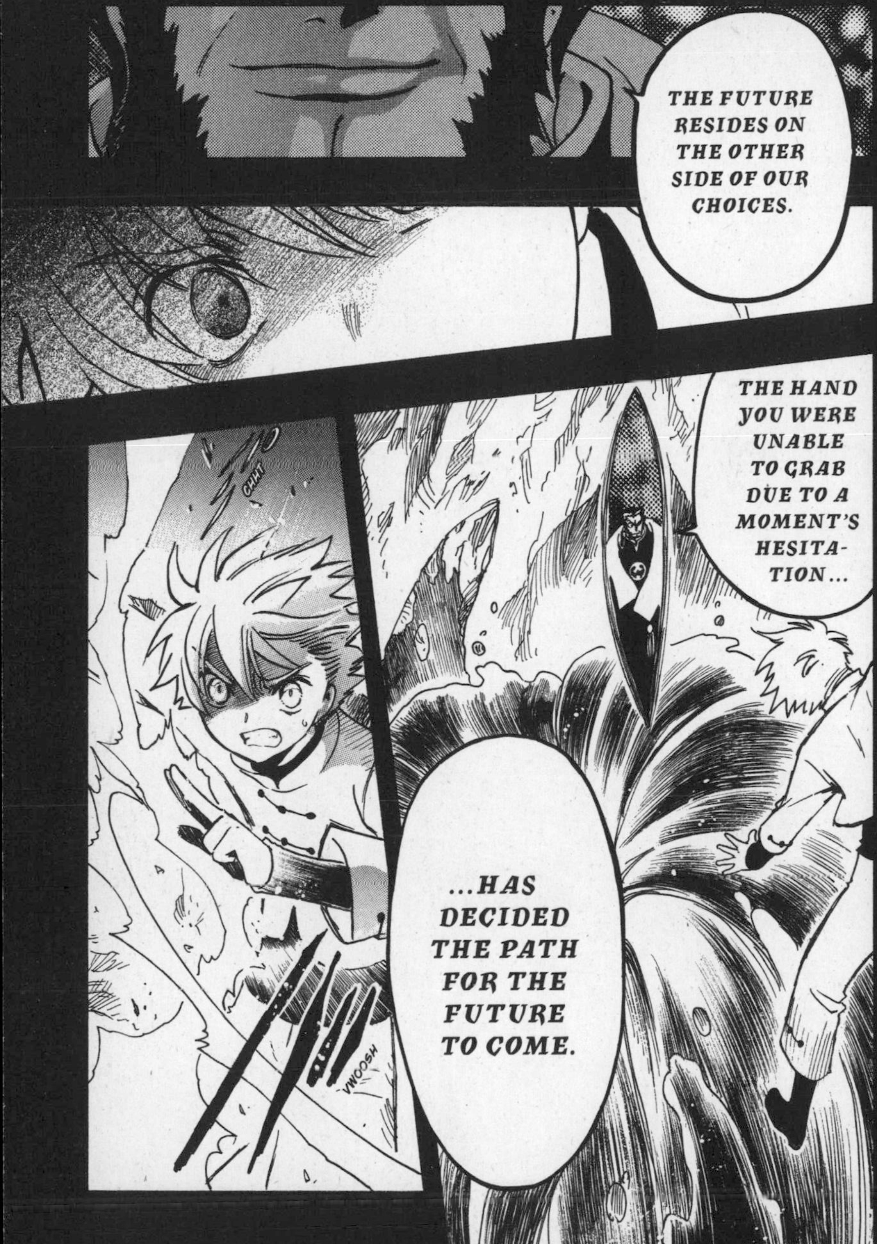
THE FUTURE RESIDES ON THE OTHER SIDE OF OUR CHOICES.
THE HAND YOU WERE UNABLE TO GRAB DUE TO A MOMENT'S HESITATION...
...HAS DECIDED THE PATH FOR THE FUTURE TO COME.
CHHT
VWOOSH

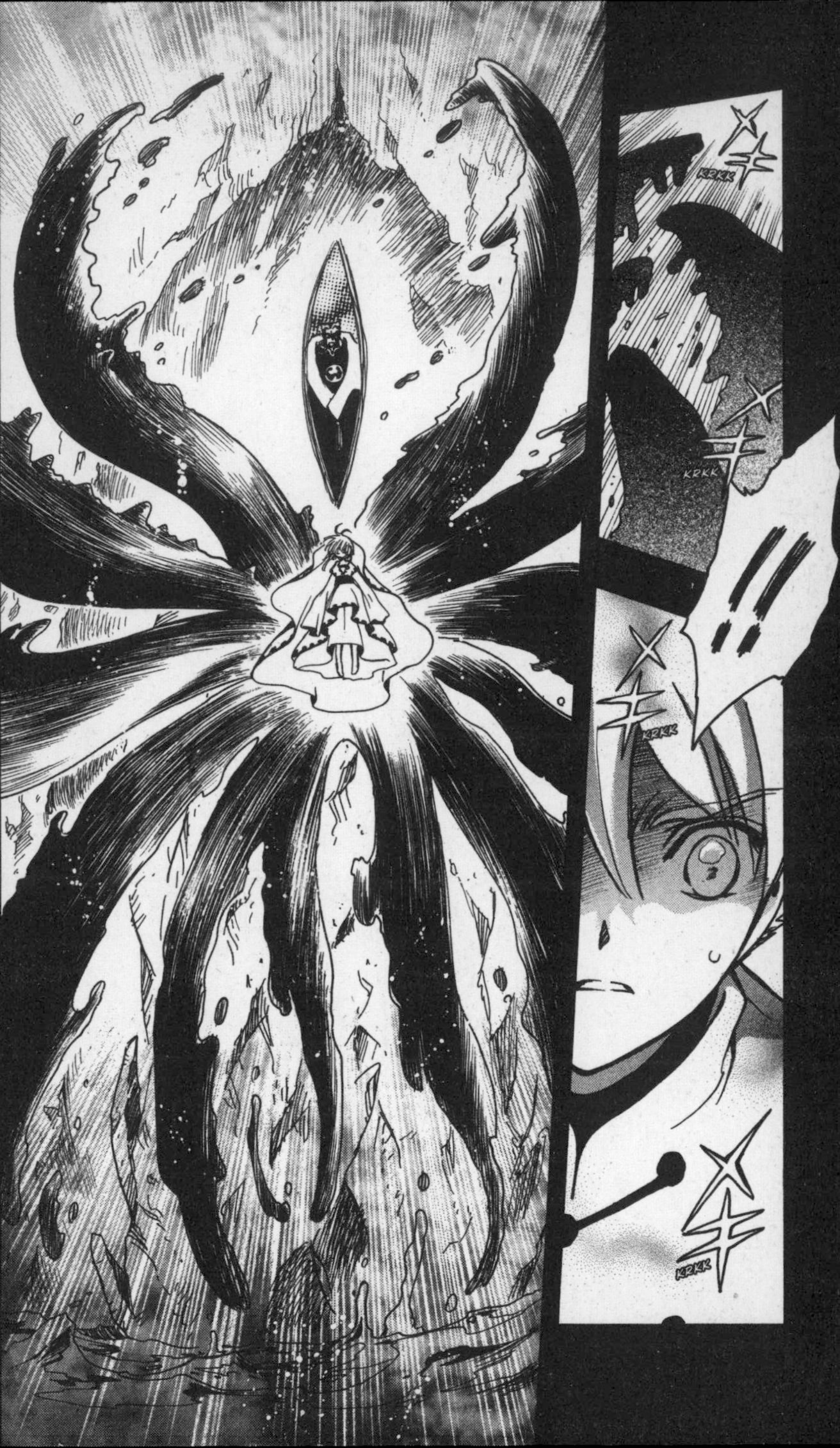
KRKK
KRKK
!!
KRKK
KRKK

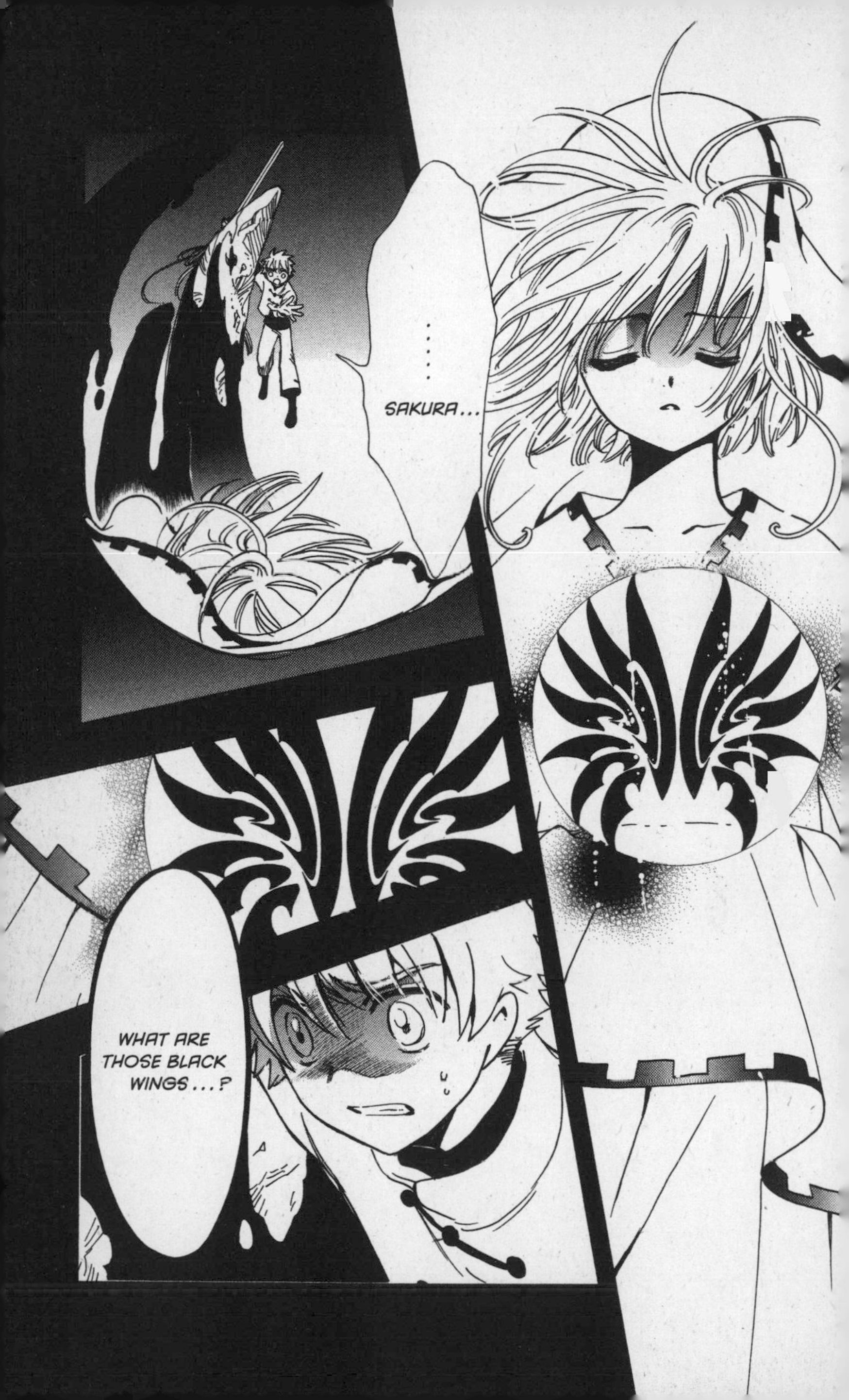

SAKURA...
WHAT ARE THOSE BLACK WINGS...?

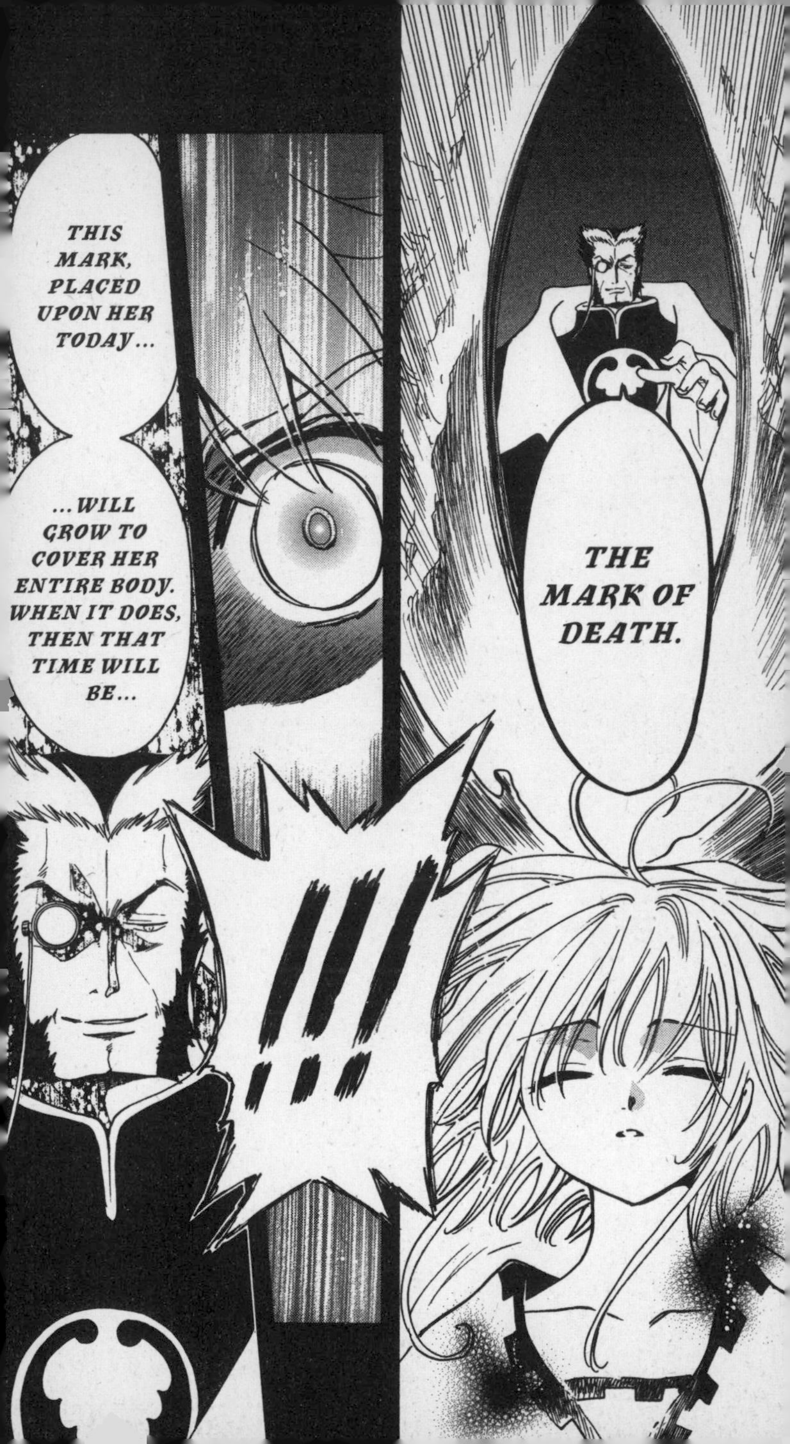
THE MARK OF DEATH.
THIS MARK, PLACED UPON HER TODAY...
...WILL GROW TO COVER HER ENTIRE BODY. WHEN IT DOES, THEN THAT TIME WILL BE...
!!!

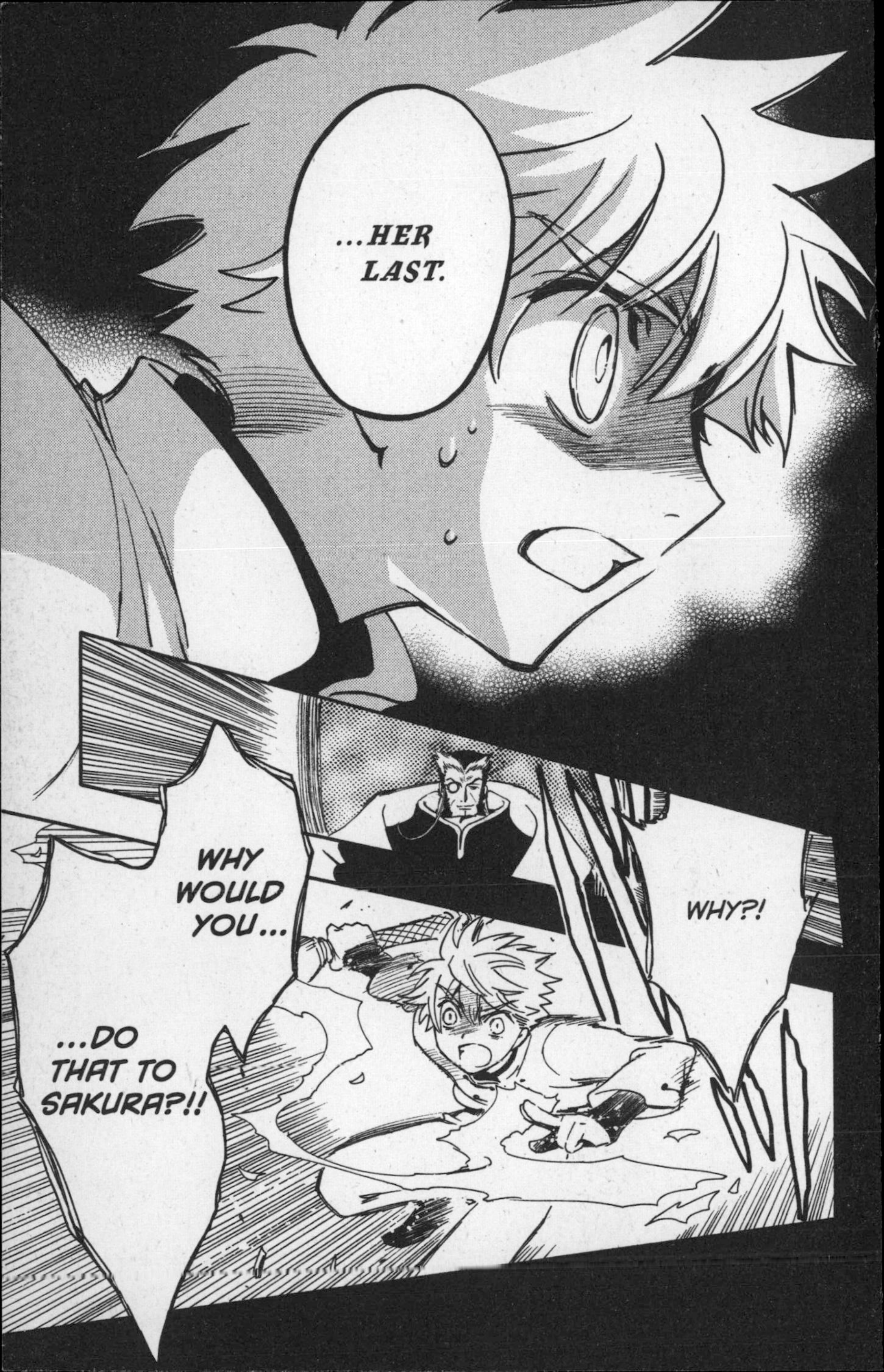
...HER LAST.
WHY?!
WHY WOULD YOU...
...DO THAT TO SAKURA?!!

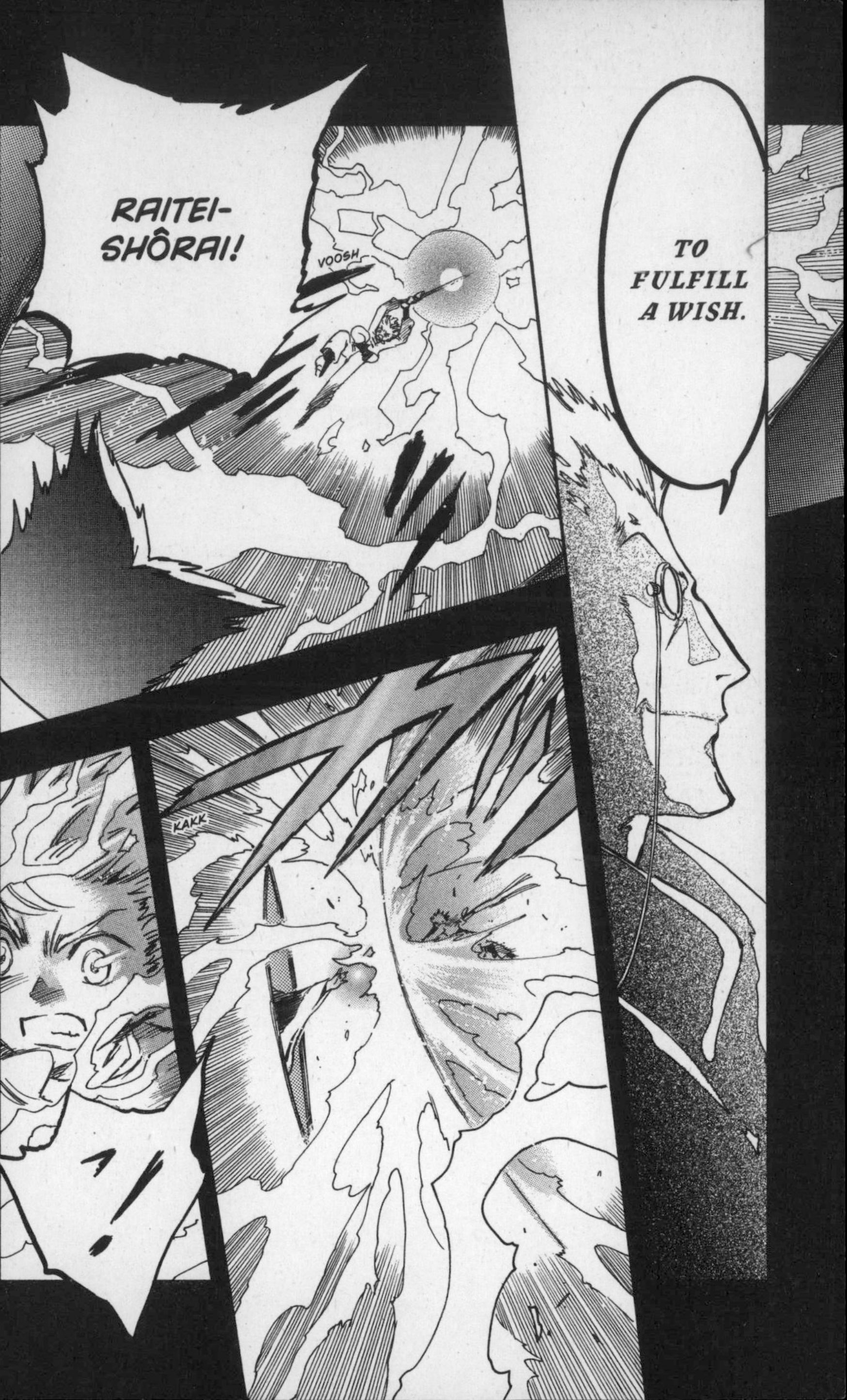
TO FULFILL A WISH.
RAITEI-SHÔRAI!
VOOSH
KAKK

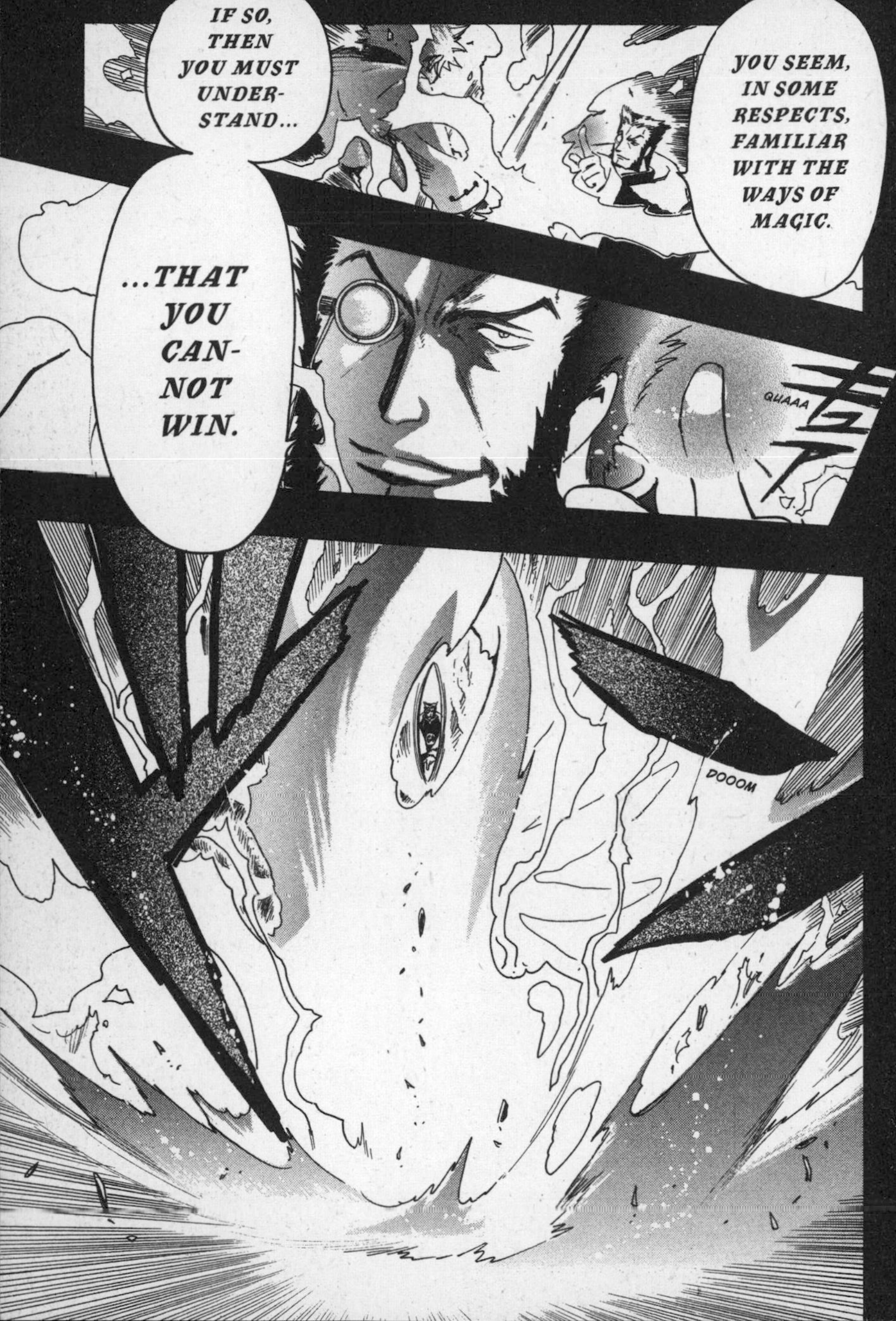
YOU SEEM, IN SOME RESPECTS, FAMILIAR WITH THE WAYS OF MAGIC.
IF SO, THEN YOU MUST UNDER-STAND...
...THAT YOU CAN-NOT WIN.
QUAAA
DOOOM

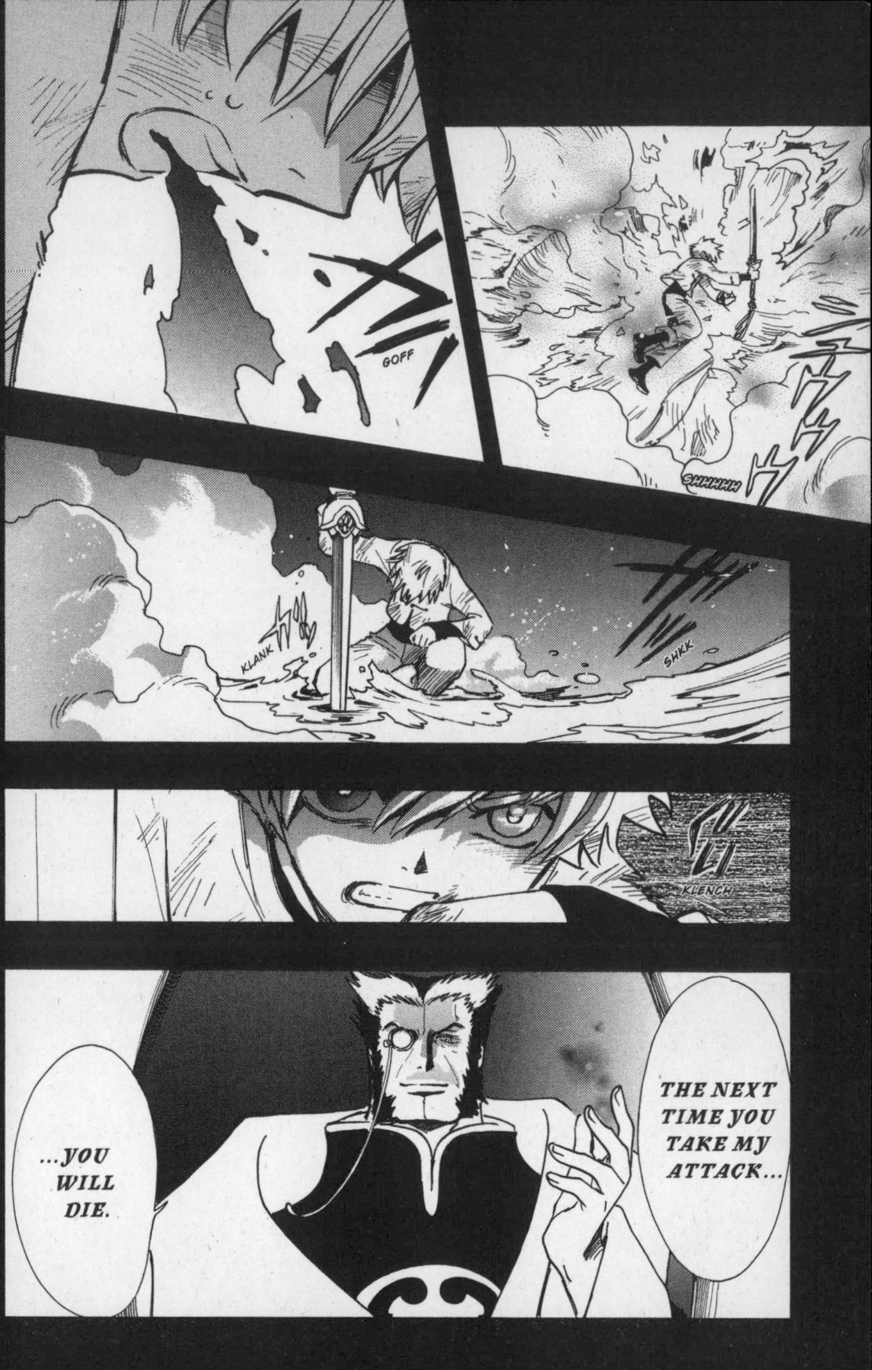
SHHHHH
GOFF
SHKK
KLANK
KLENCH
THE NEXT TIME YOU TAKE MY ATTACK...
...YOU WILL DIE.

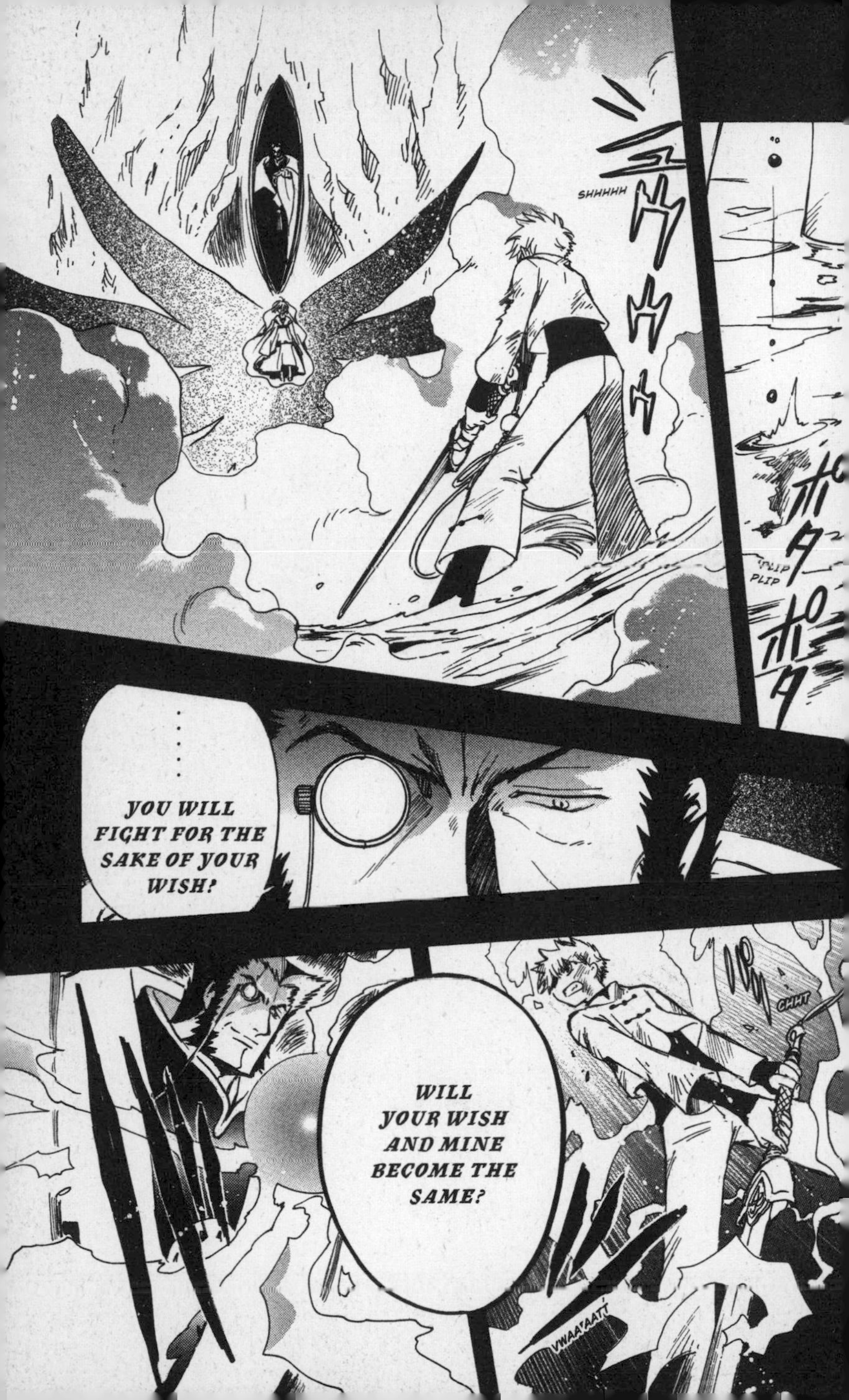
ポタポタ
PLIP PLIP
SHHHHH
. . . . .
YOU WILL FIGHT FOR THE SAKE OF YOUR WISH?
CHHT
WILL YOUR WISH AND MINE BECOME THE SAME?
VWAAAATT

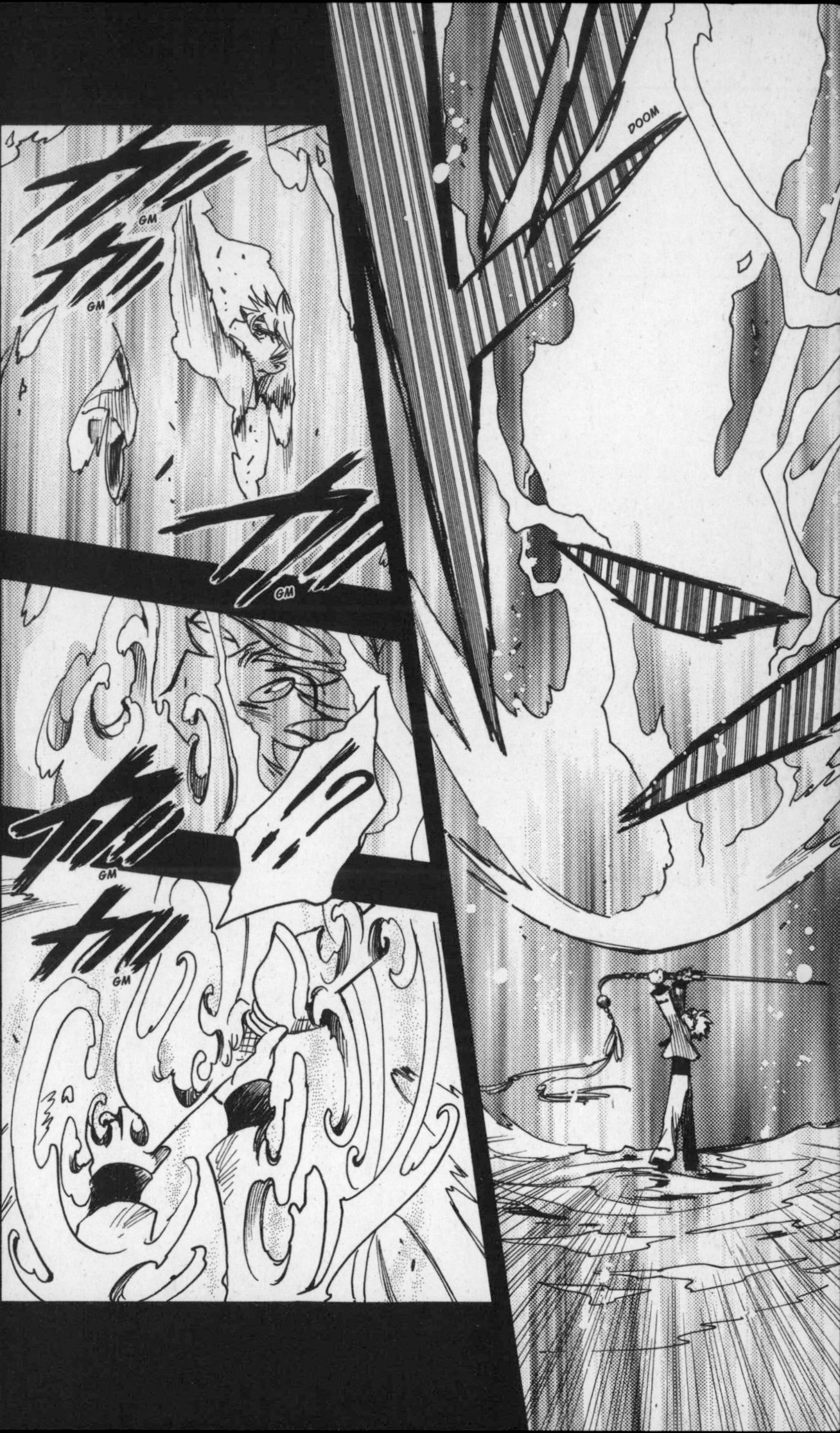
DOOM
GM
GM
GM
GM
GM

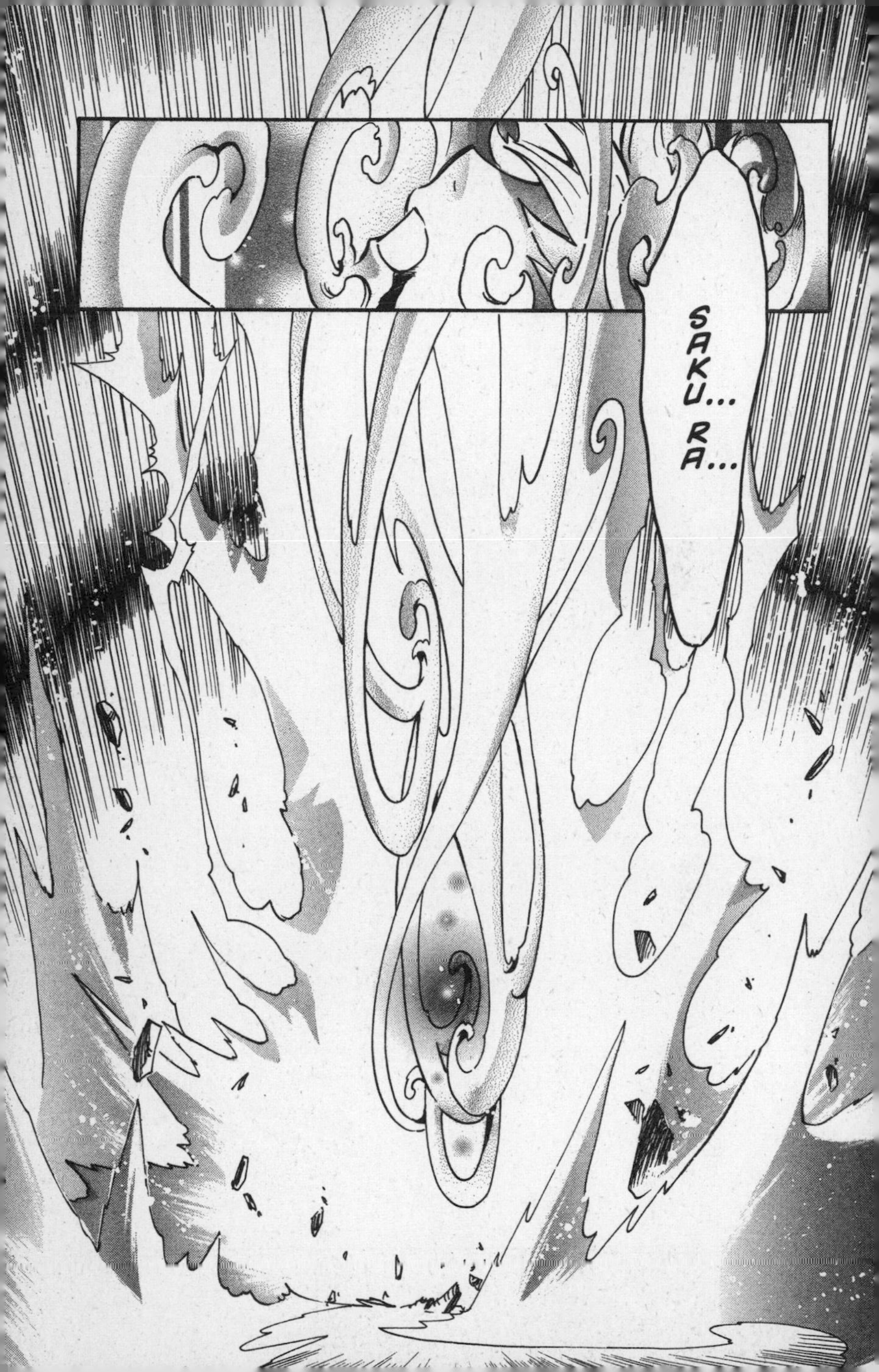
SAKU... RA...

ツバサ

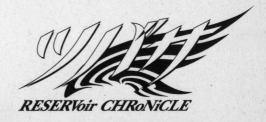

RESERVoir CHRoNiCLE

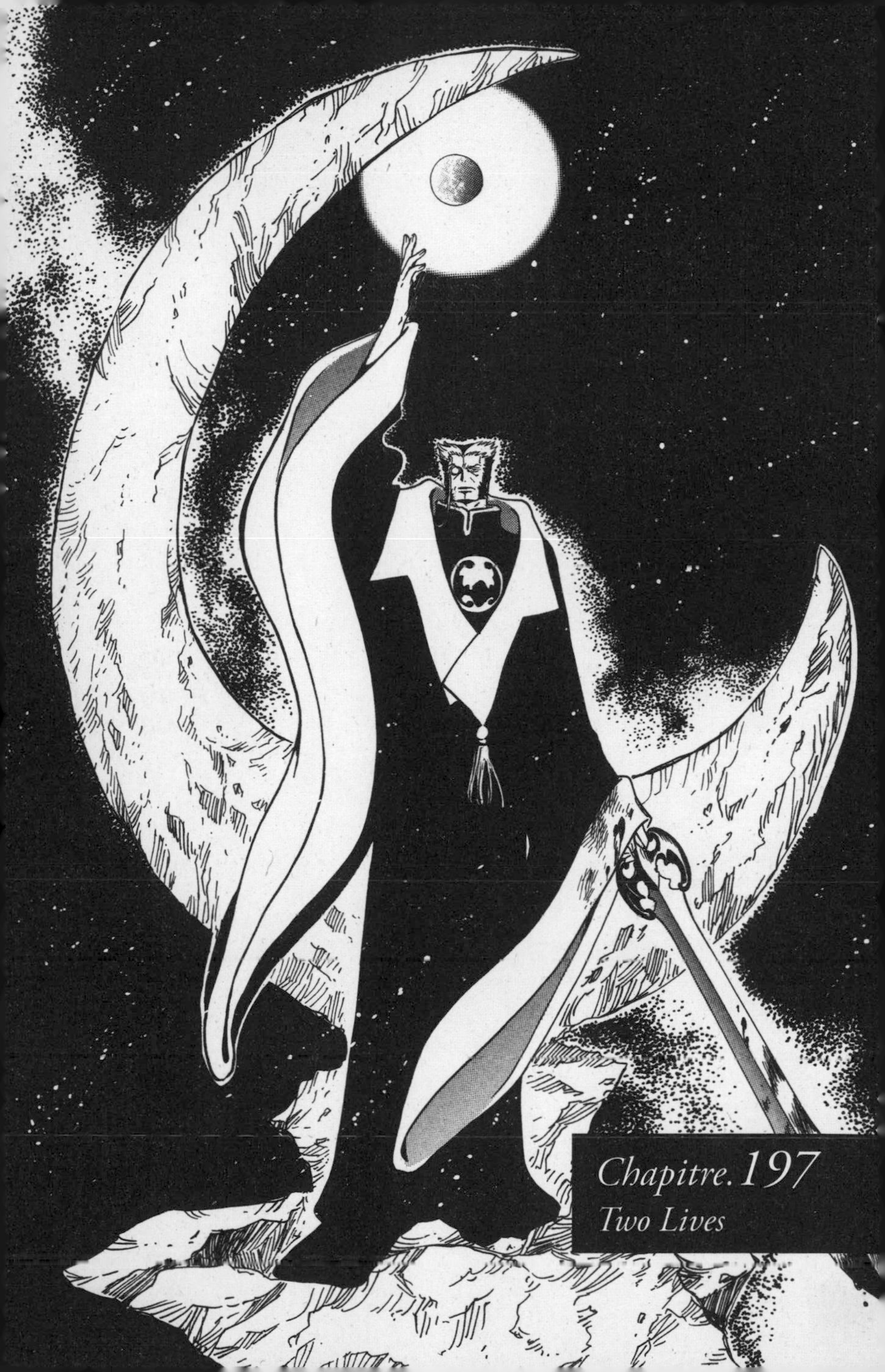
Chapitre. 197
Two Lives

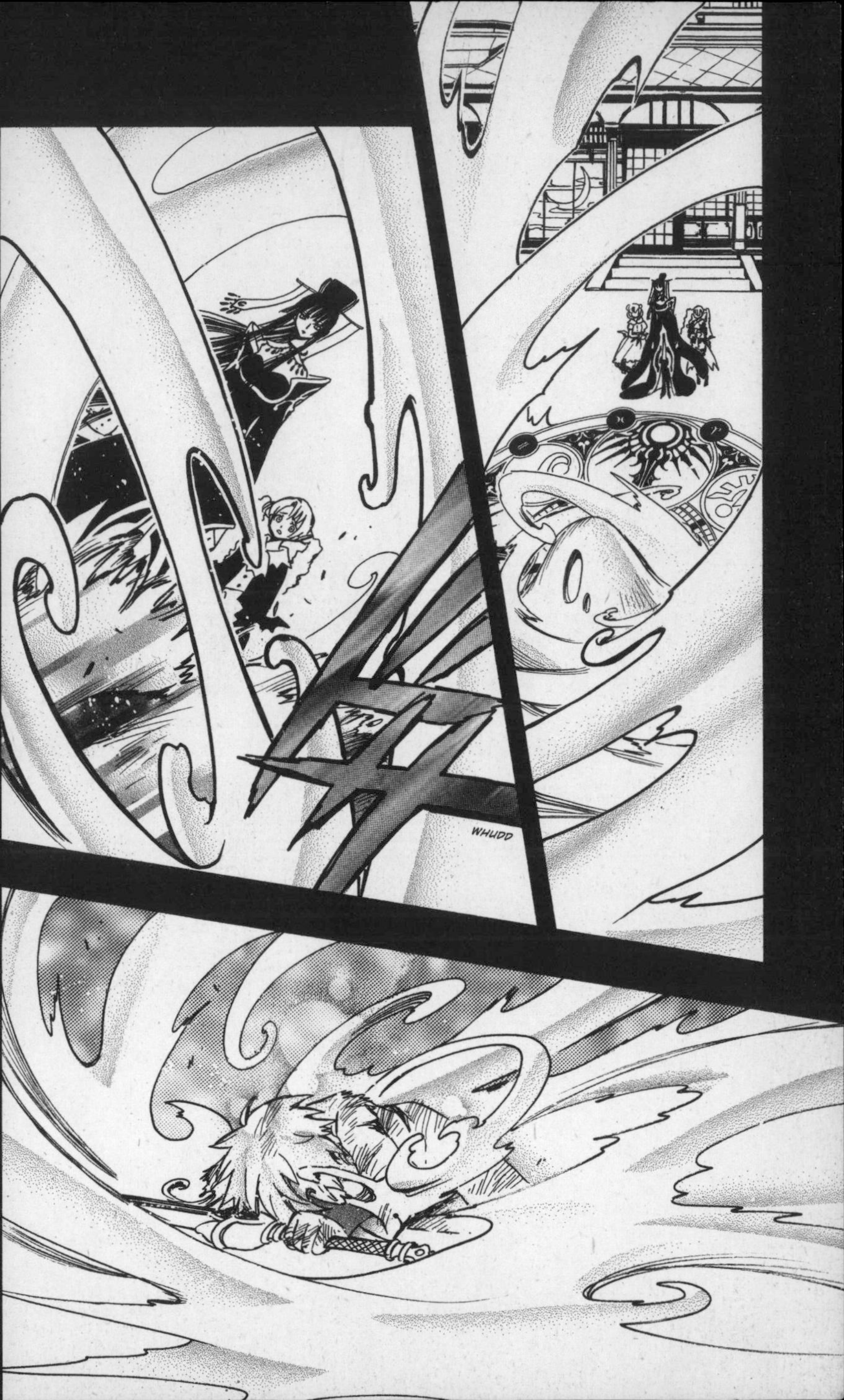
WHUDD

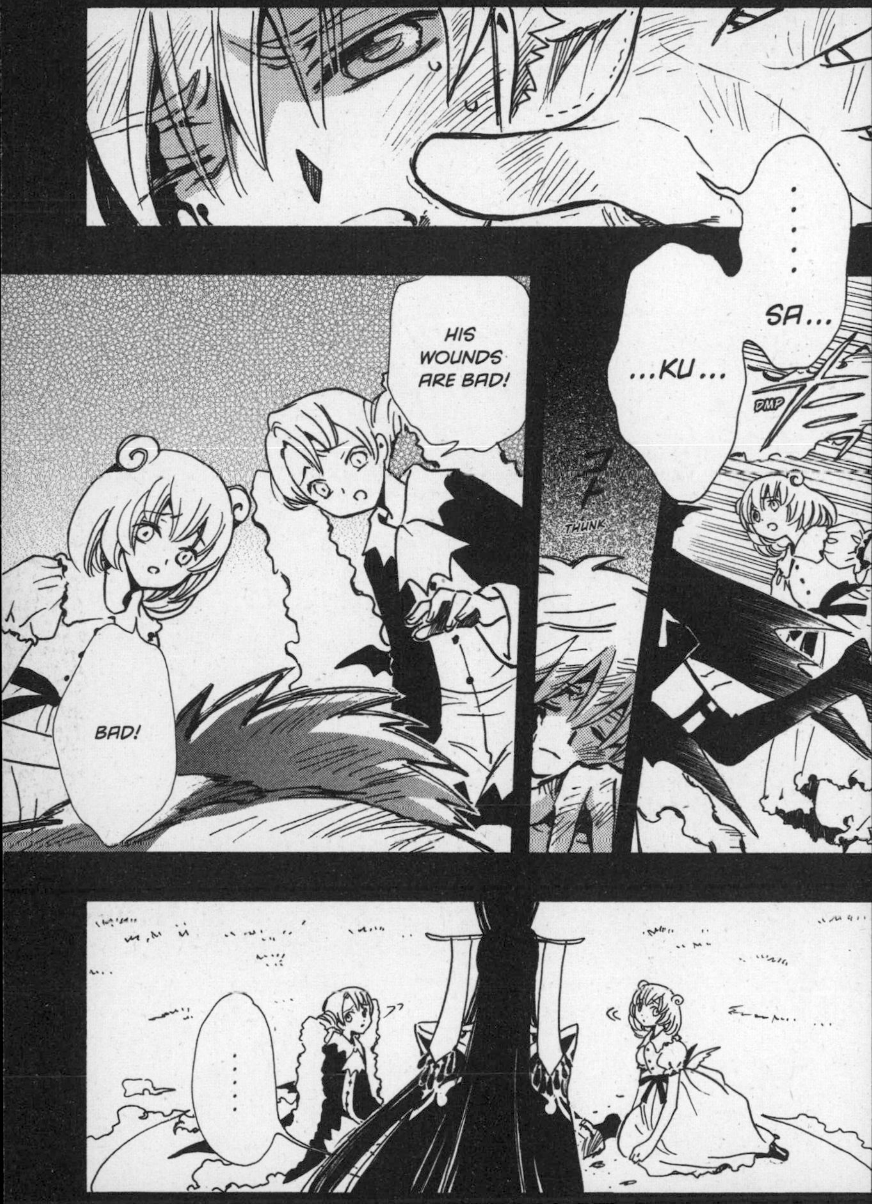
......
SA...
...KU...
DMP
THUNK
HIS WOUNDS ARE BAD!
BAD!
......

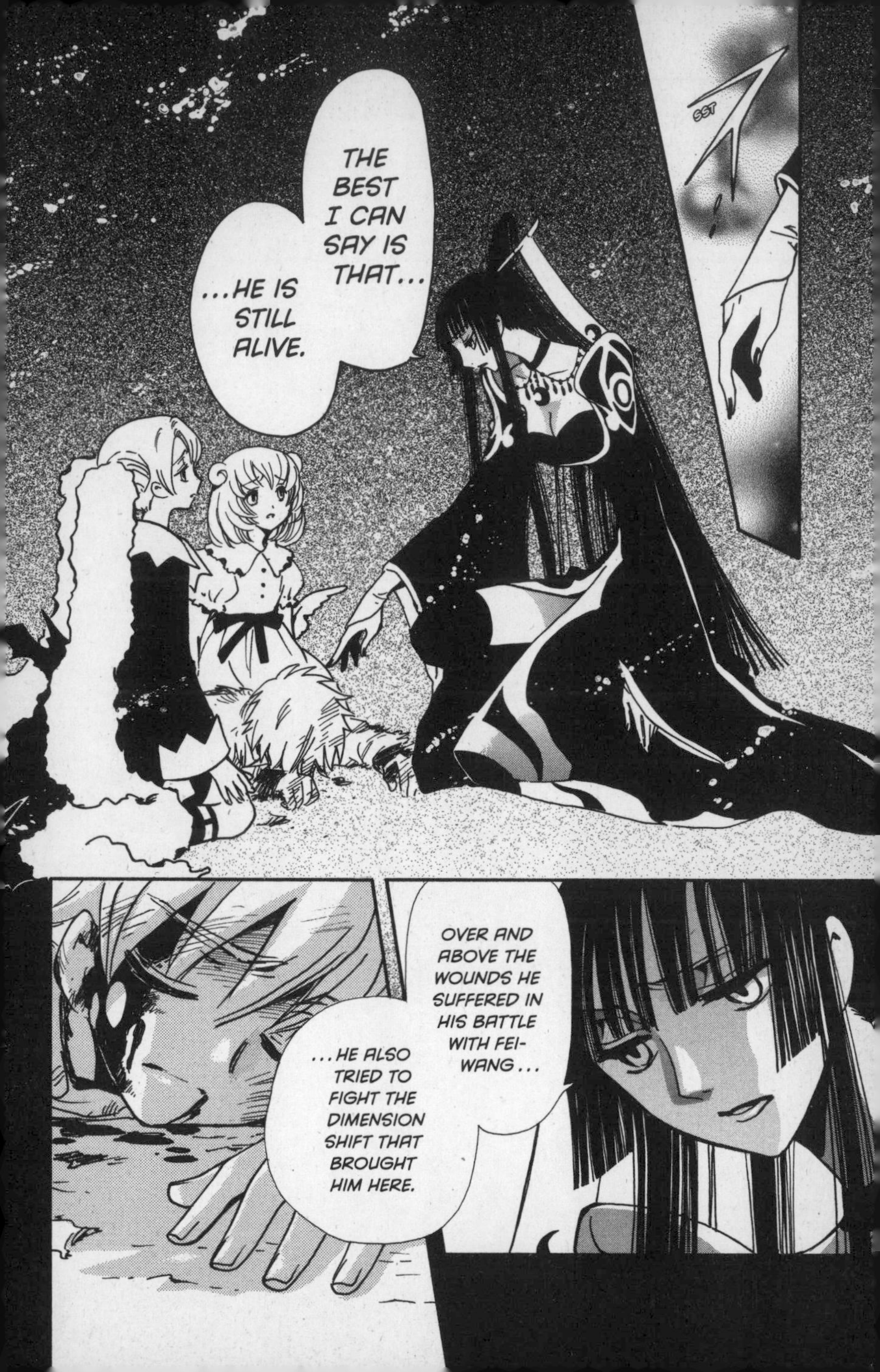
SST
THE BEST I CAN SAY IS THAT...
...HE IS STILL ALIVE.
OVER AND ABOVE THE WOUNDS HE SUFFERED IN HIS BATTLE WITH FEI-WANG...
...HE ALSO TRIED TO FIGHT THE DIMENSION SHIFT THAT BROUGHT HIM HERE.

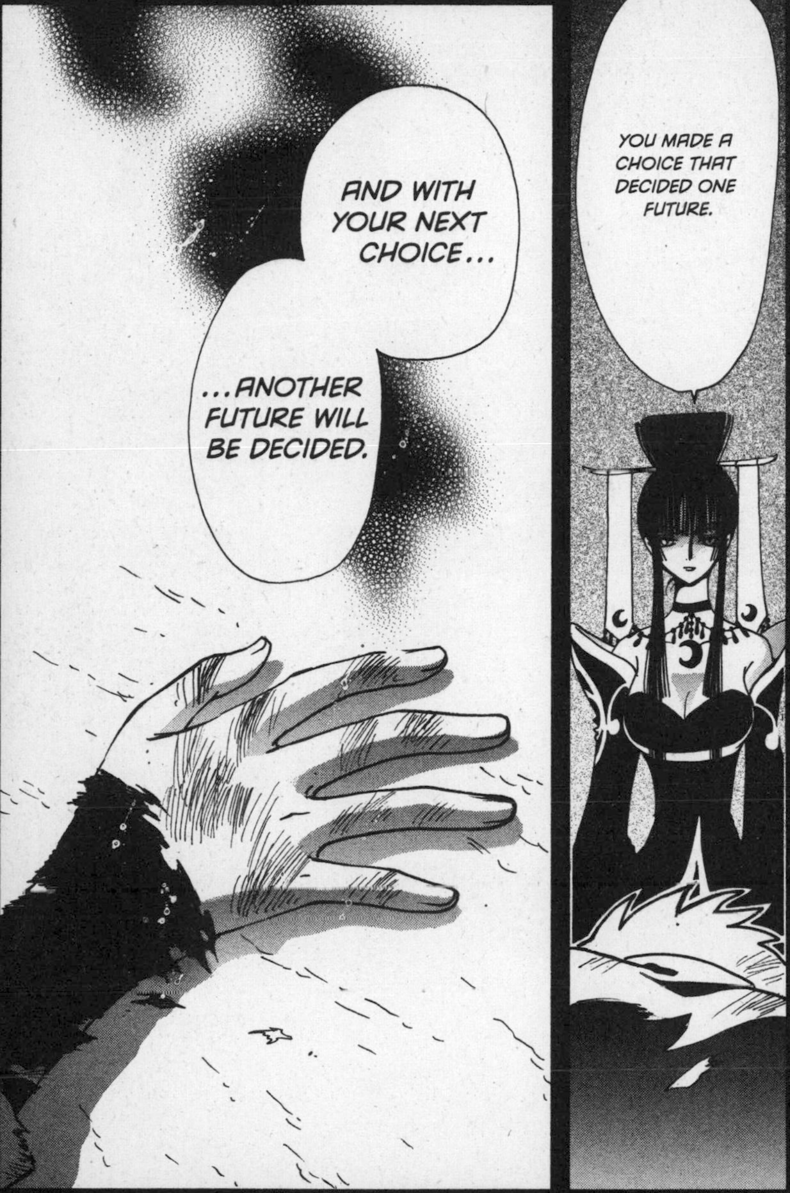
YOU MADE A CHOICE THAT DECIDED ONE FUTURE.
AND WITH YOUR NEXT CHOICE...
...ANOTHER FUTURE WILL BE DECIDED.

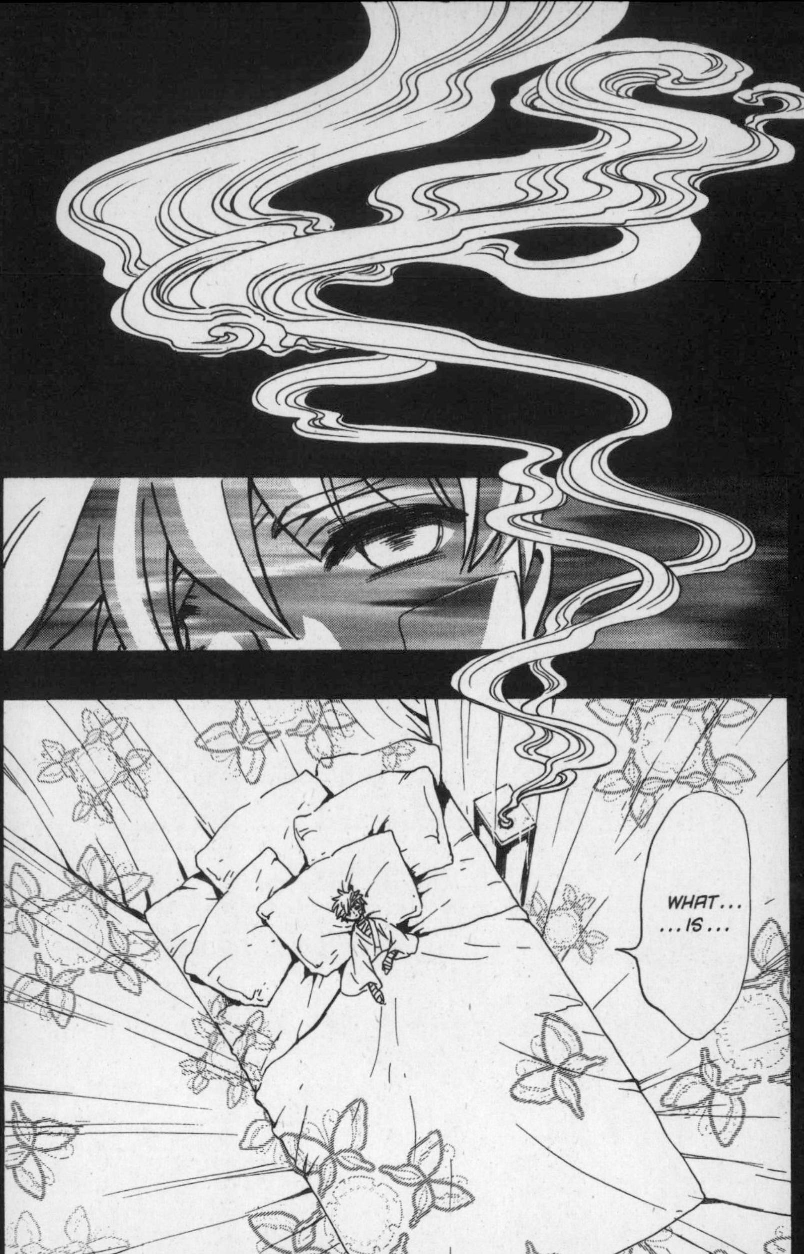
WHAT...
...IS...

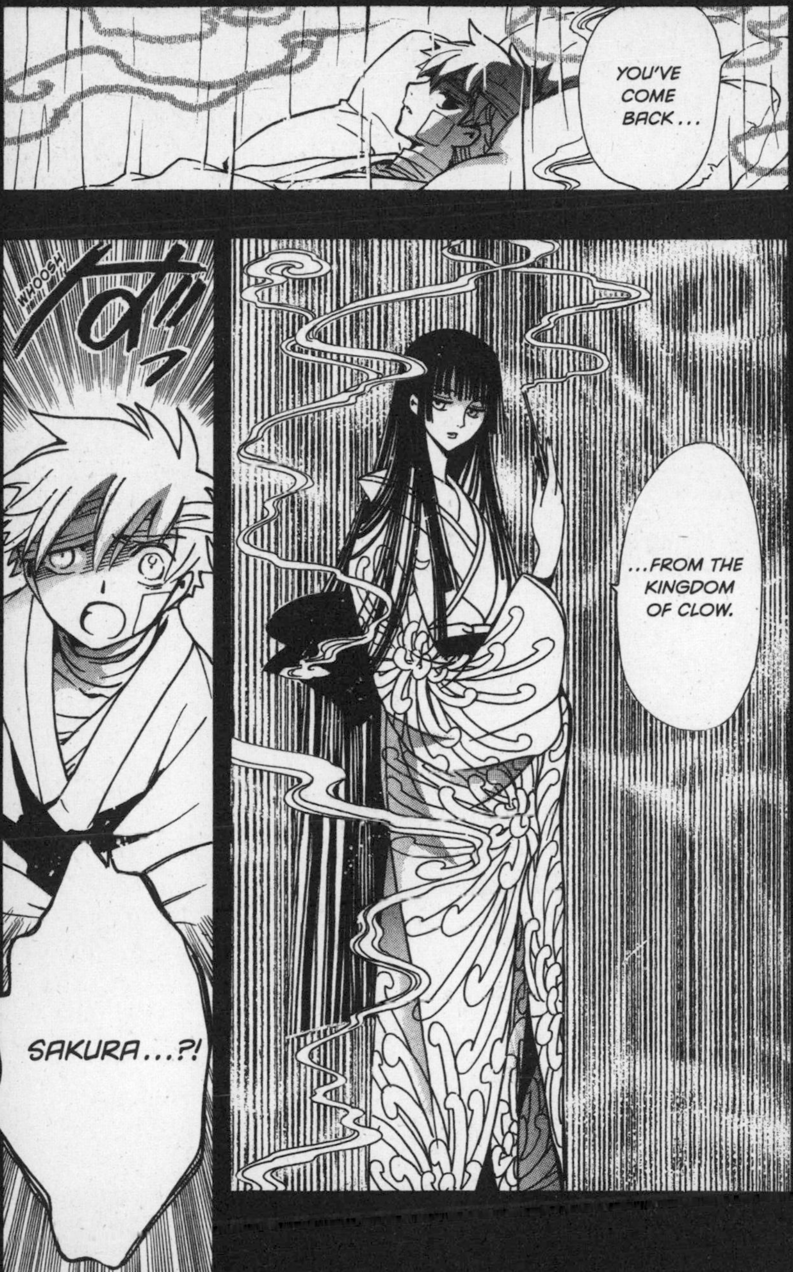
YOU'VE COME BACK...
...FROM THE KINGDOM OF CLOW.
WHOOSH
SAKURA...?!

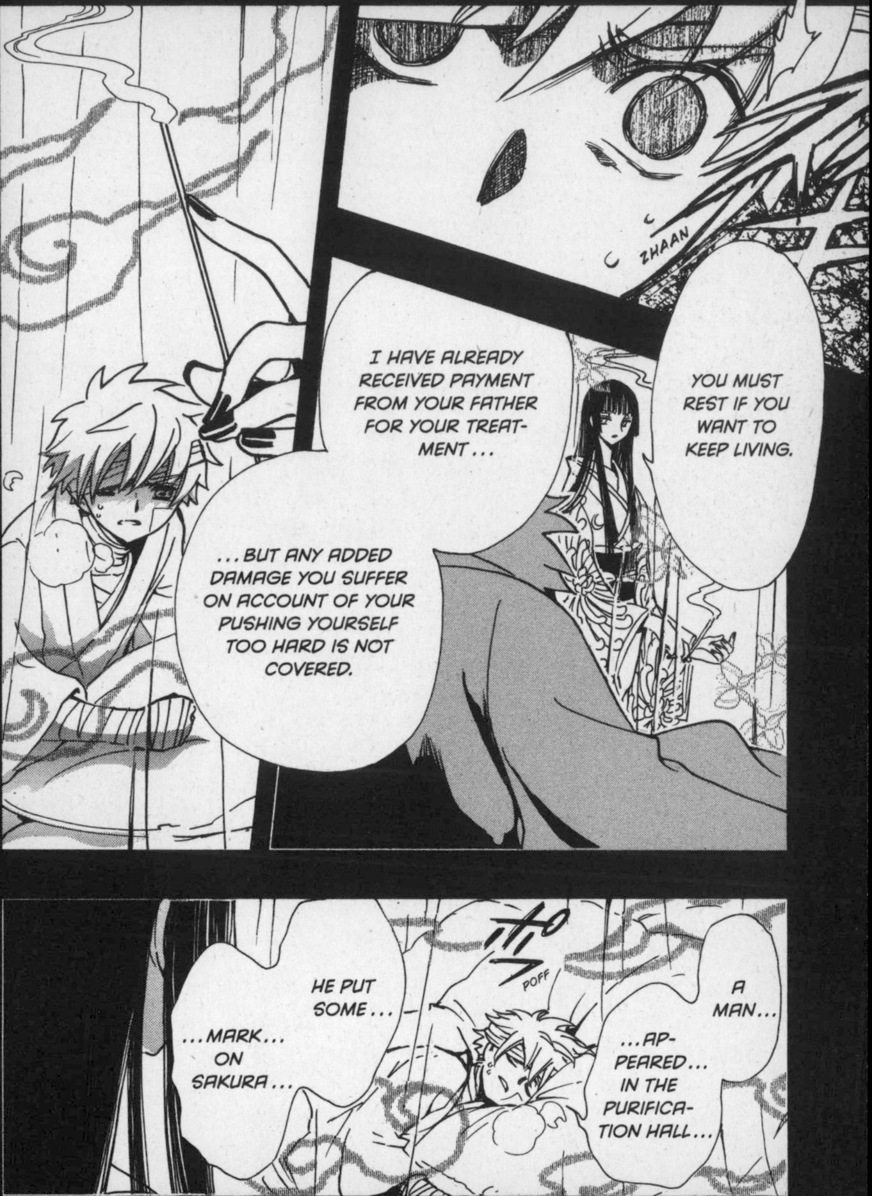
ZHAAN
YOU MUST REST IF YOU WANT TO KEEP LIVING.
I HAVE ALREADY RECEIVED PAYMENT FROM YOUR FATHER FOR YOUR TREAT-MENT...
...BUT ANY ADDED DAMAGE YOU SUFFER ON ACCOUNT OF YOUR PUSHING YOURSELF TOO HARD IS NOT COVERED.
A MAN...
...AP-PEARED... IN THE PURIFICA-TION HALL...
POFF
HE PUT SOME...
...MARK... ON SAKURA...

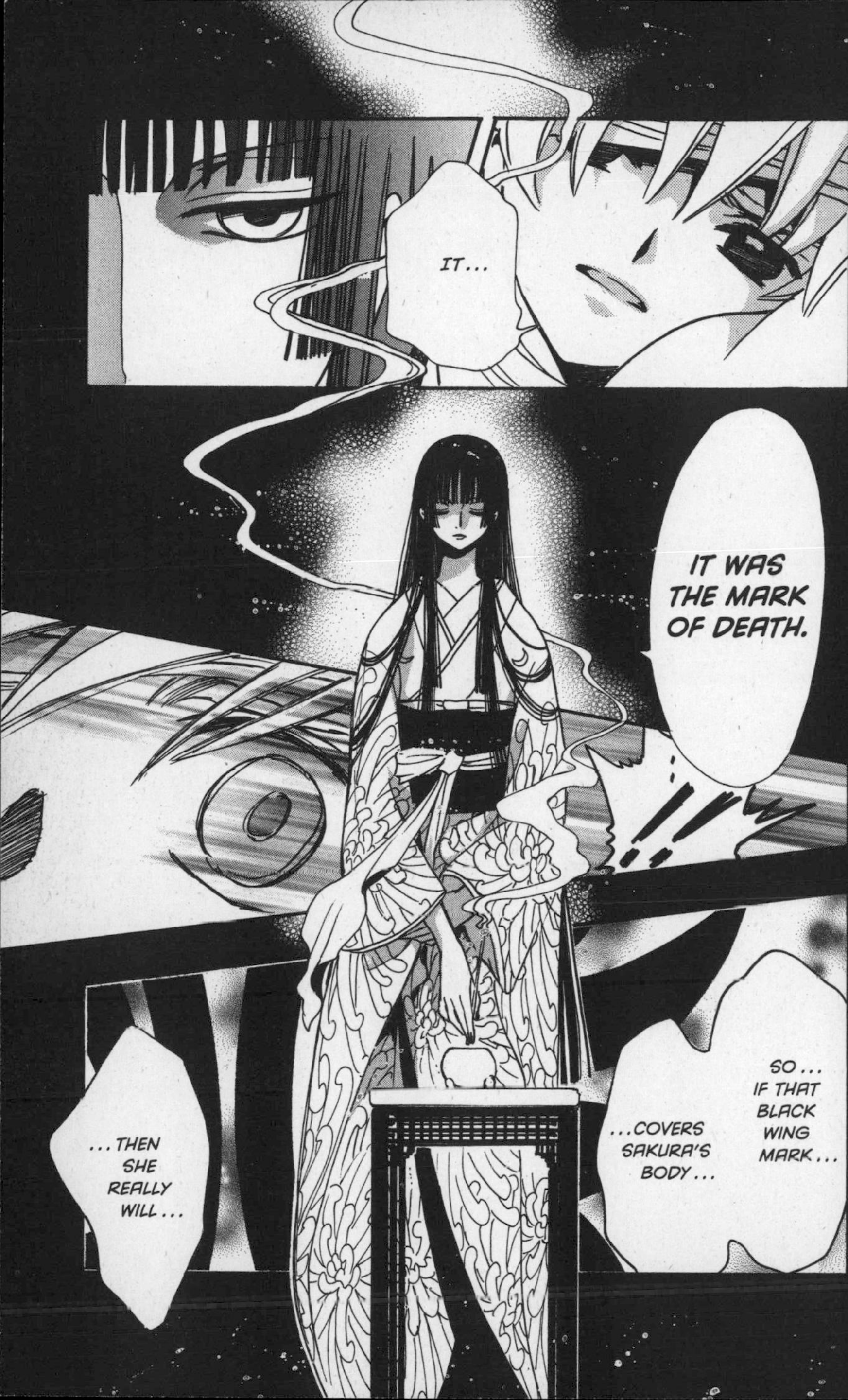
IT...
IT WAS THE MARK OF DEATH.
!!
SO... IF THAT BLACK WING MARK...
...COVERS SAKURA'S BODY...
...THEN SHE REALLY WILL...

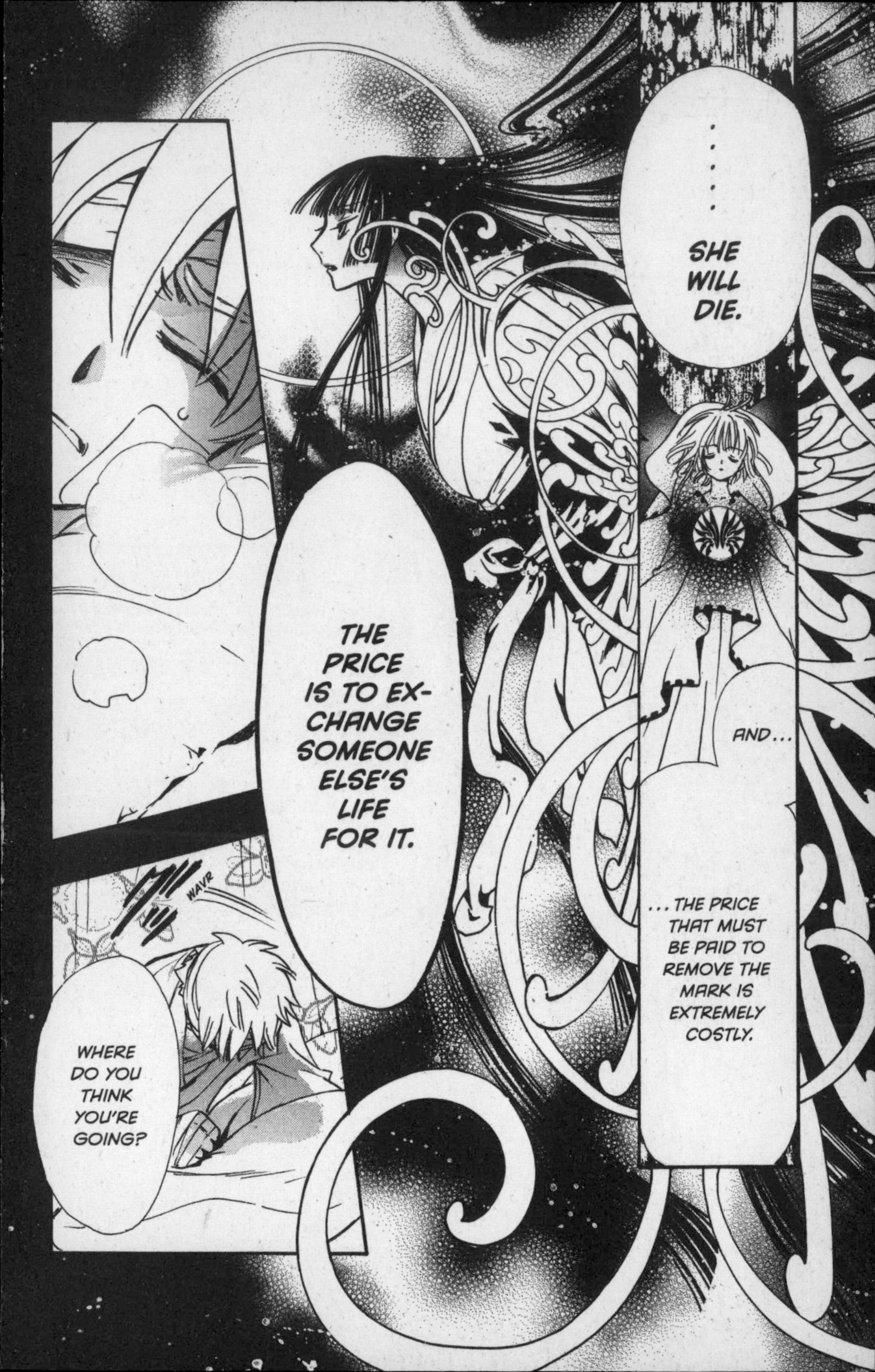
. . . . .
SHE WILL DIE.
AND...
...THE PRICE THAT MUST BE PAID TO REMOVE THE MARK IS EXTREMELY COSTLY.
THE PRICE IS TO EX-CHANGE SOMEONE ELSE'S LIFE FOR IT.
WAVR
WHERE DO YOU THINK YOU'RE GOING?

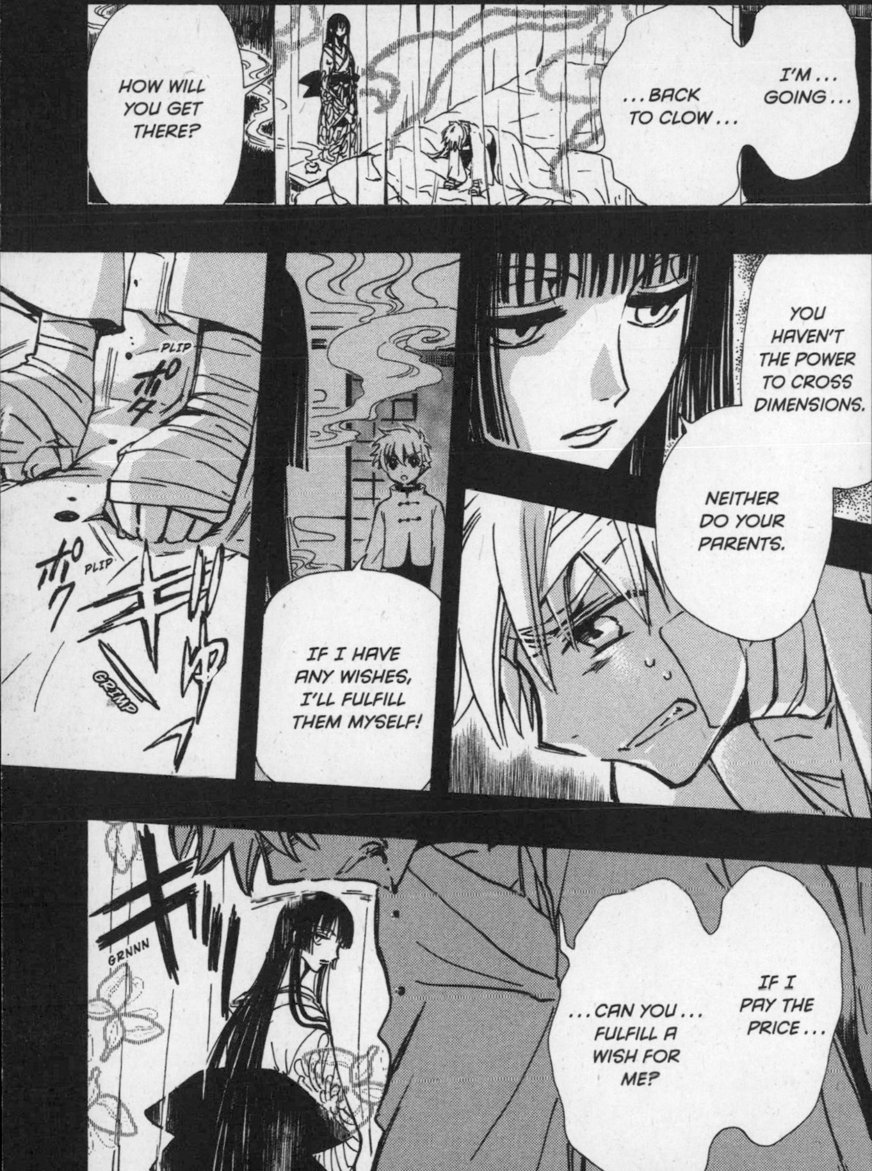
I'M . . . GOING . . .
. . . BACK TO CLOW . . .
HOW WILL YOU GET THERE?
YOU HAVEN'T THE POWER TO CROSS DIMENSIONS.
NEITHER DO YOUR PARENTS.
IF I HAVE ANY WISHES, I'LL FULFILL THEM MYSELF!
PLIP
PLIP
GRIMP
IF I PAY THE PRICE . . .
. . . CAN YOU . . . FULFILL A WISH FOR ME?
GRNNN

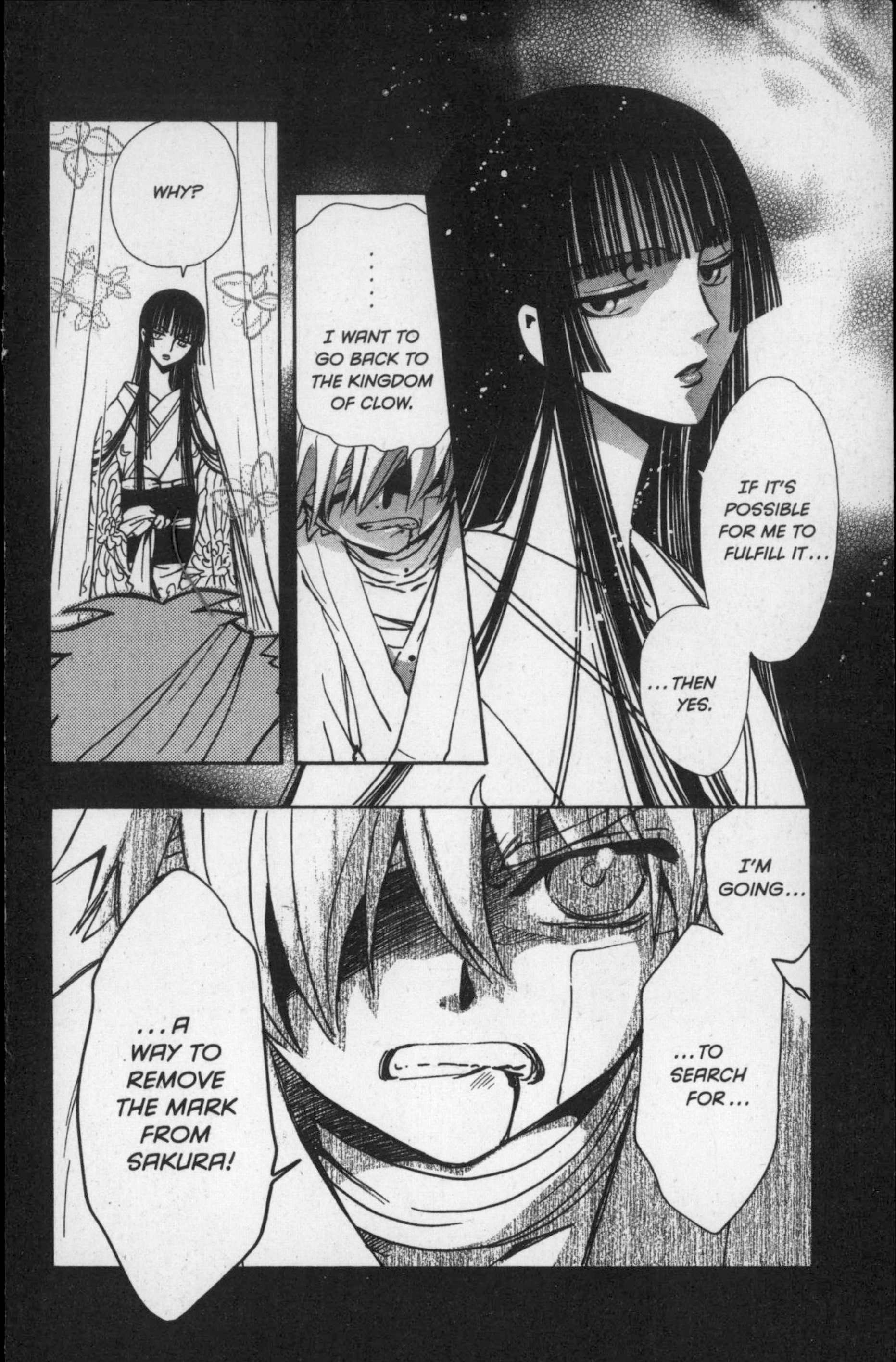
IF IT'S POSSIBLE FOR ME TO FULFILL IT...
...THEN YES.
......
I WANT TO GO BACK TO THE KINGDOM OF CLOW.
WHY?
I'M GOING...
...TO SEARCH FOR...
...A WAY TO REMOVE THE MARK FROM SAKURA!

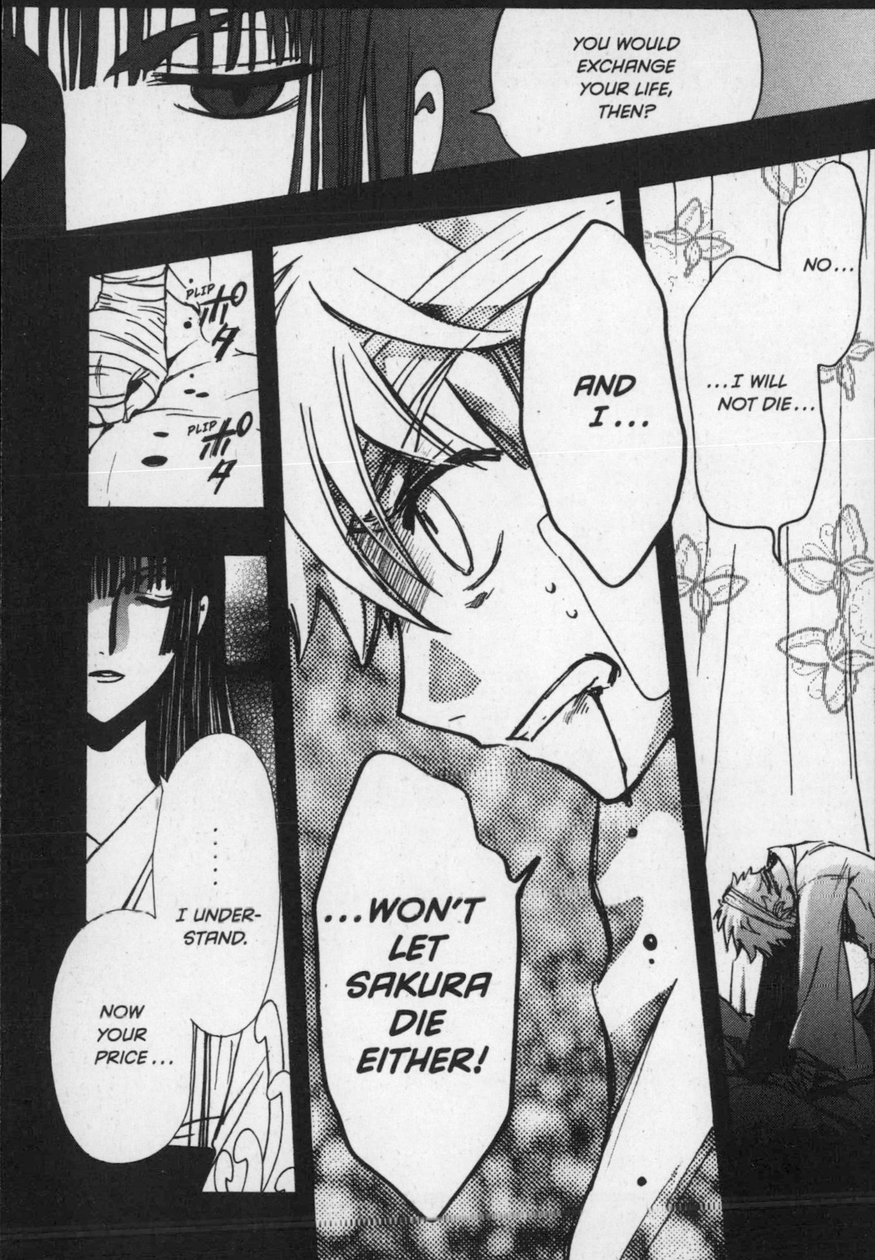
YOU WOULD EXCHANGE YOUR LIFE, THEN?
NO...
...I WILL NOT DIE...
AND I...
...WON'T LET SAKURA DIE EITHER!
PLIP
PLIP
......
I UNDER-STAND.
NOW YOUR PRICE...

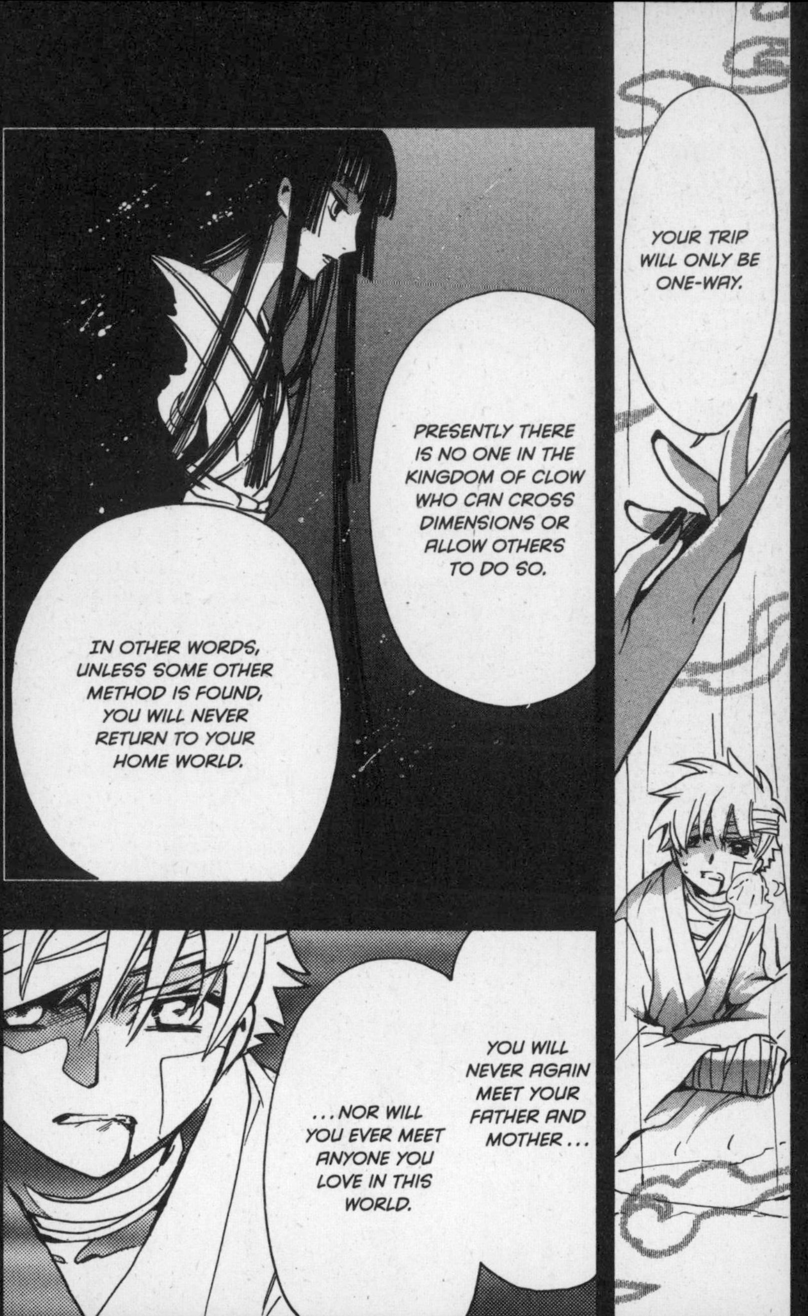
YOUR TRIP WILL ONLY BE ONE-WAY.
PRESENTLY THERE IS NO ONE IN THE KINGDOM OF CLOW WHO CAN CROSS DIMENSIONS OR ALLOW OTHERS TO DO SO.
IN OTHER WORDS, UNLESS SOME OTHER METHOD IS FOUND, YOU WILL NEVER RETURN TO YOUR HOME WORLD.
YOU WILL NEVER AGAIN MEET YOUR FATHER AND MOTHER . . .
. . . NOR WILL YOU EVER MEET ANYONE YOU LOVE IN THIS WORLD.

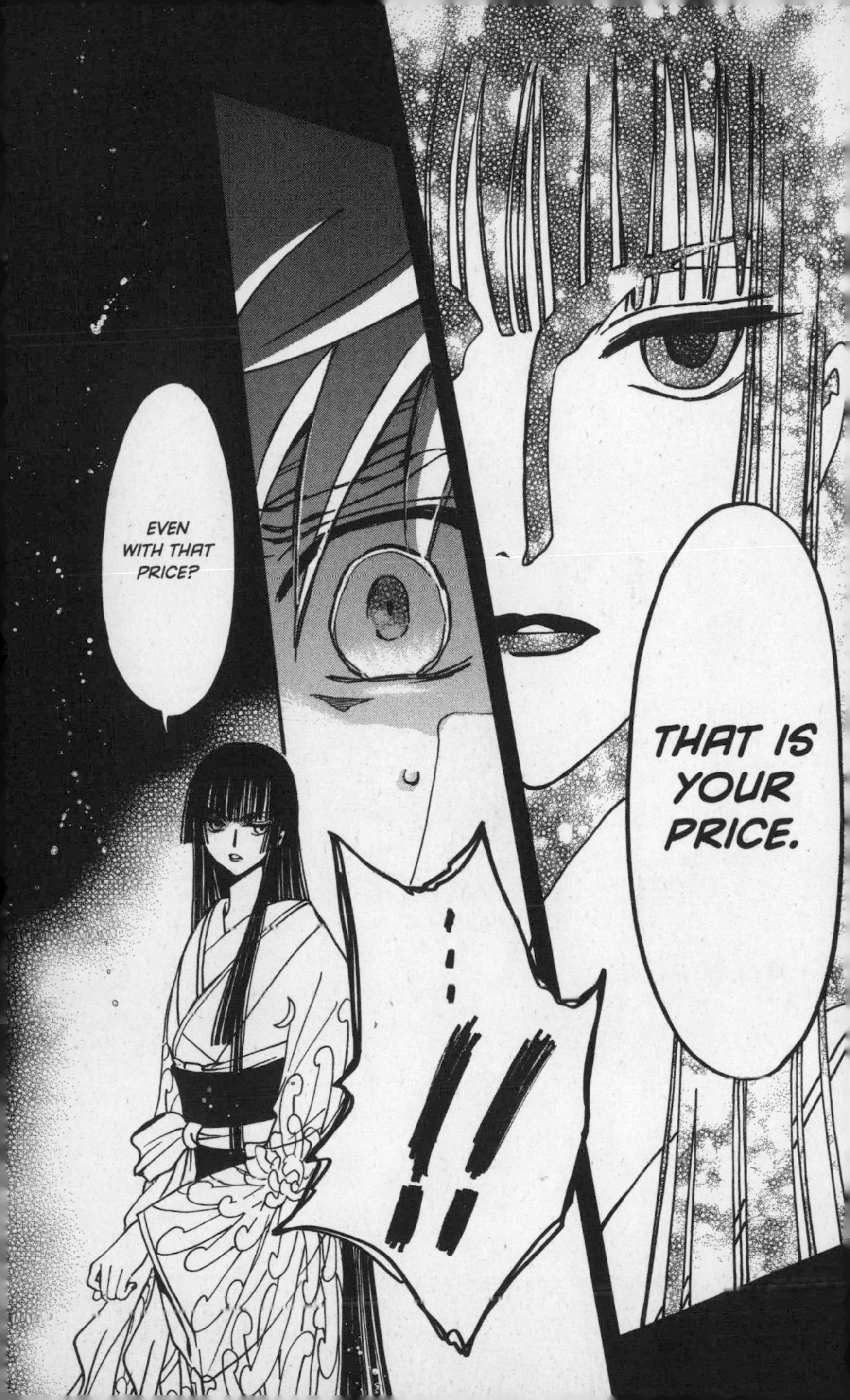
THAT IS YOUR PRICE.
...!!
EVEN WITH THAT PRICE?

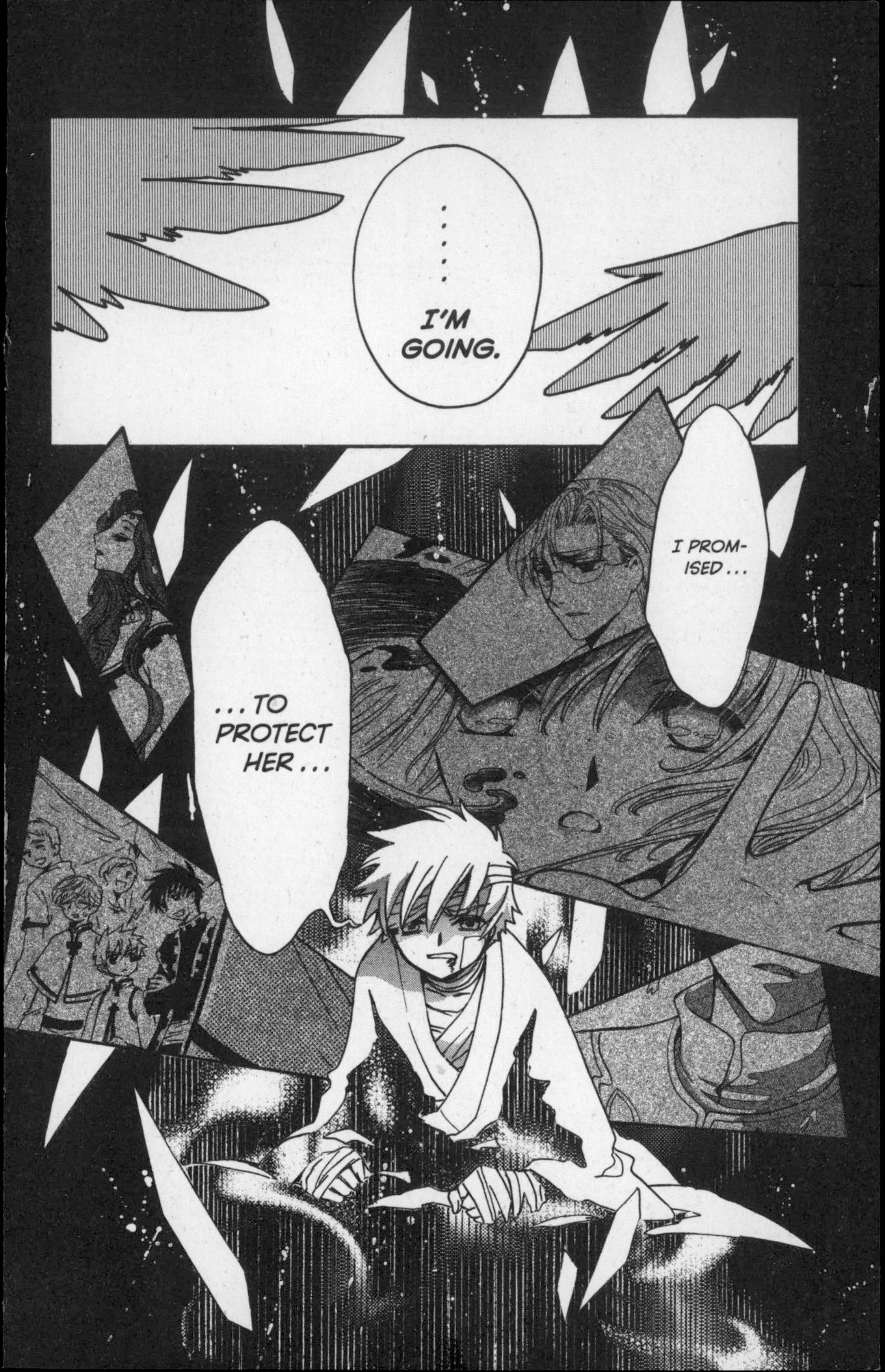
. . . . .
I'M GOING.
I PROMISED . . .
. . . TO PROTECT HER . . .

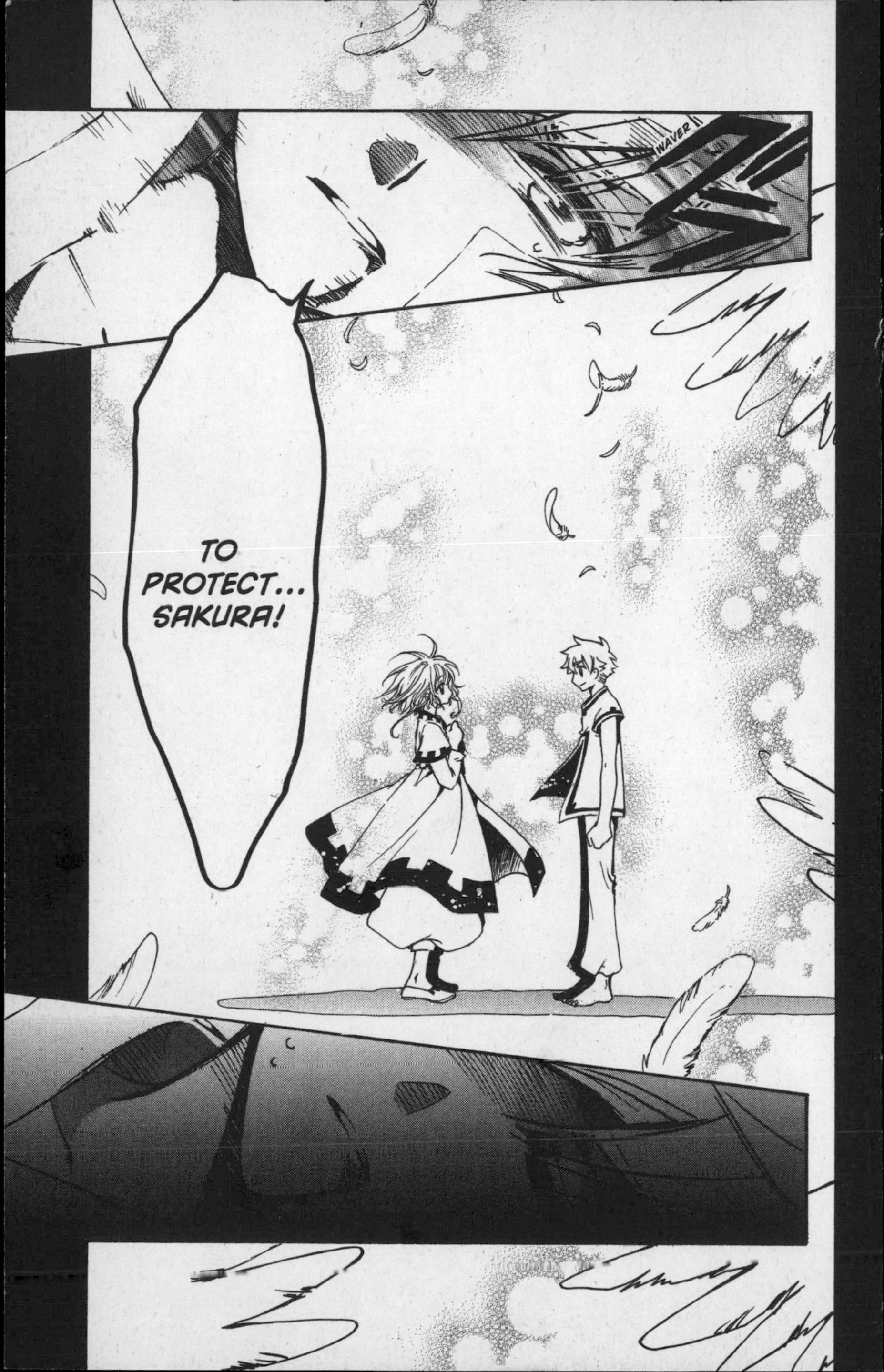
WAVER
TO PROTECT... SAKURA!

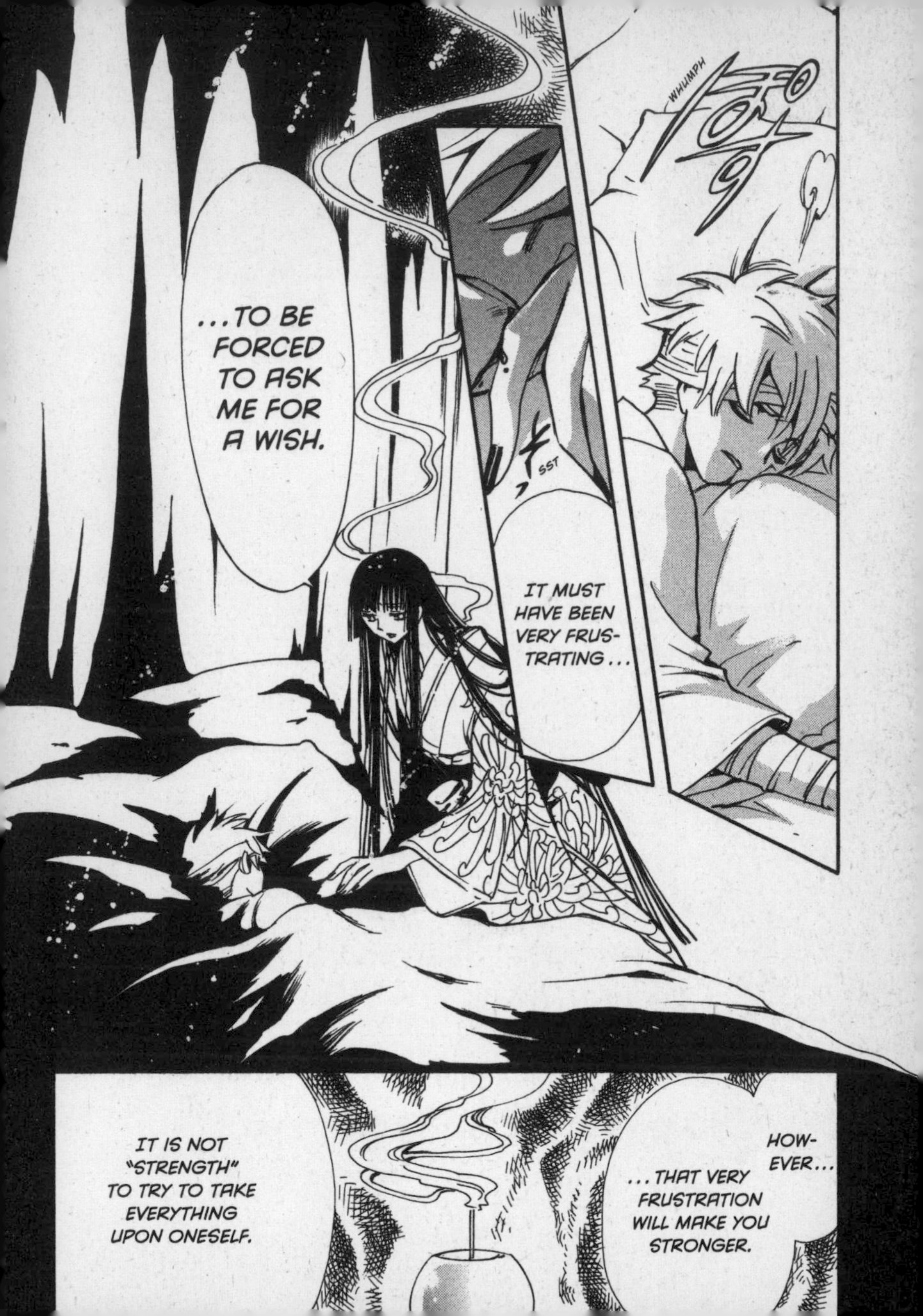
WHUMPH
SST
IT MUST HAVE BEEN VERY FRUS-TRATING...
...TO BE FORCED TO ASK ME FOR A WISH.
HOW-EVER...
...THAT VERY FRUSTRATION WILL MAKE YOU STRONGER.
IT IS NOT "STRENGTH" TO TRY TO TAKE EVERYTHING UPON ONESELF.

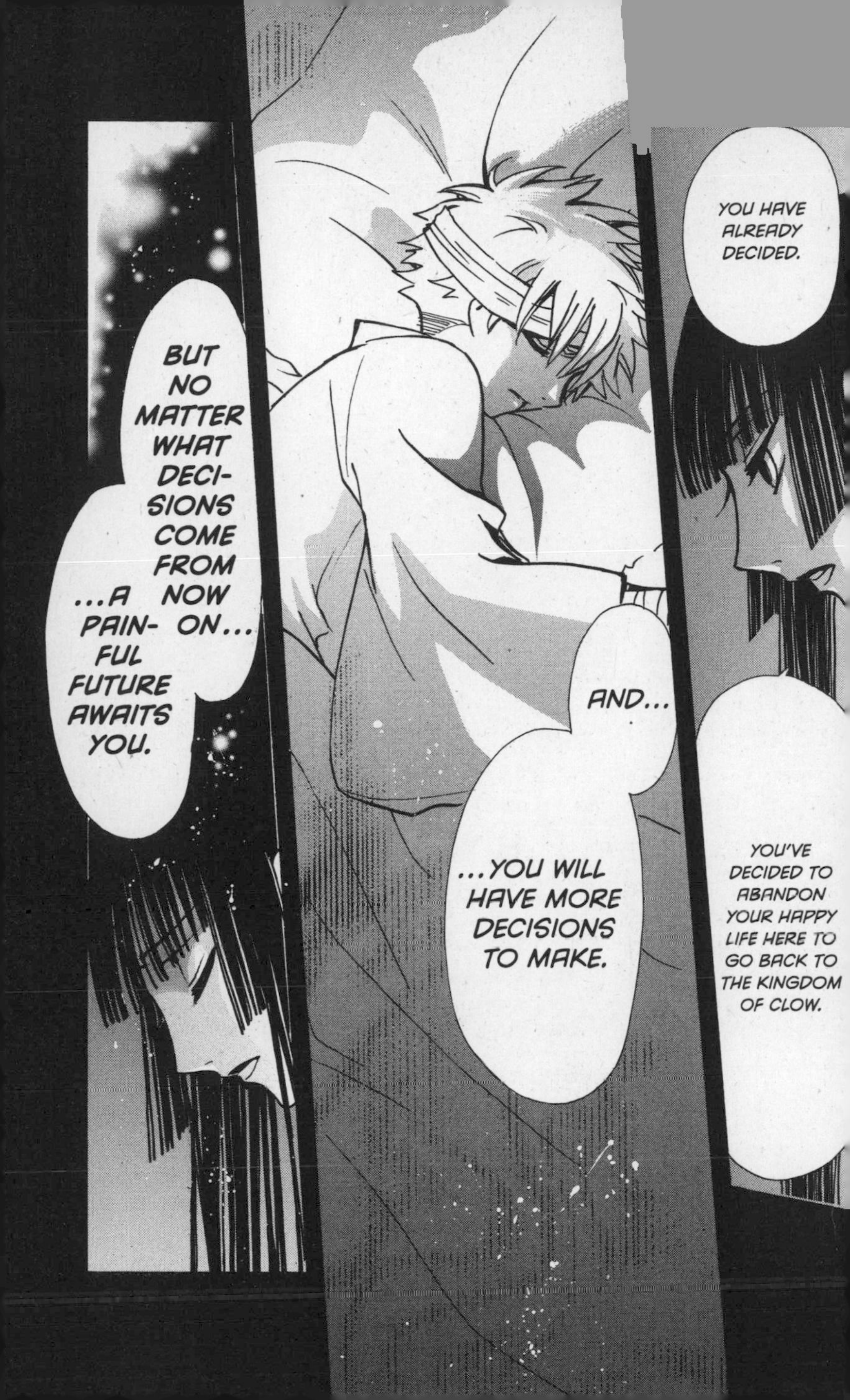
YOU HAVE ALREADY DECIDED.
YOU'VE DECIDED TO ABANDON YOUR HAPPY LIFE HERE TO GO BACK TO THE KINGDOM OF CLOW.
AND...
...YOU WILL HAVE MORE DECISIONS TO MAKE.
BUT NO MATTER WHAT DECISIONS COME FROM NOW ON...
...A PAINFUL FUTURE AWAITS YOU.

ツバサ

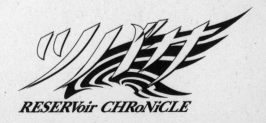

RESERVoir CHRoNiCLE

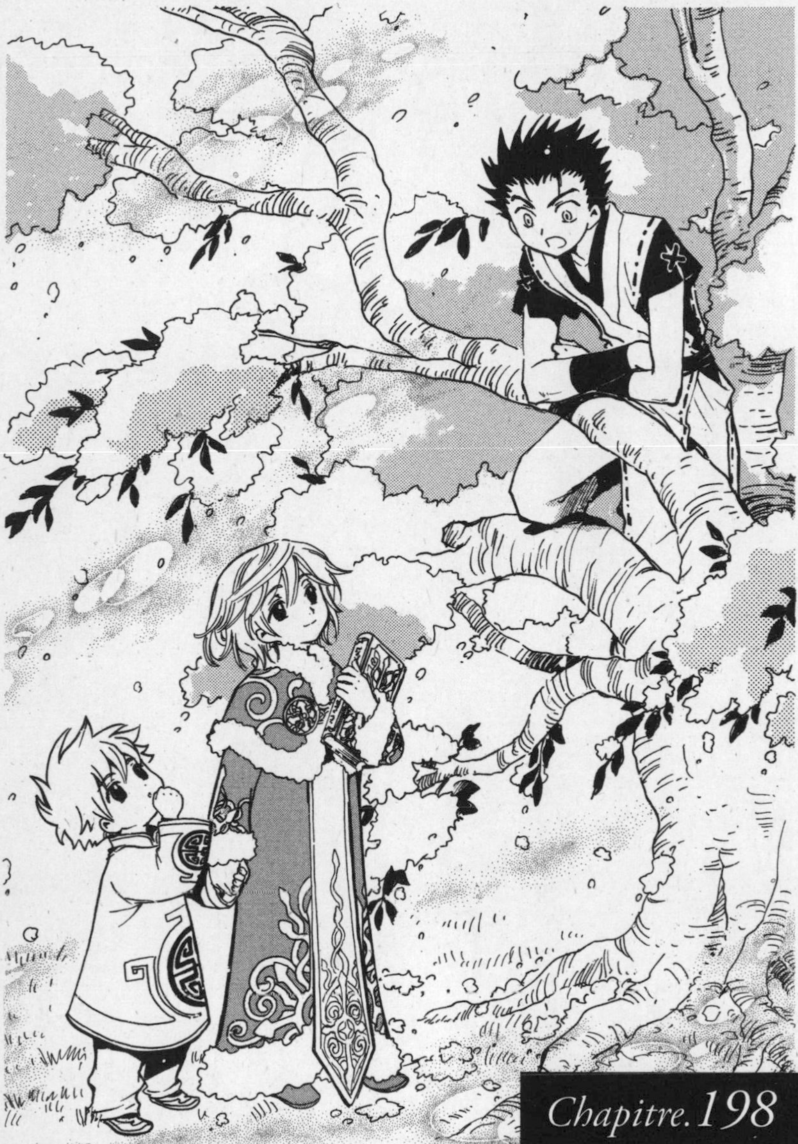

Chapitre.198
The Unseen Mark

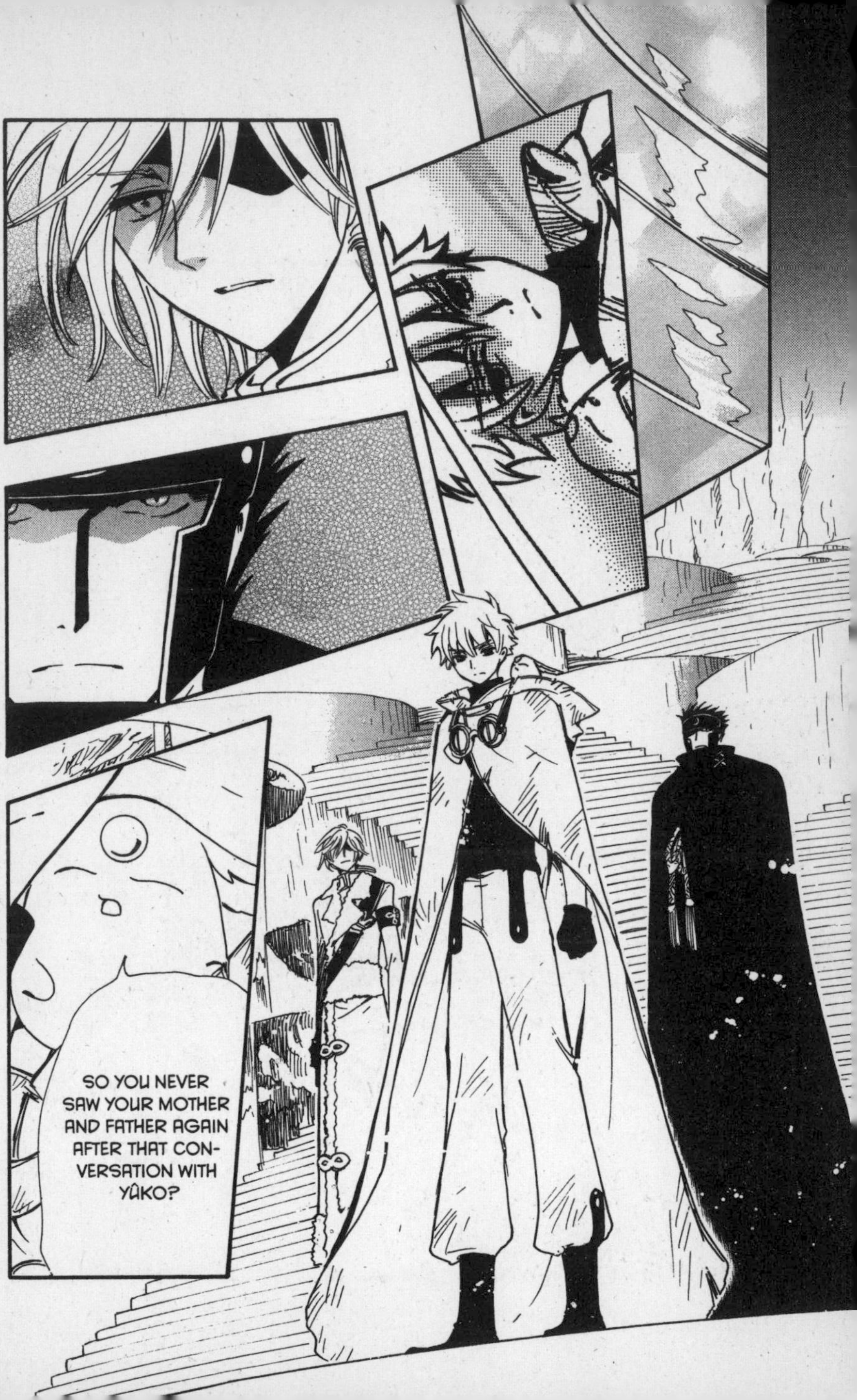
SO YOU NEVER SAW YOUR MOTHER AND FATHER AGAIN AFTER THAT CON-VERSATION WITH YÛKO?

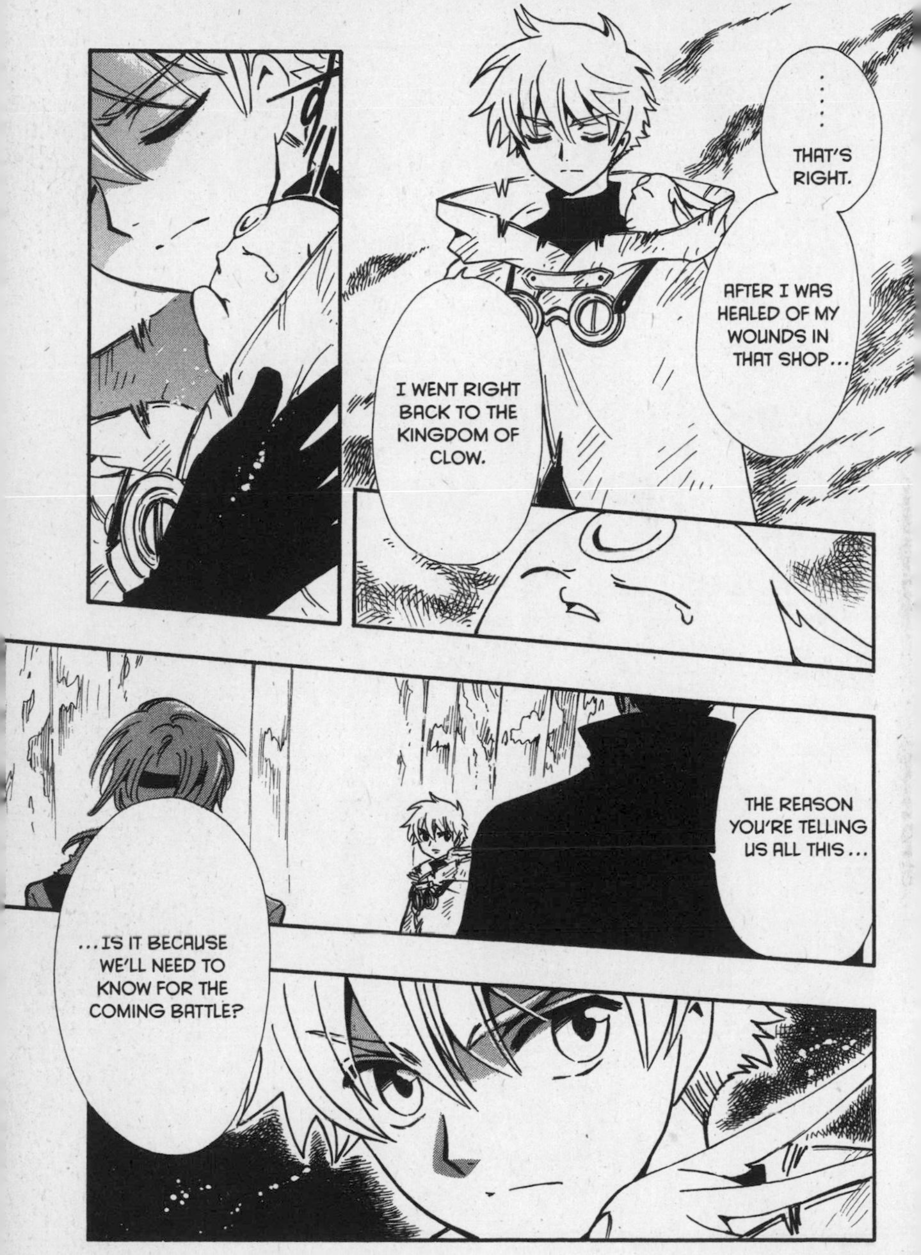
......
THAT'S RIGHT.
AFTER I WAS HEALED OF MY WOUNDS IN THAT SHOP...
I WENT RIGHT BACK TO THE KINGDOM OF CLOW.
THE REASON YOU'RE TELLING US ALL THIS...
...IS IT BECAUSE WE'LL NEED TO KNOW FOR THE COMING BATTLE?

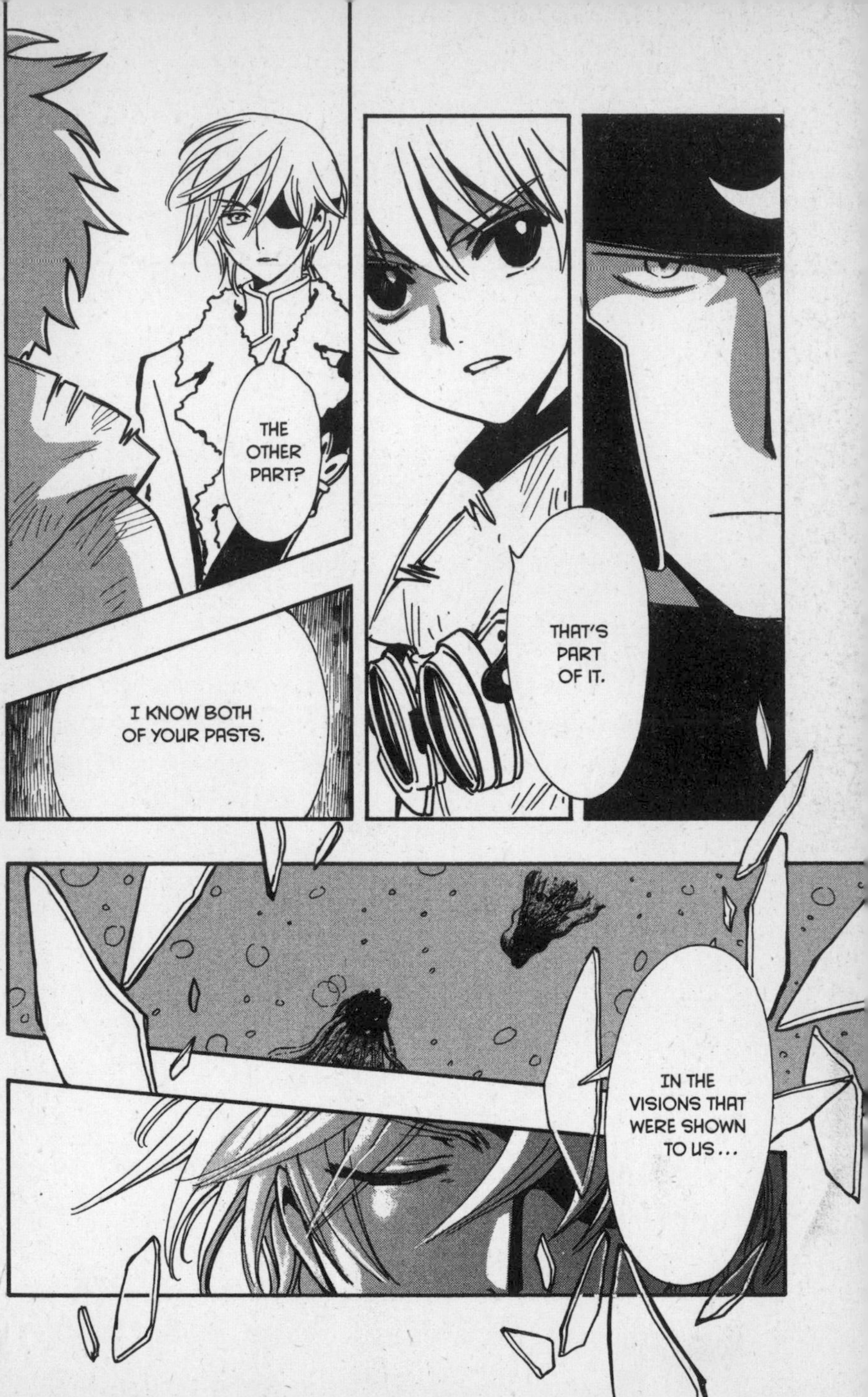
THAT'S PART OF IT.
THE OTHER PART?
I KNOW BOTH OF YOUR PASTS.
IN THE VISIONS THAT WERE SHOWN TO US...

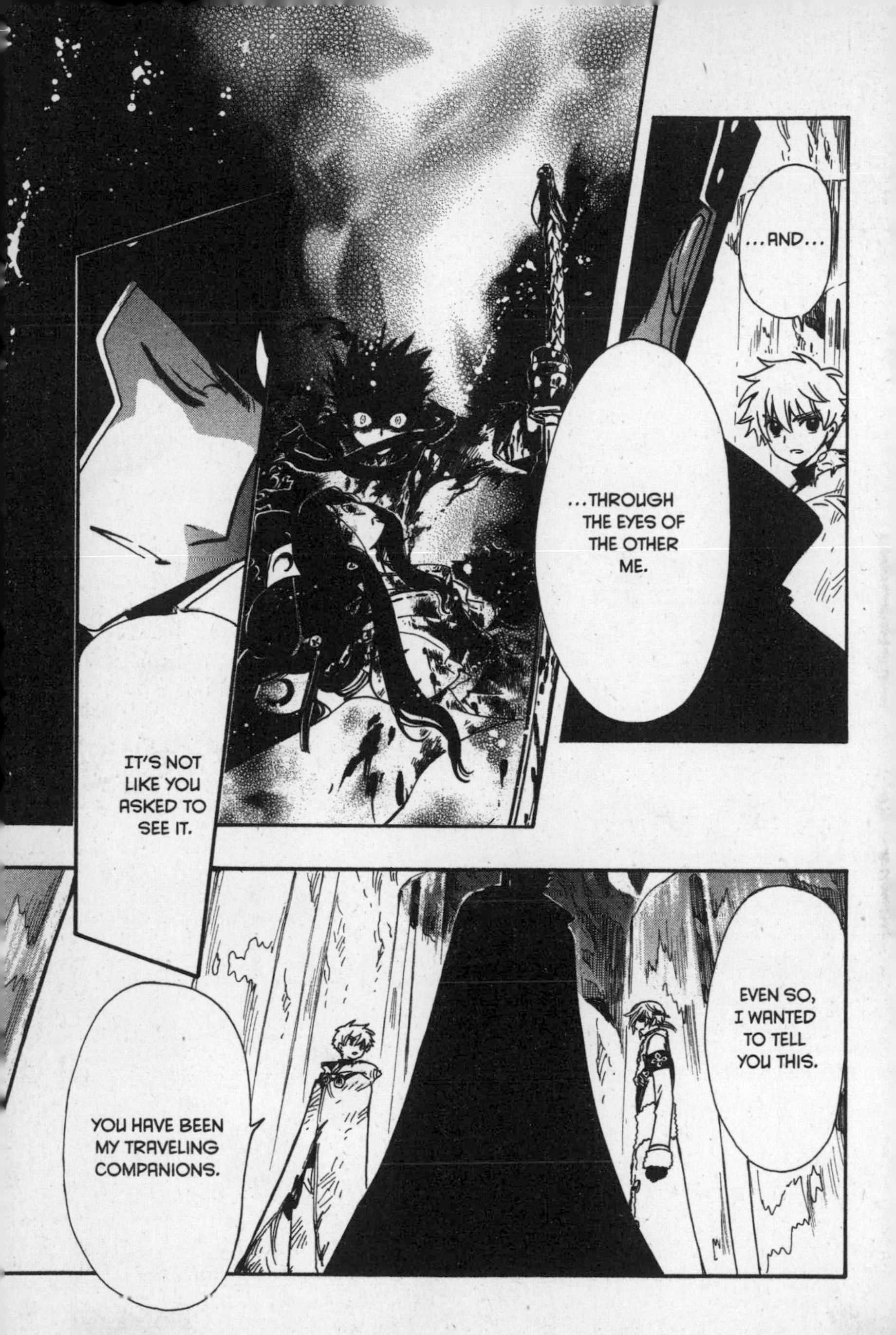
...AND...
...THROUGH THE EYES OF THE OTHER ME.
IT'S NOT LIKE YOU ASKED TO SEE IT.
EVEN SO, I WANTED TO TELL YOU THIS.
YOU HAVE BEEN MY TRAVELING COMPANIONS.

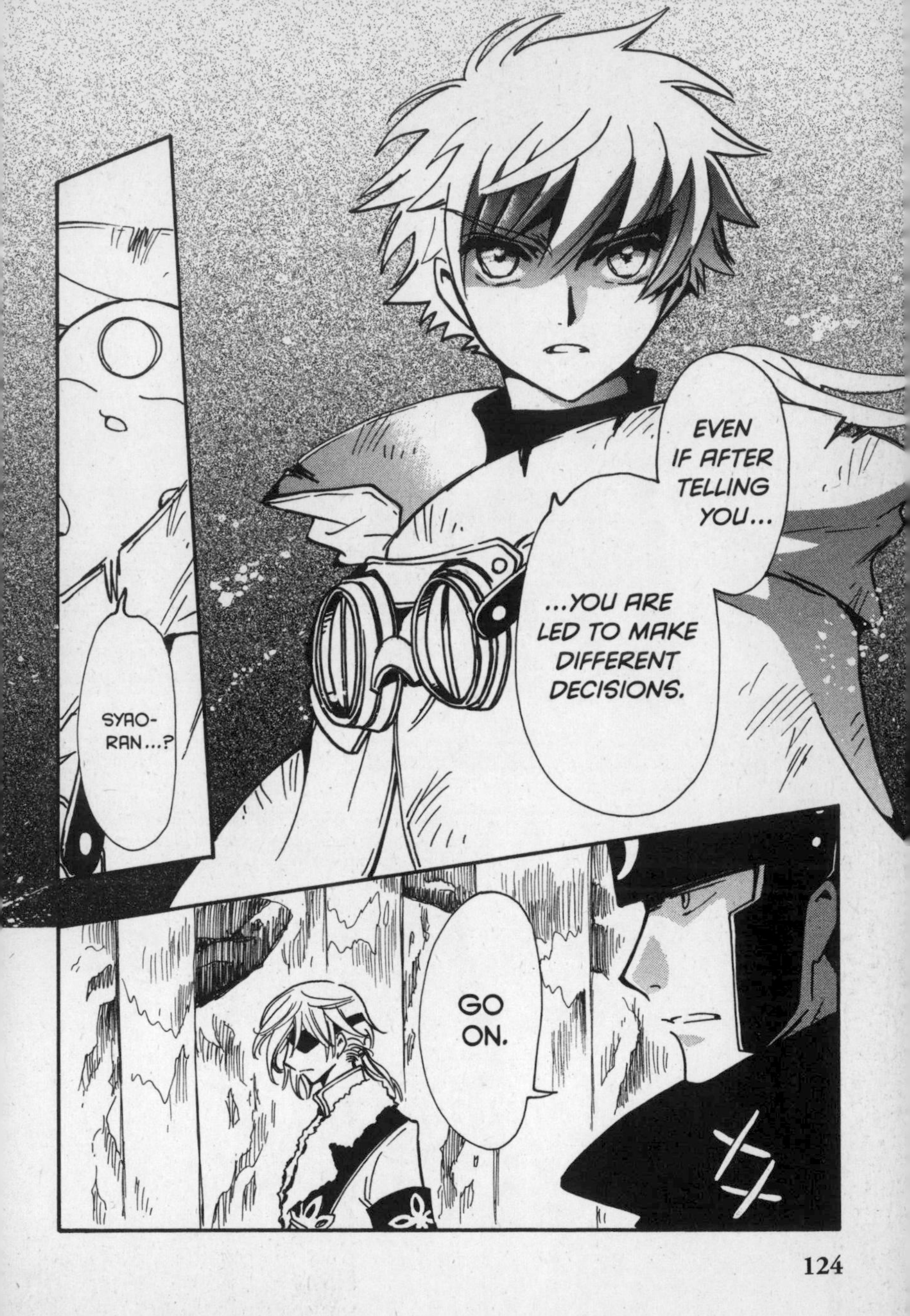
EVEN IF AFTER TELLING YOU...
...YOU ARE LED TO MAKE DIFFERENT DECISIONS.
SYAO-RAN...?
GO ON.

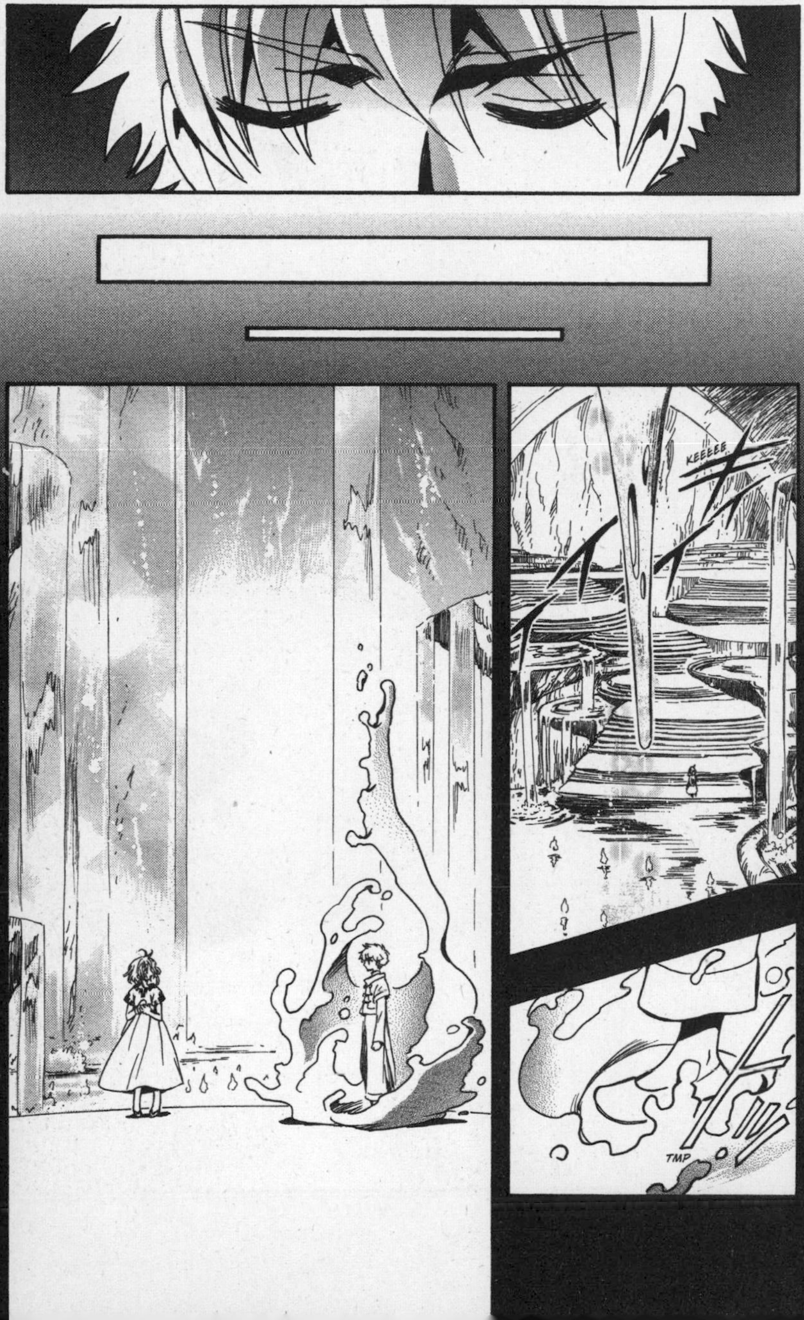
KEEEEE
TMP

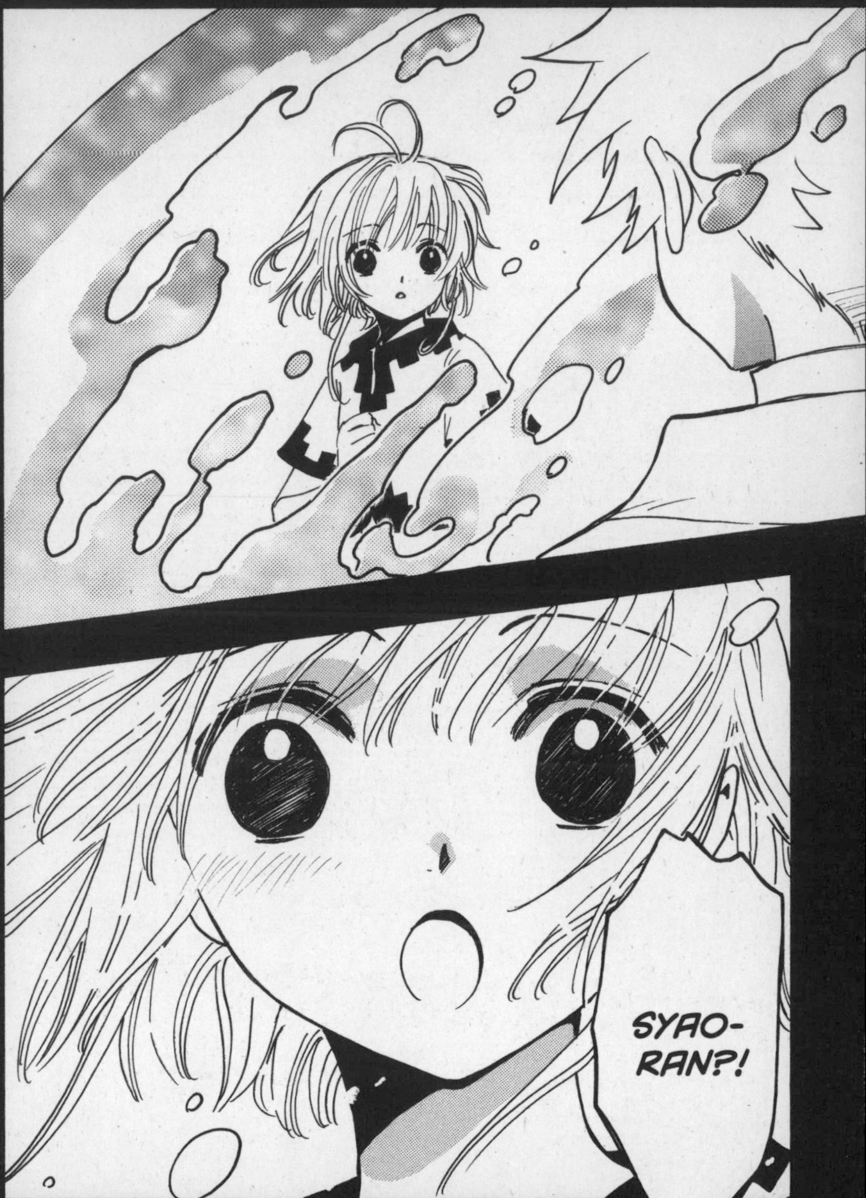
SYAO-
RAN?!

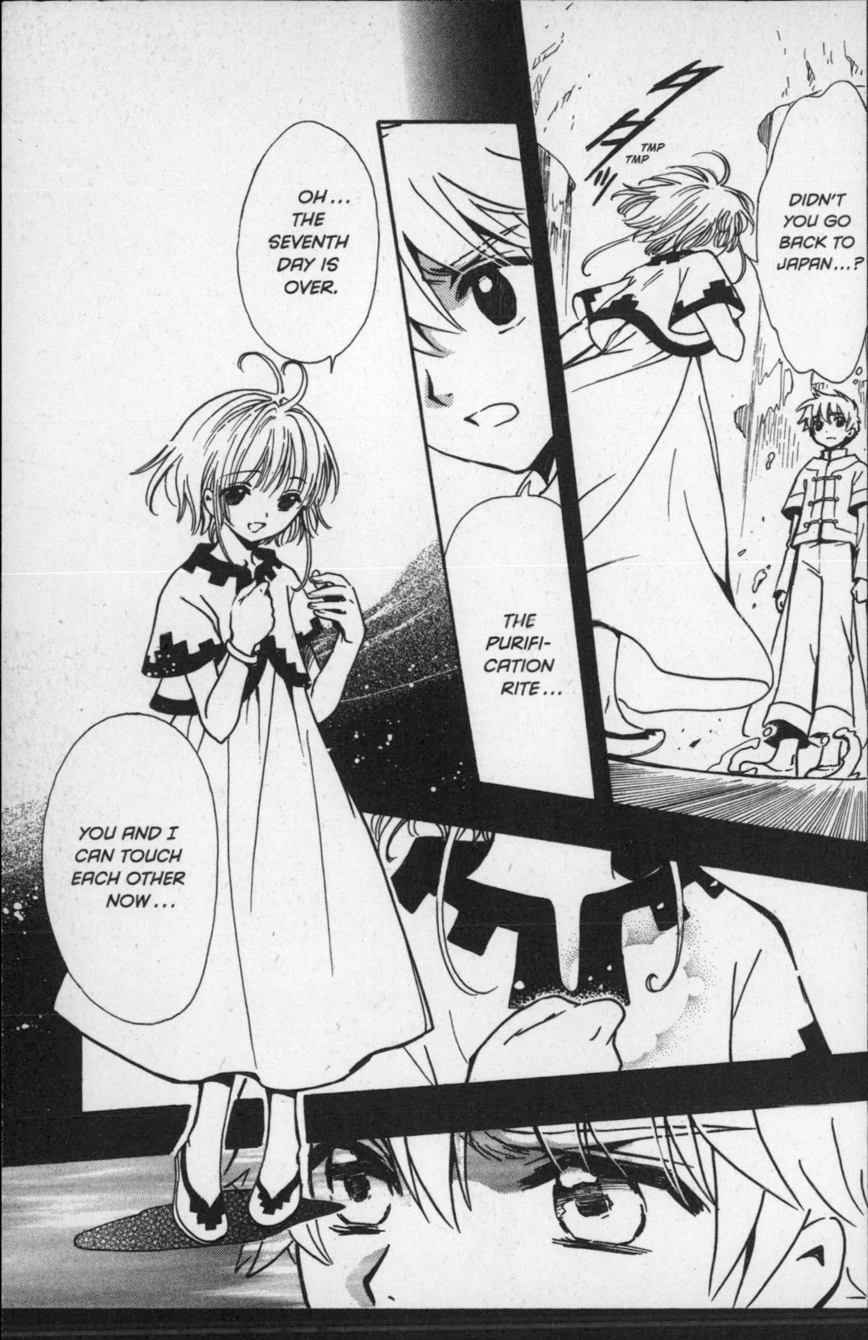
TMP TMP
DIDN'T YOU GO BACK TO JAPAN...?
THE PURIFI-CATION RITE...
OH... THE SEVENTH DAY IS OVER.
YOU AND I CAN TOUCH EACH OTHER NOW...

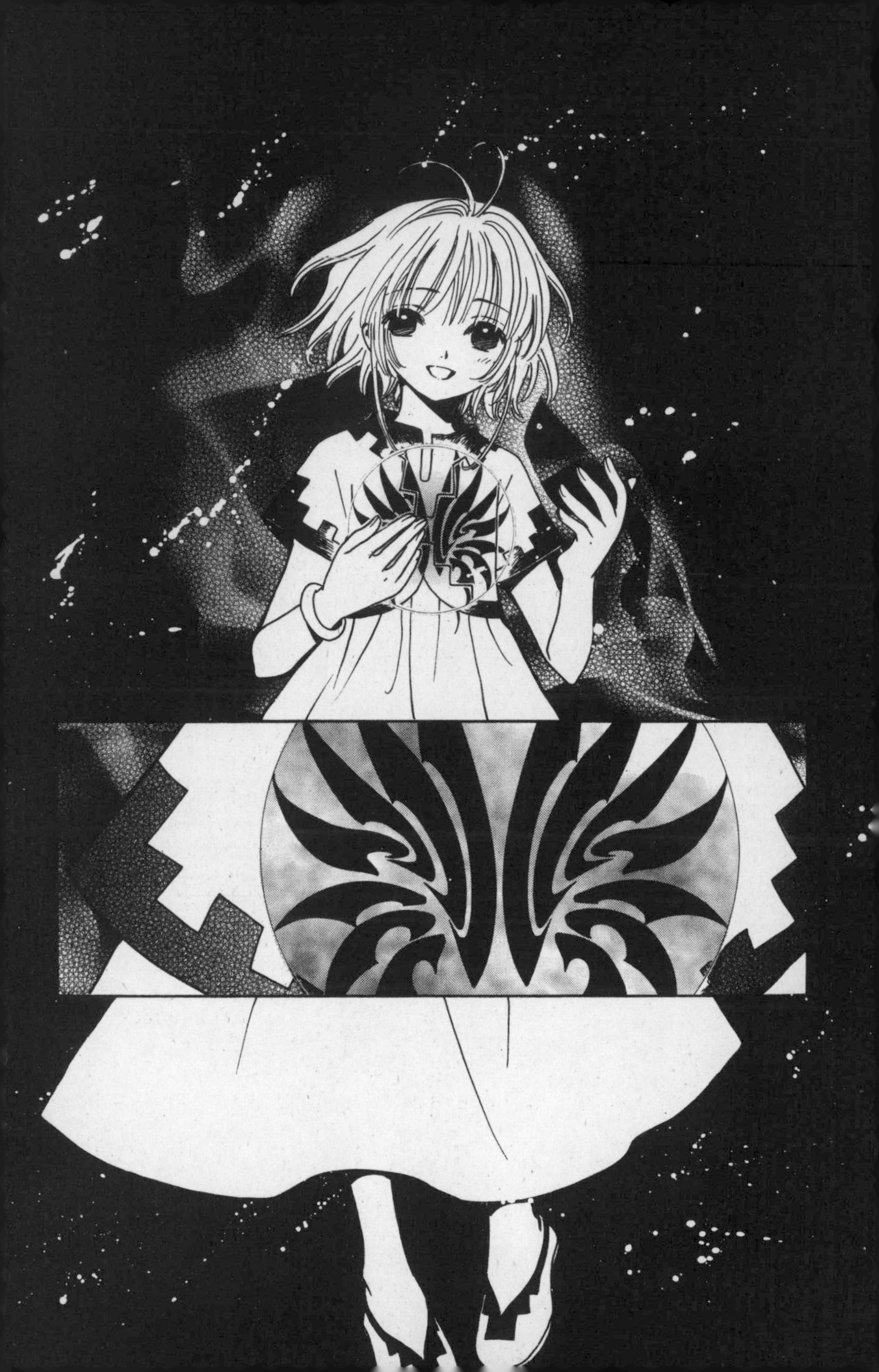

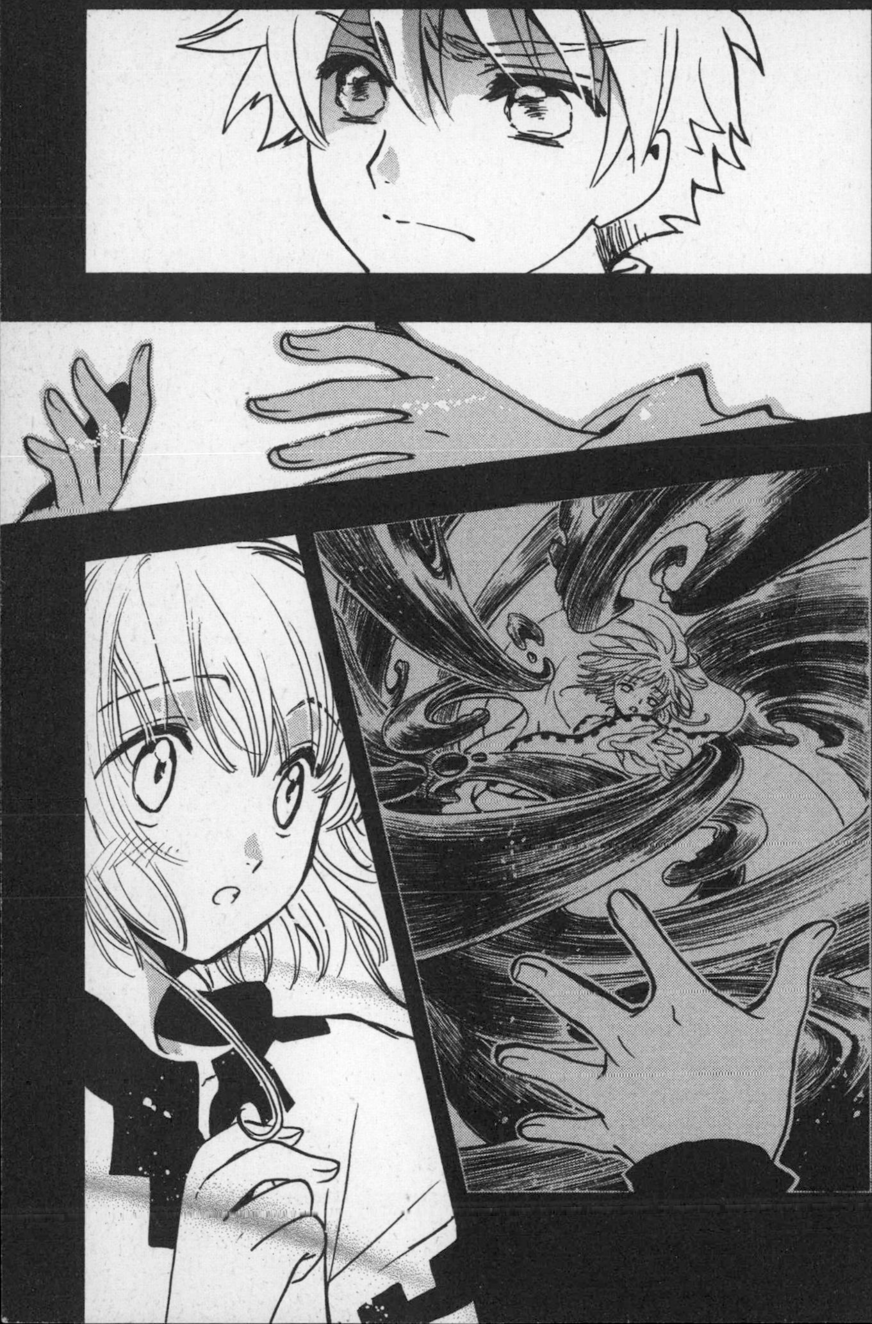

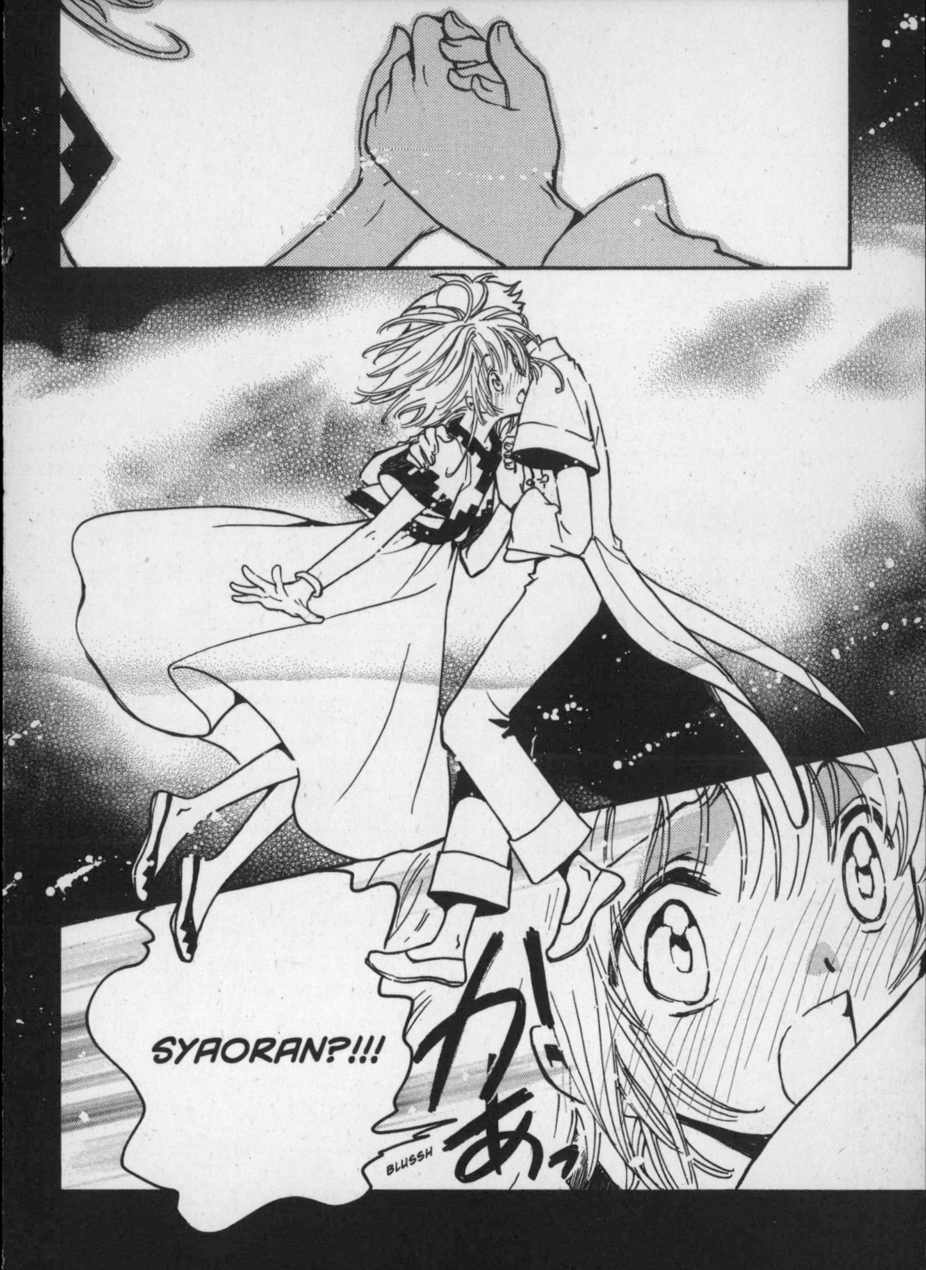
SYAORAN?!!!
わぁっ
BLUSSH

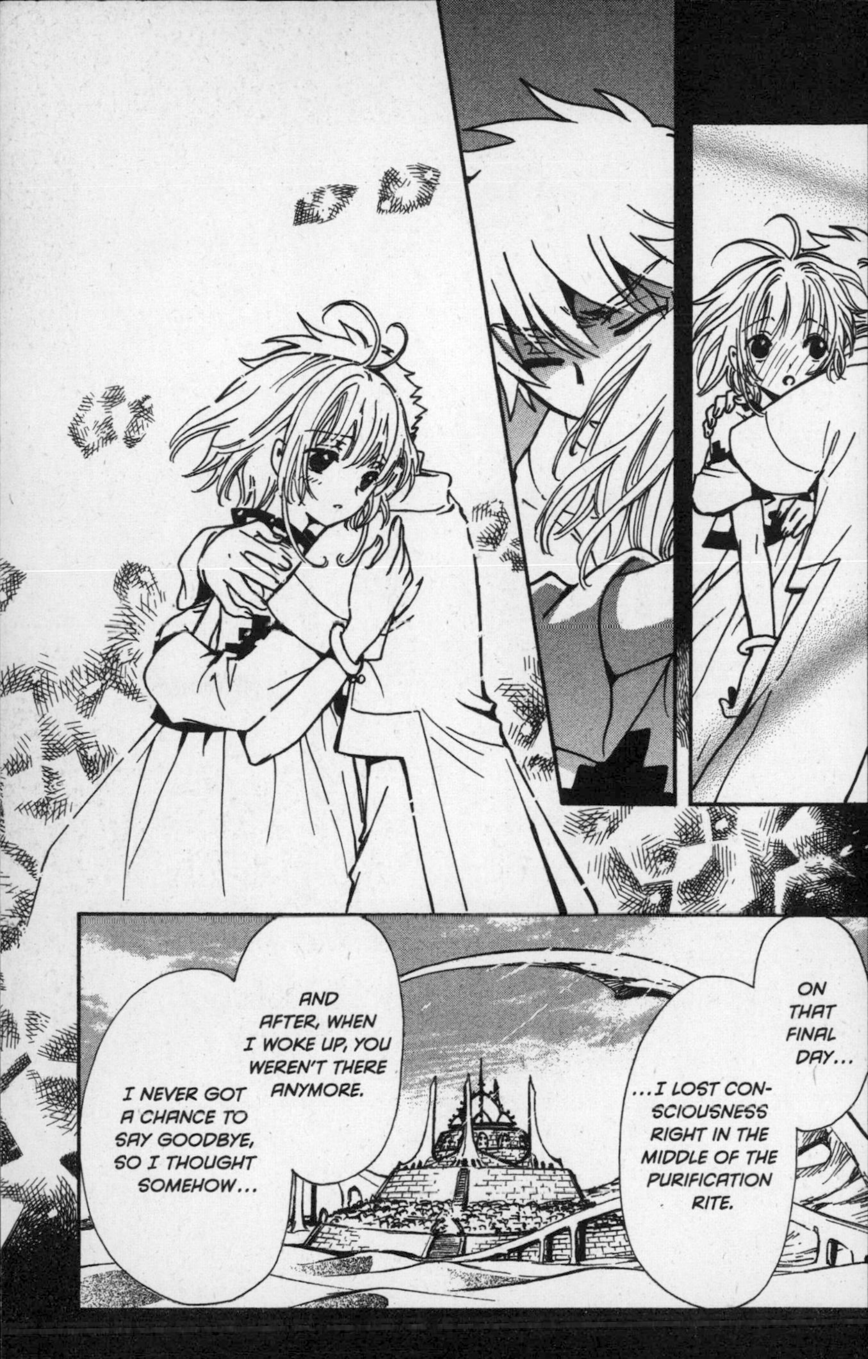
ON THAT FINAL DAY...
...I LOST CON-SCIOUSNESS RIGHT IN THE MIDDLE OF THE PURIFICATION RITE.
AND AFTER, WHEN I WOKE UP, YOU WEREN'T THERE ANYMORE.
I NEVER GOT A CHANCE TO SAY GOODBYE, SO I THOUGHT SOMEHOW...

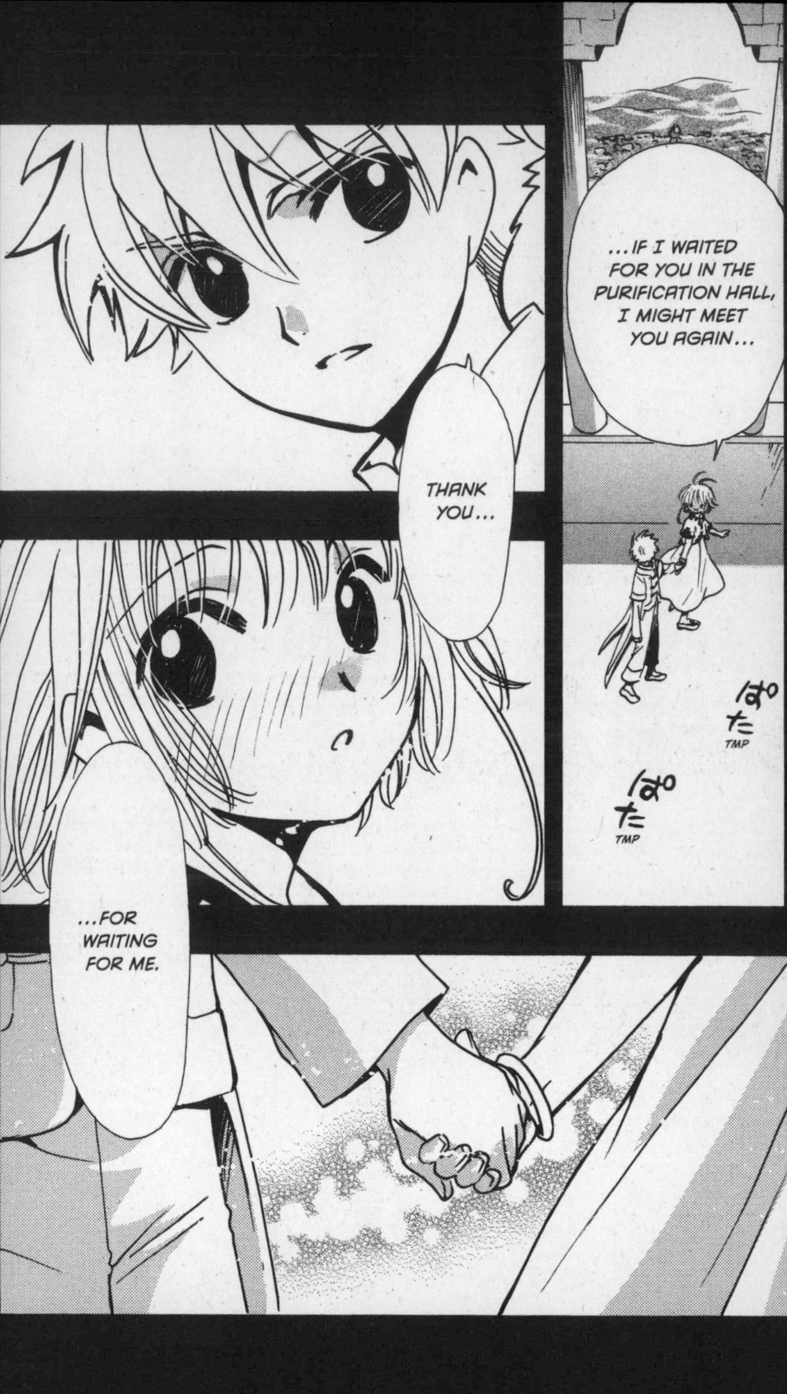
...IF I WAITED FOR YOU IN THE PURIFICATION HALL, I MIGHT MEET YOU AGAIN...
ぱた
TMP
ぱた
TMP
THANK YOU...
...FOR WAITING FOR ME.

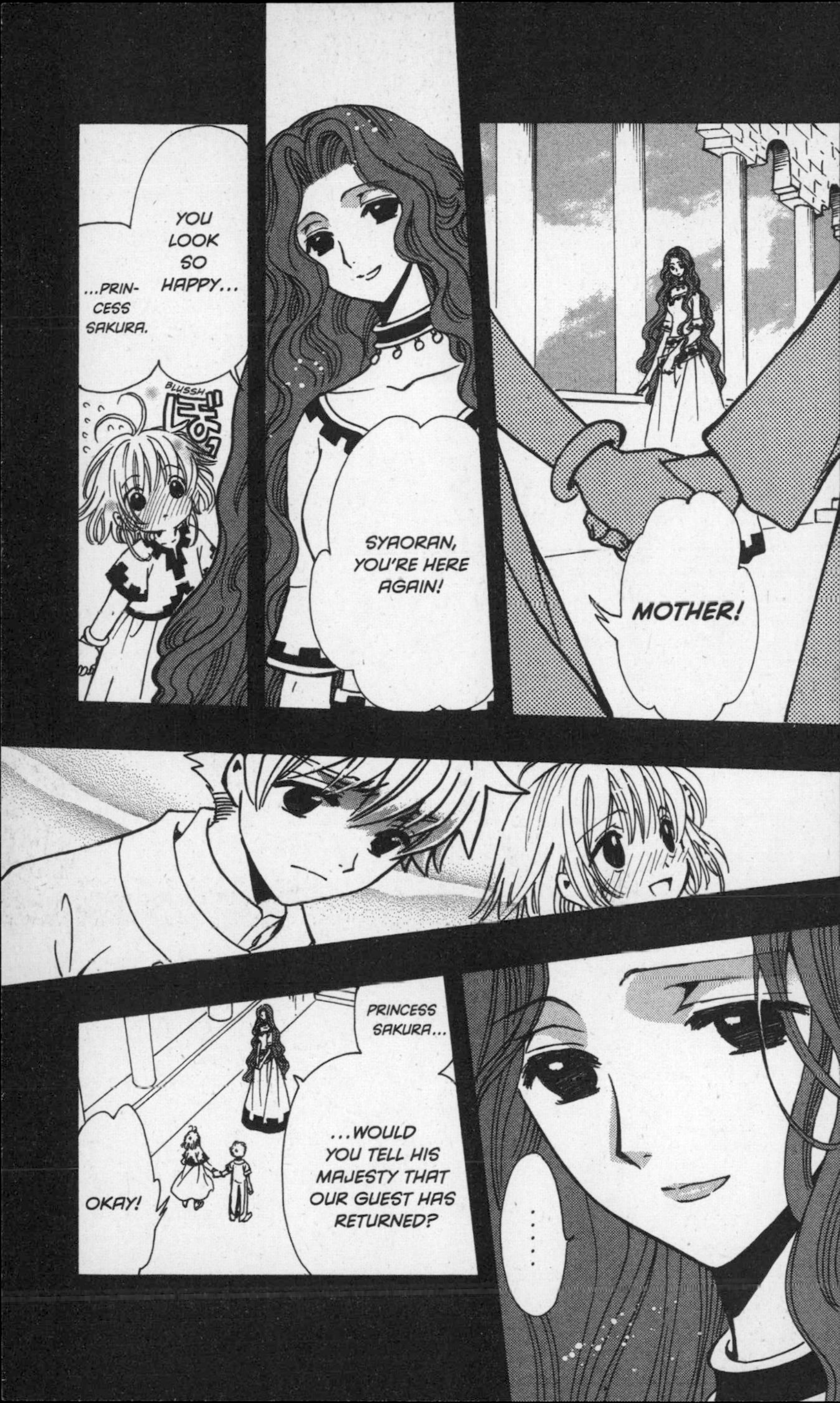
MOTHER!
SYAORAN, YOU'RE HERE AGAIN!
YOU LOOK SO HAPPY...
...PRINCESS SAKURA.
BLUSSH
.....
PRINCESS SAKURA...
...WOULD YOU TELL HIS MAJESTY THAT OUR GUEST HAS RETURNED?
OKAY!

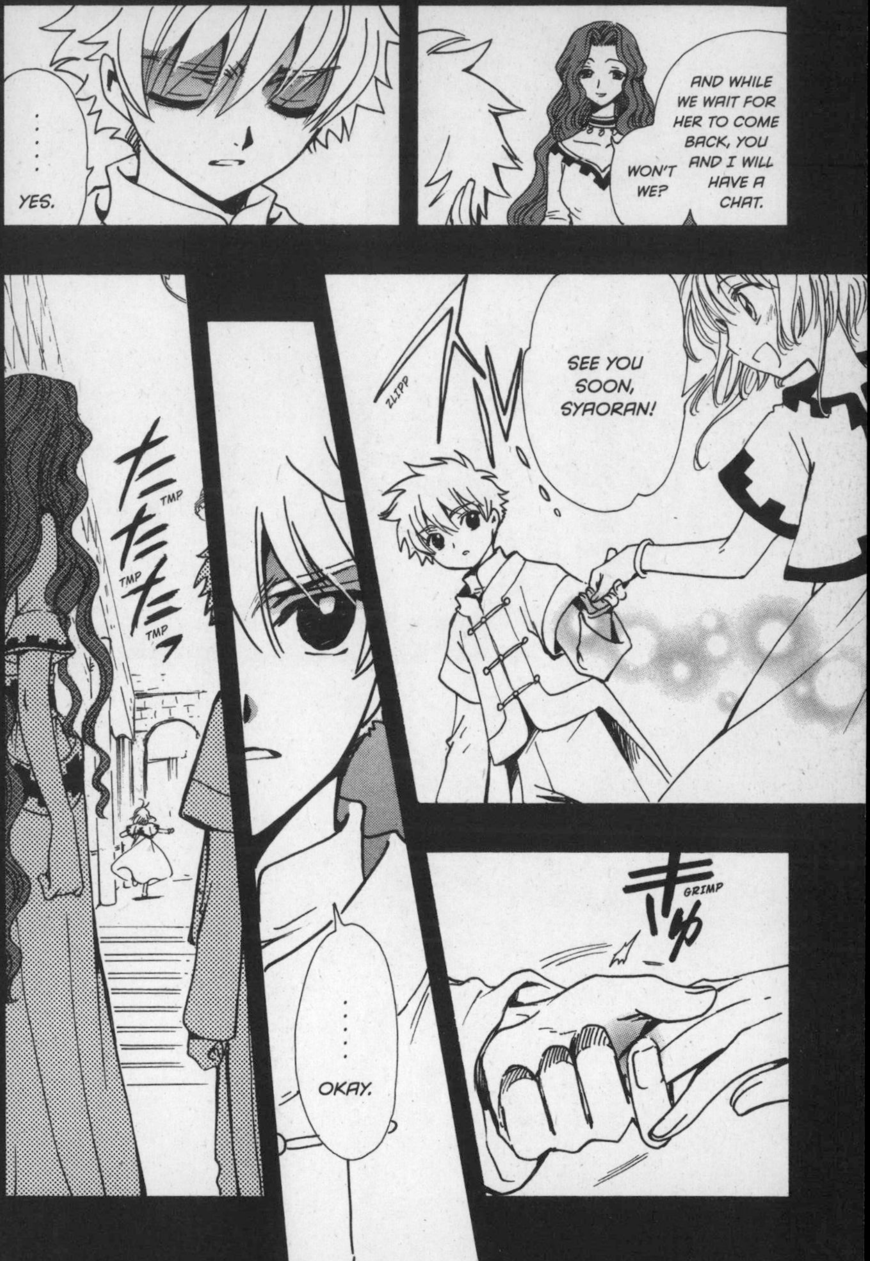
AND WHILE WE WAIT FOR HER TO COME BACK, YOU AND I WILL HAVE A CHAT.
WON'T WE?
...... YES.
SEE YOU SOON, SYAORAN!
ZLIPP
GRIMP
...... OKAY.
TMP
TMP
TMP

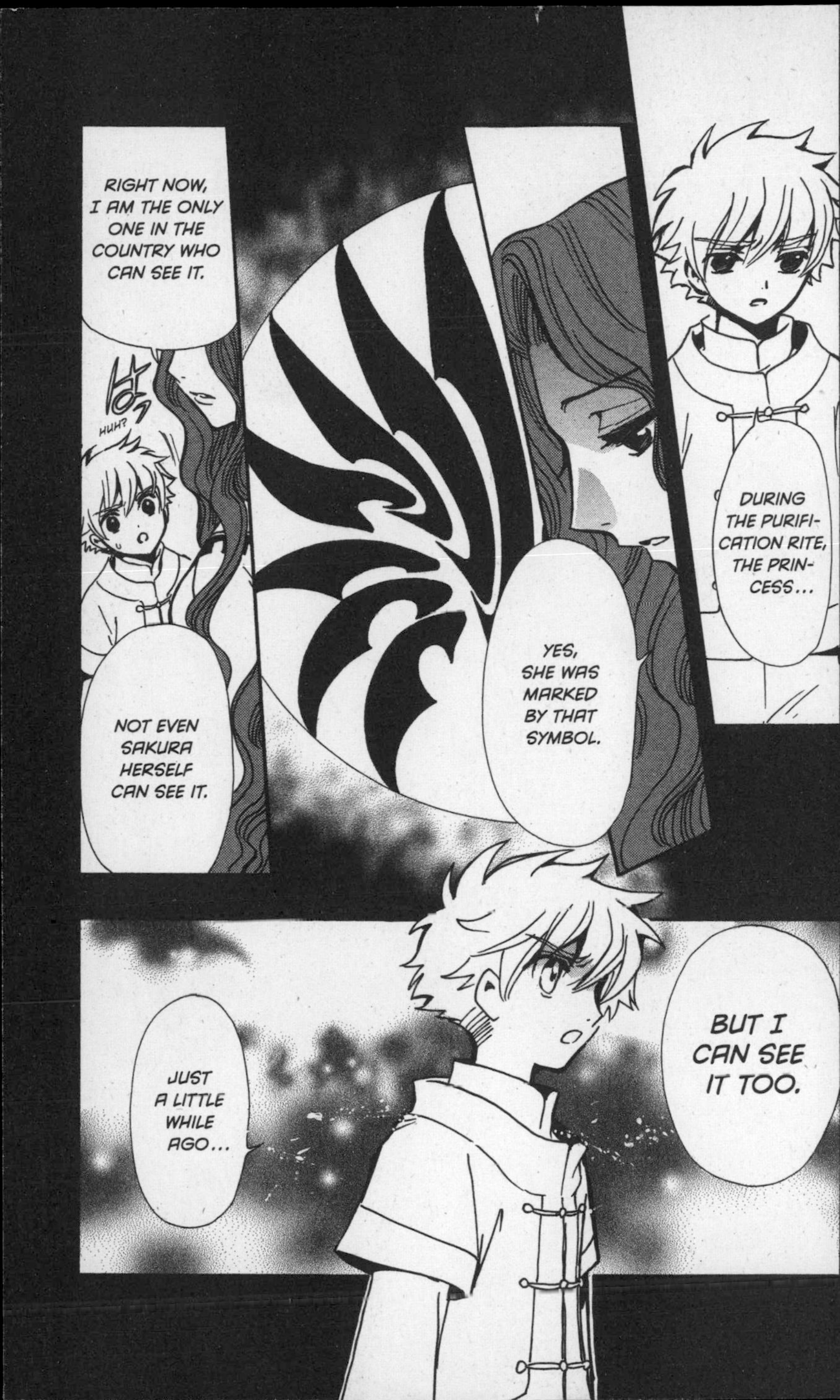
DURING THE PURIFICATION RITE, THE PRINCESS...
YES, SHE WAS MARKED BY THAT SYMBOL.
RIGHT NOW, I AM THE ONLY ONE IN THE COUNTRY WHO CAN SEE IT.
はっ
HUH?
NOT EVEN SAKURA HERSELF CAN SEE IT.
BUT I CAN SEE IT TOO.
JUST A LITTLE WHILE AGO...

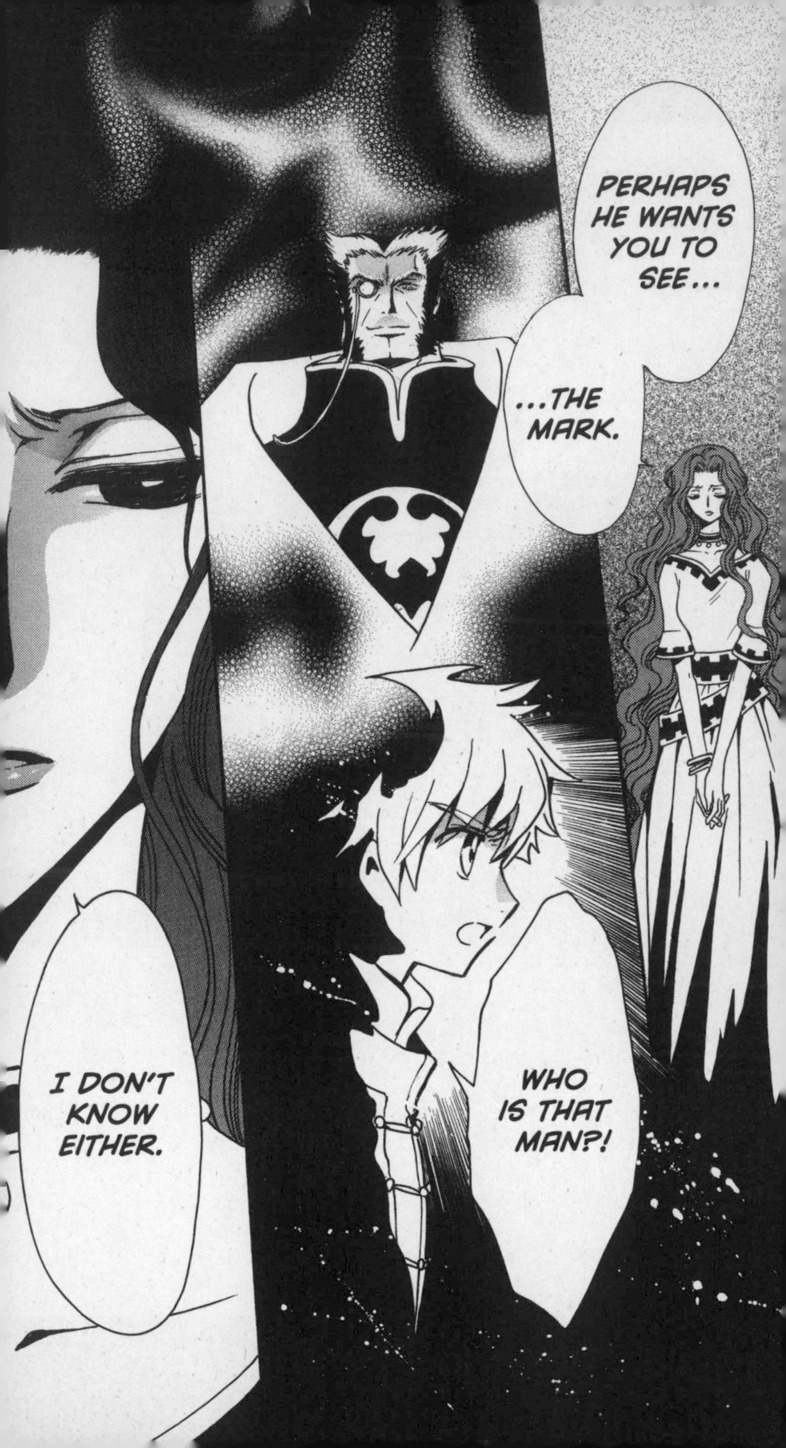
PERHAPS HE WANTS YOU TO SEE...
...THE MARK.
WHO IS THAT MAN?!
I DON'T KNOW EITHER.

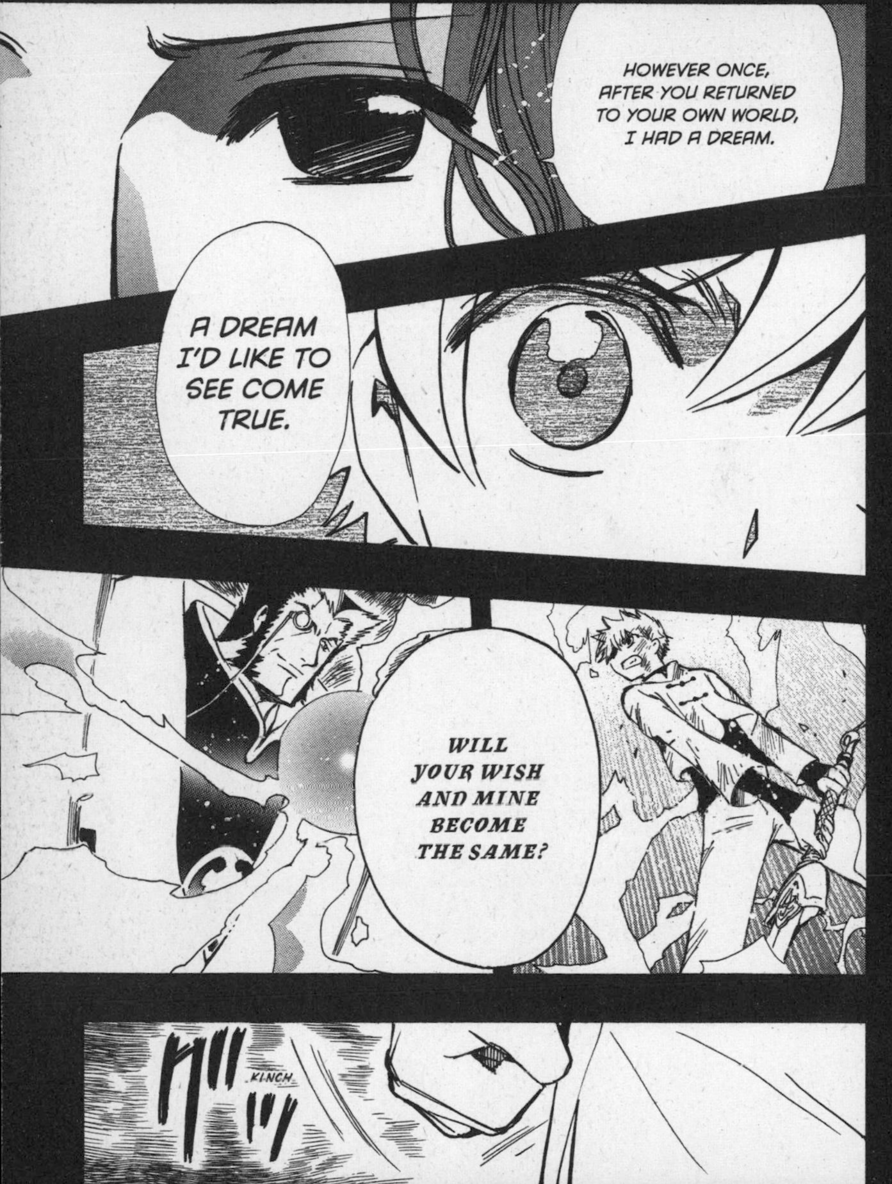
HOWEVER ONCE, AFTER YOU RETURNED TO YOUR OWN WORLD, I HAD A DREAM.
A DREAM I'D LIKE TO SEE COME TRUE.
WILL YOUR WISH AND MINE BECOME THE SAME?
KLINCH

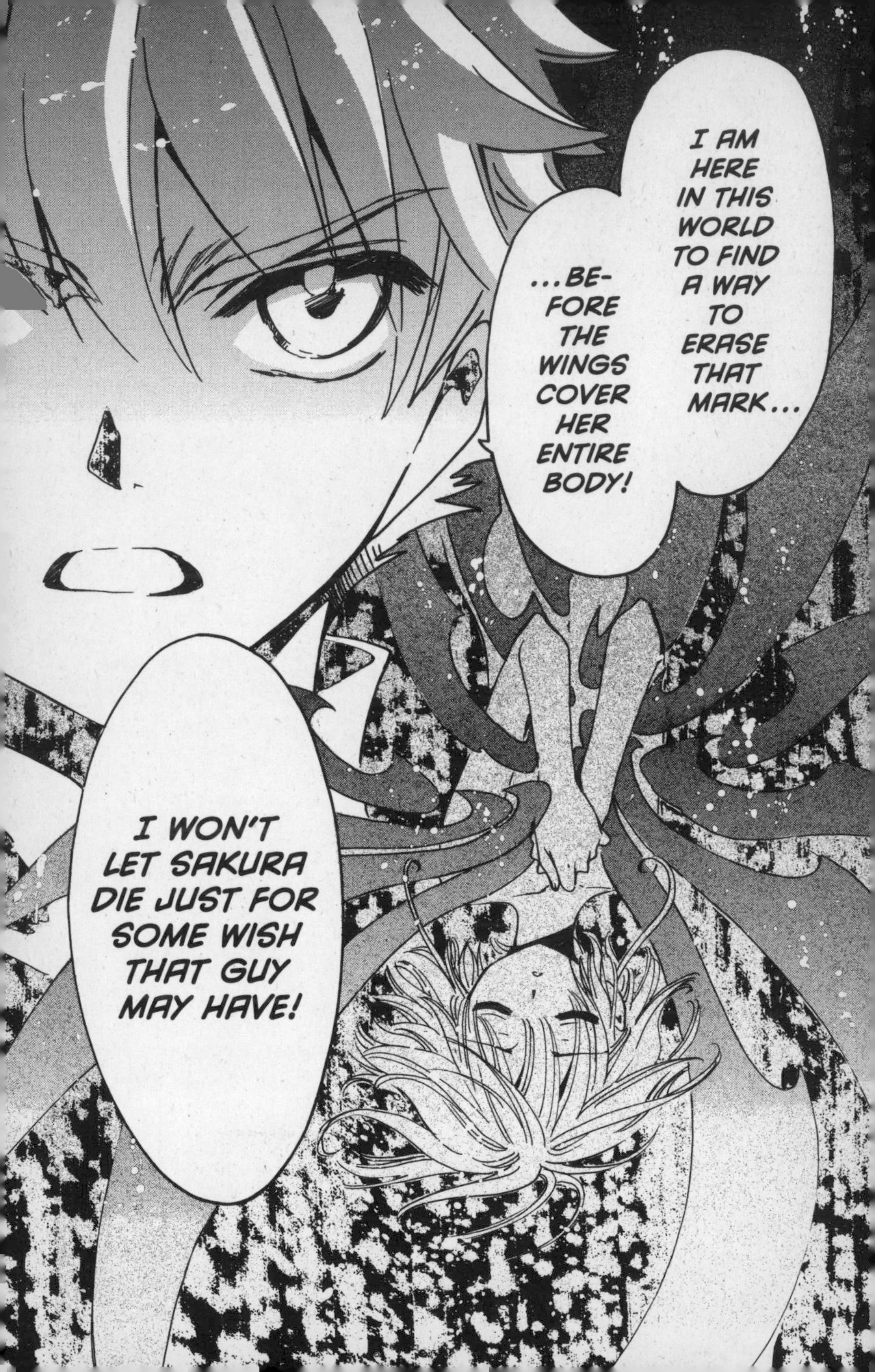
I AM HERE IN THIS WORLD TO FIND A WAY TO ERASE THAT MARK...
...BEFORE THE WINGS COVER HER ENTIRE BODY!
I WON'T LET SAKURA DIE JUST FOR SOME WISH THAT GUY MAY HAVE!

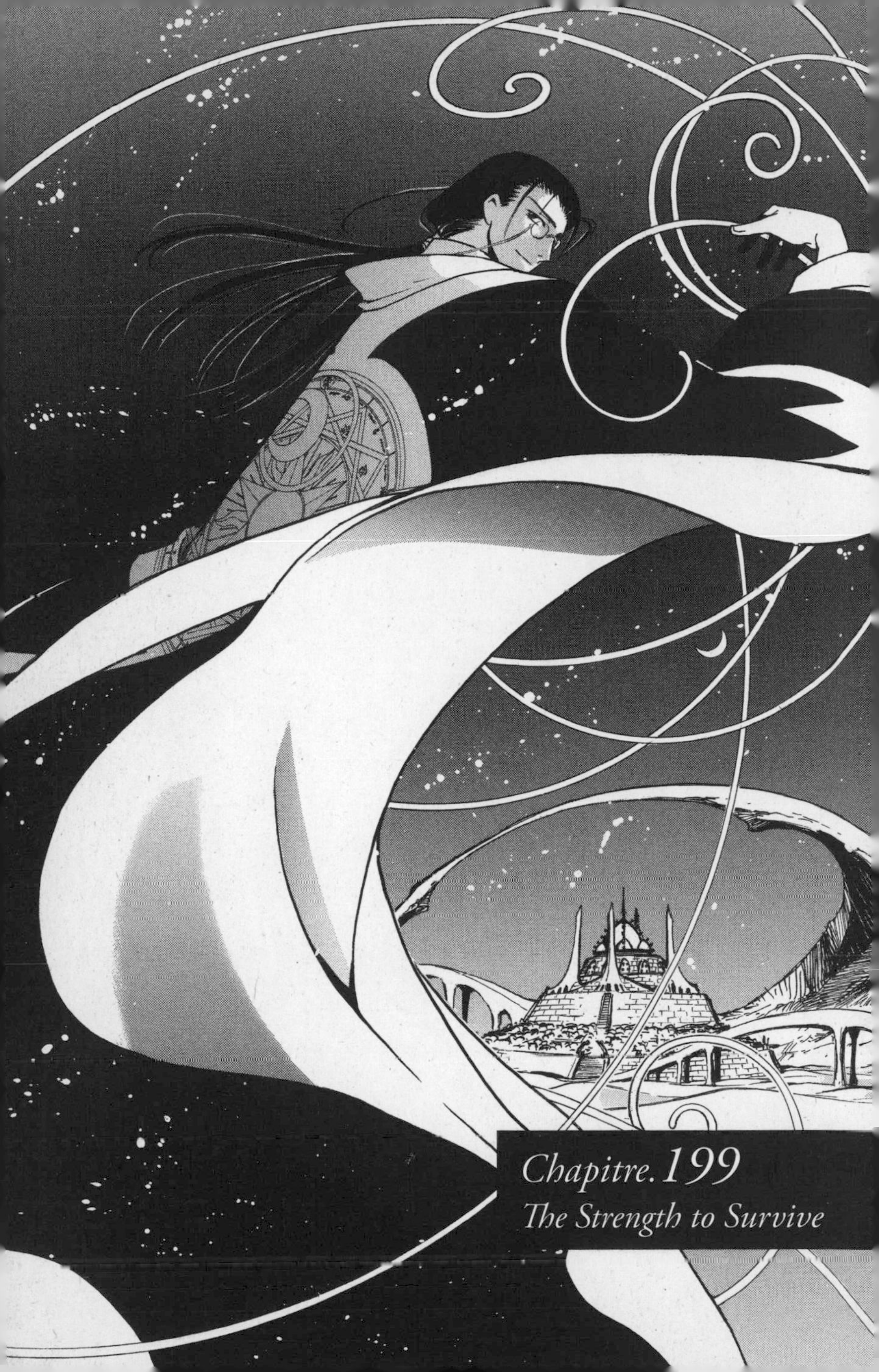
Chapitre.199
The Strength to Survive

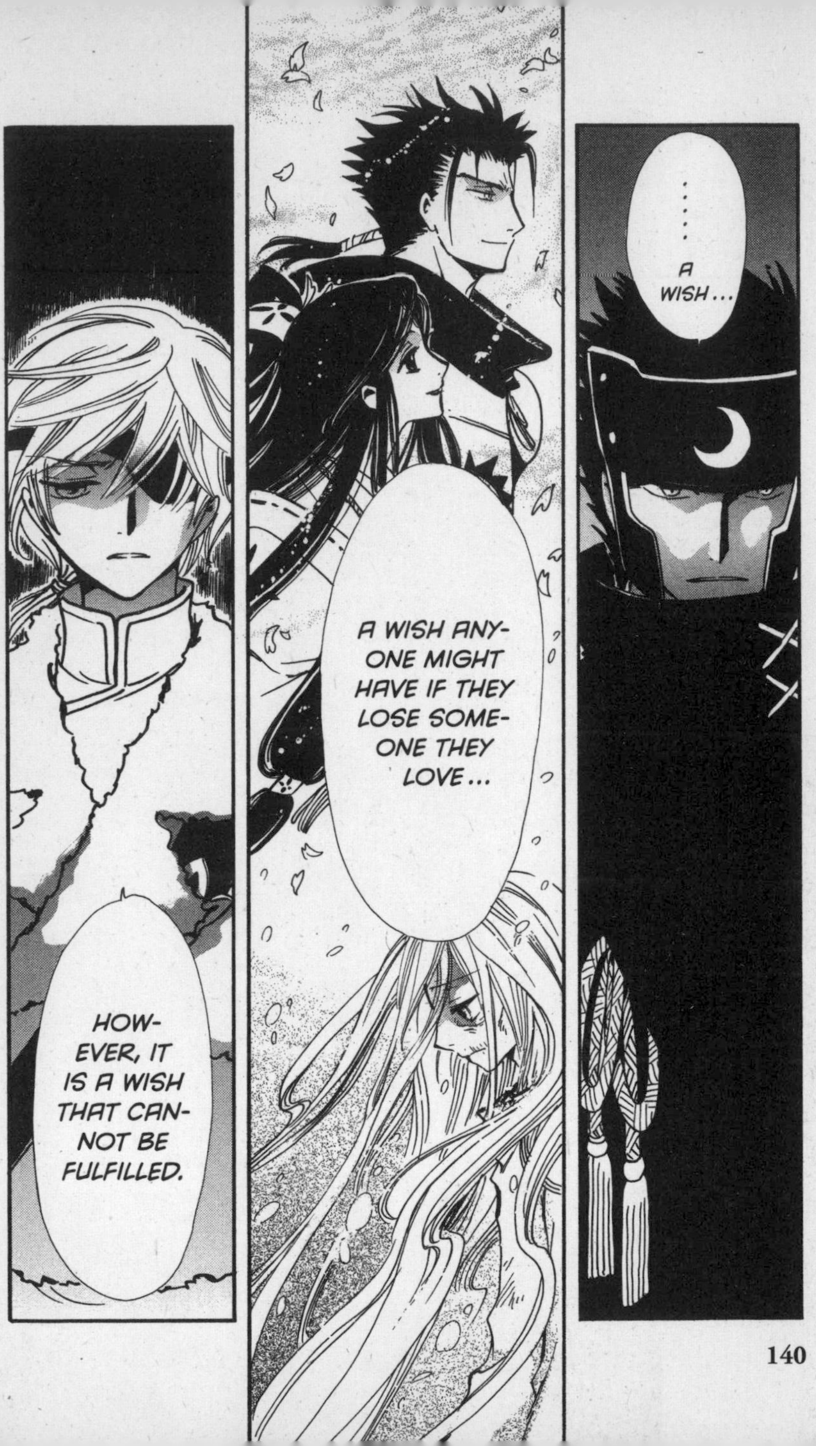

.....
A WISH...
A WISH ANYONE MIGHT HAVE IF THEY LOSE SOMEONE THEY LOVE...
HOWEVER, IT IS A WISH THAT CANNOT BE FULFILLED.

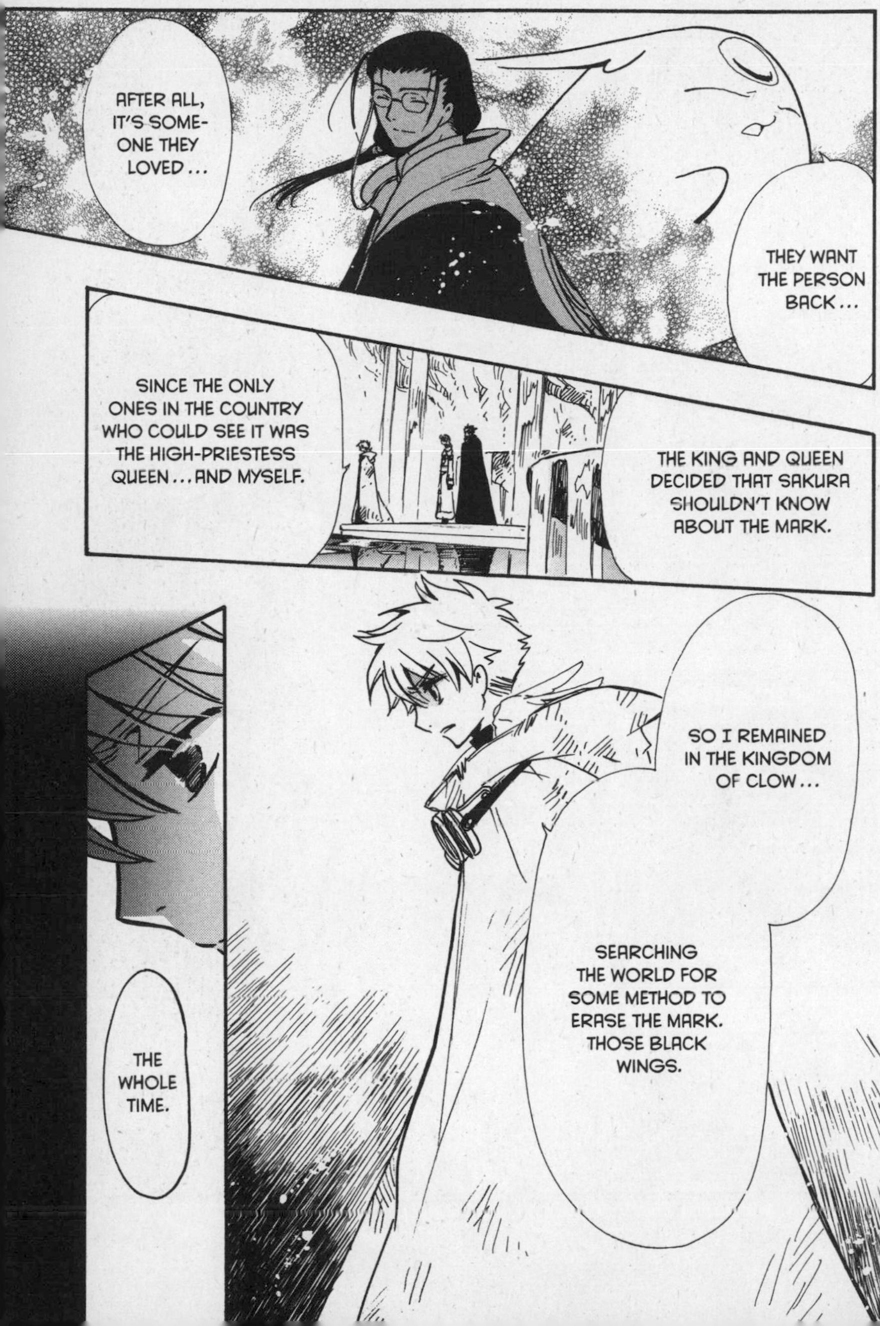
THEY WANT THE PERSON BACK...
AFTER ALL, IT'S SOME-ONE THEY LOVED...
THE KING AND QUEEN DECIDED THAT SAKURA SHOULDN'T KNOW ABOUT THE MARK.
SINCE THE ONLY ONES IN THE COUNTRY WHO COULD SEE IT WAS THE HIGH-PRIESTESS QUEEN...AND MYSELF.
SO I REMAINED IN THE KINGDOM OF CLOW...
SEARCHING THE WORLD FOR SOME METHOD TO ERASE THE MARK. THOSE BLACK WINGS.
THE WHOLE TIME.

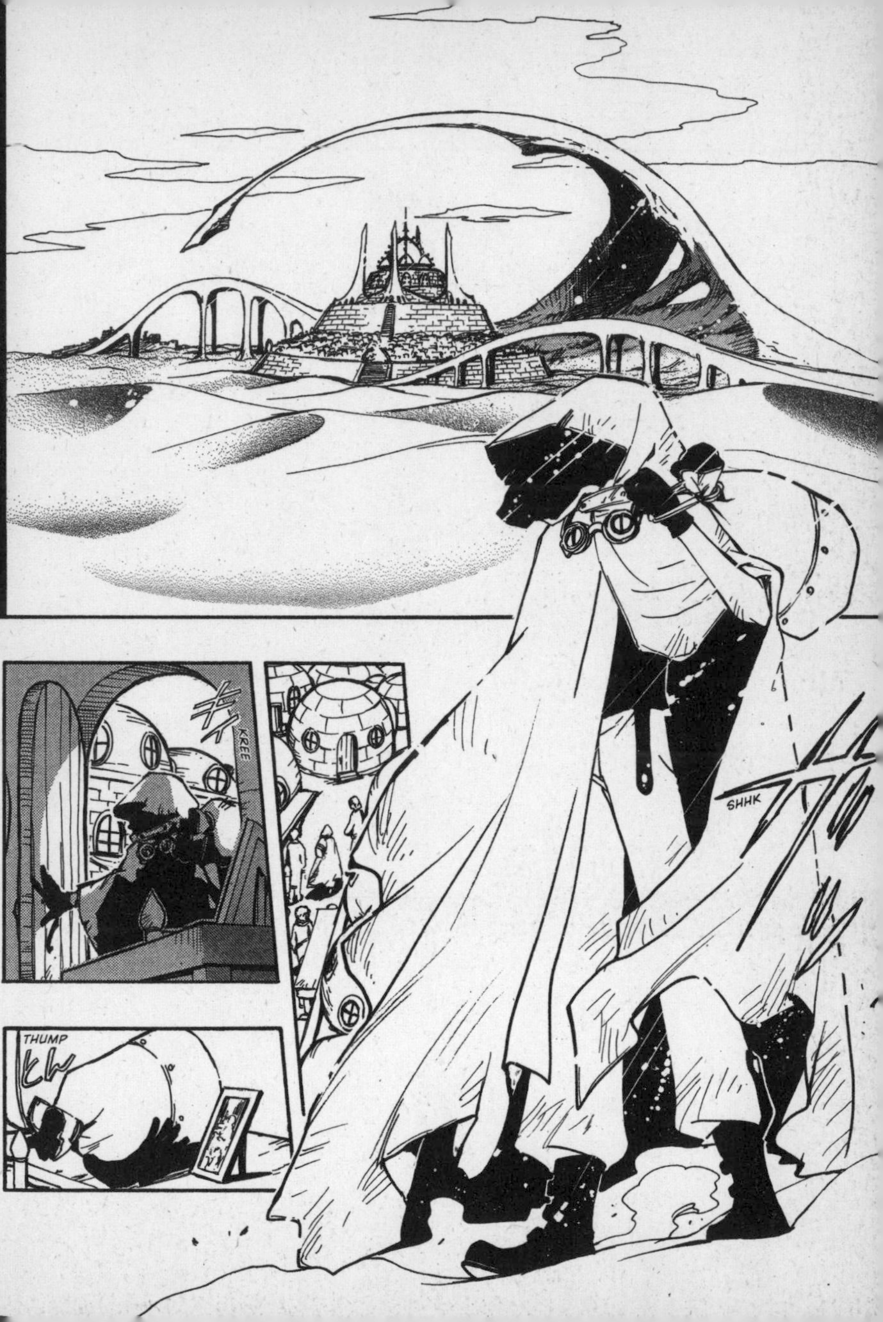
SHHK
KREE
THUMP
とん

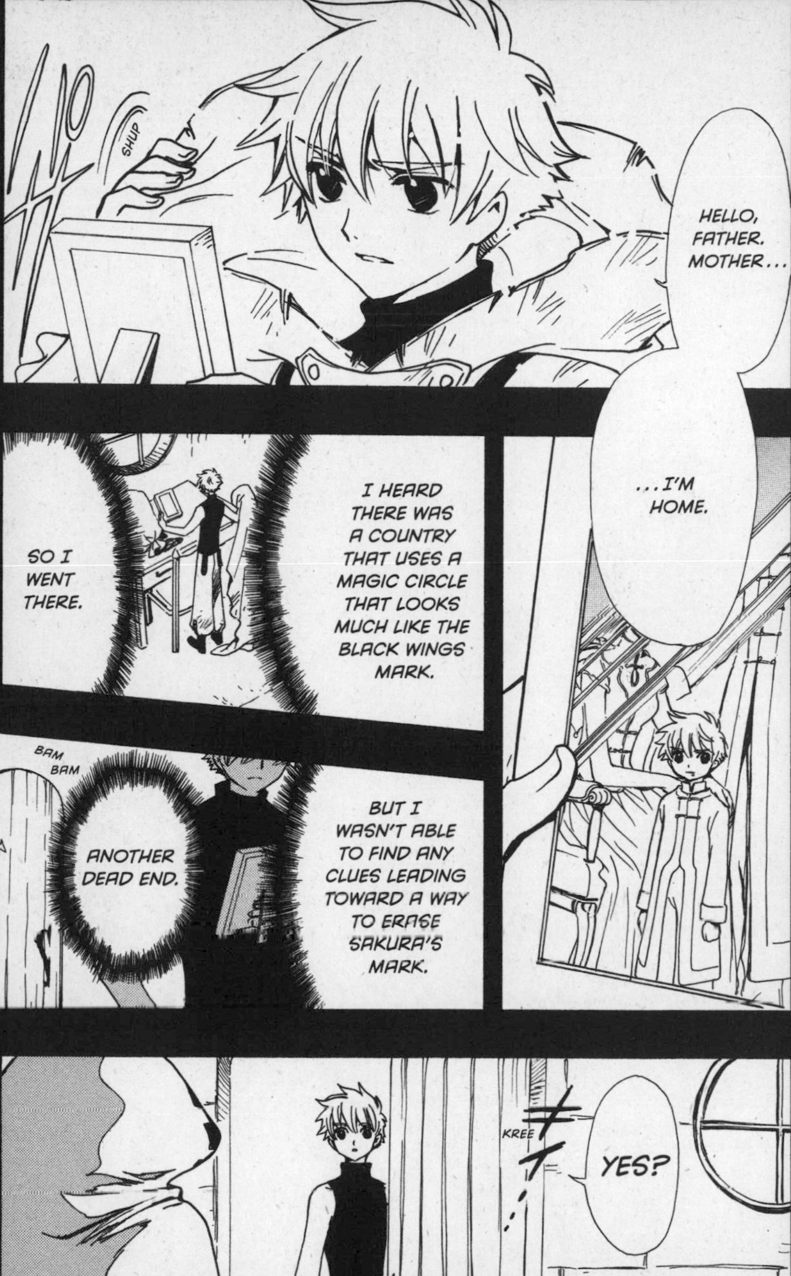
HELLO, FATHER. MOTHER...
SHUP
...I'M HOME.
I HEARD THERE WAS A COUNTRY THAT USES A MAGIC CIRCLE THAT LOOKS MUCH LIKE THE BLACK WINGS MARK.
SO I WENT THERE.
BUT I WASN'T ABLE TO FIND ANY CLUES LEADING TOWARD A WAY TO ERASE SAKURA'S MARK.
ANOTHER DEAD END.
BAM BAM
YES?
KREE

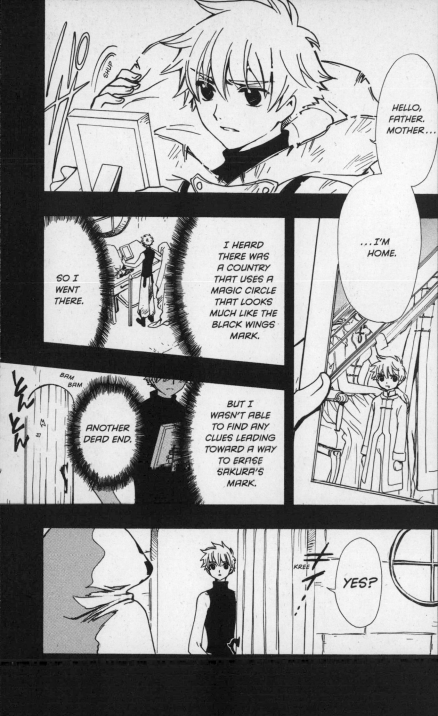

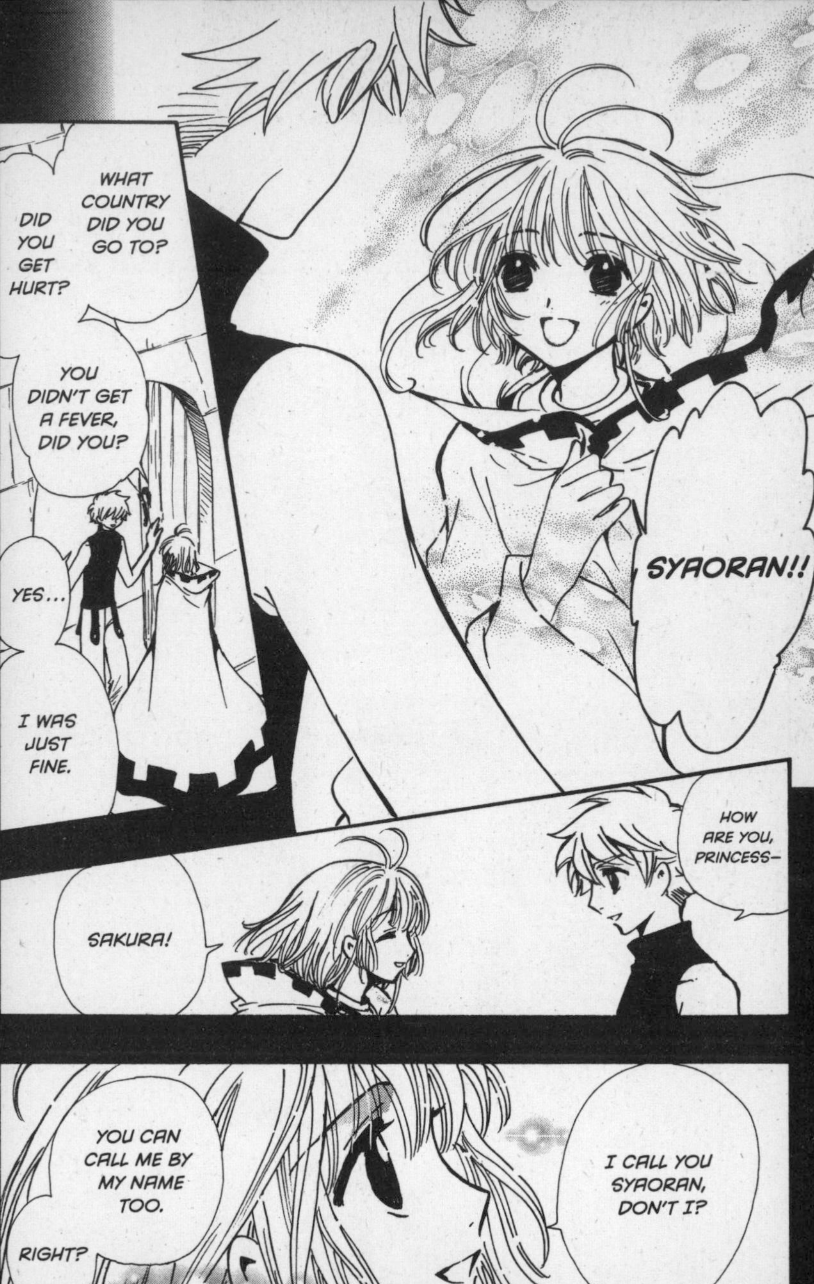
SYAORAN!!
WHAT COUNTRY DID YOU GO TO?
DID YOU GET HURT?
YOU DIDN'T GET A FEVER, DID YOU?
YES...
I WAS JUST FINE.
HOW ARE YOU, PRINCESS—
SAKURA!
I CALL YOU SYAORAN, DON'T I?
YOU CAN CALL ME BY MY NAME TOO.
RIGHT?

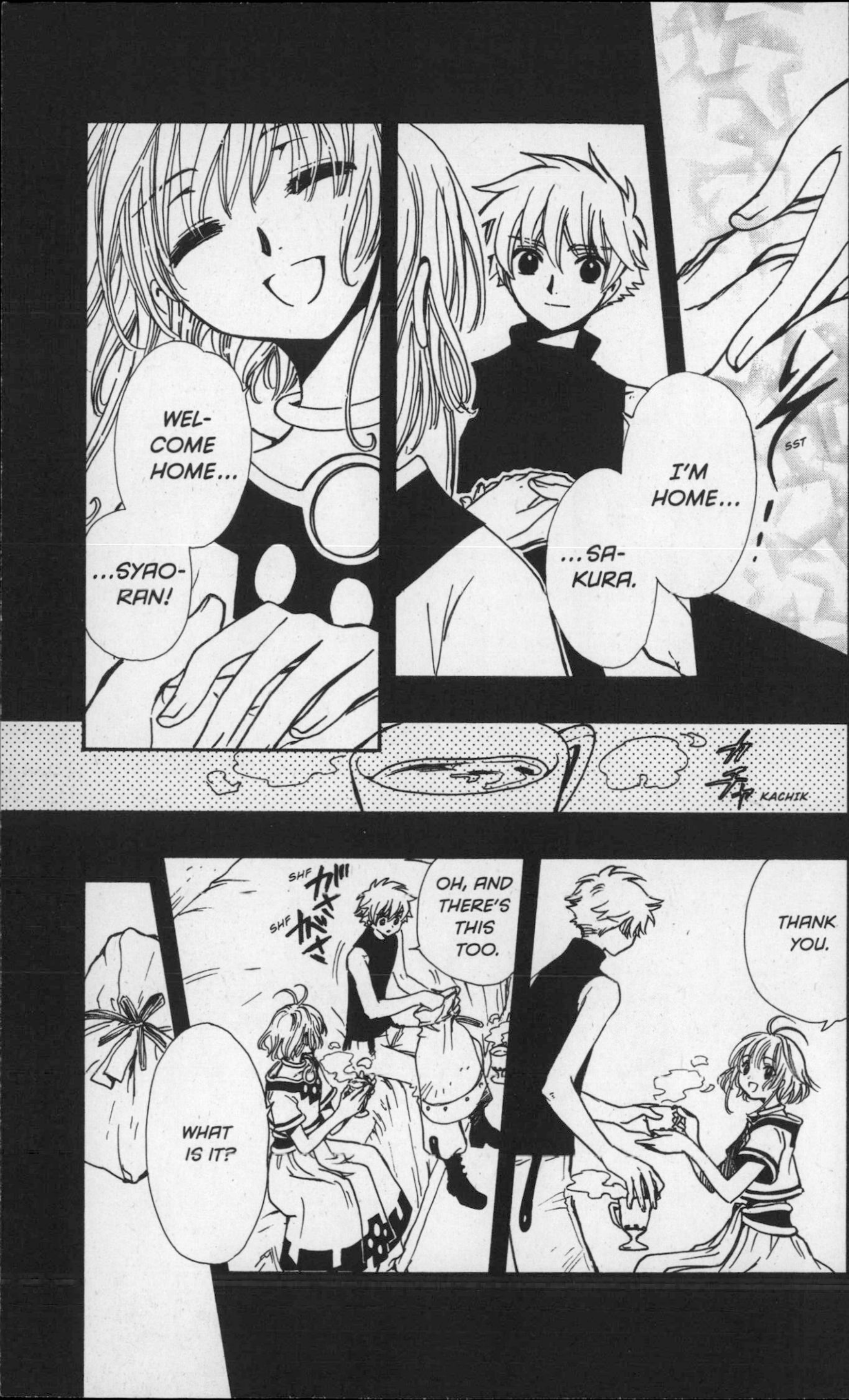
SST
I'M HOME...
...SA-KURA.
WEL-COME HOME...
...SYAO-RAN!
KACHIK
THANK YOU.
OH, AND THERE'S THIS TOO.
SHF
SHF
WHAT IS IT?

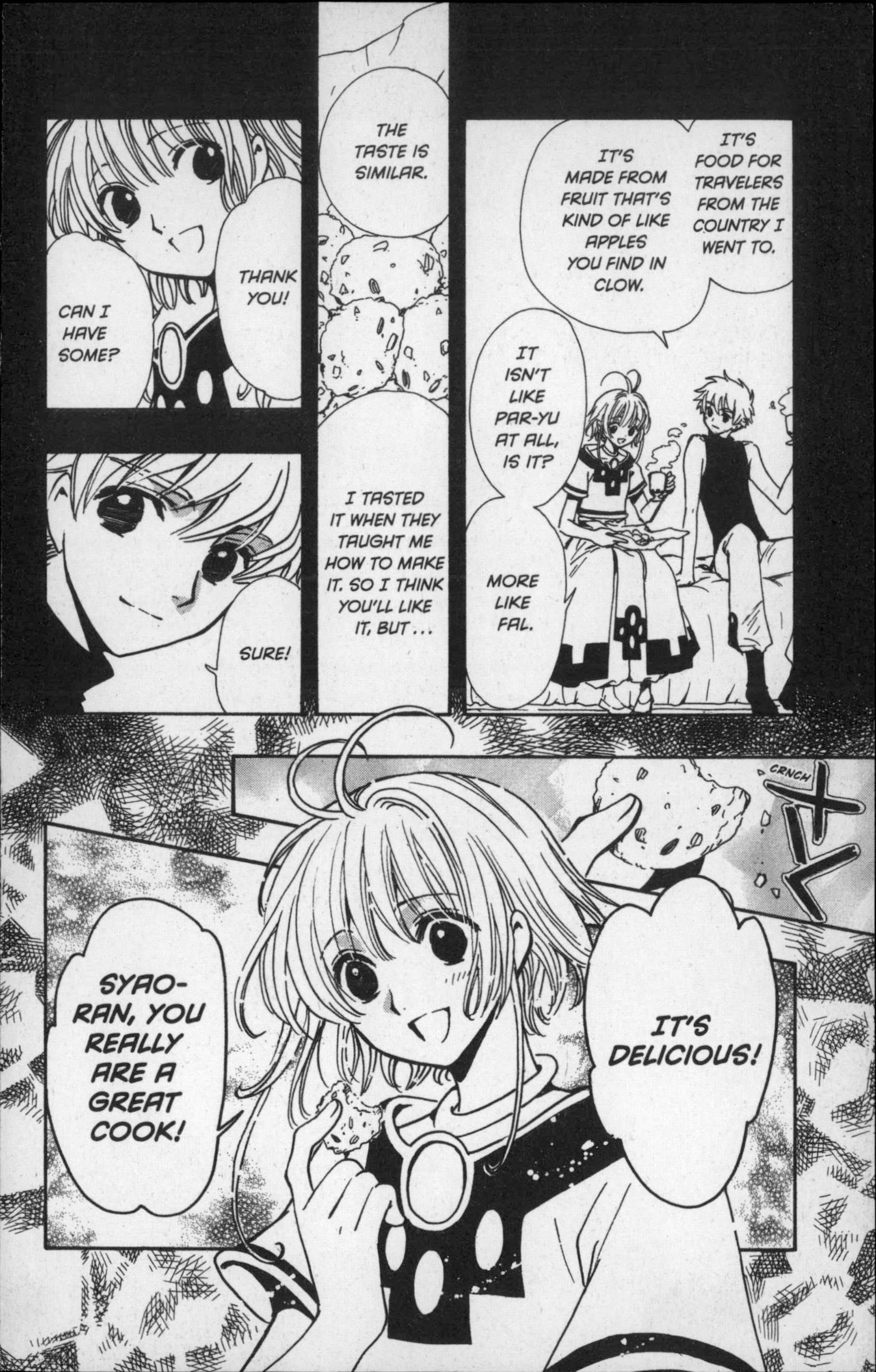
IT'S FOOD FOR TRAVELERS FROM THE COUNTRY I WENT TO.
IT'S MADE FROM FRUIT THAT'S KIND OF LIKE APPLES YOU FIND IN CLOW.
IT ISN'T LIKE PAR-YU AT ALL, IS IT?
MORE LIKE FAL.
THE TASTE IS SIMILAR.
I TASTED IT WHEN THEY TAUGHT ME HOW TO MAKE IT. SO I THINK YOU'LL LIKE IT, BUT . . .
THANK YOU!
CAN I HAVE SOME?
SURE!
CRNCH
IT'S DELICIOUS!
SYAO-RAN, YOU REALLY ARE A GREAT COOK!

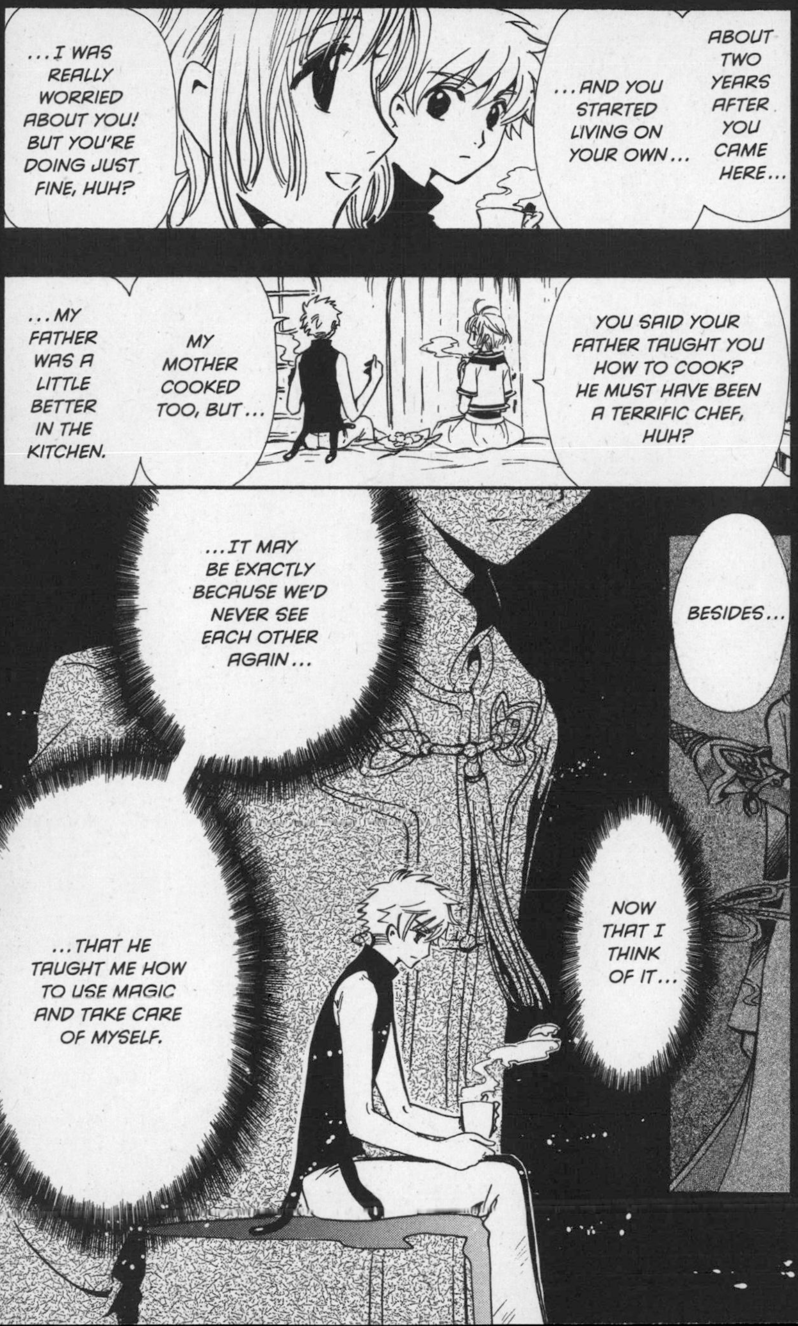
ABOUT TWO YEARS AFTER YOU CAME HERE...
...AND YOU STARTED LIVING ON YOUR OWN...
...I WAS REALLY WORRIED ABOUT YOU! BUT YOU'RE DOING JUST FINE, HUH?
YOU SAID YOUR FATHER TAUGHT YOU HOW TO COOK? HE MUST HAVE BEEN A TERRIFIC CHEF, HUH?
MY MOTHER COOKED TOO, BUT...
...MY FATHER WAS A LITTLE BETTER IN THE KITCHEN.
BESIDES...
NOW THAT I THINK OF IT...
...IT MAY BE EXACTLY BECAUSE WE'D NEVER SEE EACH OTHER AGAIN...
...THAT HE TAUGHT ME HOW TO USE MAGIC AND TAKE CARE OF MYSELF.

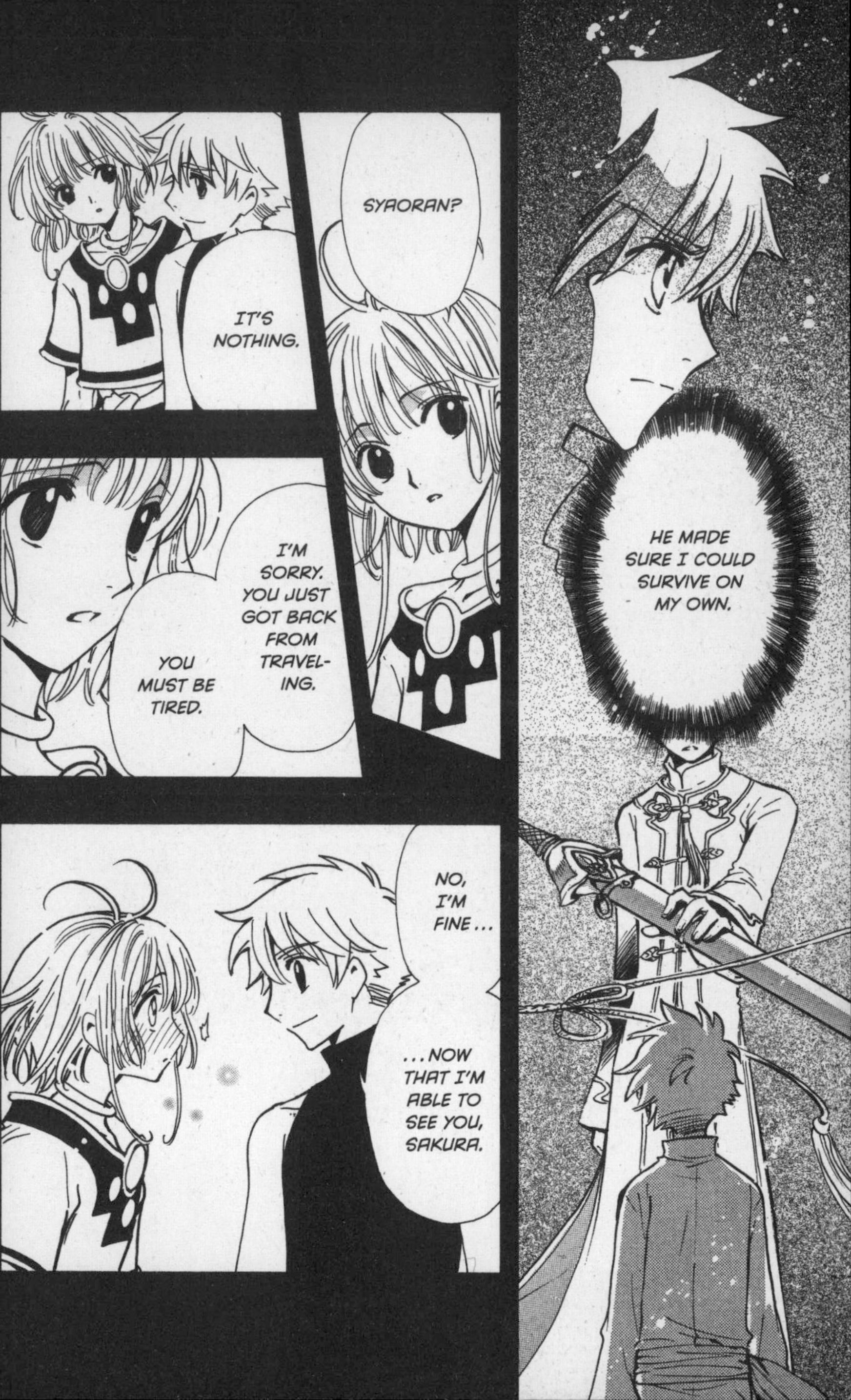
HE MADE SURE I COULD SURVIVE ON MY OWN.
SYAORAN?
IT'S NOTHING.
I'M SORRY. YOU JUST GOT BACK FROM TRAVEL-ING.
YOU MUST BE TIRED.
NO, I'M FINE...
...NOW THAT I'M ABLE TO SEE YOU, SAKURA.

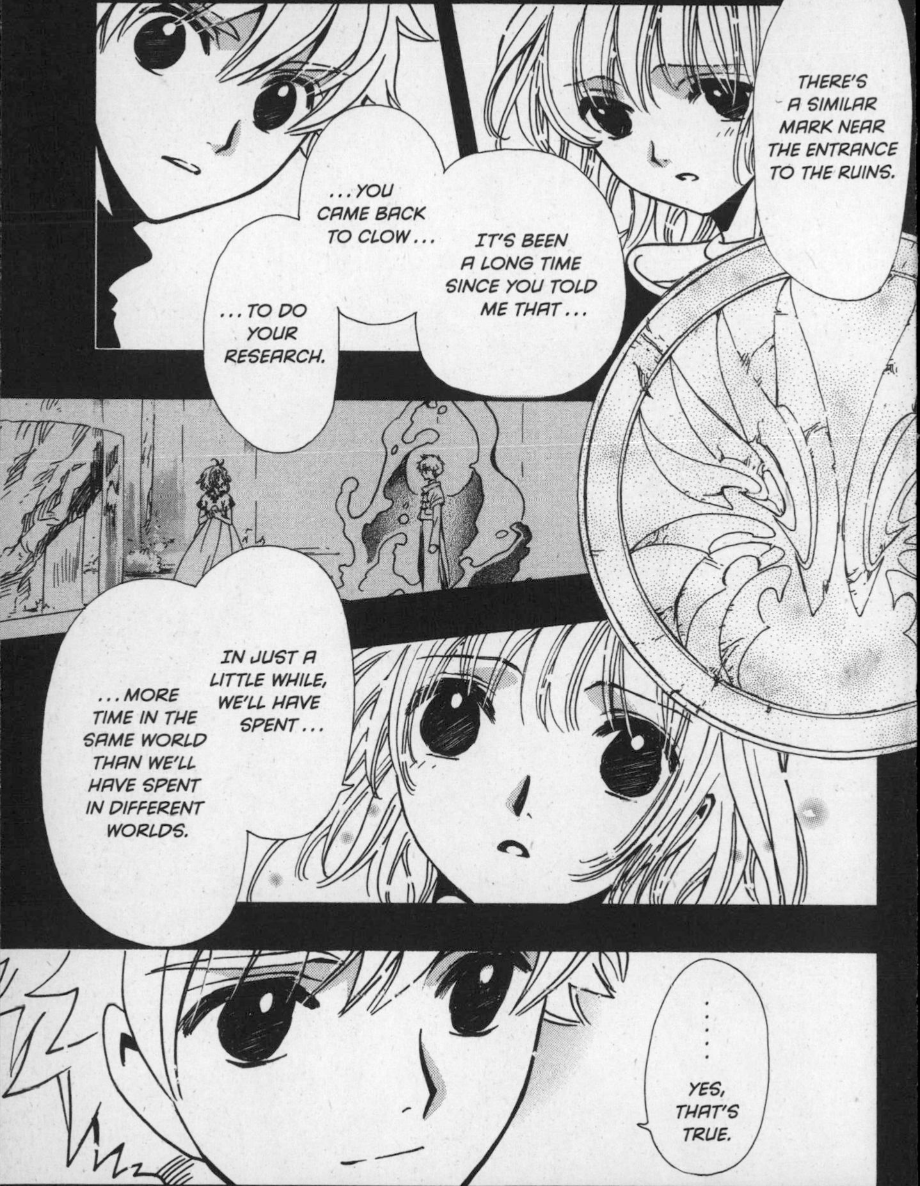
THERE'S A SIMILAR MARK NEAR THE ENTRANCE TO THE RUINS.
IT'S BEEN A LONG TIME SINCE YOU TOLD ME THAT...
...YOU CAME BACK TO CLOW...
...TO DO YOUR RESEARCH.
IN JUST A LITTLE WHILE, WE'LL HAVE SPENT...
...MORE TIME IN THE SAME WORLD THAN WE'LL HAVE SPENT IN DIFFERENT WORLDS.
......
YES, THAT'S TRUE.

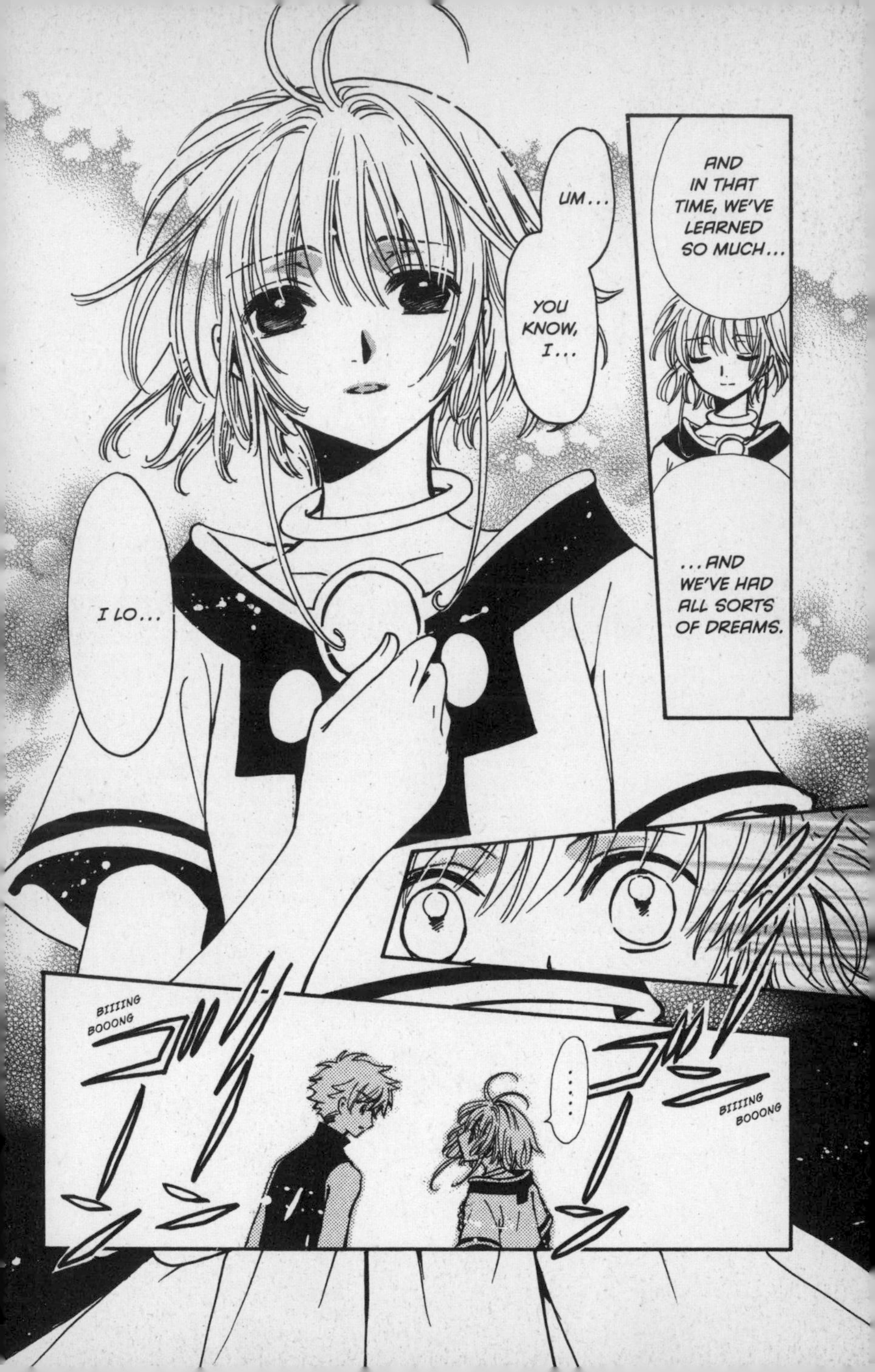
AND IN THAT TIME, WE'VE LEARNED SO MUCH...
...AND WE'VE HAD ALL SORTS OF DREAMS.
UM...
YOU KNOW, I...
I LO...
BIIIING BOOONG
.....
BIIIING BOOONG

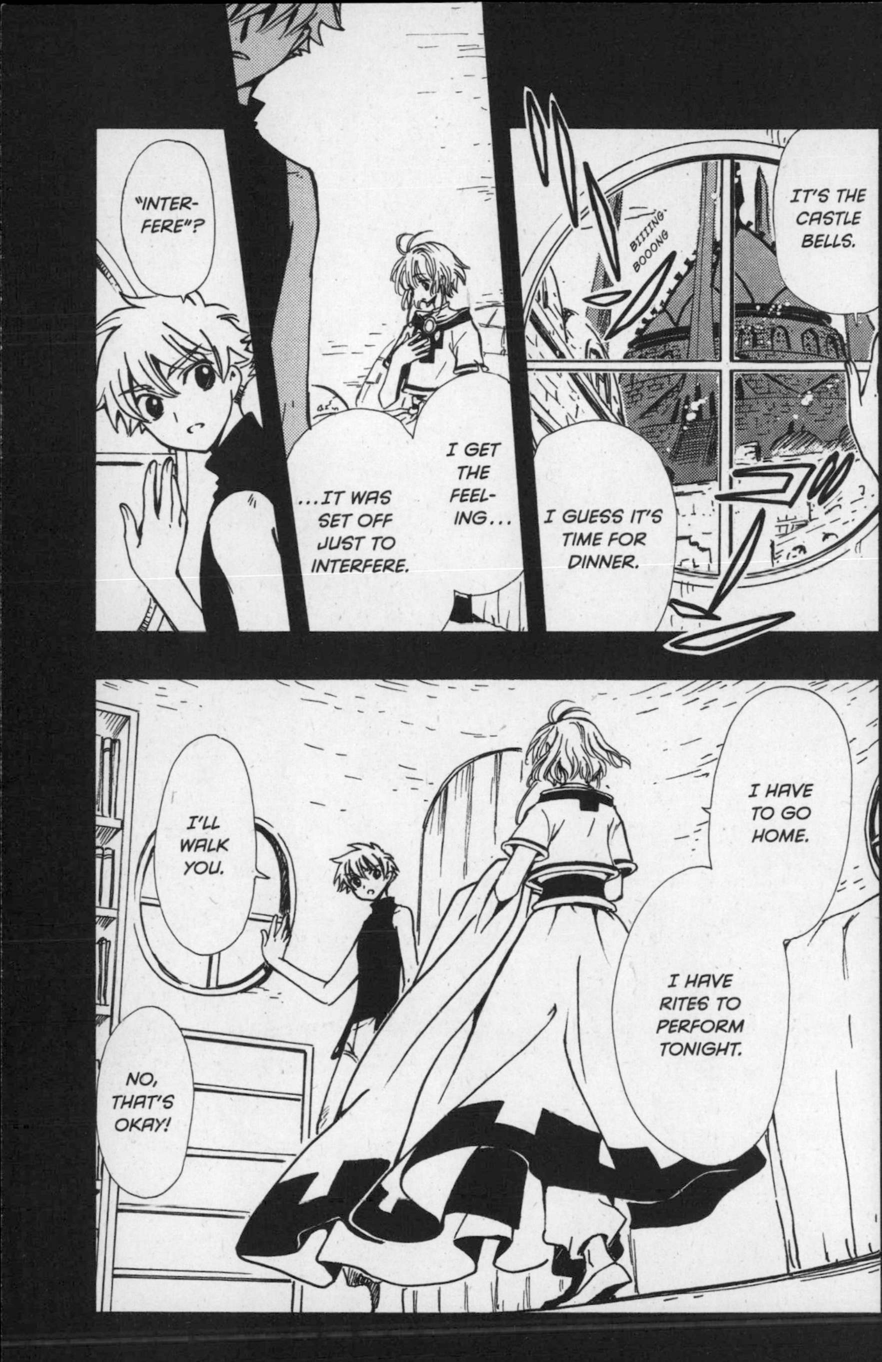
IT'S THE CASTLE BELLS.
BIIIING. BOOONG
I GUESS IT'S TIME FOR DINNER.
I GET THE FEEL-ING...
...IT WAS SET OFF JUST TO INTERFERE.
"INTER-FERE"?
I HAVE TO GO HOME.
I HAVE RITES TO PERFORM TONIGHT.
I'LL WALK YOU.
NO, THAT'S OKAY!

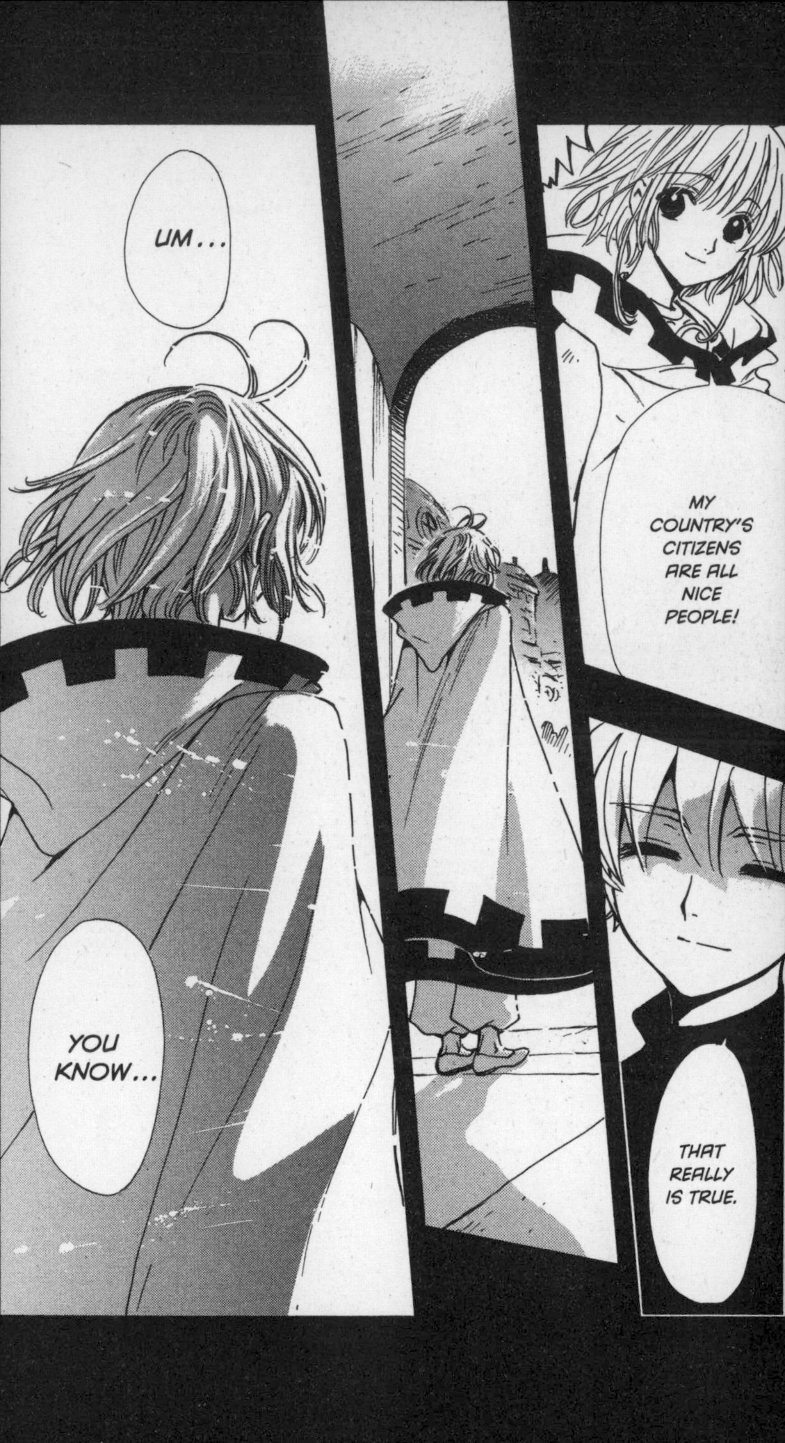
MY COUNTRY'S CITIZENS ARE ALL NICE PEOPLE!
THAT REALLY IS TRUE.
UM...
YOU KNOW...

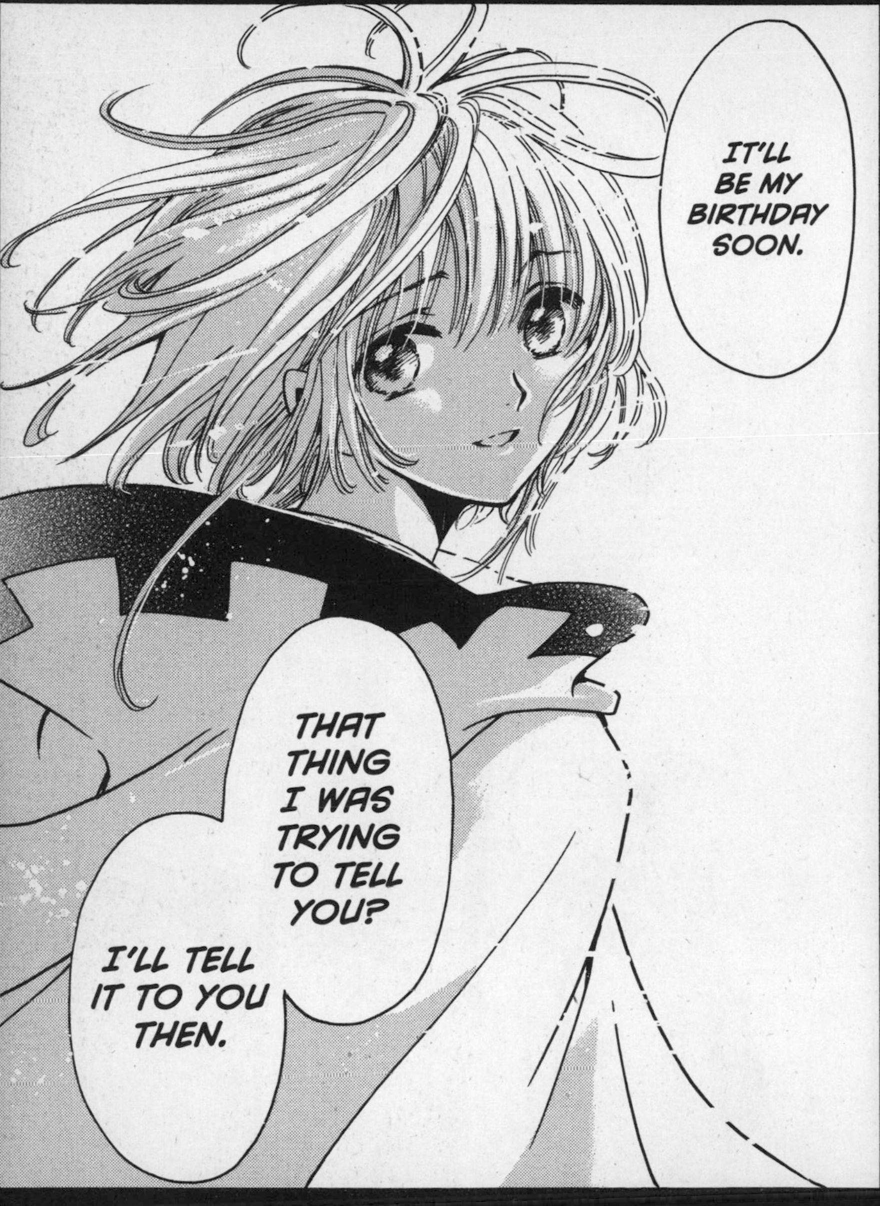
IT'LL BE MY BIRTHDAY SOON.
THAT THING I WAS TRYING TO TELL YOU?
I'LL TELL IT TO YOU THEN.

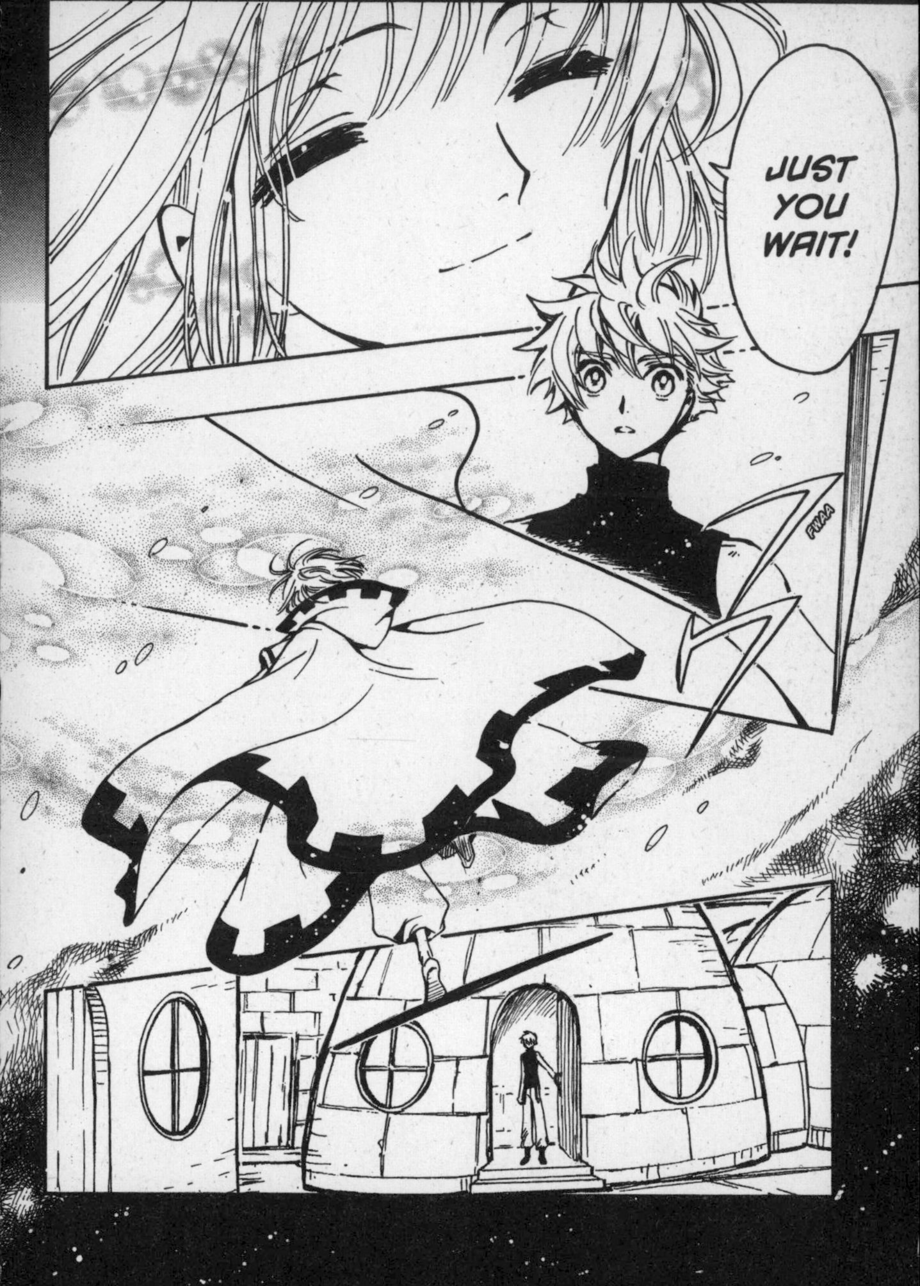
JUST YOU WAIT!
FWAA

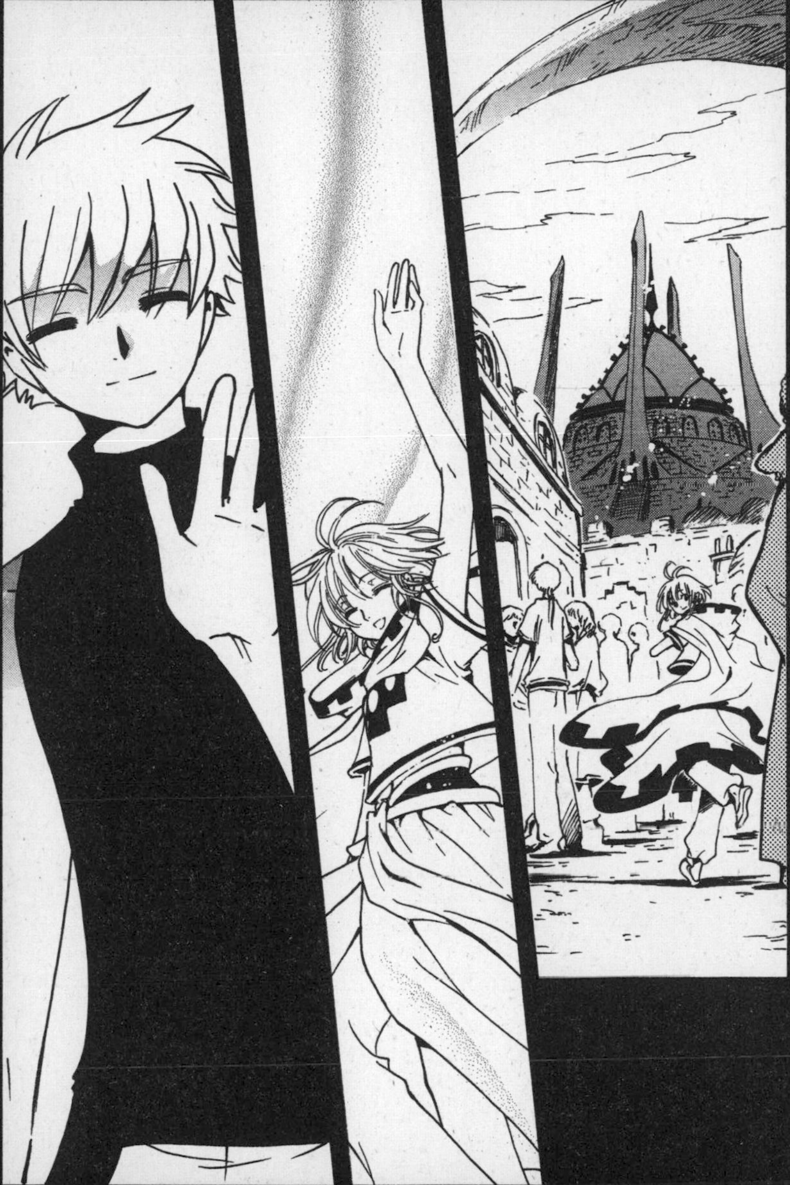

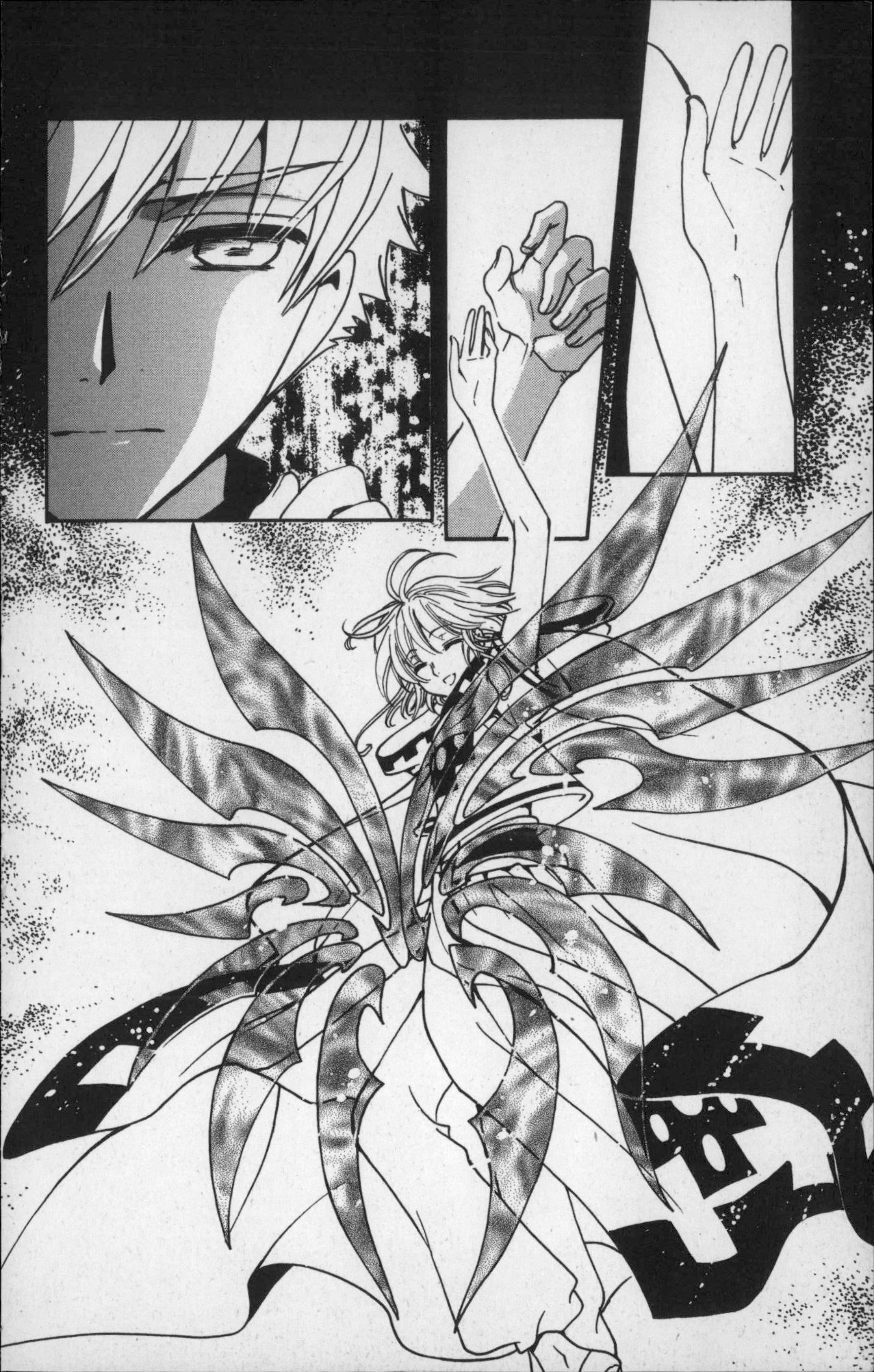

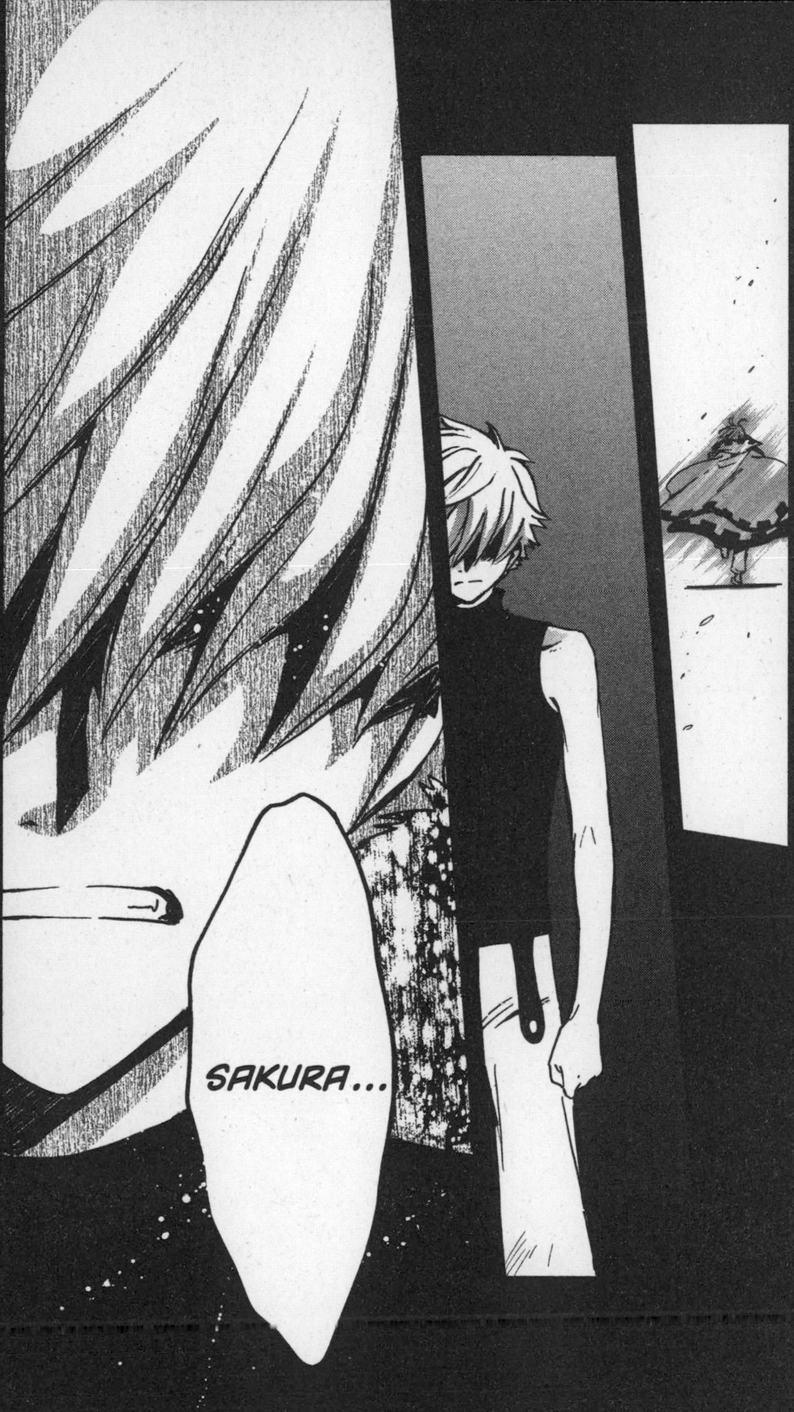
SAKURA...

ツバサ

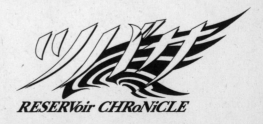

RESERVoir CHRoNiCLE

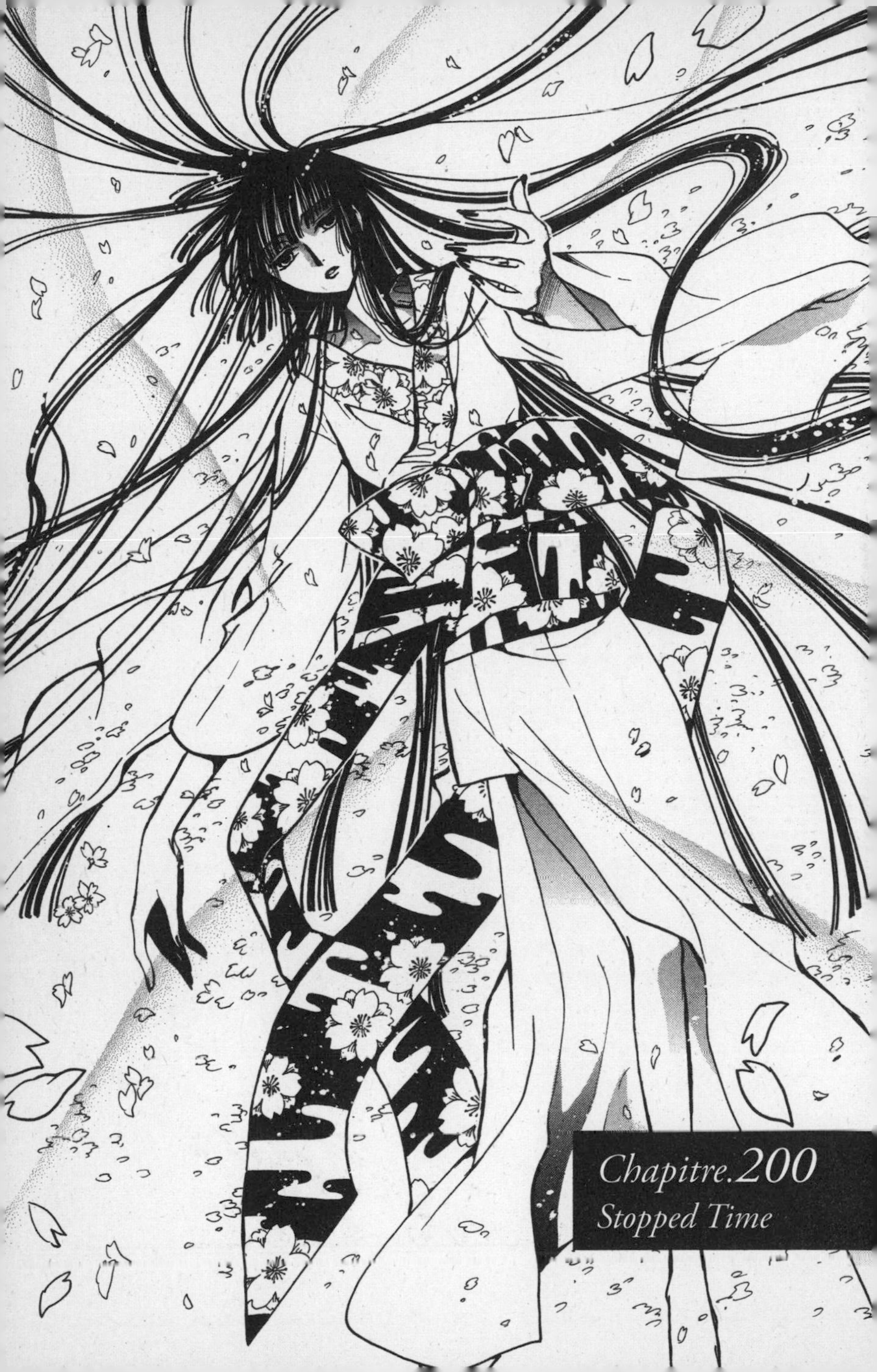
Chapitre.200
Stopped Time

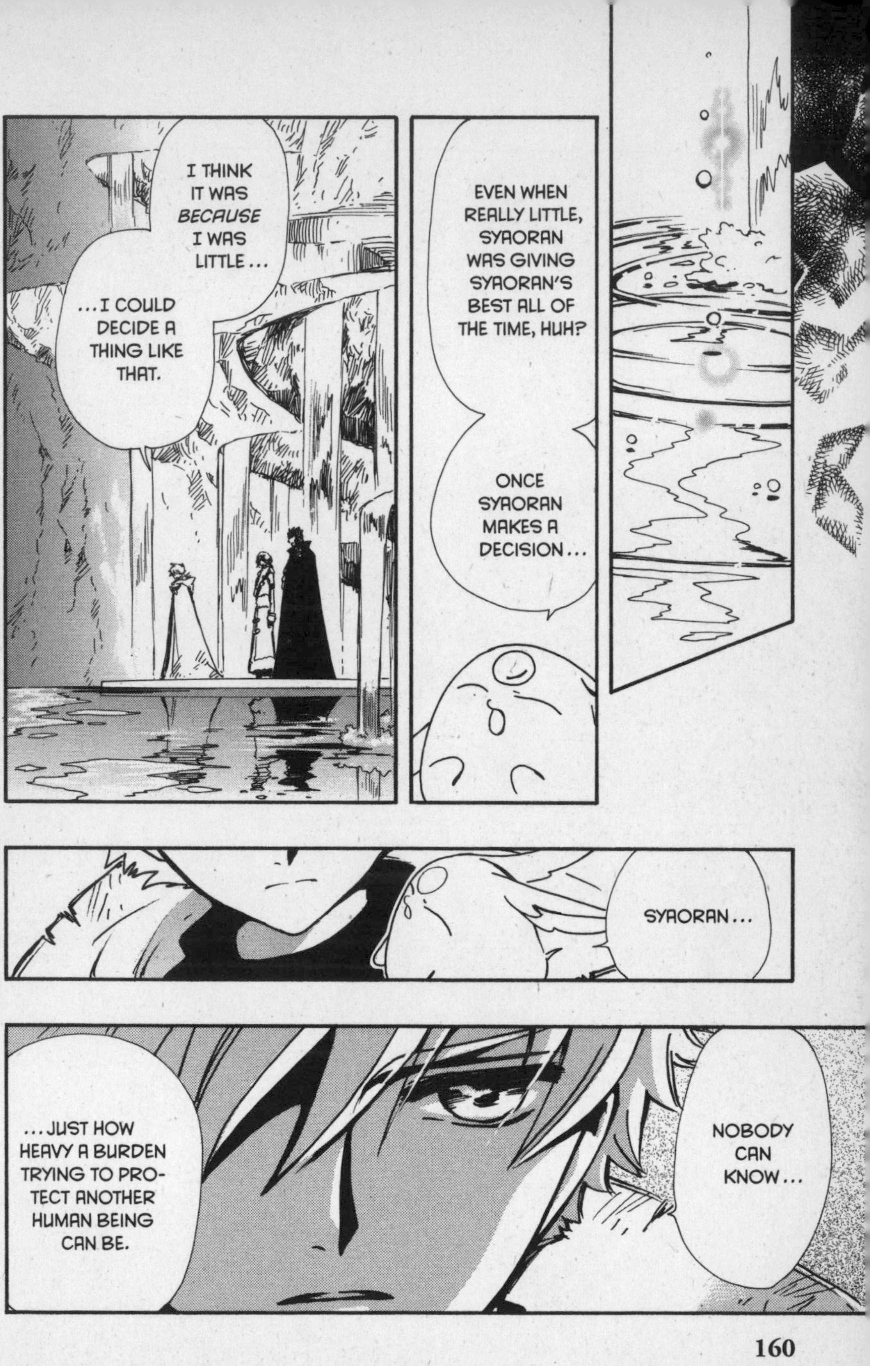
EVEN WHEN REALLY LITTLE, SYAORAN WAS GIVING SYAORAN'S BEST ALL OF THE TIME, HUH?
ONCE SYAORAN MAKES A DECISION...
I THINK IT WAS *BECAUSE* I WAS LITTLE...
...I COULD DECIDE A THING LIKE THAT.
SYAORAN...
NOBODY CAN KNOW...
...JUST HOW HEAVY A BURDEN TRYING TO PRO-TECT ANOTHER HUMAN BEING CAN BE.

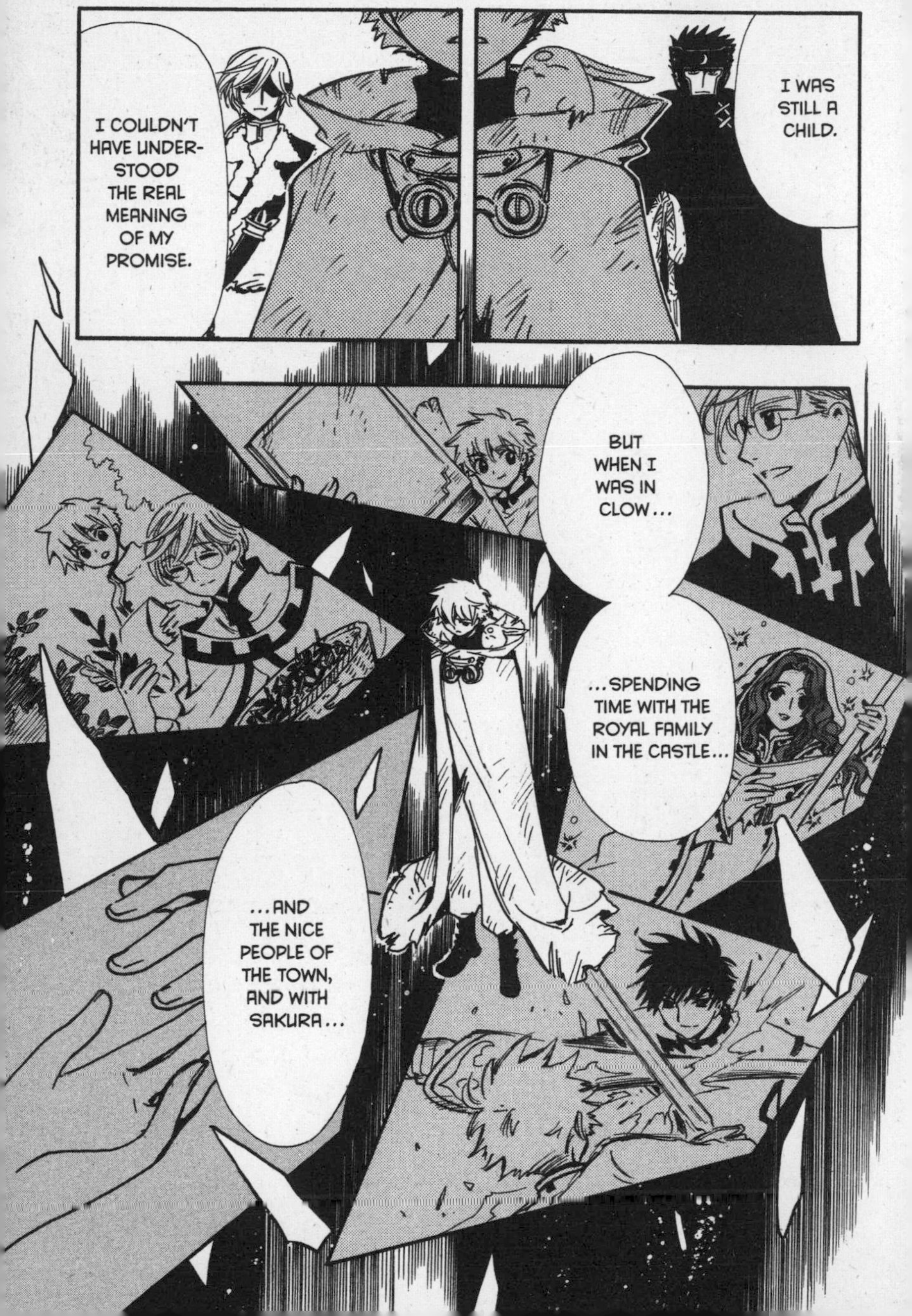
I WAS STILL A CHILD.
I COULDN'T HAVE UNDER-STOOD THE REAL MEANING OF MY PROMISE.
BUT WHEN I WAS IN CLOW...
...SPENDING TIME WITH THE ROYAL FAMILY IN THE CASTLE...
...AND THE NICE PEOPLE OF THE TOWN, AND WITH SAKURA...

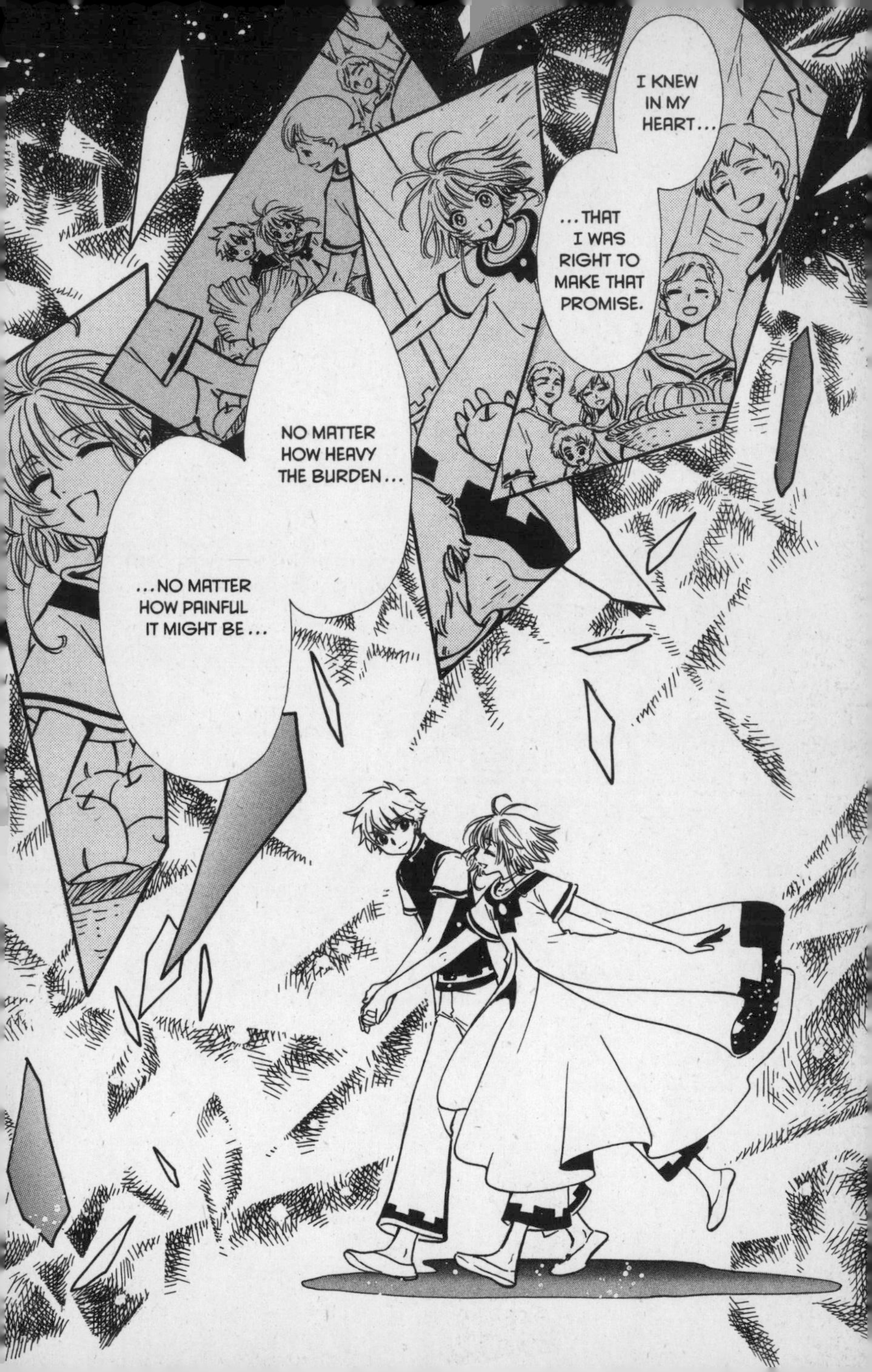
I KNEW IN MY HEART...
...THAT I WAS RIGHT TO MAKE THAT PROMISE.
NO MATTER HOW HEAVY THE BURDEN...
...NO MATTER HOW PAINFUL IT MIGHT BE...

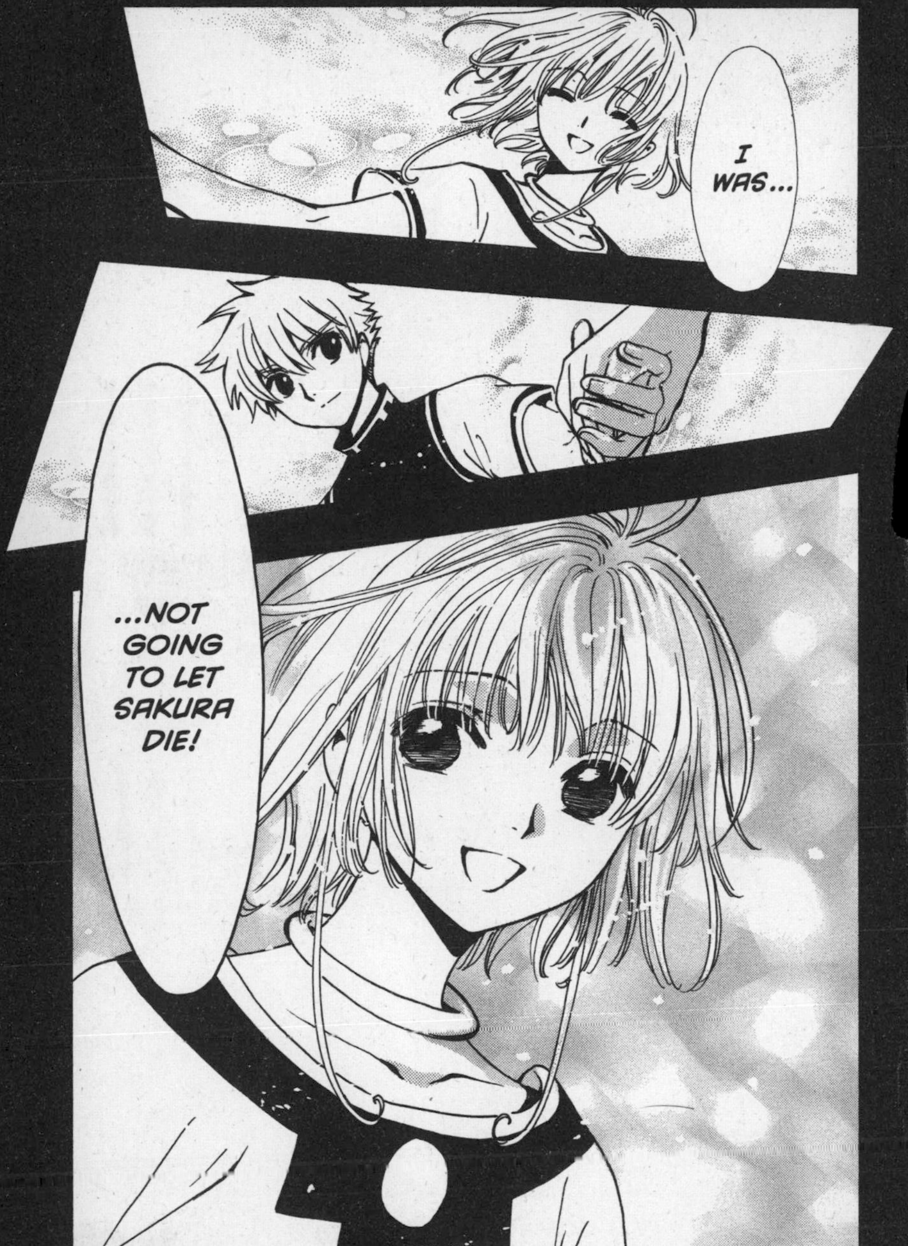
I WAS...
...NOT GOING TO LET SAKURA DIE!

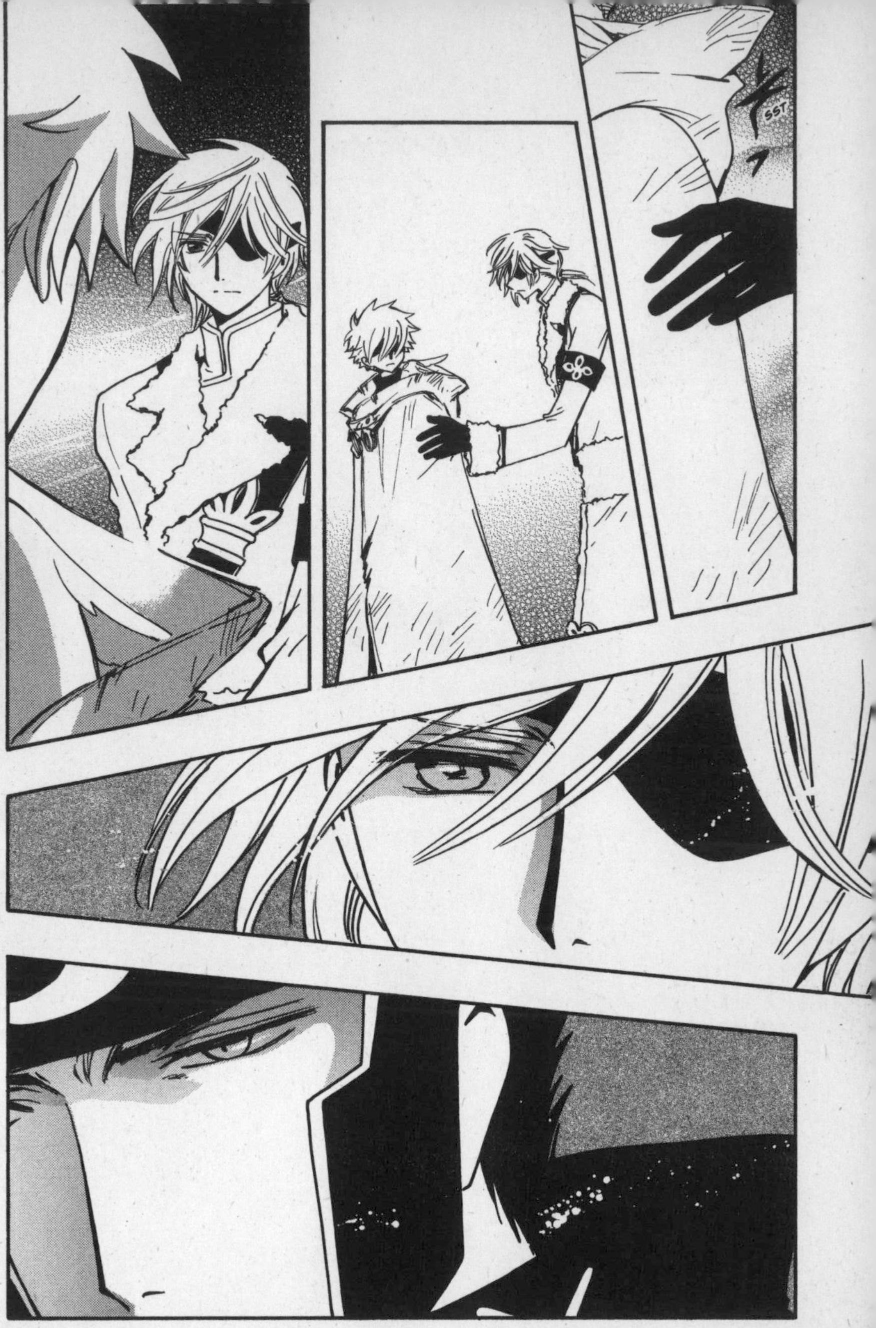
SST

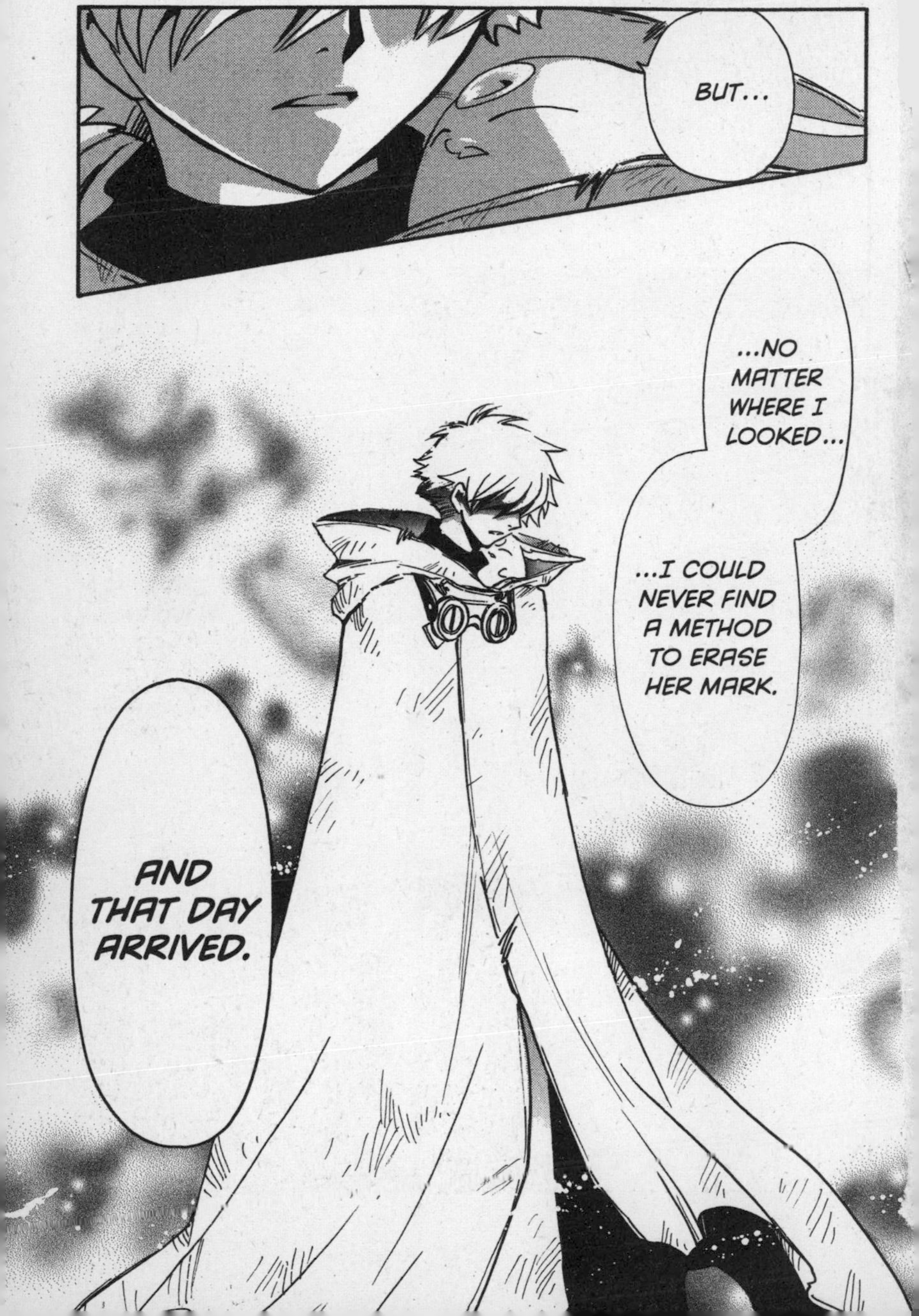
BUT...
...NO MATTER WHERE I LOOKED...
...I COULD NEVER FIND A METHOD TO ERASE HER MARK.
AND THAT DAY ARRIVED.

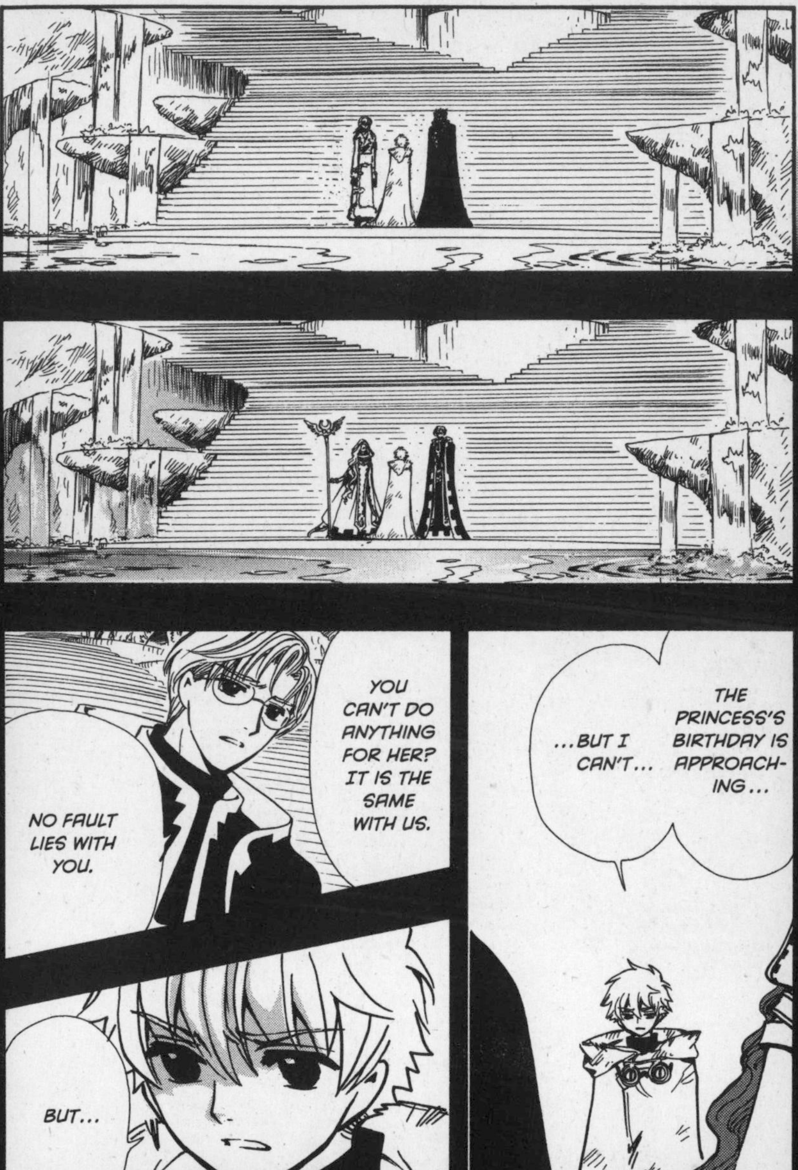
THE PRINCESS'S BIRTHDAY IS APPROACH-ING...
...BUT I CAN'T...
YOU CAN'T DO ANYTHING FOR HER? IT IS THE SAME WITH US.
NO FAULT LIES WITH YOU.
BUT...

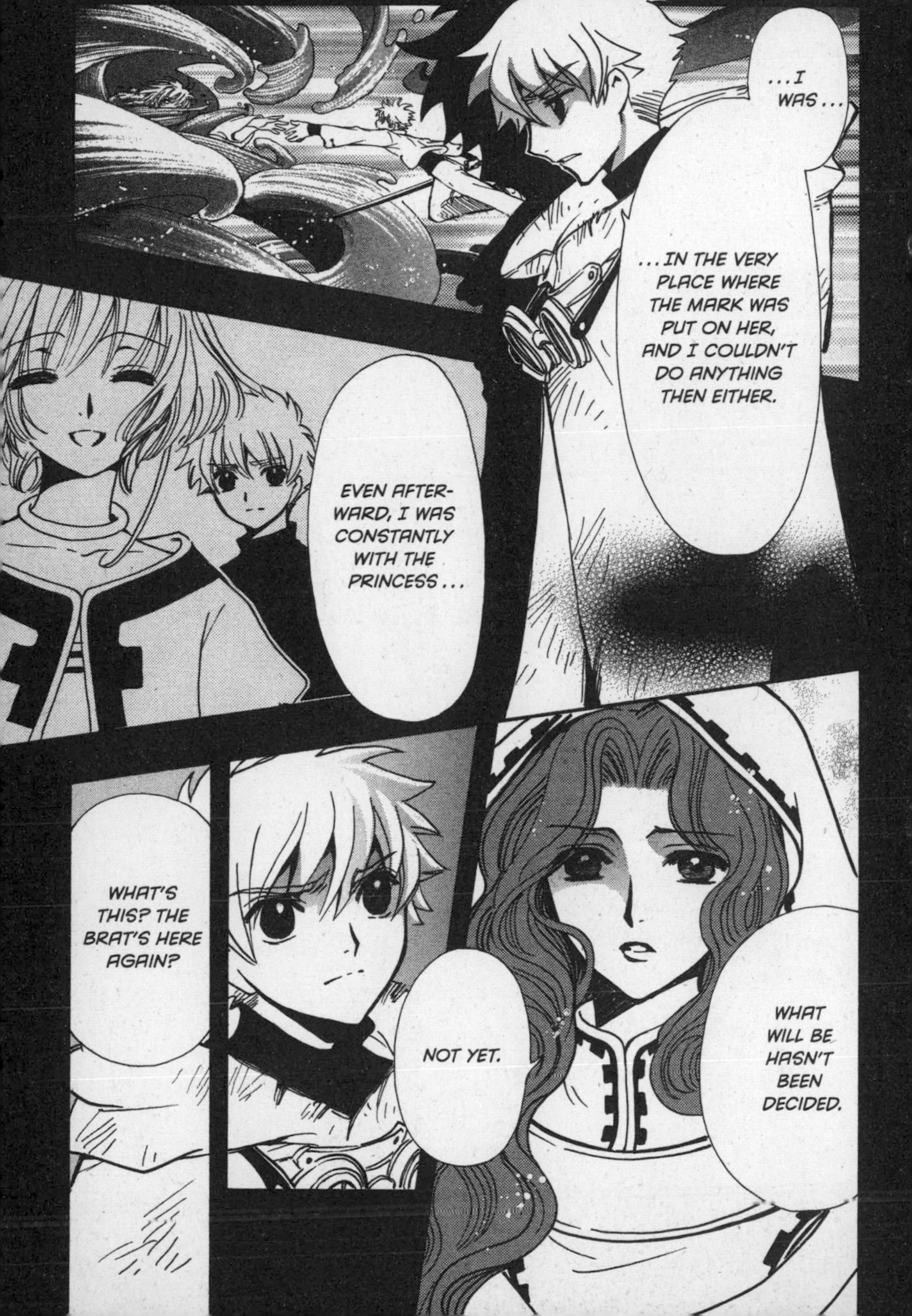
...I WAS...
...IN THE VERY PLACE WHERE THE MARK WAS PUT ON HER, AND I COULDN'T DO ANYTHING THEN EITHER.
EVEN AFTER-WARD, I WAS CONSTANTLY WITH THE PRINCESS...
WHAT WILL BE HASN'T BEEN DECIDED.
NOT YET.
WHAT'S THIS? THE BRAT'S HERE AGAIN?

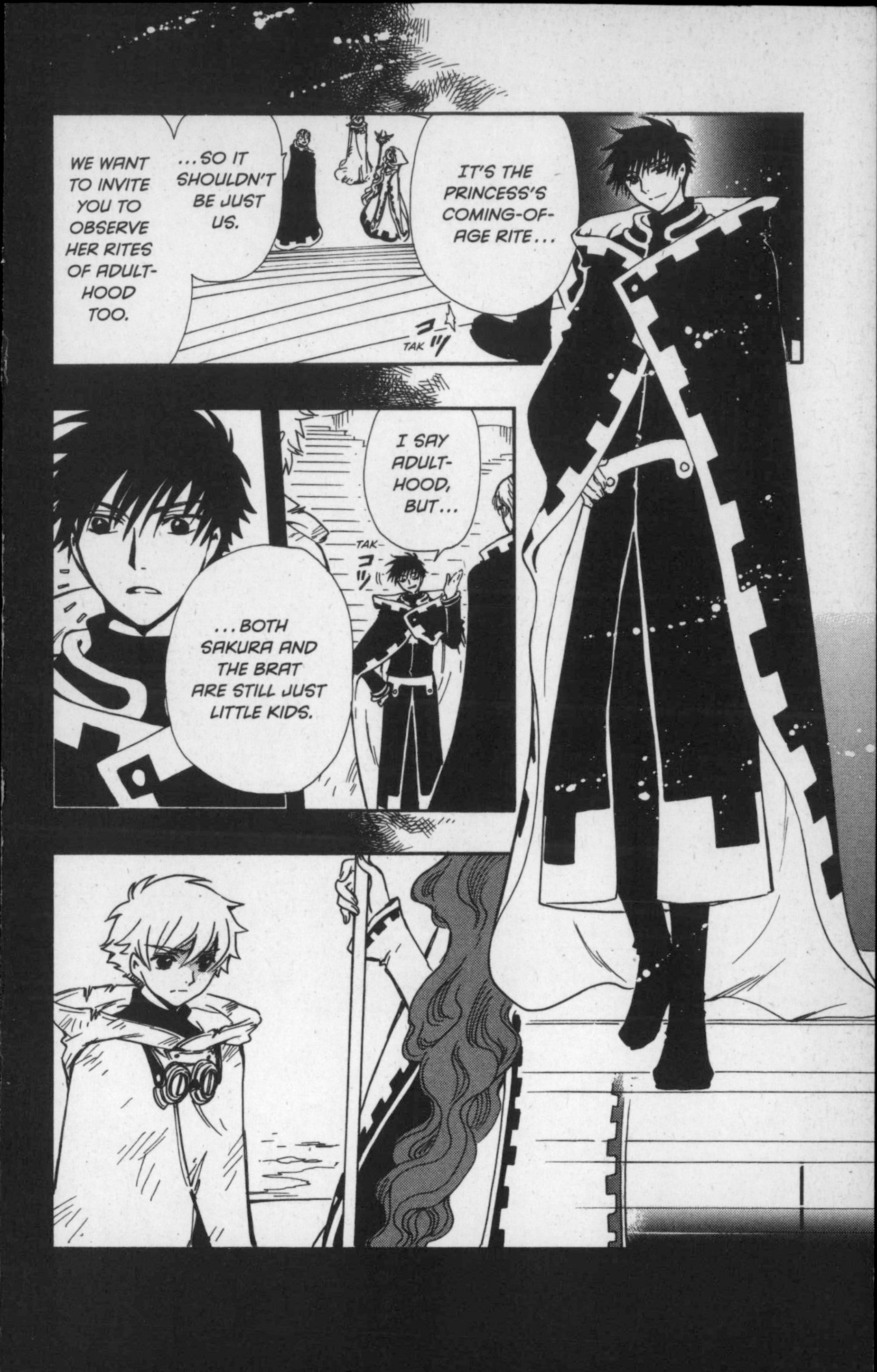
IT'S THE PRINCESS'S COMING-OF-AGE RITE...
...SO IT SHOULDN'T BE JUST US.
WE WANT TO INVITE YOU TO OBSERVE HER RITES OF ADULTHOOD TOO.
TAK
TAK
I SAY ADULTHOOD, BUT...
...BOTH SAKURA AND THE BRAT ARE STILL JUST LITTLE KIDS.

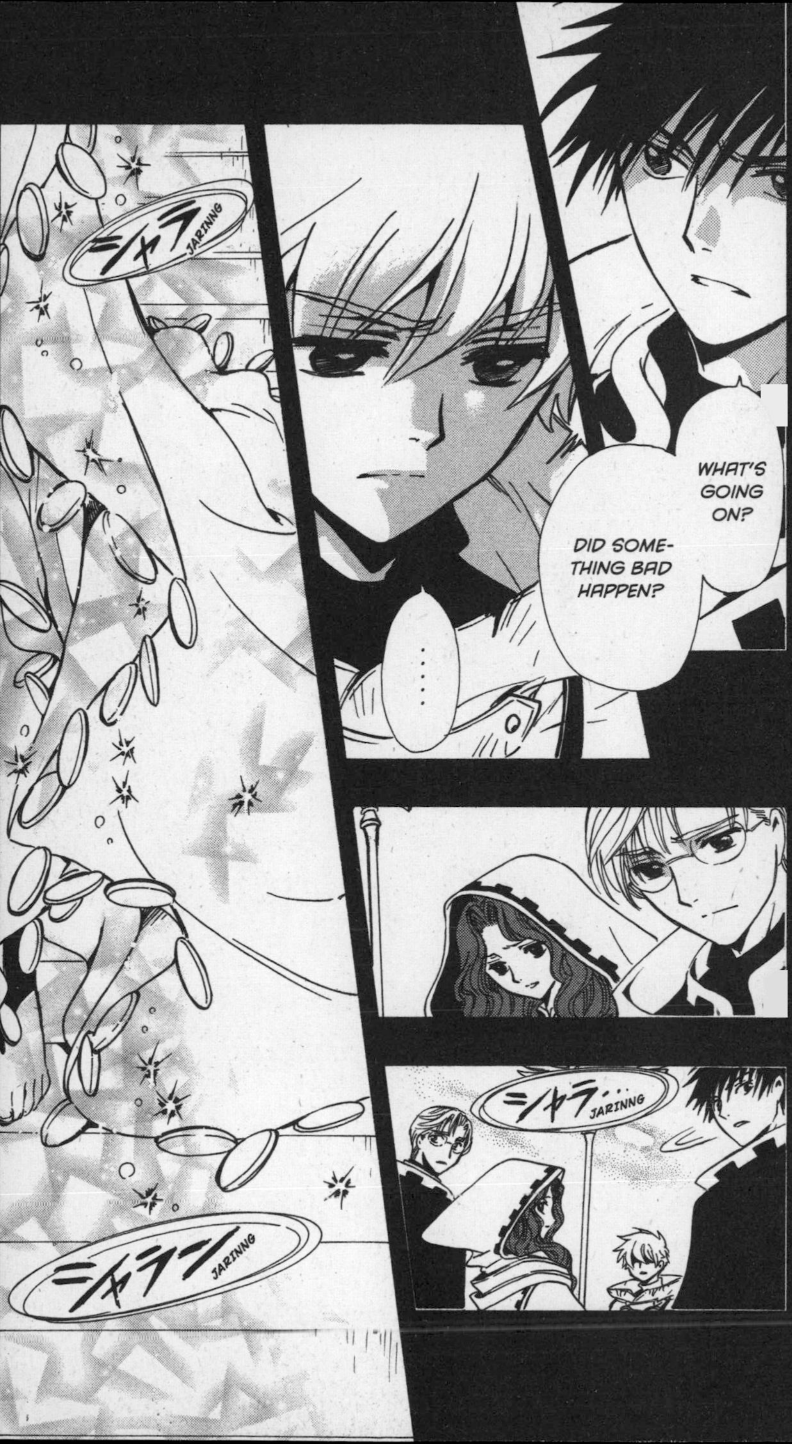
WHAT'S GOING ON?
DID SOMETHING BAD HAPPEN?
......
シャラ…
JARINNG
シャラ
JARINNG
シャラン
JARINNG

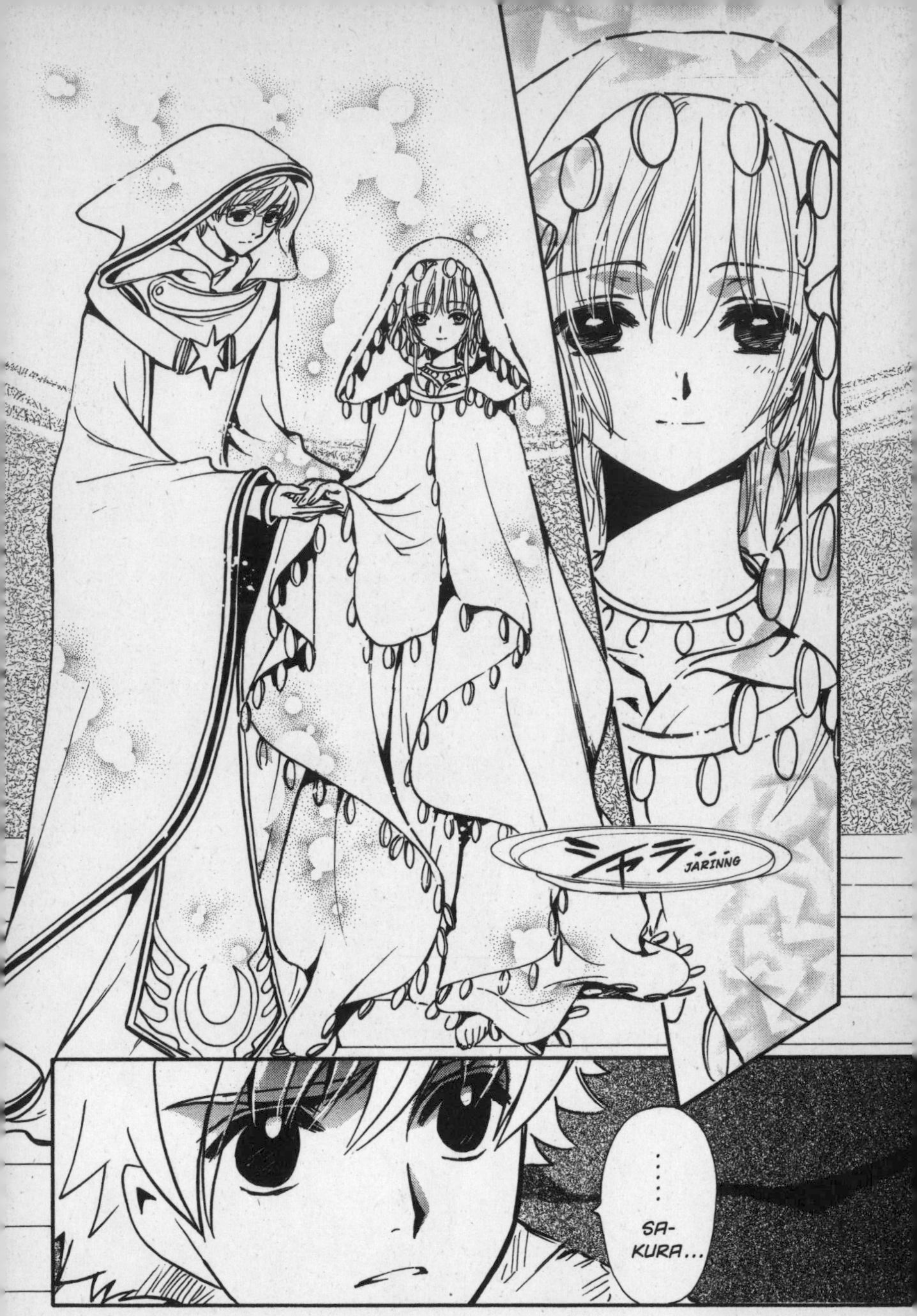
シャラ...
JARINNG
.....
SA-KURA...

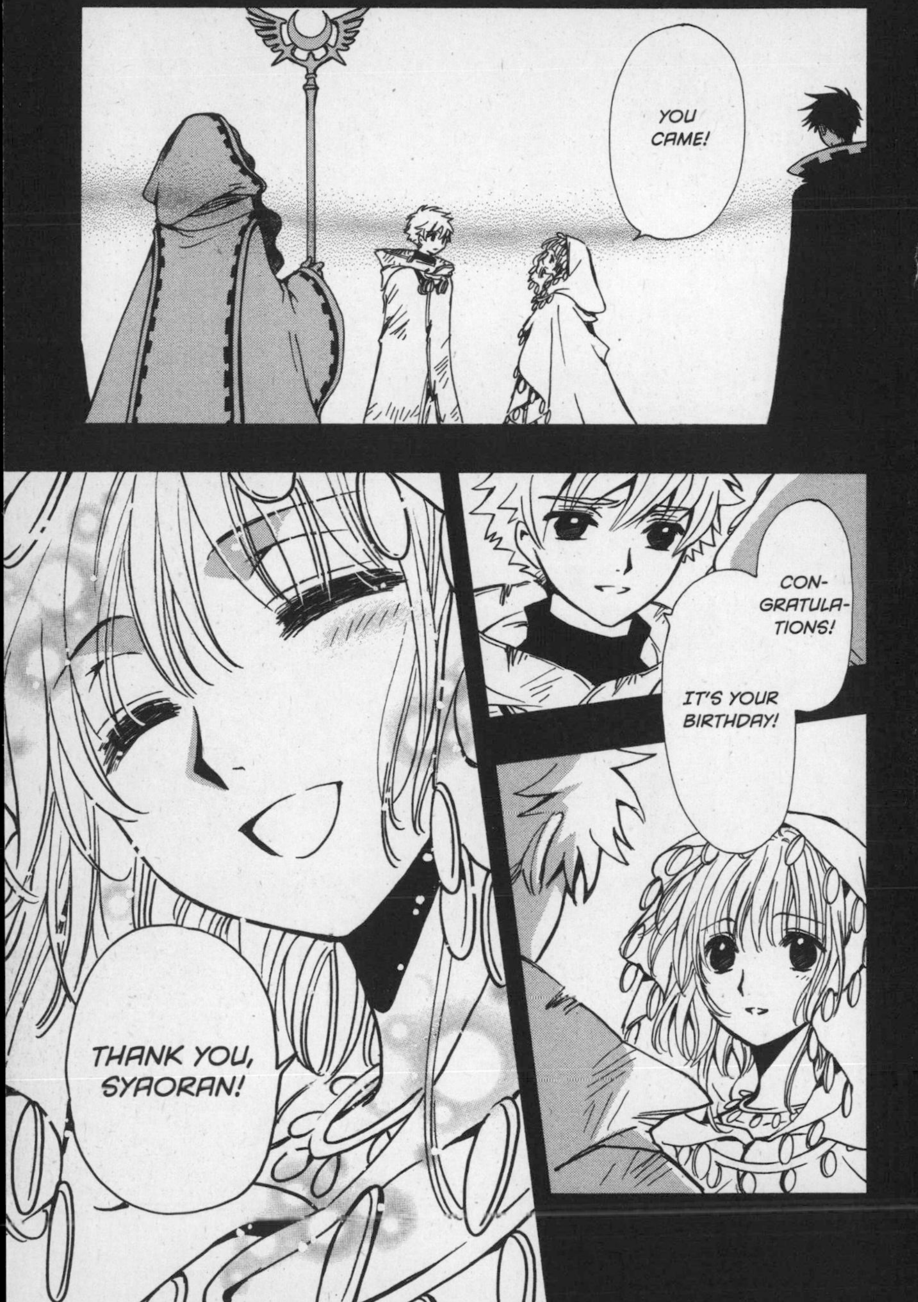
YOU CAME!
CON-GRATULA-TIONS!
IT'S YOUR BIRTHDAY!
THANK YOU, SYAORAN!

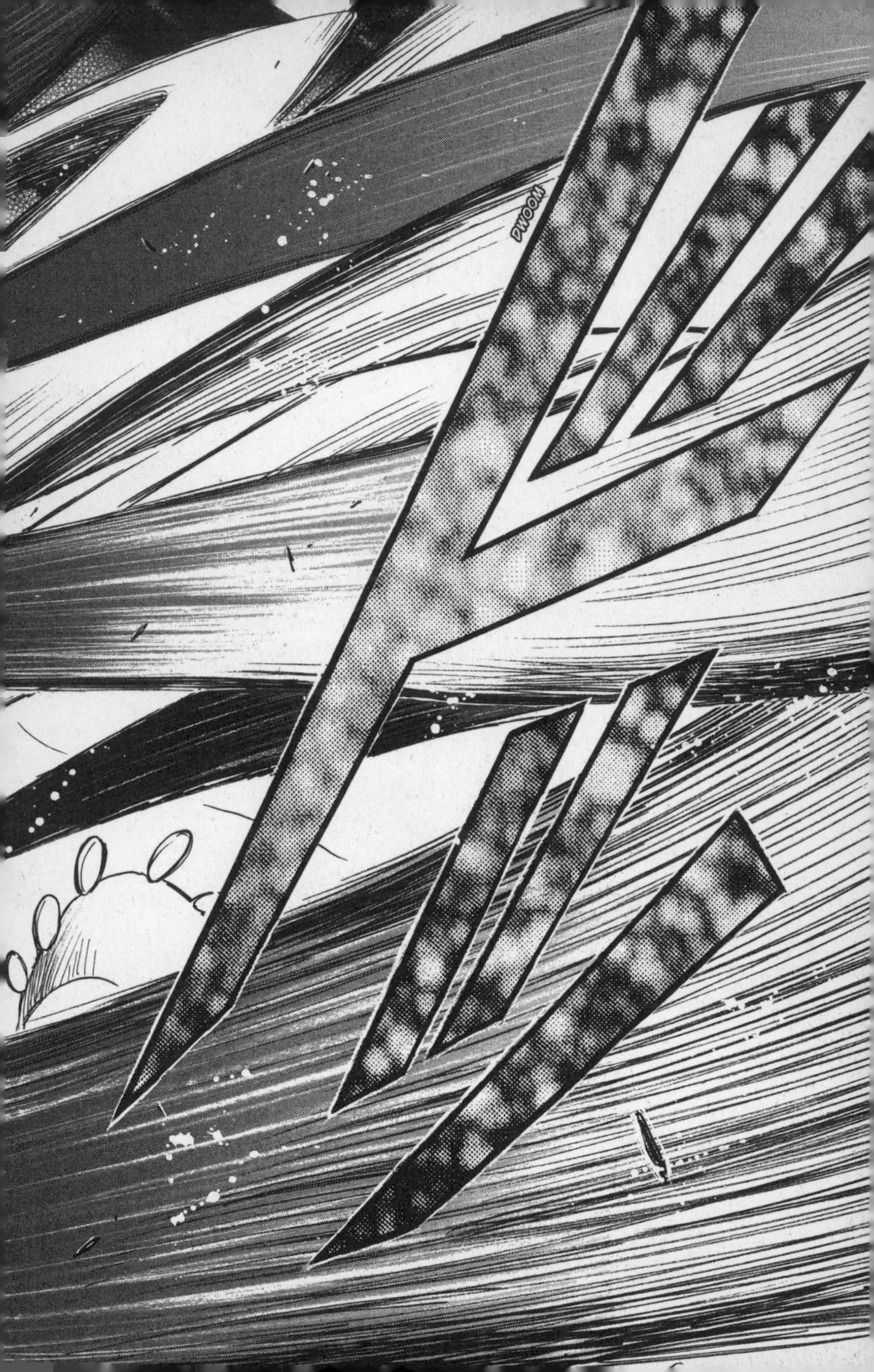
DWOOM

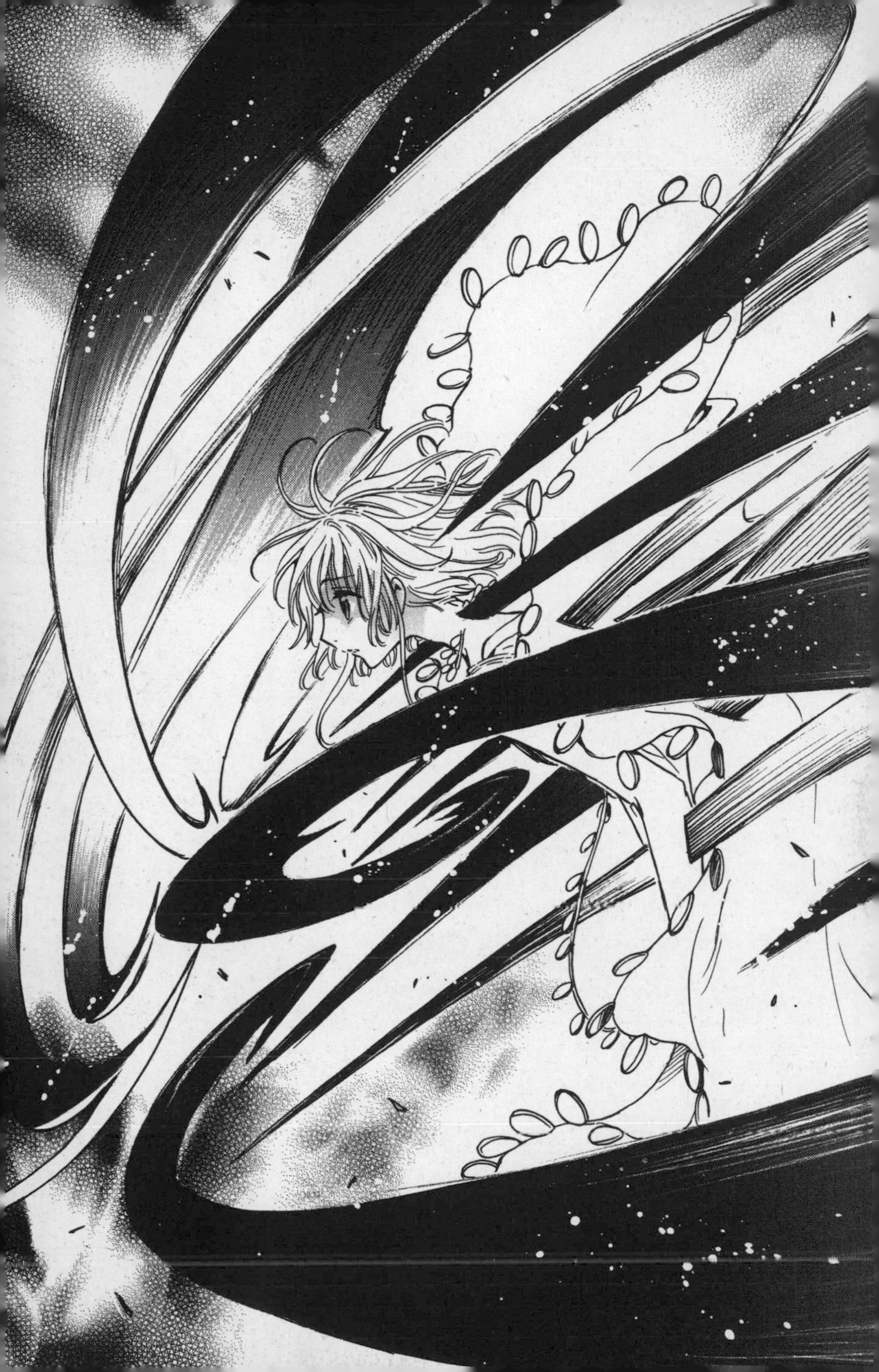

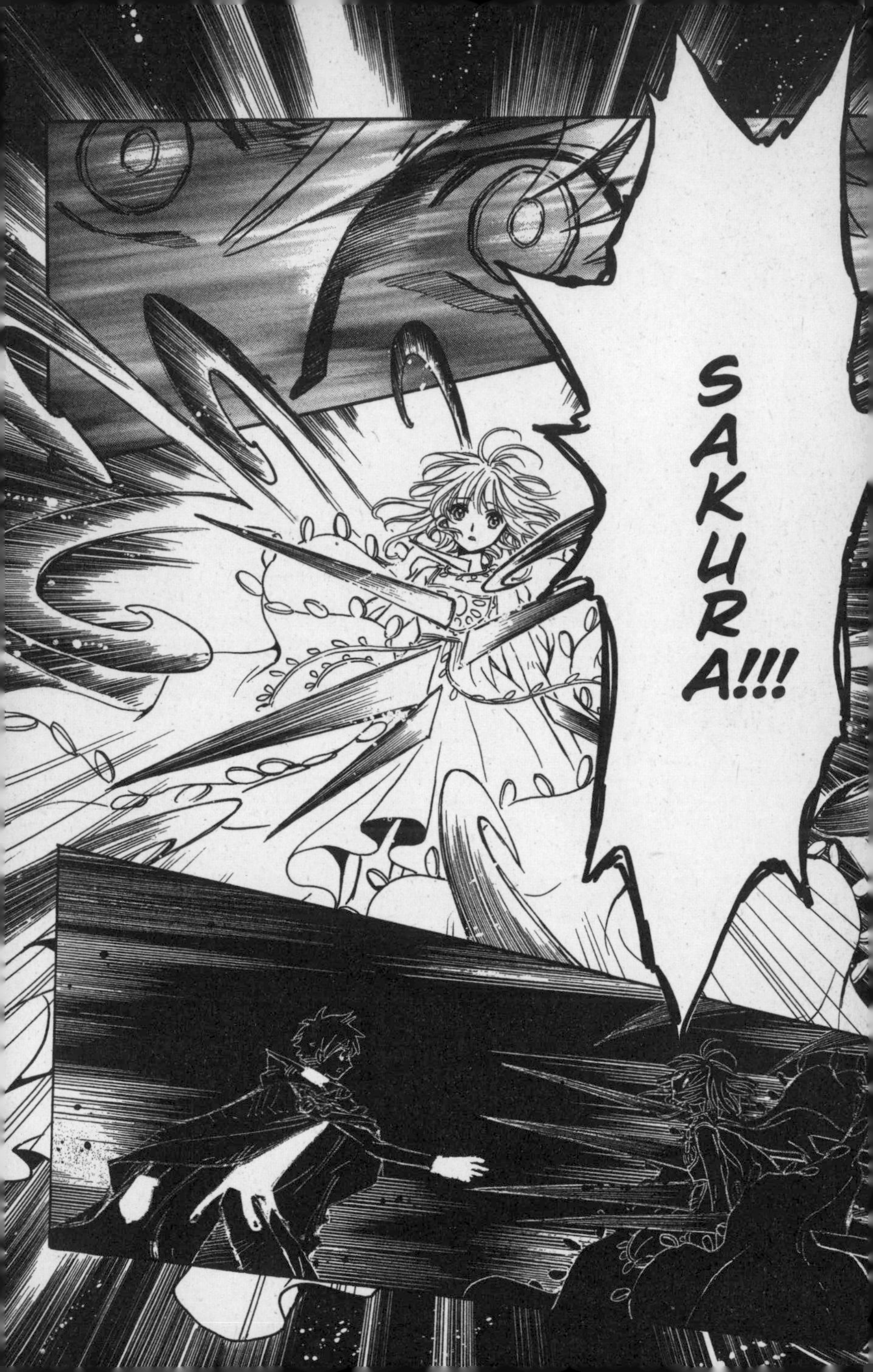
SAKURA!!!

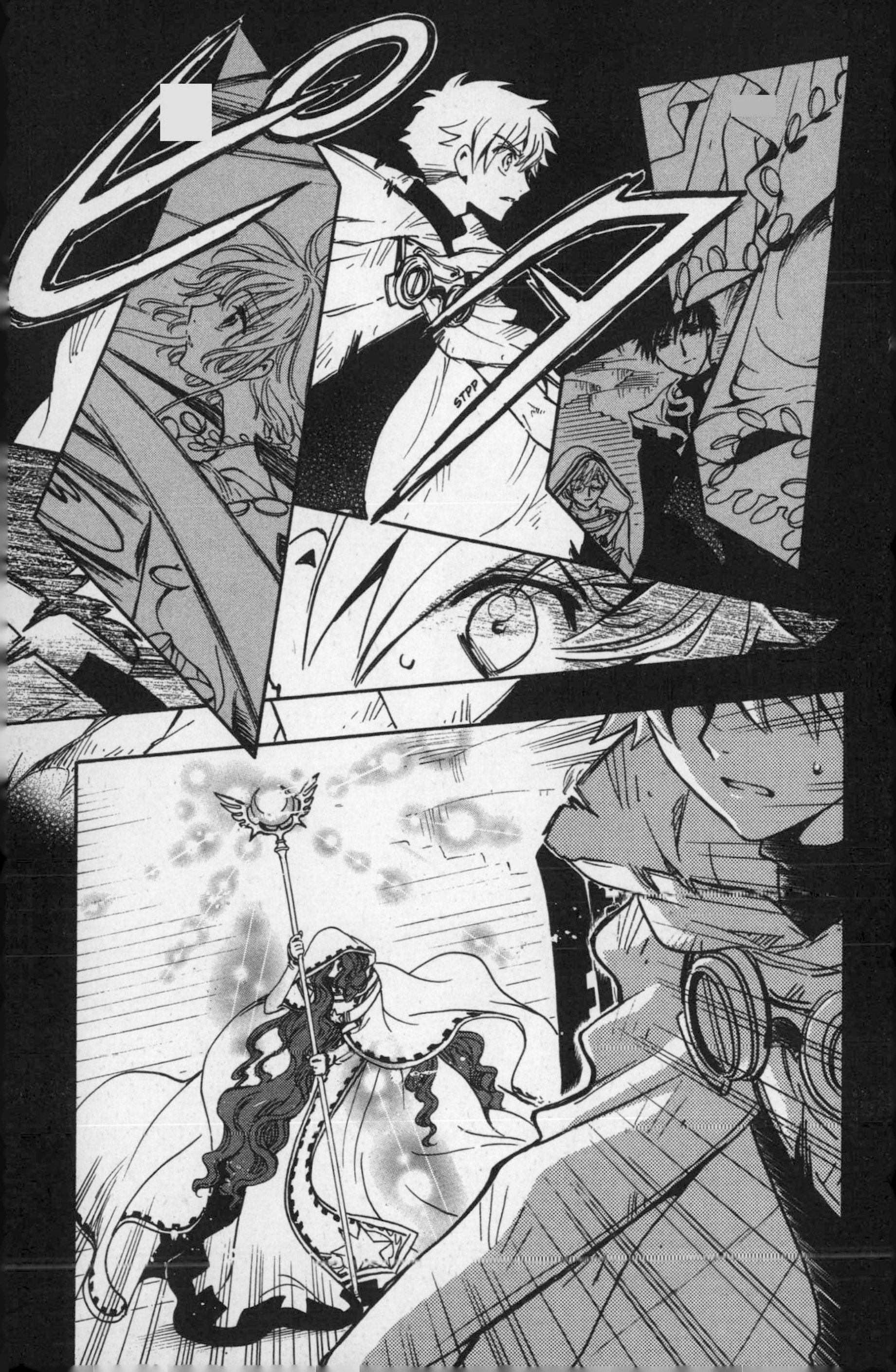
STPP

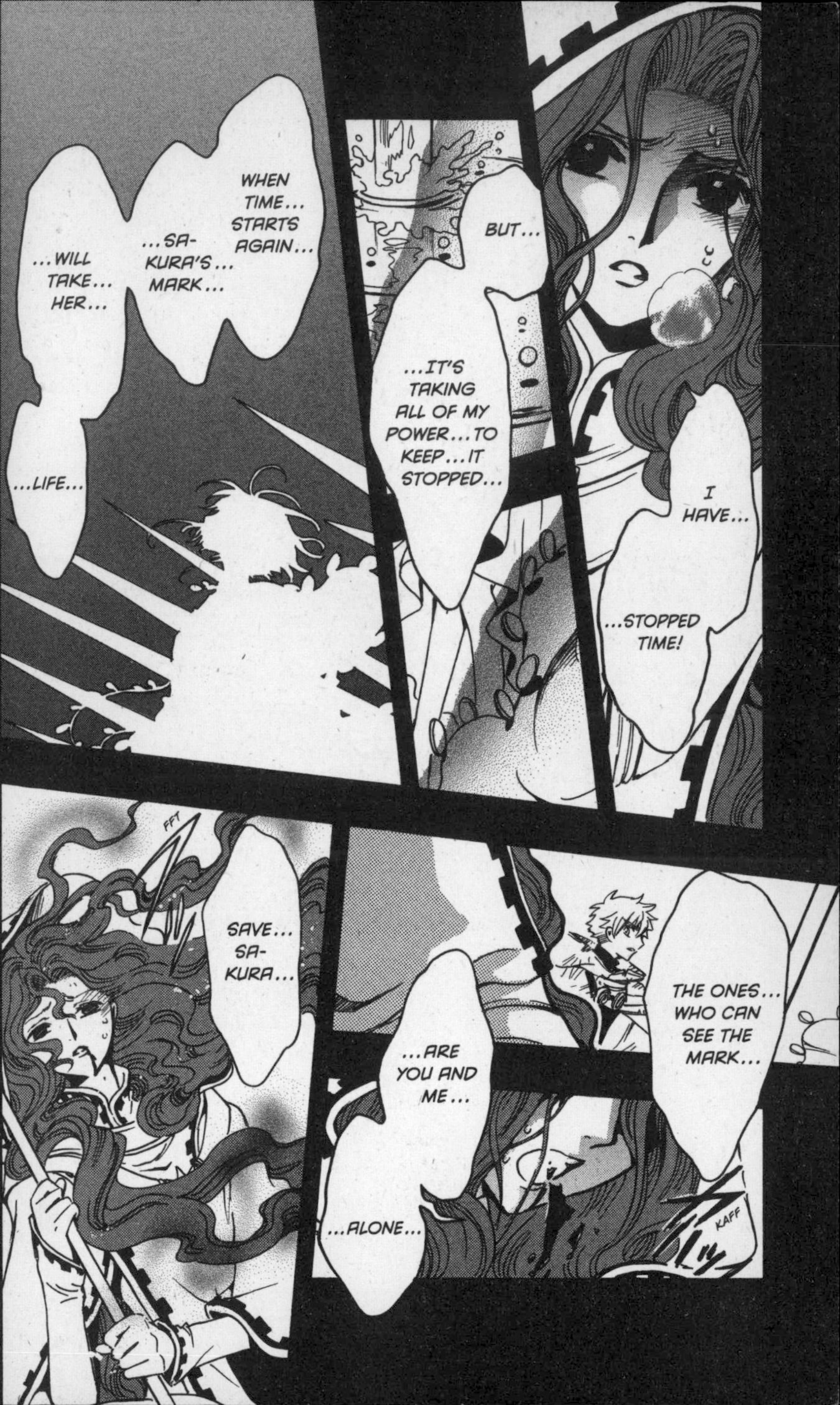
I HAVE...
...STOPPED TIME!
BUT...
...IT'S TAKING ALL OF MY POWER...TO KEEP...IT STOPPED...
WHEN TIME... STARTS AGAIN...
...SA-KURA'S... MARK...
...WILL TAKE... HER...
...LIFE...
THE ONES... WHO CAN SEE THE MARK...
...ARE YOU AND ME...
...ALONE...
KAFF
FFT
SAVE... SA-KURA...

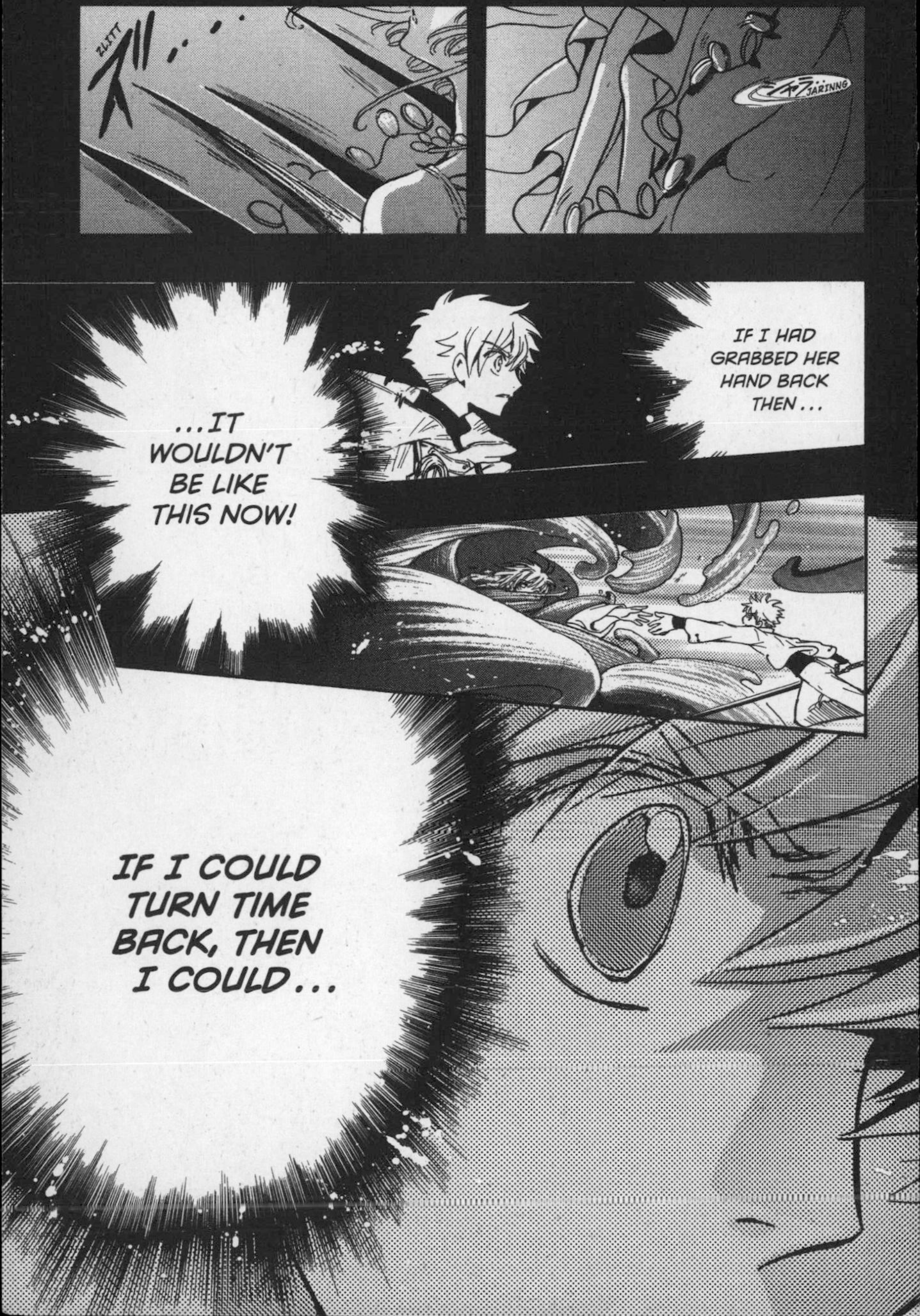
JARINNG
ZLITT
IF I HAD GRABBED HER HAND BACK THEN...
...IT WOULDN'T BE LIKE THIS NOW!
IF I COULD TURN TIME BACK, THEN I COULD...

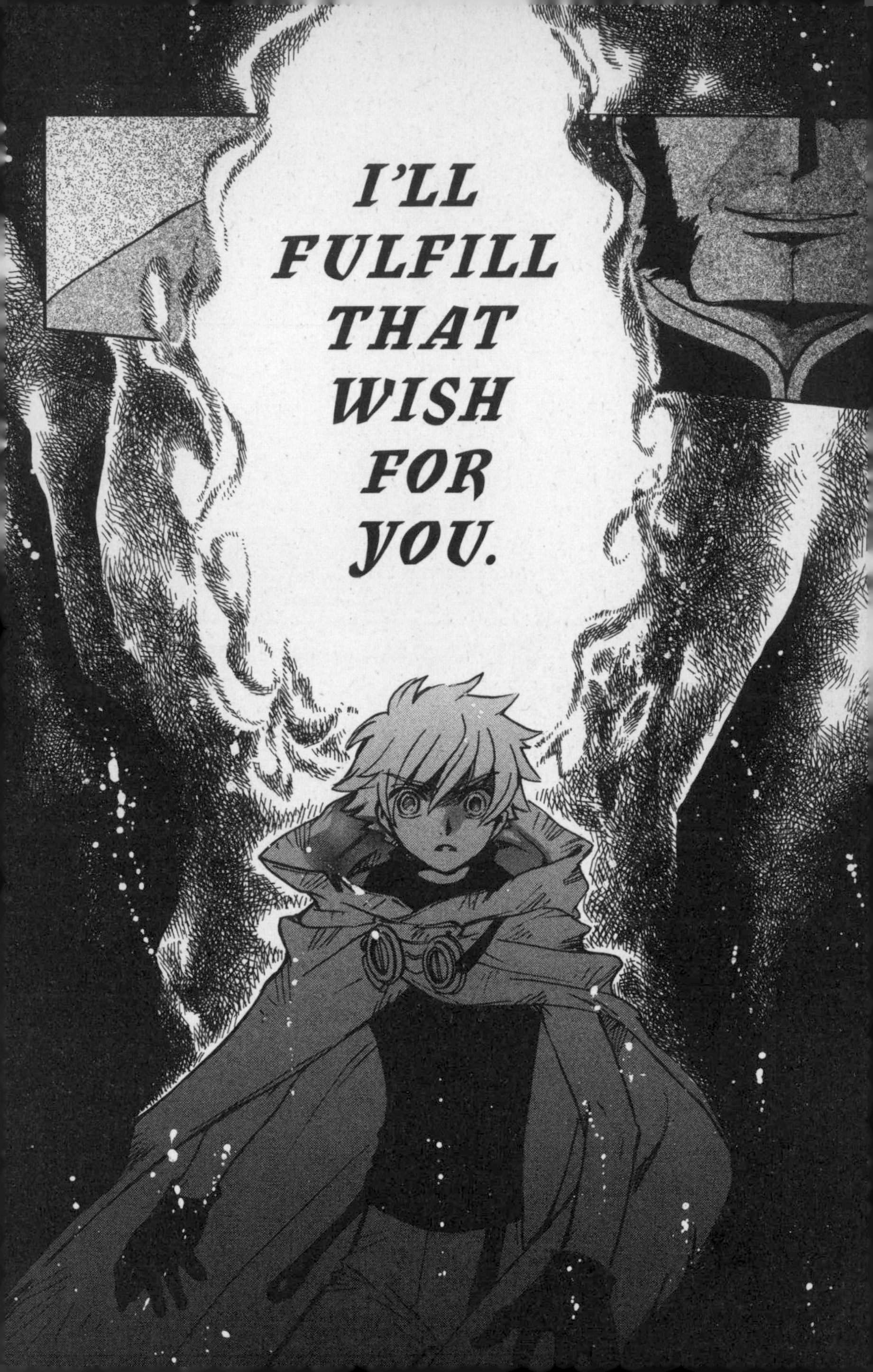
I'LL FULFILL THAT WISH FOR YOU.

To Be Continued

About the Creators

CLAMP is a group of four women who have become the most popular manga artists in America—Nanase Ohkawa, Mokona, Satsuki Igarashi, and Tsubaki Nekoi. They started out as *doujinshi* (fan comics) creators, but their skill and craft brought them to the attention of publishers very quickly. Their first work from a major publisher was *RG Veda*, but their first mass success was with *Magic Knight Rayearth*. From there, they went on to write many series, including Cardcaptor Sakura and Chobits, two of the most popular manga in the United States. Like many Japanese manga artists, they prefer to avoid the spotlight, and little is known about them personally.

CLAMP is currently publishing three series in Japan: Tsubasa and xxxHOLiC with Kodansha and Gohou Drug with Kadokawa.

Translation Notes

Japanese is a tricky language for most Westerners, and translation is often more art than science. For your edification and reading pleasure, here are notes on some of the places where we could have gone in a different direction in our translation of the work, or where a Japanese cultural reference is used.

Pinky Promise (Yubikiri), page 20

Yubikiri, which is called in English a "pinky promise" or "pinky swear," is a Japanese tradition that reportedly originated in the Edo period (1603–1868). It usually accompanies a short song which warns that the pain of ten thousand punches and of swallowing a thousand needles will be inflicted on the one who breaks the promise. Since the name *yubikiri* literally can be translated to mean "cutting a finger," it's been postulated on Internet sites that a broken promise will also mean that the promise breaker will have to cut off his/her little finger a la *yakuza* movies. But the truth seems to be the opposite. The name reportedly comes from feudal Japan when a woman working in the "water trade" (prostitutes and the like) would cut off the tip of her little finger in order to prove to the man she loves that she isn't simply faking her emotions for money. Far from punishment, the cut finger is thought to have been a sign of devotion, and that developed over time into the pinky promise known to all Japanese children today.

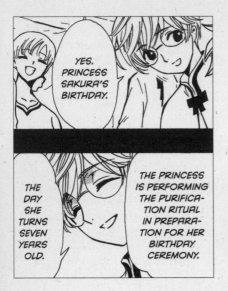

YES. PRINCESS SAKURA'S BIRTHDAY.
THE PRINCESS IS PERFORMING THE PURIFICATION RITUAL IN PREPARATION FOR HER BIRTHDAY CEREMONY.
THE DAY SHE TURNS SEVEN YEARS OLD.

Seventh Birthday, page 25

Not only is Sakura's seventh birthday significant in her rites, but she also started her training on her third birthday (see page 54). These ages are reflected in a Japanese festival called *Shichi-go-san,* which stands for the numbers 7-5-3. On this festival, only children the ages of three, five, and seven are allowed to celebrate by dressing in traditional clothes, visiting a Shinto shrine, and receiving special candy (*chitose-ame*) made for the occasion. According to the strictest rules, girls are allowed to celebrate when they are three and seven. Boys celebrate when they are three and five. But most Japanese families ignore this last restriction and both boys and girls celebrate at all three ages.

Food as a Present, page 146

One of the most popular souvenirs for Japanese tourists to bring home is the specialty food (*meibutsu*) of the region. Technically, non-food can also be *meibutsu*, but the word is so closely associated with food that the mention of the word can make one hungry. *Meibutsu* can also refer to hot meals such as Hiroshima's *okonomiyaki* or Nagoya's *miso-katsu* which are not suited to bringing home as presents, but since most Japanese destinations are aware of their tourist trade, nearly all places will have some form of *meibutsu* such as sweets or cakes that can be conveniently brought home to give to friends and family.

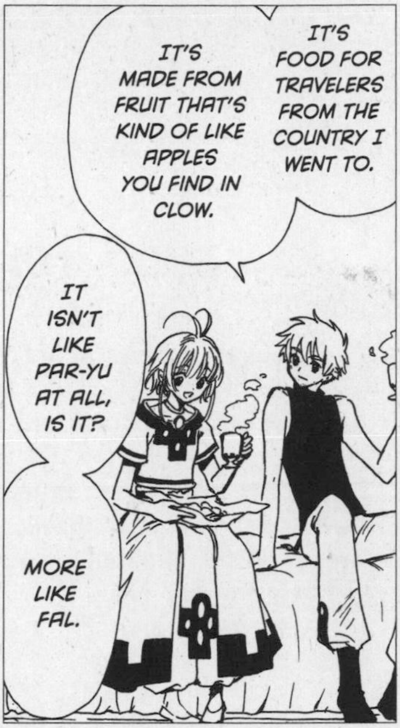
IT'S FOOD FOR TRAVELERS FROM THE COUNTRY I WENT TO.
IT'S MADE FROM FRUIT THAT'S KIND OF LIKE APPLES YOU FIND IN CLOW.
IT ISN'T LIKE PAR-YU AT ALL, IS IT?
MORE LIKE FAL.

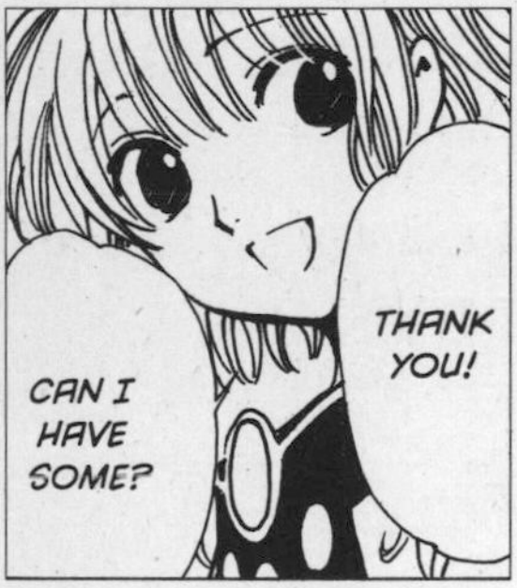
THANK YOU!
CAN I HAVE SOME?

Can I Have Some?, page 146

This sounds like an odd question to Western ears. The present is already given, so the recipient shouldn't have to ask whether she can have some or not. But it is considered only polite in Japan to ask permission of the giver before unwrapping a present or eating its contents. If the contents contain food which can be shared, it is expected of the recipient to share the gift with the giver (and with others present in the group).

TOMARE!

[STOP!]

You're going the wrong way!

Manga is a completely different type of reading experience.

To start at the *beginning*, go to the *end*!

That's right! Authentic manga is read the traditional Japanese way—from right to left. Exactly the *opposite* of how American books are read. It's easy to follow: Just go to the other end of the book, and read each page—and each panel—from right side to left side, starting at the top right. Now you're experiencing manga as it was meant to be!